MUSEUMS & GALLERIES

IN GREAT BRITAIN & IRELAND

1995 EDITION

Editor:
DEBORAH VALENTINE

Pictured above is the current holder of the:
MUSEUM OF THE YEAR AWARD
Jersey Museum
St Helier

Cover Photographs
"The Thinker" – by courtesy of Glasgow Museums: The Burrell Collection
"Pedal Harp" - G & J G Cousineau by courtesy of The Royal College of Music, London
"Early 14th century Wine Jar" - by courtesy of the Percival David Foundation, London
"A Woman Reading a Letter" - Gabriel Metsu by courtesy of The National Gallery of Ireland, Dublin
"Pair of Ladies Shoes c. 1660" - by courtesy of Northampton Museums and Art Gallery, Northampton
"Protectoral Medal" - by courtesy of The Cromwell Museum, Huntingdon
"Beefeater" - by courtesy of H. M. Tower of London
"Marmaduke" by courtesy of The Teddy Bear Museum, Stratford-upon-Avon

Published by:
Reed Information Services
Windsor Court, East Grinstead House, East Grinstead, West Sussex RH19 1XA
Telephone: (01342) 326972 Fax: (01342) 335720 Telex: 95127 INFSER G

Registered in England Number 181427
Registered Office: Church Street, Dunstable, Bedfordshire LU5 4HB

REED INFORMATION SERVICES

A Division of Reed Telepublishing Ltd.
A member of the Reed Elsevier plc group

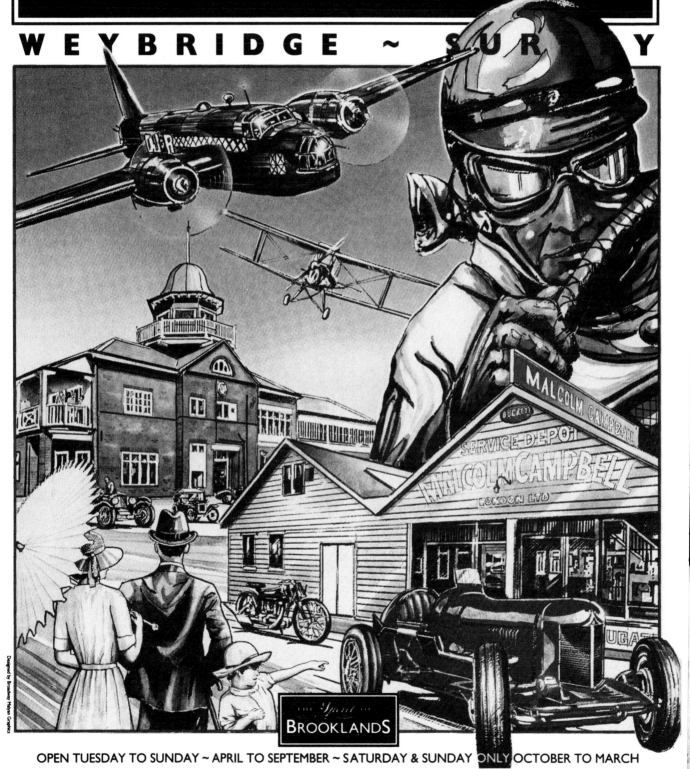

INTRODUCTION

THIS NEW EDITION has been completely revised. It includes the most comprehensive information available about collections, opening times, admission prices and, for the first time, events and exhibitions for some 1200 museums and art galleries open to the public. For ease of reference these are listed in county/town order. The subject index, found towards the end of the book, will help readers with a special interest to locate a specific type of index. Readers interested in militaria will find a separate section devoted to Service Museums.

1995 is the Festival of Arts and Culture year. Museums, as explained by the British Tourist Authority, are playing a major role in bringing their events to the attention of the public.

Much has been written about Eurotunnel. Our article looks at the visitor's experience and the future of the Exhibition Centre.

'The Golden Gallopers' are among the collections restored by The Fairground Heritage Trust, who are well advanced with their plans to open The National Fairground Museum to the public. 'A Dream Come True' is the introductory article on page iv.

The success of the educational programme at The Ryedale Folk Museum is recorded in an article by Martyn Dyer of the Heritage Education Trust.

CONTENTS

ISBN 0 948056 27 4

BRITAIN'S BIGGEST CELEBRATION
THE FESTIVAL OF ARTS AND CULTURE

by the British Tourist Authority

Sainsbury Centre for Visual Arts

Museums Play Major Role in Festival of Arts and Culture

This year's nation-wide Festival of Arts and Culture is being enthusiastically supported by Britain's museums and galleries. They are putting on more than 500 exhibitions and special events as their contribution to this year-long festival, which is the biggest celebration of the country's arts and culture ever staged. Its aim is to present - to overseas visitors, and to the British themselves - the wealth of heritage and contemporary arts which make the country one of the world's finest cultural centres.

The Festival covers the performing arts, and arts festivals; historic buildings and great gardens; religious heritage; crafts and customs; literature; and the cinema - towards the end of 1995, Cinema 100 begins, marking the first 100 years of British moving pictures.

Anniversaries

The vast programme of the Festival of Arts and Culture is much enriched by a number of other memorable anniversaries. They include the centenaries of the National Trust, Westminster Cathedral and Belfast's Grand Opera House; the bicentenaries of the birth of the poet John Keats, and the

A Midsummer Night's Dream, Edinburgh Festival

death of Josiah Wedgwood; and the tercentenary of the composer Henry Purcell. It is also, of course, 50 years since VE Day; and north of the border the Scots have the 250th anniversary of Bonnie Prince Charlie leading the Jacobite uprising which ended at the Battle of Culloden.

Other 1995 anniversaries range from 1,000 years since the founding of the diocese of Durham, and the Devon resort of Paignton's 700th birthday, to the 450th of Wilton House near Salisbury, the 60th of the De La Warr Pavilion in Bexhill, and the 35th of the National Association of Flower Arranging Societies: all good reasons for special celebrations.

Throughout 1995 when you travel to any part of the country you will be well advised to call in at local tourist information centres to get up-to-date details of Festival events of all kinds in the area you are visiting. At the time of writing, news of additional happenings is still filtering through: this brief article will give you a flavour of what is in store.

Wedgwood

Josiah Wedgwood was a hugely influential figure, and his anniversary should bring many visitors to the Potteries where a major exhibition, 'Josiah Wedgwood - The Man and His Mark', is at the City Museum & Art Gallery, Stoke-on-Trent, from June to September. Another exhibition opens at London's Victoria & Albert Museum in June; and Wedgwood will also be featured at the Lady Lever Art Gallery, Merseyside.

Symphony Hall, Birmingham

Keats

John Keats was born in the year Wedgwood died, and that poetic landmark will be commemorated with exhibitions at Dove Cottage and the Wordsworth Museum in Cumbria (April-October); at Winchester's Guildhall Gallery (June-July); and, of course, at Keats House in Hampstead.

National Trust

The most widely celebrated anniversary will undoubtedly be the 100th birthday of the National Trust - and no organisation can match its wonderful array of buildings and gardens in which to have a summer-long party. There will be several open-air theatre and opera productions; son et Lumiere at Polesden Lacey (June 16-18) and Lyveden New Bield (September 9); Fetes Champetres at West Wycombe Park (July 7-9), Claremont Landscape Garden (July 12-15), Stourhead (July 19-22) and Mottisfont Abbey Gardens (September 8-9); and a great deal of music, ranging from numerous classical concerts (several with fireworks) to Gilbert & Sullivan, and from folk music (Felbrigg Hall, May 27-28) to jazz (Clumber Park, August 5; Plas Newydd, Anglesey, August 9).

There will also be a series of lectures at the Purcell Room and other London venues from February to December, given by such distinguished speakers as Sir Crispin Tickell, Viscount Norwich, David Bellamy, Lucinda Lambton, the Duchess of Devonshire and Sir Nicholas Goodison. A National Trust centenary exhibition will be at the National Gallery from November 22-March 10, 1996; and another opens at the Royal Cornwall Museum, Truro, in March this year.

Purcell

Some of the Trust concerts will include works by Purcell, and his music will be widely heard in Britain during the year, including the Stately Homes Music Festival (May-September), which is working with Purcell Tercentenary Trust to present recitals and chamber music at various country houses. There will also be concerts and other events at All Saints' Church, Tudeley, in Kent, which has a Purcell Festival from November 17-25. Another interesting cultural event in Kent will be the very first staging of a Shakespeare play in Canterbury Cathedral - 'Romeo and Juliet' (August 7-20).

Open Air Theatre, Chatsworth House

Heritage

Wilton House in Wiltshire, which is celebrating the 450th anniversary of its Tudor origins this year, has its own link with the Bard: tradition has it that Shakespeare himself acted there, in 'As You Like It'. A house of much later vintage opens to the public for the first time at Easter: this is High Cross, on the Dartington Hall estate near Totnes, a fine example of 1930s architecture which contains Leonard and Dorothy Elmhirst's impressive collection of 20th century art, ceramics and books. It will be open for most of the year, giving visitors a chance to see paintings by Ben Nicholson and David Jones; pottery by Bernard Leach and the Japanese master, Hamada; and letters from the likes of Ghandi, Agatha Christie, Lawrence of Arabia and Bertrand Russell.

The De La Warr Pavilion at Bexhill is of similar vintage: this striking building, by the German architect Erich Mendelsohn, has just undergone careful restoration by Rother Council with English Heritage support, and there will be a series of events to mark its 60th anniversary in the Sussex resort. Another very different building will also be in the news this year: 17th century Uppark in West Sussex suffered a disastrous fire in 1989. The National Trust then embarked on its biggest ever conservation project, and you will be able to see the result when the house re-opens to the public in June.

Westminster Cathedral's centenary programme, from February to October, includes an international festival of flowers and music (May 16-20), choral and orchestral concerts, and an exhibition of Vatican treasures.

Literary Heritage

The spotlight will also be on literature during 1995, with Swansea hosting the UK Year of Literature and Writing in the fifth of the Arts Council's "Arts 2000" series (last year, Manchester was the City of Drama). Although the main emphasis is on the spoken and written word (Welsh and English) from ancient Welsh tales to Dylan Thomas and Dick Francis, there will also be music, dance and sculpture events. Literary heritage will also be a main theme in the West Country during the Festival of Arts and Culture, because the region has been home to so many writers, and the setting of so many books: from Coleridge, Wordsworth, Fielding, Jane Austen and Blackmore to Thomas Hardy, Agatha Christie, Daphne du Maurier, John Fowles and Mary Wesley. The Dorset County Museum, Dorchester, rich in memorabilia of Hardy and the local dialect poet William Barnes, is opening a new literary gallery; Devizes Museum

York Early Music Festival

is to feature Wiltshire writers; and Porlock Museum celebrates "Local Authors, Past and Present".

Bonnie Prince Charlie

Scotland's commemoration of the 1745 Jacobite uprising will include a major exhibition at Glasgow's Art Gallery and Museum, Kelvingrove (June 3-August 7); and a Jacobite Week in Inverness and Nairn in April, with exhibitions, and re-enactments of Bonnie Prince Charlie's exploits. Another important anniversary north of the border is the quincentenary of Aberdeen University - there will be a series of exhibitions in the "granite city" throughout 1995.

Museums and Galleries Festival Plans

Lastly, a glance at what some of the other museums and art galleries will be tempting you with during 1995... In London, the Barbican Art Gallery has "Impressionism in Britain" (January-April); the Crafts Council Gallery features contemporary British furniture (February-April); the National Maritime Museum unveils a new Nelson exhibition at Easter; and the Imperial War Museum will be commemorating VE Day.

The enterprising Pallant House Gallery, Chichester has "Fifty Years of Post-War British Painting" (June 6-September 2); while a few miles west Portsmouth's City Museum has exhibitions on the post-war rebuilding of the city (May-October), and 100 years of Hampshire cricket (August). "Away With the Corsets, on With the Shifts" is the provocative title of an exhibition of artistic dress 1880-1910, at the Pitville Pump Room Museum, Cheltenham (end of May to late September); and the Tate Gallery St. Ives, which opened so successfully in 1993, plans "100 Years of Images of Porthmeor Beach" (this is the beach the gallery overlooks).

The Harley Gallery, at Welbeck near Worksop, stages a British Tapestry Festival (June-July); and Sheffield's Industrial Museum has "Cutlery Capital of the World", a celebration of the cutlery, silverware and tool traders in the city (spring to September). Visitors heading a little further north-east can, for the Festival of Arts and Culture, buy a combined discounted ticket covering admission to the Captain Cook Memorial Museum, Capt. Cook Schoolroom Museum, Capt. Cook and Staithes Heritage Centre, Whitby Museum, and the Captain Cook Birthplace Museum in Middlesborough.

The Shakespeare Centre at Stratford-upon-Avon is opening a new permanent exhibition in April, in conjunction with new displays in the Birthplace, next door in Henley Street; and the Ironbridge Gorge Museum stages "Iron Mighty", an exhibition on the arts of industry (July-August). "Emigrants", a big exhibition covering two centuries of emigration to North America, is on view throughout 1995 at the Ulster American Folk Park, Omagh; while Swansea's Maritime and Industrial Museum plays its part in the city's literary year with the exhibitions on "The Art of the Book" (February-March) and "The Printed Word" (April-September).

Yes, it is going to be a vintage year, and the Festival of Arts and Culture does seem to have something for everyone.

Interpreter
Tour Guide Sound System
For visits to Museums and Galleries, Historic Houses and Castles, anywhere a tour guide is needed.
It may be used outside for Town Tours, Gardens, Parks, Woodland Trails and Nature Reserves.
Interpreter 3 Becketts Wharf, Lower Teddington Road, Hampton Wick, Surrey KT1 4ER Tel 081 977 8222 or Fax 081 977 920

SEEING IS BELIEVING

by Lord Berkeley, Eurotunnel

The Exhibition centre in Folkestone is now the second largest paying visitor attraction in Kent after Leeds Castle, and in the year of the Inauguration of the Channel Tunnel, it has been the focus of intense interest and community activity over many months.
How and where did it all start? In a back street in lower Folkestone, when we opened an information centre just three weeks after the Channel Tunnel was given the go ahead in 1986. We advertised it as a centre for local consultation, for local residents to come and find out how their homes, their businesses or environment might be changed by the construction of the Tunnel. Many residents came and over the following months they were soon outnumbered by school groups doing projects on the Tunnel. When construction started we had to comply with a parliamentary undertaking to provide in perpetuity a 'viewing platform' of the works, so we decided to go one stage better and create a tourist attraction as well.

Célébration '94 – The Schools' Challenge

The new centre conveniently near the M20 at Junction 12 and just across the motorway from the terminal, was opened in September 1988. Its objectives were:

- to provide information about the Channel Tunnel, its design, construction, operation, the environmental and economic effects it would have, all in an easily accessible format;
- to provide a place where local briefings could continue to be held, queries and complaints addressed, as well as a library where the main official and other documents produced could be studied;
- to develop and provide educationally valid facilities for schools and colleges;
- to be a shop window for Eurotunnel.

To achieve these various objectives we decided to create a tourist attraction that would have a 'worth', for which we therefore could and should make a charge to the public.

The Exhibition Content

Over the last six years, the exhibition content has had to reflect the current subjects of interest, provide updates of progress and foretastes of things to come. In the early days the main interest was in how fast the 11 tunnel boring machines were going; what was it like underground, would the sea come in, where was the spoil excavated from the tunnels going, and would the tunnels meet in the middle of the Channel?

As construction of the tunnel progressed, there was intense interest in the dredged sand being brought to it by pipeline and the massive concrete structures appearing across the road. Later still interest focused on the railway works and rolling stock that started to appear.

There was always curiosity in what was happening across the Channel, and in the special events that have marked the construction and opening of this project: the first breakthrough, when Britain became connected by land with the Continent for the first time since the Ice Age; the first train through the Tunnel; and this year the inauguration by HM The Queen and President Mitterrand.

We have tried to update the Exhibition to reflect progress and changing interests, but there are some parts that have always remained popular: the history of many previous attempts, what it was like down the 1880 tunnel, and the boring machine that was used in the 1922 trial that was rescued from Folkestone Warren, refurbished and is now displayed at the Centre.

Eurotunnel Exhibition Centre

The model railway layout of the complete system, constructed to almost exact scale for N-gauge operation, required us to go into the model railway business to keep it operating! Now we have mock-ups of shuttles and Eurostar trains, locomotive driver's simulator and information about the wider European transport scene.

The Developing Model Railway

Interpretation

Whatever we have shown has had to be done in a way that demonstrates quality, is accessible to the widest range of audiences and cultures, and is as interactive as the budget allows. In this way, we hope that the visitor's experience is as 'in depth' as they wish to take it.

We planned on ensuring that a visit is considered to be educationally valid, and we were pleased to receive approval of the French Ministry of Education for visits by groups of French students.

Everything is bilingual English/French and our intention is to allow visitors to pass through the Exhibition at any speed they want. We try to have a variety of interactive modes, to allow visitors to touch and feel, and to have staff available to answer questions and generally help.

Whatever the actual subject, we are always aware that visitors may be interested in technology, the environment, transport or languages and find that the Channel Tunnel is a unique subject in which to bring these themes together.

Facilities

Since 30 - 40% of our visitors are school groups, we make special provisions for them. We provide worksheets for different student age groups visiting the Centre. We also run practical workshops in our education rooms for groups of up to 25 students, in geography, technology and environmental studies. They last two hours and are taught in English or French. They are so popular that they are often booked up three months in advance. Last year they were the highlights of a 'Seeing is Believing' visit by Business in the Community.

Two former Intercity railway coaches now serve as static 'school dinner rooms'. These coaches are still the most modern design of rolling stock in the whole of the Kent Coast network. For some families it is the first time that they have been in a train.

We welcome disabled visitors and all facilities are accessible to them except the viewing tower, where a lift could not be installed. Instead we have provided a remote control video camera and monitor so that those unable to climb to the top of the tower can see the view at ground floor level.

The shop and cafe are always popular. The shop's most popular lines are publications about the Channel Tunnel, ranging from the highly technical to educational books, popular picture books, postcards and games. This year we have started 'Terminal Tours', hourly coach tours around the Folkestone Channel Tunnel Terminal.

Célébration '94

The Centre was never as busy as in April and May of this year, when we organised a Community Festival to mark the inauguration of the Channel Tunnel. The event based at the Centre was for, and with the active participation of, the local community. We had two marquees for indoor events, 3 000 participants and many more visitors to a programme of events in education, the environment, tourism, the arts and sport. The Centre was also a place from which to view the 'official events' taking place on the terminals, and for Eurotunnel to throw a party afterwards for its many local friends as a way of saying 'thank-you'.

Our Visitors

Over the six years that we have been open, visitor numbers have fluctuated between 250,000 and just over 300,000. Probably because of the topicality of the Channel Tunnel, we have been less affected by the recent downturn in visitor numbers than other local attractions.

Over the same period, the proportion of cars has reduced and coaches increased, and we find that about half our visitors come from within the county of Kent. We also have a loyal band of local regulars who make many return visits with friends staying with them.

The Future

The Exhibition Centre has been a great success, not only for Eurotunnel's community and public relations, but as a tourist attraction in its own right. However, it has certain problems which will have to be addressed if it is to have a long-term future, as we hope it will.

The content of the Exhibition must change; there is no point in having a large mock-up of a shuttle of a train when one can travel in the real thing across the road. Most importantly, we have no temporary exhibition, event or conference area, and we are well aware of the importance of these for attracting return visits.

"Tele heads" tell young visitors about the Tunnel

We are collecting some exciting pieces of machinery, equipment and memorabilia used in the development or construction of past and present channel tunnels, as well as a veritable archive of documents, photos and videos, some donated and some loaned. These all need proper archiving and curatorial treatment, not least the large boring machine outside the Centre which still says it is 'for sale, one careful owner'.

The Channel Tunnel is a subject that evokes interest far beyond its construction: for example the environment, rabies, tourism, transport, languages and 'Europe'. It is seen as an example (good or bad) of how to achieve major projects, and we are encouraged by the level of support from professionals in the museums business for the transformation of the Centre into a museum of 'The Story of the Channel Tunnel'. It should and must have an educational bias, and we hope for links with the Science Museum in London, the National Railway Museum in York, the University of Kent at Canterbury, as well as with museums and educational establishment across the channel.

Most important of all, such a museum must provide facilities for events, temporary exhibitions and conferences, and be seen to serve and be part of the local community.

The Centre is in an ideal location, next to the M20 at Junction 12 and the Channel Tunnel Terminal where by 1996, we expect to have over 15 million car and coach passengers using *Le Shuttle* every year. On the other side of the Centre is the Folkestone-Ashford railway line - all it needs is a station, and we should go for that as well!

Six exciting years after it opened, we are now addressing the challenge of its longevity!

4073

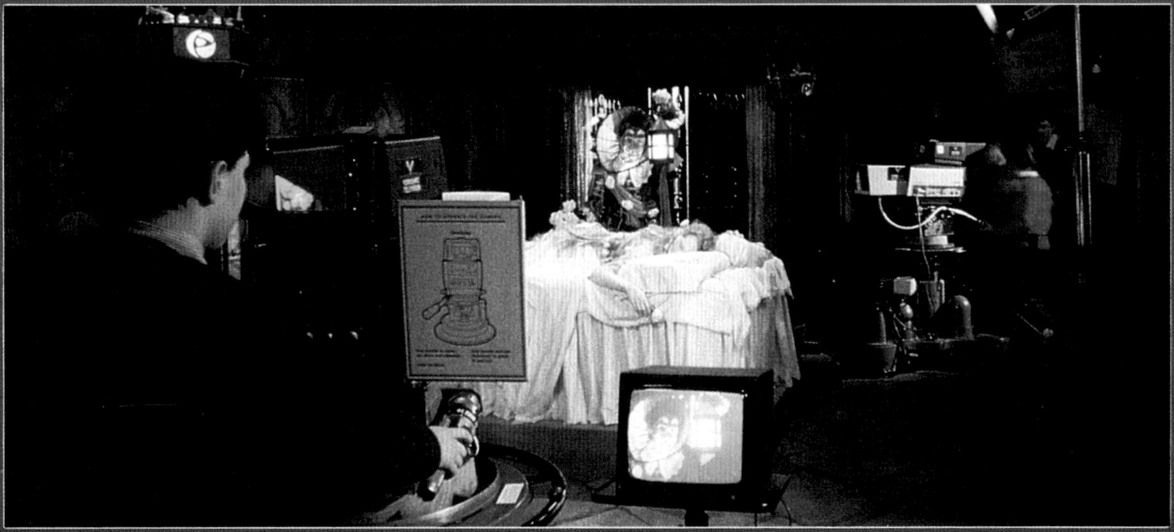

A DREAM COME TRUE

by Valerie Bott, Curator of The Fairground Heritage Trust

A long-standing dream will become reality when the National Fairground Museum opens to visitors. During 1995 a purpose built home will be erected on a riverside site just outside Northampton for the Fairground Heritage Trust's collections and two thousand years of fairs and fairground people will provide the theme for an exciting exhibition.

How it all Began

While researching the subject of fairground art and decoration Geoff Weedon and Richard Ward began to realise how quickly our heritage of fine rides, shows and stalls was disappearing. Some fairground equipment was being destroyed when it was no longer wanted, some was exported or broken up for sale by antique dealers, some earlier decoration was being painted over with new designs. In the late 1960's there were about thirty traditional galloping horse roundabouts still in use - there are only about a dozen today. Their research resulted in the magnificent book, "Fairground Art", published in 1981 (White Mouse Publications) and in 1986 the Fairground Heritage Trust was established and the idea of a National Fairground Museum was born.

In less than a decade the Trust had established a major collection of fairground equipment and amusements drawn from all over the British Isles. No other museum collects actively in this field although one or two own individual rides and examples of fairground art. Because of its unique role, the Trust has been helped by extremely generous grants from such sources as the Science Museum's PRISM Fund, the Victoria and Albert Museum's Purchase Fund and the National Heritage Memorial Fund, and by charities like the Manifold Trust, the Radcliffe Trust and the Material World Foundation. A large number of individual donors supported the restoration project for the Edwards Golden Gallopers, pledging £100 per horse or cockerel.

Edwards' Gallopers

Hatwell Panel

Growing Collections

Such material presents some difficult logistical problems compared with that held by many other museums! These are not exhibits which can be packed into boxes and placed on shelves in a museum store. Rides travelled on their own purpose-built packing trucks, drawn in convoy by steam traction engines or early diesel lorries. They are masterpieces of prefabrication, designed to be built up and dismantled in hours. The Museum's Dodgem set is 96 feet long when built up. It is one of the largest ever made and this alone has four trucks, a lorry and a mobile ticket office to move from fair to fair. But as the collection began to grow, showmen provided space in their winter quarters to enable rides to be safely stored while other supporters have offered space in their homes and garages for smaller items that were being rescued. Even the Science Museum provided a temporary home for the Edwards' Gallopers at its huge Wroughton stores.

Edwards' Dodgems

Since the end of 1993 the National Fairground Museum has had its own warehousing with workshops at Three Mills in East London. The first curator was appointed in early 1994, with the task of assembling the collection in one place, establishing a catalogue of the Trust's holdings and preparing the material for display. The Northampton site will house display galleries, teaching and study facilities, cafe and shop, plus a spectacular tented area under which the fairground rides and stalls can be set out and operated for visitors to enjoy. Funding for the new building is coming from Wilson Bowden, the developers of the adjoining site as a major retail park, and from charitable trusts and sponsors.

'The Shopping List'

So what will visitors see? There are still some items which are on the "shopping list" for the future, like a Razzle-Dazzle and a Helter Skelter or "Slip", but the collection already includes examples of almost every kind of fairground equipment. As much as possible will be on show. The oldest known British ride, the Rodeo Switchback, the only surviving spinning top switchback and one of the first to be converted to electricity, was exported to America but brought back by enterprising enthusiasts and eventually bought for the museum. The Bioscope wagon is probably the last surviving wagon of its kind, extravagantly decorated to form, with a matching wagon, a spectacular showfront to draw the crowds in for early moving film shows in the 1890's. It has lost all its colour and gilding, having served as a farm labourer's home in a Lincolnshire field since the 1920's, but the Trust plans a special fund-raising drive to get it restored, build a replica to match and eventually recreate the early Bioscope shows in a tent behind this wonderful front. It might even show an audio-visual introduction to the museum in this unusual setting! Few fairground boxing booths survive but Billy Woods' "International Boxing Academy", constructed in the 1920's with a colourful showfront depicting prize bouts and past champions, is now owned by the Trust.

Four rides from the fair operated by the Edwards family out of Swindon are now in the museum. The Golden Gallopers are very special because they represent the work of Arthur Anderson, a Bristol carver, and Charlie Gaze, a Swindon signwriter. The Gallopers were put away in 1933 when a new ride proved more successful with the punters, and were never brought out again until the Trust acquired them in 1986. The decoration of the horses in soft rich colours with gilding, is very beautiful now that the old browning varnish has been removed. The restoration of the centre engine, which drove the ride is almost complete, and the Verbeeck steam organ bought for it in the early 1930's has come to the Museum as well. The collection also includes their Dodgems and their Skid.

All of these can be used and enjoyed but the operation of the rides will have to be very carefully managed. When they are static you can see their superb detail but it needs movement and noise to recreate the impression of the fairground action. Safety will be of paramount importance and the preservation of the rides will have to be balanced with care against their use. The Rodeo Switchback which spent the summer season of 1994 at the Hollycombe Steam Collection in Hampshire, illustrates this very well. This revolving ride with two "hills" and two "valleys" is now rather disappointing as the wear on its aging wheels makes for a rather uncomfortable ride. But the glamour which drew people to it in the 1890's, with its spectacularly carved carriages and their bizarre animal heads, some replaced in the 1930's with cowboy figures, still attracts a modern crowd - and replacement wheels will probably solve the worst of the discomfort!

Visitors' Enjoyment

The Galloping Horses may have to be removed from the roundabout and displayed as fairground art in the galleries to avoid damage to their painted and carved decoration. Alongside other examples of the work of painters, carvers and engineers this will enable the museum to celebrate the skills of the fairground world. Modern replica horses can be provided for people to climb onto so that the Gallopers can work while the originals are protected. The Dodgems were designed to be bumped into one another and they are no fun if they don't! But they will eventually suffer damage if used frequently. In this case the cars were replaced in the 1970's and it may be possible to build 1930's-style replicas for use if funds allow.

Rodeo Switchback

The side shows and stalls include a shooting gallery which still has all its "swag": the 1930's, '40's and '50's ornaments and prizes it once proudly displayed, and small round stalls or "hoop-las" with "roll-em in" boards. A mushy pea stall from Yorkshire, which was still travelling in 1993, fortunately still has its pre-decimal coinage price cards for peas, candy floss and hot dogs. There is also the original banner which formed a back drop to the stall before it was extended to half as long again as its original size.

What this museum alone can offer is a chance to find out more about the private world of the fairground. The building up and pulling down of rides, with the workers using their packing trucks as a high-level platform to work from, is often done overnight or early in the morning, unseen by those who have gone home to bed. The museum can demonstrate this in action to show the skill of the operation and ingenuity of the construction. The strange and frightening effects of the Ghost Train can all be revealed to show how simple the tricks they play really are. Models and film can show how the complex mechanisms of a Cakewalk or a Razzle-Dazzle actually work. The operation of the steam organs can be demonstrated with programmes of the special punched cardboard music. Repairs and redecoration were the showmen's winter task; the museum can have demonstrations of some of these special fairground techniques, such as "flamboyant" painting or the carving of galloping horses, by bringing in today's fairground craft workers. In addition performers can recreate some of the earlier shows and illusions where original material does not survive.

Special Effects

Victorian and Edwardian showmen and fairground manufacturers showed great inventiveness in achieving special effects. It was the showmen who harnessed steam to pull new larger rides along the improved tarmacadam roads and to drive the rides round the fairground. And for many people at the turn of the century, the fairground was the first place where they saw electric light. The Savage & Co archive of technical drawings, now owned by the Trust, includes detail designs of a variety of fairground equipment manufactured by this ingenious company in King's Lynn. Alongside other illustrations and photographs from the museum's growing collection, and even some of the company's rides, the construction and technology of the fairground can be shown.

Life on the Road

How did the showmen's families live on the roads? The Museum already has two living wagons, one of 1902 which belonged to Violet Davies and another of about 1922 which Elizabeth Ashley inherited from her father. Both have superb interior decoration which visitors will be able to see. While some operated rides and stalls of their own, other women played a major role on the road managing the family's finances as well as the children, while their husbands and sons concentrated on the technical business of maintaining and operating rides. Great strides have been taken in improving education for the children of occupational travellers and the Museum hopes to contribute to this work. The Museum will, after all, be the only museum recording the showmen's lives. Using photographs, personal possessions, news cuttings and reminiscences the Museum hopes to enable visitors to imagine vividly "life on the road".

Edwards' Gallopers

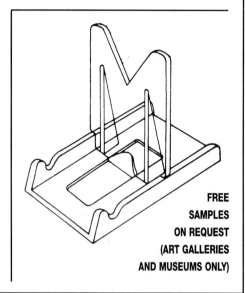

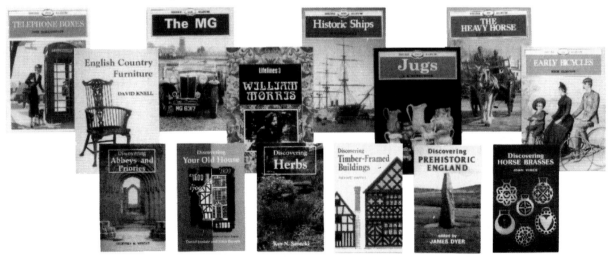

HERITAGE EDUCATION TRUST

EDUCATION AND LOCAL ENTERPRISE IN A NORTH YORKSHIRE VILLAGE

THE RYEDALE FOLK MUSEUM, a 1994 winner of the Sandford Award for excellence in Heritage Education is situated in what must be one of the prettiest and most unusual villages in Yorkshire and therefore in England: Hutton-le-Hole. The Museum itself could be described in similar terms.

As you step into the light, welcoming reception area you see beyond the glass-panelled entrance what looks like another village. A pathway winds in front of you: on the right is a blacksmith's forge, a yeoman's cottage, and a cruck house, brought up-to-date for nineteenth century living. On the left are workshops for the cobbler and the tin-smith, with the village shop, post office and chemist next door. Beyond these buildings are further delights set round a maypole in the centre of a greensward. Beyond that again you discover an Edwardian photographic studio, (presented by Mr. Raymond Hayes, one of the museum's trustees) a barn complete with horsewheel (a massive piece of nineteenth-century technology for separating grain and husk), and a wagon-shed housing by gone farm vehicles. All the buildings are either originals moved from other parts of Ryedale or careful replicas.

Hutton-le-Hole – One of the prettiest and most unusual villages in Yorkshire and therefore in England

THE CROSLAND FOUNDATION: a local trust

This unusual museum has its origins in a local family, the Croslands. Before the Second World War, Wilfred Crosland assembled a collection of about 100 rural artifacts in his house (now part of the museum) which he would show to interested visitors. When he died Mr. Bertram Frank, MBE., set about developing the collections as the foundation for a future museum. In 1964 the Ryedale Folk Museum opened its doors with Mr Frank as founder and first Curator on property bequeathed to him.

From the start therefore the Ryedale Museum was rooted in local energy, pride and imagination and this tradition is preserved today by the Trustees of the Crosland Foundation: it is the guiding light and source of all their store. The present Curator, Martin Watts, explains the policy for developing the collections which now number over 10,000 pieces: 'Additions must complement existing collections and they must come from Ryedale. We take pains not to overlap other collections and we do not include art, original documents or costume. We have an army of volunteer helpers and all the objects are given by local people.'

Ryedale Folk Museum is a success story and Martin Watts believes this success depends on the local contacts and the enthusiasm of all involved and their willingness to do anything.

The Ryedale Manor House

Nowhere is this local commitment better illustrated than in the story of one of the most striking buildings to make up this museum, the Manor House. This now fine looking

Brownies at Ryedale grapple with the problems of Cruck construction as part of a "Brownies Challenge" programme in aid of the Spastics Society

building stands near the maypole and dominates the scene. It was originally built in the late sixteenth century. It stood in Harome, a village about eight miles south west of Hutton-le-Hole. A photograph dated 1970 shows it in a state of dilapidation. It was in this state that it was transplanted to its new home to be rebuilt on its present site by local volunteers as a fine example of the cruck construction and a sixteenth century manor house. This leads naturally to the place of Heritage Education in the Museum. Visitors who coincide with a school party may well find themselves threading their way round a group of children in the Manor House manhandling hefty wooden beams. They are grappling with constructional problems similar to those which sixteenth century builders would have faced. Among the education service equipment is a pile of wooden beams, braces, pegs and purlins which form a kind of do-it-yourself cruck construction kit. All the pieces are hewn (by local volunteers of course) to match the actual construction of the Manor House itself. They are colour-coded and prepared with dowels and peg-holes all fashioned and ready to find their mates. When put together (it usually takes a school group about two hours work) the children will have built a section of the house within a house, replicating the cruck construction all around them.

Heritage Education At It's Best

To the layman such an exercise might appear as no more than yet another example of the much derided trendiness in education. In truth it is no such thing. It is an example of Heritage Education at its best: it is history where it happened and could not have taken place in the classroom. When the children have completed their exercise they will have a fuller understanding of what they are looking at when they study the Manor House and therefore be better placed to appreciate its contents and history. They will also know what text books are talking about when manor houses are mentioned. They will have worked together to solve a practical problem. They will have added to their vocabulary: ridge-tree, saddle, purloin, collar-plate, wall-plate and tie-beam are just some of the words they will be using. They will learn from this the importance of precision in the use of words if language is to mean anything, and they will then be able to use their new words when, as they usually do, they come back to the museum with their fathers, mothers, their cousins and their uncles and their aunts. This is not trendiness. It is education of a depth and breadth that is simply not attainable with a text-book alone studied within the four walls of a classroom.

Of course, none of these rewards is available if the teachers regard such a visit as no more than an outing and if the museum staff look upon school parties as no more than bodies through the turnstiles. Teachers and museum staff must come together to plan visits in advance and conduct them properly when they are taking place and follow them up with further study in the classroom when they are over. This is one of the requirements for the Sandford Award. Helen Mason, Education Officer, and her helpers at the Ryedale

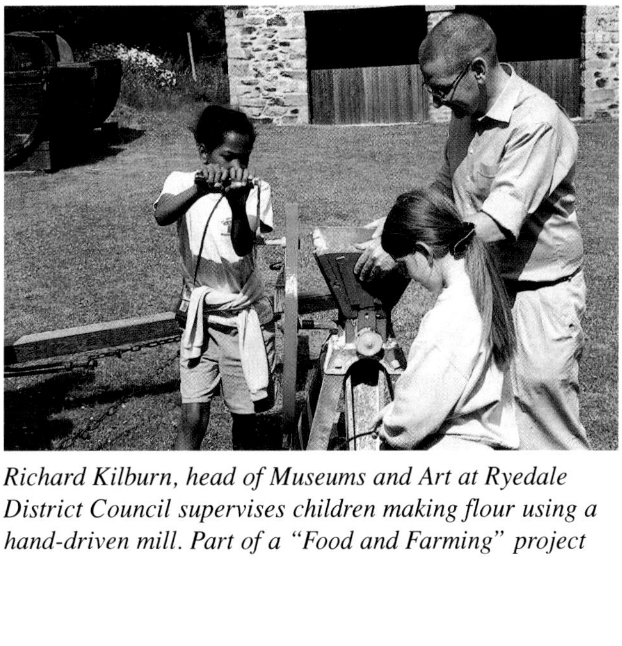

Richard Kilburn, head of Museums and Art at Ryedale District Council supervises children making flour using a hand-driven mill. Part of a "Food and Farming" project

Museum leave nothing to be desired under this heading. They have developed a whole range of practical projects based on the museum collections all of which are hands on, of which the cruck construction described above is only one example. Care has been taken to match the projects to curriculum demands and suggestions from schools are welcomed. There is a close co-operation with schools and Local Authority Advisers. The museum is also involved in in-service training and stages discussion sessions with local teachers. Information sheets are provided to help teachers plan visits and Helen Mason will also visit schools before and after their visits to help in the presentation and follow-up classroom work.

One of Those Wonderful Places

The focus at the Ryedale Folk Museum is local but its appeal is nation-wide and schools come from all over the country to benefit from its marvellous resources and splendid educational services. Schools from Essex book in every year as part of their field-work studies and yet another part of the service provided is advice on other sites and activities available in the area.

It is sometimes said that Heritage Education is of no relevance to inner-city children. The Heritage Education Trust has always regarded this criticism as ill-founded and dependant on narrow orthodoxy. Fortunately this view is not widespread among teachers and perhaps the last word on Ryedale should be given to an inner-city deputy head, Mr Ken Talbot of Matthew Murray High School, Leeds.

'I have personally taken many groups of inner-city youngsters to Hutton-le-Hole and district. It appears nothing is too much trouble and all my pupils without exception have returned to the City much better for their experience, especially for their hands-on work. To those of us in cities working with the less fortunate it is vital that there are facilities to allow us to provide them with very different experiences. Ryedale Folk Museum is one of those wonderful places.'

Children from South Kilvington C of E School, Thirsk, dressed in costumes provided at the museum play the parts of Richard and Mary Morrett. Two occupants of The Manor House in 1642

Melanie Grey and Mark Denness from St Wilfred's R C School, Ripon, prepare a plague remedy

Visit the best!
Culross, Fife
Free brochures and helpful service from the
Travel Trade Department
The National Trust for Scotland
5 Charlotte Square Edinburgh EH2 4DU
Telephone 0131 226 5922 Fax 0131 243 9302
The National Trust for Scotland

BUCKINGHAM PALACE
Originally the home of an English Duke, Buckingham Palace is the official London residence of the Sovereign and is one of the best known, and most potent symbols of the British Monarchy.
For details of opening arrangements and admission charges for The Queen's Gallery, the Royal Mews and the Summer Opening of the State Rooms telephone our 24 hr information line on 071-799 2331.

Museums and Art Galleries
in Great Britain and Ireland

Collections are listed in alphabetical order of Counties, and Towns within Counties, followed by a list of Service Museums, Subject, Location and Alphabetical Indices.

AVON

BATH

AMERICAN MUSEUM IN BRITAIN
Claverton Manor, Bath **Tel:** (01225) 460503 Education Dept (01225) 463538

he American decorative arts from the late 17th to the mid 19th century seen in a eries of furnished rooms and Galleries of special exhibits. Paintings, furniture, lass, woodwork, metalwork, textiles, hatboxes, folk art, miniature rooms. Marine oom. Fire exhibit. Dallas Pratt Collection of Historical Maps. American gardens tc.
)pen: End Mar-end Oct daily (except Mon) 2-5 Bank Holiday weekends Sun and 1on 11-5 During winter on application only school tours all year by previous rrangement except in Jan Gardens open throughout the season (except Mon) 1-6 eekends 12-6.
dmission: House Grounds and Galleries adults £5 OAPs £4.50 children £2.50 irounds and Galleries only adults £2 children £1 parties of children not admitted uring normal opening hours. Adult parties by previous arrangement with Special 'isits Secretary (1994 prices).
ocation: 2.5 m from Bath station via Bathwick Hill 3.75 m south-east of Bath via Varminster road (A36) and Claverton village (coaches must take the route via athwick Hill Bath as turning off A36 is not suitable for coaches) Bus 18 (to niversity) from bus station - alight at The Avenue 10 minutes walk to museum.
efreshments: Teas and refreshments at the house. Light lunches at weekends.
xhibitions/Events: Seasonal exhibitions in the New Gallery.

ATH POSTAL MUSEUM
8 Broad Street, Bath BA1 5LJ **Tel:** (01225) 460333
he story of the post, from earliest times to the present. Changing exhibitions. chool and other parties welcomed. Advance bookings requested. Video.
pen: All year Mon-Sat 11-5 & Mar-Dec Sun 2-5.
efreshments: Tea/coffee available.
ift Shop.

THE BOOK MUSEUM
(Hylton Bayntun-Coward)
Manvers Street, Bath **Tel:** (01225) 466000
Showing the craft of bookbinding, and Bath in Literature, and featuring a reconstruction of Dickens's study at Gadshill.
Open: Office hours Mon-Fri and Sat morning.
Admission: Adults £2 students/children £1.

THE BRITISH FOLK ART COLLECTION
(Andras Kalman)
Countess of Huntingdon Chapel, The Vineyard, Paragon, Bath BA1 5NA
Tel: (01225) 446020
The British Folk Art Collection, a comprehensive selection of 19th century paintings and artifacts depicting people and animals with a direct simplicity, both revealing and entertaining.
Open: All year Tues-Sat and Bank Hols 10.30-5 also Apr-Oct Sun 2-5.
Shop open throughout season selling prints, books, postcards and interesting things.

FASHION RESEARCH CENTRE
(Bath City Council)
4 Circus, Bath **Tel:** (01225) 461111 Ext. 2752
Facilities for study and research, including extensive reference library and study collection of costume.
Open: Mon-Thurs 9.30-5 Fri 9.30-4.30 (by appointment).
Admission: Free.

GEORGIAN GARDEN
(Bath City Council)
Gravel Walk, Bath **Tel:** (01225) 461111 Ext. 2760
Authentic 18th century town garden layout, discovered by excavation and recreated using plants of the period.
Open: May-Oct Mon-Fri 9-4.30.
Admission: Free.
Location: Gravel Walk.

GUILDHALL
(Bath City Council)
High Street, Bath BA1 5AW **Tel:** (01225) 461111 Ext. 2785
18th century Banqueting Room.
Open: Mon-Thurs 8.30-5 Fri 8.30-4.30 subject to bookings.
Admission: Free.
Refreshments: By arrangement.

HOLBURNE MUSEUM AND CRAFTS STUDY CENTRE
Great Pulteney Street, Bath **Tel:** (01225) 466669

HOLBURNE MUSEUM & CRAFTS STUDY CENTRE

Great Pulteney Street,
Bath BA2 4DB
Tel: 01225-466669

Elegant 18th century building housing an excellent collection of 17th-18th century fine and decorative art. Work by British 20th century artist-craftsmen on view in the Crafts Study Centre including pots by Bernard Leach. Temporary exhibitions throughout year.

Open weekdays 11-5, Sundays 2.30-6. Closed mid-December - mid February and Mondays November to Easter.

Licensed Teahouse, Garden. Free Parking.

Queen Charlotte (1744-1818) by Johann Zoffanny 1733-1810

The Holburne Museum, Bath, is a successful combination of ancient and modern. Set in an elegant 18th century building the collection of decorative and fine art which it contains was made by Sir Thomas William Holburne (1793-1874) and includes superb English and continental silver and porcelain. Italian maiolica and bronzes, together with glass, furniture, miniatures and old master paintings. Fine examples of work by British 20th century artist craftsmen are also on view in the Crafts Study Centre. This collection and archive embraces printed and woven textiles, pottery, furniture and calligraphy. Study facilities by appointment. Temporary exhibitions and events throughout the year.
Open: Mon-Sat 11-5 Sun 2.30-6 open Bank Holidays except Christmas closed mid Dec-mid Feb and Mons Nov-Easter.
Admission: Adults £3.50 OAPs £3 unemployed/students £2 children £1.50.
Refreshments: Licensed tea-house in lovely garden.
Free Parking. Coaches welcome by prior appointment.

THE MUSEUM OF EAST ASIAN ART
12 Bennett Street, Bath B1 2QL **Tel:** (01225) 464640 **Fax:** (01225) 461718

THE MUSEUM OF EAST ASIAN ART

12 Bennett Street,
Bath BA1 2QL
Tel: 01225 464640

Over 500 East Asian art treasures in pottery, stoneware, porcelain, bronze, gold, silver, enamel, cloisonne, jade, bamboo and lacquer, beautifully displayed in 5 galleries in a restored Georgian house close to Bath's famous Circus.

Museum shop. Facilities for visitors with special needs including wheelchair access to all floors.

Open weekdays 10-6. Sundays 10-5. (Last admission half an hour before closing time). Closed for the Christmas and New Year period.

Groups welcome. Rates on application.

Over 500 East Asian Art treasures displayed in a restored Georgian house close t Bath's famous Circus. The Museum houses a wide range of Chinese ceramic (2500BC to 1820AD), jades (5500BC TO 1800AD), metalwares (1900BC t 1881AD) and decorative arts. Art objects from Japan, Korea, Thailand, Indochina Tibet and Mongolia are also represented in the collection.
Open: Mon-Sat 10-6 Sun 1-5 (last admission 30 minutes before closing time).
Admission: Adults £3 children 8-16 £1.50 (under 8's free) family ticket £8 con cessions for OAP's. Group and educational visits are welcome by arrangement.
Location: 12 Bennett Street, Bath just off Bath Circus.
Exhibitions/Events: Major exhibition 'Jades from China' featuring 354 Jade ranging from Neolithic times to early 19th century. Until at least Mar 1995. Facilities for people with special needs. Accompanied wheelchair lift access to a floors. For further information please telephone above number. Introductory vide in six languages.

MR BOWLER'S BUSINESS - BATH INDUSTRIAL HERITAGE CENTRE
Julian Road, Bath BA2 6RN **Tel:** (01225) 318348
The entire stock-in-trade of J.B. Bowler, Victorian brass founder, engineer and mineral water manufacturer, displayed in authentic settings - some working machinery.
Open: Easter-Oct daily 10-5 Nov-Easter weekends only 10-5 closed Dec 24 25 26.
Admission: Adults £3 children/OAPs/students £2 family ticket £7.50 (up to 6 family members 2 adults).
Location: Set back off Julian Road.
Refreshments: Cafe/tea-room.
Exhibitions/Events: Temporary exhibitions throughout year.
Parties all year by appointment, apply for educational facilities.

MUSEUM OF COSTUME
(Bath City Council)
Assembly Rooms, Bennett Street, Bath **Tel:** (01225) 461111 Ext. 2785
The Museum of Costume is one of the largest and most prestigious in this country and is housed in Bath's famous 18th century Assembly Rooms, designed by John Wood the Younger in 1769. The Museum's extensive collections are devoted to fashionable dress for men, women and children from the late 16th century to the present day.
Open: Daily 10-5 except Sun 11-5 last tickets half an hour before closing.
Admission: Adults £3.20 children £2 reduction for parties family ticket (2+4) £16.
Refreshments: By arrangement.
Specialist shop on site.

NO. 1 ROYAL CRESCENT
(Bath Preservation Trust)
Bath BA1 2LR **Tel:** (01225) 428126

No. 1 ROYAL CRESCENT

BATH, BA1 2LR
Museum telephone Bath (01225) 428126

Number 1 was presented to the Bath Preservation Trust in 1968 and has been restored to its original position as one of the grandest and most beautiful houses in the World Heritage City of Bath. The Royal Crescent, started in 1767 by John Wood the Younger, is a perfect example of Palladian architecture. Visitors to Number 1 can enjoy a house redecorated and furnished so that it appears as it might have been soon after the house was completed.

A Georgian Town House in Bath's most magnificent crescent; redecorated and furnished to show the visitor how it might have appeared in the late 18th century.
Open: 1 Mar-30 Oct Tues-Sun and Bank Hol Mons 10.30-5 31 Oct-10 Dec Tues-Sun 10.30-4 (last admission .5 an hour before closing).
Admission: Adults £3.50 concessions £2.50.
Museum Shop.

ROMAN BATHS MUSEUM
(Bath City Council)
Abbey Church Yard, Bath **Tel:** (01225) 461111 Ext. 2785 **Fax:** (01225) 448521
Adjoins the extensive remains of the Roman Baths and temple and includes material from that and other Roman sites, including architectural fragments, inscriptions, metalware and offerings from the sacred spring.
Open: Winter Mon-Sat 9-5 Sun 10-5 summer daily 9-6 (Aug late opening 8-10).
Admission: Adults £5 children £3 (including entrance to Museum in Pump Room Roman Baths and Temple Precinct) admission to Pump Room free. Family ticket (2+4) £13. Reductions for parties.

THE ROYAL PHOTOGRAPHIC SOCIETY
The Octagon, Milsom Street, Bath BA1 1DN **Tel:** (01225) 462841 **Fax:** (01225) 448688
Five Galleries with changing exhibitions, museum, restaurant and shop.
Open: All year seven days a week except Christmas Day and Boxing Day 9.30-5.30.
Admission: Adults £3 concessions £1.75 accompanied children under 16/disabled free.
Location: Central Bath.
Refreshments: Available.
Exhibitions/Events: Continuous.
Facilities for the disabled. Museum shop.

VICTORIA ART GALLERY
(Bath City Council)
Bridge Street, Bath **Tel:** (01225) 461111 Ext. 2772 **Fax:** (01225) 469982
Exhibitions from permanent collections and temporary exhibitions frequently changed. Paintings, prints and drawings, glass, ceramics and watches. Local topography.
Open: Mon-Fri 10-6 Sat 10-5.30 closed Sun and Bank Holidays.
Admission: Free.

BRISTOL

ARNOLFINI GALLERY
16 Narrow Quay, Bristol **Tel:** (0117) 929 9191

BRISTOL CITY MUSEUM AND ART GALLERY
(City of Bristol)
Queen's Road, Bristol BS8 1RL **Tel:** (0117) 922 3571 **Fax:** (0117) 922 2047
Permanent collections represent applied art, fine art, oriental art, archaeology, ethnography, Egyptology, geology and natural history. Displays include dinosaurs, Bristol ceramics, silver, the Bristol School of Artists, 19th century French paintings, Chinese and Japanese ceramics. Changing temporary exhibitions in the Solaglas Gallery.
Open: Daily 10-5 (inc Sun).
Admission: Adult £2 free Leisure Card holders and under 16.
Refreshments: Available.
Museum Shop.

DAVID CROSS GALLERY
7 Boyces Avenue, Clifton, Bristol BS8 4AA **Tel:** (0117) 973 2614
Specialists in traditional British paintings and drawings.
Open: Mon-Sat 9-6.
Please telephone for details of forthcoming exhibitions.

THE EXPLORATORY HANDS-ON SCIENCE CENTRE
Bristol Old Station, Temple Meads, Bristol BS1 6QU **Tel:** (0117) 925 2008 Info. Line: (0117) 922 5944 **Fax:** (0117) 925 7342
Over 150 exhibits on two floors. All exhibits are Hands-On.
Open: 10-5 7 days a week.
Admission: Adults £4 children £2.50 discounts for group bookings.
Location: Next to B.R. Temple Meads railway station in the Centre of Bristol.
Refreshments: Cafe on site (weekends & school holidays only).
Exhibitions/Events: Throughout the year.
Shop. Disabled access.

GUILD GALLERY
68 Park Street, Bristol BS1 5JY **Tel:** (0117) 926 5548
Monthly exhibitions by mainly, but not exclusively, West Country artists and craftspeople.
Open: Mon-Sat 9.30-5 closed Bank holidays.
Admission: Free.
Location: Second Floor.
Refreshments: Shop, restaurant.
Not suitable for the disabled.

WESTON-SUPER-MARE

THE INTERNATIONAL HELICOPTER MUSEUM
Weston Airport, Locking Moor Road, Weston-super-Mare BS22 8PP **Tel:** (01934) 635227 **Fax:** (01934) 822400
The Country's only dedicated helicopter museum, with more than 50 full-sized exhibits, restoration hangar, model and interior displays and Ride Simulator. Open Cockpit Days second Sunday each month April-October.
Open: Daily 10-6 (Nov-Mar 4) closed Christmas Boxing Day and New Years Day.
Admission: Adults £3 OAPs £2.50 children £2 and 15% reduction for 15 people or more.
Location: A371 on town's east boundary and 5 mins from J 21/M5.
Refreshments: Cafeteria with hot and cold snacks.
Exhibitions/Events: Annual Helidays Helicopter Show July 29/30 1995.

WESTON-SUPER-MARE HERITAGE CENTRE
(Weston-super-Mare Civic Society)
3-6 Wadham Street, Weston-super-Mare BS23 1JY **Tel:** (01934) 412144
The story of the resort, the coast, and local countryside in models and pictures from prehistory to modern times. An introduction to discovering the district, with special treatment of the Victorian resort. Audio-visual presentation.
Open: Mon-Sat 10-5.
Admission: Adults £1 accompanied children under 16 free unaccompanied children under 16 50p parties by arrangement group rate of 30+ 50p.
Location: Wadham Street (bottom of Grove Park).
Refreshments: Cornish coffee house - tea coffee and light lunches.
Shop and information point with local trails, guides, books on local subjects and gifts. Public car park 50 yds. Shop and cafe suitable for disabled persons.

BEDFORDSHIRE

BEDFORD

BEDFORD MUSEUM
(Bedford Borough Council)
Castle Lane, Bedford MK40 3XD **Tel:** (01234) 353323
The Museum for North Bedfordshire with displays of local material including archaeology, social history, natural history and geology. Programme of temporary exhibitions, children's activities and other events.
Open: Tues-Sat 11-5 Sun and Bank Hol Mons 2-5.
Admission: Free.

BROMHAM MILL
(Bedfordshire County Council Leisure Services)
Bromham, Bedford **Tel:** (01234) 228330
Restored water mill and Art Gallery with varied contemporary exhibitions changing each month. Milling demonstrations on the last Sunday of each month and Bank Holidays during the open season and by arrangement. Natural history room, special exhibitions, and craft cabinets. Nature sanctuary and adjoining picnic area.
Open: Apr-Oct Wed-Fri 10.30-4.30 Sat Sun and Bank Hols 11.30-6.
Admission: (1994 rates) Adults 70p children/OAPs 35p party rates on application.
Refreshments: Fresh filter coffee.
Exhibitions/Events: National Apple Day celebrated each Oct.
Car parking for 30 cars. Some parts of this property are not suitable for disabled.

THE BUNYAN MEETING LIBRARY AND MUSEUM
(Trustees of Bunyan Meeting)
Mill Street, Bedford MK40 3EU **Tel:** (01234) 358870/212485
Open: Apr-Oct inc Tues-Sat 2-4 also Jul-Sept Tues-Sat 10.30-12.30.
Admission: Adults 50p OAPs/children 30p.
Location: Mill Street Bedford.
Items relating to John Bunyan's life and works, including 'The Pilgrim's Progress' in 168 languages.

CECIL HIGGINS ART GALLERY AND MUSEUM
(Bedford Borough Council and the Trustees of the Gallery)
Castle Close, Bedford MK40 3NY **Tel:** (01234) 211222 **Fax:** (01234) 221606
Award winning re-created Victorian Mansion, displayed in room settings to create a 'lived-in' atmosphere, including a room with furniture designed by the Victorian architect, William Burges. Adjoining gallery with changing displays of important watercolours, prints and drawings, and permanent displays of English and Continental ceramics and glass which are particularly rich in 18th century pieces. Some objets d'art, metalwork and jewellery, and fine collection of Bedfordshire lace.
Open: Tues-Sat 11-5 Sun and Bank Holiday Mon 2-5 closed Mon Good Friday and Christmas.
Admission: Free.
Location: Centre of Bedford, just off the River Embankment.
Refreshments: For groups booking in advance only.
Exhibitions/Events: Telephone Gallery for details.
Sandford Award winner, 1989 and 1993. Special arrangements for group or evening visits, and lectures. Facilities for the disabled. Gallery shop.

LUTON

JOHN DONY FIELD CENTRE
(Luton Museum Service)
c/o Bushmead Community Centre, Hancock Drive, Luton LU2 7SF **Tel:** (01582) 483986 **Fax:** (01582) 483178
Interpretation of local environment and educational facility.
Open: Mon-Fri 9.30-4.30 Sun 9.30-1.
Admission: Free.
Location: On Bushmead Estate, 3 miles north of Luton town centre.
Refreshments: Pre-booking only.
Facilities for people with disabilities. Please telephone for further information. Educational enquiries: telephone Dr T. Tween at the above number.

LUTON MUSEUM AND ART GALLERY
(Luton Museum Service)
Wardown Park, Luton LU2 7HA **Tel:** (01582) 36941 **Fax:** (01582) 483178
Collections/displays archaeology, costume, dolls and toys, fine and decorative art, local history, social history, military (Beds and Herts Regiment), natural history/geology, lace, straw plait, changing exhibitions.
Open: Weekdays and Sat 10-5 Sun 1-5 for Christmas/New Year closures and further details please phone museum.
Admission: Free.
Location: 1 mile north of Luton town centre, regular buses, free parking.
Refreshments: Tea area for light refreshments.
Study access to reserve collections by appointment only. Educational group visits welcome by prior booking. Facilities for people with disabilities: lift to first floor. Free parking. Gift shop.

STOCKWOOD CRAFT MUSEUM AND GARDENS HOME OF THE MOSSMAN COLLECTION
(Luton Museum Service)
Stockwood Park, Farley Hill, Luton LU1 4BH **Tel:** (01582) 38714 **Fax:** (01582) 483178
The largest collection, on public display, of horse-drawn vehicles and carriages in the UK. Collections/displays rural crafts and trades including thatching, saddlery, shoemaking, rushwork, blacksmithing, wood crafts, wheelwrighting and agriculture. Also to be seen: craft workshops, regular weekend craft demonstrations, period gardens and sculptures by Ian Hamilton Finlay.
Open: Apr-Oct weekdays and Sat 10-5 Sun 10-6 closed Mons (except Bank holiday Mons) open Nov-Mar Sat Sun 10-4.
Admission: Free.
Location: Near M1 exit 10.
Refreshments: Conservatory tea-room.
Exhibitions/Events: Events programme in summer months.
Gift shop. Access facilities for people with disabilities. Guided tours for pre-booked groups.

BERKSHIRE

BRACKNELL

THE LOOK OUT COUNTRYSIDE AND HERITAGE CENTRE
(Bracknell Forest Borough Council)
The Look Out, Nine Mile Ride, Bracknell RE12 7QW **Tel:** (01344) 868222
The Look Out houses a permanent exhibition featuring the story of Bracknell. It explores the history of the local area as well as its natural environment. There is also

a section on the local industries. The centre also has a series of changing exhibitions featuring historical and environmental topics. These are developed with children in mind complete with 6 quizzes and childrens games.
Open: Daily 10-5 closed Christmas Day and Boxing Day.
Admission: Exhibition/special exhibition and Tower adults 50p children/OAPs 50p disabled free. Groups welcome at above rates
Exhibitions/Events: Childrens holiday events and workshops. Craft Fairs.
The Look Out is situated in a large area of woodland with walks, nature trails, picnic area, gift shop, Tourist Information, lookout tower and mountain bike hire.

COOKHAM-ON-THAMES

STANLEY SPENCER GALLERY

King's Hall, Cookham-on-Thames SL6 9SJ **Tel:** (01628) 520890/520043
Major Spencer collection (The Last Supper 1920, Christ Preaching at Cookham Regatta 1959, etc) in village immortalized by the artist.
Open: Easter-Oct daily 10.30-5.30 Nov-Easter Sat Sun and Bank Holidays 11-5.
Admission: Fee charged.
Location: Cookham, Berks.

Refreshments: Available in High Street.
Gallery shop. Enquiries, telephone on the above number.

READING

BLAKE'S LOCK MUSEUM

(Reading Borough Council)
Gasworks Road, off Kenavon Drive, Reading RG1 3DH **Tel:** (01734) 590630 **Fax:** (01734) 590630
Displays the history of the industrial and commercial life of Reading in the 19th and early 20th centuries, and the development of its waterways.
Open: Tues-Fri 10-5 Sat and Sun 2-5 Bank Hol Mon 2-5.
Admission: Free.
Location: On north bank of River Kennet, 15 minutes walk from central Reading.
Exhibitions/Events: In Caravan Gallery: Roman Silchester until Mar 95. Exhibitions also in Screens House.
Full education programme available for schools.

MUSEUM OF ENGLISH RURAL LIFE
(The University of Reading)
Whiteknights, Reading **Tel:** (01734) 318660
Part of The Rural History Centre, this is a national collection of material relating to the history of the English countryside, including agriculture, crafts, domestic utensils and village life. There is a permanent exhibition open to the general public and, in addition, study collections of objects and documentary material which may be consulted on application to the Secretary.
Open: Tues-Sat 10-1 and 2-4.30 closed Sun Mon and Public Holidays.
Admission: Adults £1 children free.

THE MUSEUM OF READING
(Reading Borough Council)
Blagrave Street, Reading RG1 1QH **Tel:** (01734) 399800 **Fax:** (01734) 399881
The Museum of Reading re-opened in September 1993. Displays feature Britain's Bayeux Tapestry, Reading's faithful victorian replica The Story of Reading Gallery which traces Reading's development from a Saxon settlement on the banks of the River Kennet to the commercial heart of today's Thames Valley.
Open: Tues-Sat 10-5 Sun & Bank Hols 2-5.
Admission: Free.
Location: In Town Centre adjacent to Town Hall; 5 mins from rail station.
Refreshments: Available on site in 3B's Cafe
Exhibitions/Events: In Link Gallery and Earley Charity Room.
Full education programme available for schools.

NATIONAL DAIRY MUSEUM
Wellington Country Park, Riseley, Reading RG7 1SP **Tel:** (01734) 326444
Exhibits and displays showing the growth of the dairy industry from a small rural activity to a large countrywide industry.
Open: Mar 1-Oct 31 daily 10-5.30 also weekends in winter.
Admission: Includes entry to Country Park. Adults £2.80 children £1.30 (under 5's free) party reduction for 20 or more £2.25 children £1.10 (1993 charges).

SLOUGH

SLOUGH MUSEUM
23 Bath Road, Slough SL1 3UF **Tel:** (01753) 526422
Did you know that 3 famous 18th century astronomers lived in Slough? Just one of the surprising facts we tell in Slough's story from mammoths to modern town.
Open: Wed-Fri 12-4 Sat and Sun 2-5 Bank Holidays 2-5.
Admission: Free.
Parties free by arrangement. Free parking at weekend. Access by wheelchair possible but no disabled toilet.

BUCKINGHAMSHIRE

AYLESBURY

BUCKINGHAMSHIRE COUNTY MUSEUM
(Buckinghamshire County Council)
Church Street, Aylesbury HP20 2QP **Tel:** (01296) 696012 **Fax:** (01296) 696012
Displays illustrating local history and temporary exhibitions.
Open: Mon-Sat 10-1.30 and 2-5 closed Bank Hols Christmas Day Boxing Day New Year's Day and Good Friday.
Admission: Free.
Location: 4 minutes walk from railway station.
Undergoing major refurbishment to be complete in Oct 1995.

CHALFONT ST. GILES

CHILTERN OPEN AIR MUSEUM
Newland Park, Gorelands Lane, Chalfont St Giles **Tel:** (01494) 871117 (office)/875542 (Education Dept)/872163 (Information Line)

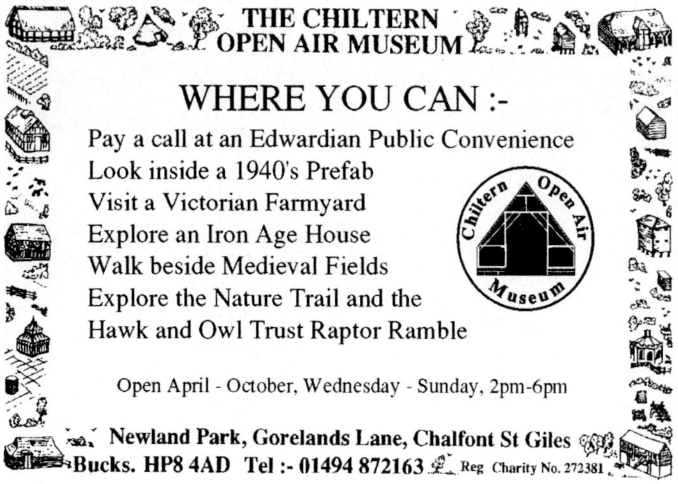
THE CHILTERN
OPEN AIR MUSEUM
WHERE YOU CAN :-
Pay a call at an Edwardian Public Convenience
Look inside a 1940's Prefab
Visit a Victorian Farmyard
Explore an Iron Age House
Walk beside Medieval Fields
Explore the Nature Trail and the
Hawk and Owl Trust Raptor Ramble
Chiltern Open Air Museum
Open April - October, Wednesday - Sunday, 2pm-6pm
Newland Park, Gorelands Lane, Chalfont St Giles
Bucks. HP8 4AD Tel :- 01494 872163
Reg Charity No. 272381

Historic buildings and rural life of the Chilterns from the Iron Age to the Victorian era. Barns, granaries, stables, cartsheds, toll house, cottages, public convenience and furniture factory rescued from demolition and re-erected in 45 acres of beautiful countryside.
Open: Apr-Oct Wed-Sun and Bank Holidays 2-6.
Admission: Fee charged.
Location: Signposted on A413 at Chalfont St. Giles & on leaving J17 M25.
Refreshments: Available.
Special events are held during the season. School parties welcome all year round. Free car park. Gift Shop. Interpret Britain Award Winner 1992.

MILTON'S COTTAGE
Chalfont St. Giles **Tel:** (01494) 872313
Open: Mar 1-Oct 31 Wed-Sun and Bank Holiday Mons 10-1 and 2-6 closed Mon & Tues and Nov Dec Jan and Feb.
Admission: Adults £2 children under 15 60p parties of 20 or more £1.50

HIGH WYCOMBE

THE DISRAELI MUSEUM
(The National Trust)
Hughenden Manor, High Wycombe **Tel:** (01494) 532580
Home of Benjamin Disraeli, Earl of Beaconsfield (1847-81). Disraeli relics, furniture, pictures and books.

WYCOMBE LOCAL HISTORY AND CHAIR MUSEUM
(Wycombe District Council)
Castle Hill House, Priory Avenue, High Wycombe HP13 6PX **Tel:** (01494) 421895 **Fax:** (01494) 421808

WYCOMBE •MUSEUM•

Attractive 18th century house built on a medieval site and set in Victorian gardens with a nature trail. Exhibitions on the crafts and history of the local area highlighting the furniture industry. Displays on archaeology, art and much more.
Open: All year Mon-Sat special events only Suns and Bank Holiday.
Admission: Free.
Exhibitions/Events: Programme of temporary exhibitions and events.

MILTON KEYNES

MILTON KEYNES EXHIBITION GALLERY
(Buckinghamshire County Council)
Milton Keynes Library, 555 Silbury Boulevard, Milton Keynes MK9 3HL
Tel: (01908) 835025 **Fax:** (01908) 835028
Programme of exhibitions changing monthly, covering art, craft, social and local history.
Open: Tues Wed Fri Sat 10-5 Thurs 10-8 closed Mon Sun Christmas Day Boxing Day New Year's Day and Good Friday.
Admission: Free.
Location: In central library building.
Facilities for the disabled.

MILTON KEYNES MUSEUM OF INDUSTRY & RURAL LIFE
Stacey Hill Farm, Southern Way, Wolverton, Milton Keynes MK12 5EJ
Tel: (01908) 316222
An extensive collection of industrial, agricultural and domestic items including tractors, implements, stationary engines, lawnmowers, and photographic, printing and telephone equipment. Exhibitions include Wolverton & Stony Stratford Tram, Salmons-Tickford, E & H Roberts.
Open: Apr 14-Oct 29 Wed-Sun 1.30-4.30 Bank Holiday Mon 1.30-4.30 also at Christmas and Lent half term. Please ring for details. Schools and group visits at all times by arrangement.
Admission: Charges.
Location: Access off MK Grid Road H2, Millers Way.
Refreshments: Available.
Exhibitions/Events: May 21 July 16 Aug 20 Sept 17 11.30-5.30. Special exhibitions and craft displays.
Free car park. Souvenir shop.

OLNEY

COWPER AND NEWTON MUSEUM
Orchard Side, Market Place, Olney MK46 4AJ **Tel:** (01234) 711516
Personal belongings of 18th century port, William Cowper, and Rev. John Newton (author of 'Amazing Grace'). Exhibitions of bobbin lace. Two gardens. one containing Cowper's summer house.
Open: Apr 1-Oct 31 Tues-Sat 10-1 and 2-5 Nov 1-Mar 31 1-4 closed Dec 15-Jan 31 and Good Fri open Bank Holiday Mon.
Admission: Adults £1.50 OAPs/unemployed £1 children/students (on production of a student card) 50p parties of 12+ £1.
Location: Market Place, Olney; N of Newport Pagnell on A509.
Refreshments: None at museum but several nearby.
Free Car Parking on Market Place opposite, except Thurs.

CAMBRIDGESHIRE

CAMBRIDGE

CAMBRIDGE AND COUNTY FOLK MUSEUM
2/3 Castle Street, Cambridge CB3 OAQ
The museum's collections reflect the everyday life of the people of Cambridge and Cambridgeshire from the seventeenth century to the present day.
Open: Apr-Sept Mon-Sat 10.30-5 Sun 2-5 Oct-Mar closed Mons Tues-Sun as above.
Admission: Adults £1 children/OAPs/students/unemployed/disabled 50p.

DUXFORD AIRFIELD
Duxford Airfield, Duxford, Cambridge CB2 4QR **Tel:** (01223) 835000 (information line)
Once a famous RAF station which played a vital role in the Battle of Britain, Duxford Airfield is now home to the finest collection of military and civil aircraft in Britain - from First World War fighters to Concorde. Also on display are military vehicles, artillery and large naval exhibits. Among the other attractions are a unique Showscan Dynamic Motion Theatre, an adventure playground, a 1940's pre-fab furnished in Utility style and many special exhibitions.
Open: Daily summer (end Mar-mid Oct) 10-6 winter 10-4 (or dusk if ealier) closed Dec 24-26.
Location: Junction 10 off the M11.
Refreshments: Restaurant picnic areas.
Souvenir shop. Ample free parking.

KETTLE'S YARD
(University of Cambridge)
Castle Street, Cambridge CB3 0AQ **Tel:** (01223) 352124
20th Century Art in a domestic setting with furniture, decorative arts, pebbles and shells. Artists include Alfred Wallis, Ben Nicholson, Barbara Hepworth, Christopher Wood, Henri Gaudier-Brzeska and Henry Moore. Contemporary and 20th century exhibitions in the gallery.
Open: Gallery Tues-Sat 12.30-5.30 Sun 2-5.30 closed Mon and Bank Hols **House** daily 2-4 closed Mon and Bank Hols.
Admission: Free.
Location: Corner of Castle Street and Northampton Street.
Refreshments: Coffee machine.
Exhibitions/Events: 6/7 20th century exhibitions per year. Leaflet produced.
Parties £2.50 per head for out of hours tours. Car Parks and metres in town.

ELY

ELY MUSEUM
High Street, Ely CB7 4HL **Tel:** (01353) 666655
Displays covering the social and natural history of the Isle of Ely. Collections include local archaeology, Fenland farm and craft instruments, the bicycle which won the world's first bicycle race, video films of Fenland life and much more besides. Something for everybody!
Open: Summer Tues-Sun 10.30-1 and 2.15-5 winter Tues-Fri 11.30-3.30 weekends 11.30-4.
Admission: Party reductions.
Limited access for disabled.

THE STAINED GLASS MUSEUM
North Triforium, Ely, Ely Cathedral CB7 4DN **Tel:** (01353) 778645
Stained glass from medieval to modern times, displayed at eye level. Models of a workshop, origins and history of the craft. Children's activity table. Audio tour.
Open: Mar-Oct Mon-Fri 10.30-4 Sat and Bank Holidays 10.30-4.30 Sun 12-3 plus every weekend throughout the year and local school holidays.
Admission: Entry charge. Party reductions.
Location: North triforium gallery in Ely Cathedral.
Refreshments: Available in Cathedral.
Access is difficult for disabled.

HUNTINGDON

THE CROMWELL MUSEUM
(Cambridgeshire County Council)
Grammar School Walk, Huntingdon **Tel:** (01480) 425830

CROMWELL
Museum
Grammar School Walk, Huntingdon
Open every day except Monday
Free admission 01480-425830

Oliver Cromwell was born in Huntingdon in 1599, and spent his early life in the town. The Museum illustrates the life of Oliver Cromwell and the Parliamentary side of the Puritan Revolution 1642-1660.
Open: All year round. Apr-Oct 11-1 and 2-5 Tues-Fri 11-1 and 2-4 Sat & Sun Nov-Mar 1-4 Tues-Fri 11-1 and 2-4 Sat 2-4 Sun.
Admission: Free.
Location: The Museum is in Cromwell's old school in the centre of the town.
Refreshments: Available nearby.
Party bookings are welcome. Coach parking. For further details and leaflet write or telephone above number.

MARCH

MARCH AND DISTRICT MUSEUM
(March Town Council)
High Street, March PE15 9JJ **Tel:** (01354) 55300
Situated in mid 19th century school buildings. The museum has a large collection of domestic and agricultural artifacts, and a number of restored Fen buildings.
Open: All year Wed 10-12 Sat 10-12 and 2-4.30.
Admission: Free.
Parties welcome by arrangement. Telephone (01354) 54783.

PETERBOROUGH

RAILWORLD
Oundle Road, Peterborough PE2 9NR **Tel:** (01733) 344240
'Railworld': Exhibitions on modern trains and the environment and modern trains, the role of rail in tomorrow's global society, and an international heritage section.
Open: Daily 11-4 Nov-Feb only Mon-Fri.
Admission: Adults £1.50 with usual reductions.
Location: Peterborough City Centre, good parking off A605 Oundle road.
Refreshments: 5 minutes walk away is an ASDA restaurant.
Exhibitions/Events: 'PR150' throughout 1995 Peterborough celebrates its 150 railway years.
Facilities for the disabled.

SACREWELL FARM AND COUNTRY CENTRE
Sacrewell, Thornhaugh, Peterborough PE8 6HJ **Tel:** (01780) 782222
Large open air museum on attractive farm site. Working 18th century watermill on Domesday site. Very large collection of hand implements, tools, and equipment relating to farming, and the Mill's history, housed in 18th century farm buildings; traditional building materials.
Open: Always.
Admission: Adults £2.50 OAPs £2 children (2-16) 75p family maximum £8.
Location: Easily accessible from A47, 8m W of Peterborough.
Refreshments: Available.
Ample parking, toilets and gift shop. Farm, nature and general interest trails. Aviary, maze and other entertainments for children.

ST. IVES

NORRIS MUSEUM
(St. Ives Town Council)
The Broadway, St. Ives PE17 4BX **Tel:** (01480) 465101
Local history of Huntingdonshire: fossils, archaeology, bygones, crafts, research library.
Open: Mon-Fri 10-1 and 2-5 (winter closes at 4) Sat 10-12 May-Sept also open 2-5 Sat and Sun.
Admission: Free.

WISBECH

WISBECH AND FENLAND MUSEUM
Museum Square, Wisbech **Tel:** (01945) 583817
Local history, archaeology, natural history, geology, ceramics, bygones, Clarkson and the Abolition of Slavery, African Art, Egyptology (library by appointment only).
Open: Tues to Sat 10-5 (closes at 4 in winter).

CHANNEL ISLANDS

GUERNSEY

CASTLE CORNET
St. Peter Port, Guernsey **Tel:** (01481) 721657
Medieval castle with important Elizabethan, Georgian, Victorian and Second World War additions. Major new maritime museum; museums with military, CI Militia, RAF, German Occupation collections; picture galleries; refectory and shop.
Open: Apr-Oct daily 10.30-5.30 Noon-day Gun conducted parties at 10.45 and 2.30.
Admission: Adults £4 children £1.50 OAPs £2.
Location: St. Peter Port
Refreshments: Refectory

FORT GREY SHIPWRECK MUSEUM
Rocquaine Bay, St. Peter's, Guernsey **Tel:** (01481) 65036
Napoleonic fort restored as a maritime museum specialising in west coast shipwrecks.
Open: Apr-Oct daily 10.30-12.30 1.30-5.30.
Admission: Adults £1.50 children 50p OAPs 75p.
Location: Rocquaine Bay, St. Peter's.

GERMAN OCCUPATION MUSEUM
Forest, Guernsey
Open: Apr-Oct daily 10-5 winter Sun and Thurs afternoons 2-4.30.
Admission: Adults £2.50 children £1 (including German Fortifications).
Refreshments: Tea-room and garden.
Also Pleinmont Tower and fortifications (summer only).

GUERNSEY MUSEUM & ART GALLERY
St. Peter Port, Guernsey GY1 1UG **Tel:** (01481) 726518
Guernsey's new museum tells the story of the island and its people. It also includes an art gallery and audio-visual theatre. Frequent special exhibitions.
Open: Daily 10.30-5.30 (4.30 winter).
Admission: Adults £2 children 75p OAPs £1.
Location: Candie Gardens, St. Peter Port.
Refreshments: Tea-room.

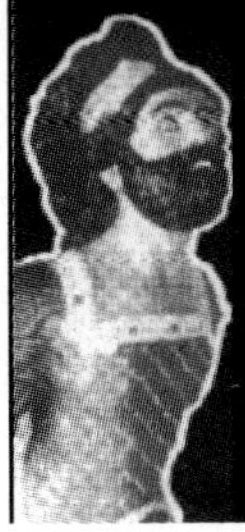

JERSEY

SIR FRANCIS COOK GALLERY

(Jersey Museums Service)

Route de la Trinité, Augrès, Jersey **Tel:** (01534) 863333 **Fax:** (01534) 864437

Converted methodist chapel - permanent collection of work of Sir Francis Cook.

Open: As advertised locally.

Admission: Free.

Location: Augres, Trinity.

Car parking. Director of Museums Michael Day B.A., A.M.A.

ELIZABETH CASTLE

(Jersey Museums Service)

St. Aubins Bay, Jersey **Tel:** (01534) 23971 **Fax:** (01534) 610338

Elizabethan fortress built on an islet about one mile from shore. Eighteenth century garrison buildings with interpretive displays and museum of Jersey militia, refortified by the German occupying forces in 1940-44. New permanent exhibition 'In War and Peace' opened in the officers' quarters July 1989.

Open: Apr-Nov daily 9.30-6 including Bank Hols.

Admission: Adults £2.50 children/OAPs £1.25 children under 10 free.

Refreshments: Cafe.

Parties by arrangement. Director of Museums Michael Day B.A., A.M.A.

HAMPTONNE

(Jersey Museums Service)

Rue de la Patente, St Lawrence, Jersey **Tel:** (01534) 863955 **Fax:** (01534) 863935

In the rural heart of Jersey a farmstead, lived and worked in for six centuries, has been restored and furnished to be a living museum. Exhibition, architectural playground.

Open: Apr-Nov daily 10-5.

Admission: Adults £2.50 students/senior citizens £1.25 children to 10 years free.

Refreshments: Cafe, licensed, picnics.

Car park (free) bus access, access to most of the site for disabled visitors. Conference and lecture facilities.

JERSEY MUSEUM

(Jersey Museums Service)

Weighbridge, St. Helier, Jersey **Tel:** (01534) 30511 **Fax:** (01534) 66085

Purpose built museum opened spring 1992. Permanent exhibition 'Story of Jersey'. A.V. Theatre, art gallery, temporary exhibition gallery. National Heritage IBM Museum of the Year 1993.

Open: Mon-Sat 10-5 Sun 2-5 throughout the year.

Admission: Adults £2.50 children/OAPs £1.25 children under 10 free.

Location: The Weighbridge, St. Helier.

Refreshments: Available in cafe - teas, coffees, lunches, snacks.

Parties by arrangement. Car parking at nearby multi-storey in Pier Road. Director of Museums Michael Day B.A., A.M.A. Fully accessible for disabled visitors. Conference and lecture facilities.

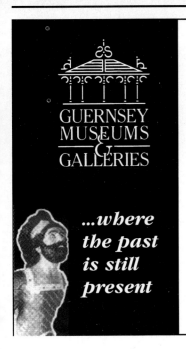

LA HOUGUE BIE MUSEUM
(Jersey Museums Service)
Grouville, Jersey **Tel:** (01534) 853823 **Fax:** (01534) 856472
3,850 B.C. Neolithic tomb - open to the public. Medieval chapel, museums of archaeology, geology, agriculture and the German occupation.
Open: Apr-Nov daily 10-5.
Admission: Adults £2 children/OAPs £1 children under 10 free.
Location: Grouville.
Refreshments: Tea, coffee, ice cream and snacks.
Parties by arrangement.Director of Museums Michael Day B.A., A.M.A.

MONT ORGUEIL CASTLE
(Jersey Museums Service)
Gorey, St. Martins, Jersey **Tel:** (01534) 53292
Medieval fortress. Small archaeological museum of local finds. Tableaux illustrating the Castle's history.
Open: Apr-Oct daily 9.30-6 and Nov-Jan Sat Sun Mon.
Admission: Adults £2.50 children/OAPs £1.25 children under 10 free.
Refreshments: Available.
Parties catered for. Director of Museums Michael Day B.A., A.M.A.

CHESHIRE

CHESTER

CHESTER HERITAGE CENTRE
St. Michael's Church, Bridge Street Row, Chester **Tel:** (01244) 317948
New displays from prehistoric times to modern day in this converted church on the Historic Rows illustrate Chester's history and architecture.
Open: 11-5 Mon-Sat 12-5 Sun.
Admission: Fee charged.
Access: steps to entrance and stairs to upper floor. Souvenir shop.

GROSVENOR MUSEUM
Grosvenor Street, Chester **Tel:** (01244) 321616
Whitbread North West Museum of the Year 1993 '...a real pleasure to visit' Award winning Roman Galleries, largest collection of Chester related Silver including Race Cups, Period House displays with scenes from 1680's-1920's. New Charles Kingsley Natural History Gallery.
Open: Mon-Sat 10.30-5 Sun 2-5.
Admission: Free but donations welcome.
Location: City Centre.
Refreshments: Tea/coffee only.
Exhibitions/Events: Major Civil War exhibition Apr-Sept 1995.
Shop access: steps at entrance and on ground floor. Stairs to 1st and 2nd floors.

KING CHARLES TOWER
City Walls, Chester **Tel:** (01244) 321616
Built c.13th or 14th centuries: heavily damaged during the Civil War and subsequently rebuilt in its present form. From the roof King Charles I watched the defeat of his army at the Battle of Rowton Moor in 1645. Displays on the Civil War and the Siege of Chester.
Open: Open high season only 11-4 telephone for details.
Admission: Fee charged.
Access: steps to upper chamber. Shop

WATER TOWER
City Walls, Chester **Tel:** (01244) 321616
Built in 1324 to protect ships on the River Dee, these two linked Towers retain their medieval appearance. Audio Guide tells scenes from local history together with small display on City Walls.
Open: High Season only 11-4 telephone for dates.
Admission: Fee charged.
Access: many steep steps within Tower.

ELLESMERE PORT

THE BOAT MUSEUM
(Britains Premier Canal Museum)
Dockyard Road, Ellesmere Port L65 4EF **Tel:** 0151-355 5017 **Fax:** 0151-355 4079
A working museum in the old docks at the junction of the Shropshire Union and Manchester Ship Canals. Over 60 historic canal boats, steam driven pumping engines; exhibitions, including worker's cottages, and blacksmith's forge; The Tom Rolt education conference centre.
Open: Summer 10-5 daily winter 11-4 closed Sat-Wed.
Admission: Adults £4.50 students & OAPs £3.50 children £3 family £14.
Location: Access from junction 9 of M53.
Refreshments: Available.
Exhibitions/Events: Programme of special events throughout the year.
Tel for bookings and information. **Best Small Attraction of the Year (NWTB).**

MACCLESFIELD

JODRELL BANK SCIENCE CENTRE & ARBORETUM
(University of Manchester)
Macclesfield SK11 9DL **Tel:** (01477) 571339 **Fax:** (01477) 571695
Marvel at the 76m Lovell radio telescope, a landmark in astronomy and Cheshire. See displays on astronomy, space energy and the environment. Experience hands-on exhibits and a journey through the Solar system in the Planetarium. Explore the Environmental Discovery Centre. Follow trails through the beautiful Arboretum.
Open: Winter weekends and Christmas holidays 11-4.30 Mid Mar-end Oct daily 10.30-5.30.
Admission: Adults £3.50 children £1.90 OAPs £2.50 family ticket (2 + 3) £10.50 Schools - child rate + 1 adult free with every 10 children discount for 20 or more in the party (prices on application).
Location: A535, junction 18 of the M6
Refreshments: Available.
Free car parking. Suitable for the disabled. Museum shop

MACCLESFIELD SILK MUSEUM AND HERITAGE CENTRE
(Trustees of Macclesfield Museums Trust)
Roe Street, Macclesfield **Tel:** (01625) 613210 **Fax:** (01625) 617880

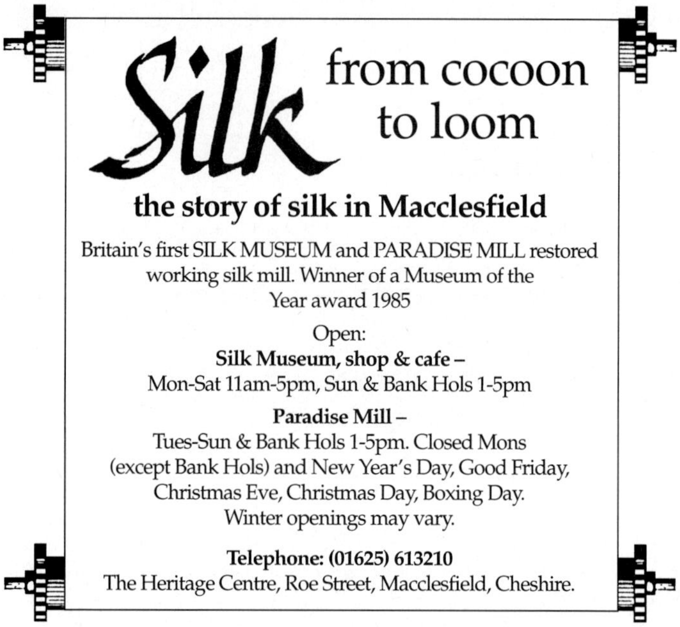

Silk Museum (Britain's first) - The story of silk in Macclesfield, audio visual, models and costume displays, silk shop. *Heritage Centre* - Free exhibitions on the history of the Sunday School movement.
Open: Mon-Sat 11-5 Sun 1-5 closed Christmas Day Boxing Day New Year's Day and Good Friday.
Admission: Fee charged.
Refreshments: Coffee Shop
Parties at other times by arrangement. *Victorian Schoolroom* - Educational parties by appointment only. Director: Moira Stevenson.

PARADISE MILL

(Trustees of Macclesfield Museums Trust)

Old Park Lane, Macclesfield **Tel:** (01625) 618228

26 silk hand looms with Jacquards, demonstrations of hand weaving, room settings of 1930s, design and card cutting rooms, Manager's office. Silk Shop.
Open: Tues-Sun 1-5 closed Mon (except Bank Hols 1-5) Christmas Eve Christmas Day Boxing Day New Year's Day Good Friday.
Admission: Fee charged.
Refreshments: Coffee shop in Heritage Centre 5 minutes walk.
Parties by arrangement, mornings and evenings. 1985 Museum of the Year Award for achievement with limited resources. Director: Moira Stevenson.

WEST PARK MUSEUM

(Trustees of Macclesfield Museum Trust)

Prestbury Road, Macclesfield **Tel:** (01625) 619831

Fine and decorative art, Egyptology. Work by C.F. Tunnicliffe, R.A.
Open: Tues-Sun 2-5 closed Mon (except Bank Holiday 2-5) Christmas Eve Christmas Day Boxing Day New Year's Day and Good Friday.
Admission: Free.
Refreshments: In the Park.
Director: Moira Stevenson.

RUNCORN

NORTON PRIORY MUSEUM

(Norton Priory Museum Trust)

Tudor Road, Runcorn WA7 1SX **Tel:** (01928) 569895

A fulfilling place for a family visit - excavated remains of the medieval priory are set in beautiful and peaceful woodland gardens and an attractive and colourful Georgian walled garden is close by. Contemporary art responding to the environment is sited throughout the gardens. Indoor displays on the life and work of the canons who moved to Norton in 1134 and on the Brooke family who made the priory their home from 1545-1921. Events throughout the year.
Open: From 12 noon closed Dec 24-26 and Jan 1 Walled Garden as above but closed Nov-Feb.
Admission: Fee charged.
Refreshments: Available, picnic area.
Exhibitions/Events: Year round changing programme.
Special packages for school and party visits. Gift shop, facilities for disabled people, free car park.

STOCKPORT

BRAMALL HALL, STOCKPORT ART GALLERY AND MUSEUM

(Stockport Heritage Services)

See entries under Stockport, Greater Manchester.

STYAL

QUARRY BANK MILL

(Quarry Bank Mill Trust Ltd as tenants of The National Trust)

Styal **Tel:** (01625) 527468 What's On and Information Line (01426) 981359

18th century cotton mill, fully restored and producing cloth by water power, now an award-winning working museum of the cotton industry housed in a 200 year-old spinning mill. Skilled demonstrators operate vintage machinery showing cotton processes from carding and spinning to weaving on Lancashire looms. Display on water power, the lifestyle of the mill-owning Greg family plus the millworkers' world at home and at work in the 19th century. Giant 1850 waterwheel restored to working order. Renovated Apprentice House. The millworkers' village of Styal and the mill are set in the 284 acre Styal Country Park. Mill shop.
Open: Mill: All year Apr-Sept daily 11-6 (last admission 4.30) Oct-Mar Tues-Sun 11-5 (last admission 3.30) open all Bank Hols. Pre-booked parties from 9.30 throughout the year (not Sun or Bank Holidays) and specified evenings May-Sept. Apprentice House and Garden as Mill opening times during school holidays Tues-Fri 2-Mill closing time during term time Sat and Sun as Mill opening times.
Admission: (No dogs)**Mill and Apprentice House** adults £4.50 children/concessions £3.20 family £13.50 **Mill only** adults £3.50 children/concessions £2.50 family £10 **Apprentice House and Garden only** Adults £3 children/concessions £2.30 family £9. Advance booking essential for all groups of 10 or more (please apply for a booking form at least 3 weeks in advance; guides may be booked at the same time, fee per guide per 20 persons). Groups of 20 or more at a concessionary rate.
Refreshments: Licensed restaurant.
Please note that due to fire and safety regulations a maximum of 30 people can be accommodated in the Apprentice House at one time. Admission is by timed ticket ONLY available from Mill Reception. Shop, newly sited and refurbished, open as Mill. Stocks goods made from cloth woven in mill. *Disabled access:* Exterior and special route through part of interior using step-lift. Please telephone for access details and leaflet. Cars may set down passengers in Mill yard. Disabled lavatory by Education Resource Centre. Mill unsuitable for guide dogs. Taped tour available at reception.

WARRINGTON

MUSEUM AND ART GALLERY

(Warrington Borough Council)

Bold Street, Warrington WA1 1JG **Tel:** (01925) 442392 or 442398 **Fax:** (01925) 442399

WARRINGTON MUSEUM AND ART GALLERY

BOLD STREET, WARRINGTON

Toy Shop Front c. 1940 with 19th and 20th century items displayed in a new Social History Gallery.

Rich collections of Art, Natural History and Ethnology displayed in a period Museum. Of particular interest are the rare Roman Actor's Mask, the Egyptian Coffin and 'Still Life' by Van Os. Of appeal to specialists are the extensive Bronze Age and Roman collections while examples of an early fire-engine, stocks, gibbet iron and bicycle mean there is something here for everyone.

General collections of natural history, geology, ethnology and Egyptology. Local history is well represented in the Prehistory, Roman and Medieval periods. Good collections of pottery, porcelain, local glass and clocks. Recently refurbished art galleries now house special exhibitions and a selection of the town's fine collection of oil paintings and watercolours. A new Social History Gallery reflects on life in Victorian times in a most dramatic way. Museum Education service operates.
Open: Mon-Fri 10-5.30 Sat 10-5 closed Suns and Bank Holidays.
Admission: Free.
Location: Near shopping centre, multi storey car parks, bus station and railway stations
Refreshments: Available.
Disabled access, public lift and toilets. Shop.

CLEVELAND

GUISBOROUGH

MARGROVE SOUTH CLEVELAND HERITAGE CENTRE

(Cleveland County Council)

Margrove Park, Boosbeck, Saltburn TS12 3BZ **Tel:** (01287) 610368 **Fax:** (01287) 610368

This award winning centre on the edge of the North Yorks National Park promotes the upland valley and coastal landscapes of South Cleveland, charting humans' impact on the environment. A changing exhibition schedule and busy events programme.
Open: Summer Mon-Thurs 10-4.30 Sun 12-5 Winter Mon-Thurs 1-4.30 Sun 12-4.30.
Admission: Free.
Location: Off the A171 Guisborough to Whitby Road.
Refreshments: Hot and cold drinks.
Exhibitions/Events: Advertised in a twice yearly leaflet.
Shop, local walks and picnic areas. Events programme.

MIDDLESBROUGH

CAPTAIN COOK BIRTHPLACE MUSEUM

(Middlesbrough Borough Council)

Stewart Park, Middlesbrough **Tel:** (01642) 311211 or 813781

CAPTAIN COOK BIRTHPLACE MUSEUM

MIDDLESBROUGH

This award winning Museum traces the story of James Cook R.N., F.R.S. (1728-1779) and illustrates the ethnography and natural history of the many countries he visited.

Illustrating Captain Cook's early life and voyages of exploration; Cook personalia; natural history and ethnography of Australia, New Zealand, North America and Pacific Islands.
Open: Tues-Sun 10-5.30 summer 9-4 winter.
Admission: Adults £1.20 children/OAPs 60p family £3 last tickets 0.75 hour before close.
Refreshments: Cafeteria.
Changing exhibitions. Souvenir Shop. Full access for the disabled. Major refurbishment of 1st floor gallery and addition of educational resource centre.

CLEVELAND CRAFTS CENTRE

57 Gilkes Street, Middlesbrough TS1 5EL **Tel:** (01642) 226351/262376 **Fax:** (01642) 262376

cleveland gallery
cleveland crafts centre
margrove heritage centre

Three splendid museums and galleries holding the County's collections of Studio Pottery, Contemporary Jewellery, Fine Art, Maps and Lace. Busy exhibition programmes and specialist retailing outlets.

For details please see Listings.

Cleveland Gallery
TS1 3QS
Tel (01642) 225408
Fax (01642) 253661

Cleveland Crafts Centre
Tel (01642) 226351/262376
Fax (01642) 262376

Margrove South Cleveland Heritage Centre
Tel (01287) 610368
Fax (01287) 610368

CLEVELAND
COUNTY COUNCIL
an equal opportunity employer

The centre has major collections of studio pottery and contemporary jewellery, a good part of each are on permanent display. There is a strong exhibition programme, current details of which can be found in Crafts Magazine. The Crafts

Council Selected Shop is comprehensively stocked. Twelve practising craftsworkers are based in the first floor workshops.
Open: Tues-Sat 10-5.
Admission: Free.
Location: By Middlesbrough Bus Station and BBC Radio Cleveland.
Please telephone.

CLEVELAND GALLERY
(Libraries & Leisure Dept)
Victoria Road, Middlesbrough TS1 3QS **Tel:** (01642) 225408 **Fax:** (01642) 253661
Exciting range of temporary exhibitions of national and international contemporary art. The Gallery houses the County's permanent collection of modern drawings and paintings and decorative art from the seventeenth century to the present day, all of which are exhibited from time to time.
Open: Tues-Sat 10-5.
Admission: Free.
Location: Victoria Road.
Refreshments: Hot drinks available.
Exhibitions/Events: Comprehensive range of events and creative activities.
Largest art and design bookshop in the region.

DORMAN MUSEUM
(Middlesbrough Borough Council)
Linthorpe Road, Middlesbrough TS5 6LA **Tel:** (01642) 813781
Local, social, industrial and natural history. Permanent display of regional and Linthorpe pottery. Temporary exhibition programme.
Open: Tues-Sat 10-5.30.
Admission: Free.

MIDDLESBROUGH ART GALLERY
(Middlesbrough Borough Council)
Linthorpe Road, Middlesbrough **Tel:** (01642) 247445
Exhibitions of regional and national importance. Permanent collection of British 20th Century art and 17th to 19th Century collection. Both shown through temporary exhibitions. Outdoor Sculpture Court.
Open: Tues-Sat 10-5.30 and a temporary exhibition programme of touring and in-house organised exhibitions.
Admission: Free.

REDCAR

KIRKLEATHAM OLD HALL MUSEUM
(Langbaurgh-on-Tees Borough Council)
Kirkleatham, Redcar TS10 5NW **Tel:** (01642) 479500 **Fax:** (01642) 474199

KIRKLEATHAM OLD HALL MUSEUM

Local History Museum for Langbaurgh-on-Tees district. 1995 exhibitions as follows: Jan-Mar 'Life in a Medieval Castle', Apr-Sept 'A Staithes Summer' with paintings of Staithes by various artists, and Sept-Dec 'The Redcar Jazz Club' featuring images of The Who, Marc Bolan, David Coverdale and more.

Open: Times available on request.
Admission: Free.
Refreshments: Museum cafe.
Car Parking for 80 cars. Ground floor access for disabled.

STOCKTON-ON-TEES

BILLINGHAM ART GALLERY
(Stockton Borough Council)
Queensway, Billingham, Stockton-on-Tees TS23 2LN **Tel:** (01642) 555441
A purpose built modern art gallery with a constantly changing programme of exhibitions.
Open: Mon-Sat 9-5 during exhibitions closed Sun and Bank Holidays.

GREEN DRAGON MUSEUM AND TOURIST INFORMATION CENTRE
(Stockton Borough Council)
Finkle Street, Stockton-on-Tees **Tel:** (01642) 674308
Local history museum showing the development of Stockton. Experience the sights, sounds and smells at the dawn of the railway era in an exciting audio/visual show '1825 - the birth of railways', the story of the Stockton and Darlington, the world's first public railway built for steam power. Other exhibits include an extensive display of local pottery, an exhibition showing the life of John Walker, the inventor of matches, and a rebuilt nineteenth century school room for pre-booked parties.
Open: Mon-Sat 9-5 closed Sun and Bank Hols.
Admission: Free.
Location: Town centre off High Street.

PRESTON HALL MUSEUM
(Stockton Borough Council)
Yarm Road, Stockton-on-Tees TS18 3RH **Tel:** (01642) 781184 **Fax:** (01642) 789907

Preston Hall Museum

Return to a bygone age at Preston Hall Museum, stroll down a recreated Victorian high street with period shops and working craftsmen or explore over 100 acres of picturesque parkland overlooking the River Tees.

Extensive galleries throughout the museum show life as it was in Victorian times, with the highlight, a recreated high street featuring period shops and working craftsmen. Among the museum's other exhibits are collections of arms and armour, costume and fine art which includes Georges de la Tour's enchanting painting 'The Dice Players'. The Museum stands in over 100 acres of picturesque parkland with picnic areas, a tropical bird aviary, riverside walks, children's play area with 'safety surfaces' and a historical walk along a length of original Stockton & Darlington Railway trackbed - the world's first railway built for passenger travel.
Open: Summer (Easter-Sept 30) Mon-Sun 10-5.30 winter (Oct 1-Easter) Mon-Sun 10-4.30 last admission 0.5 hour before closing closed New Year's Day Good Friday Christmas Day Boxing Day.
Admission: Free.
Refreshments: Cafe in park.
Party bookings Tel: (01642) 781184/791424

CORNWALL

BOLVENTOR

POTTERS MUSEUM OF CURIOSITY

(Five Star Management Ltd)

Bolventor, Bodmin Moor EX4 3SQS **Tel:** (01392) 216167 **Fax:** (01392) 423480

Humorous life work of Victorian naturalist and taxidermist, plus numerous curiosities from all over the world.

Open: All year except Jan low season 11-4 high season 10-8.

Location: Jamaica Inn Bolventor nr. Launceston Cornwall PL15 7TS Tel (01566) 86838/86250.

Refreshments: Available.

Party bookings by request during winter months by telephoning above number. Toilets, shop and partially disabled facilities.

CAMBORNE

CAMBORNE SCHOOL OF MINES GEOLOGICAL MUSEUM AND ART GALLERY

(University of Exeter)

Pool, Redruth TR15 3SE **Tel:** (01209) 714866 **Fax:** (01209) 716977

Collection of minerals, rocks and ores. Art exhibitions, Cornish mineral gallery.

Open: Mon to Fri 9-5. Closed Bank Hols.

Admission: Free.

CAMELFORD

NORTH CORNWALL MUSEUM AND GALLERY

The Clease, Camelford **Tel:** (01840) 212954

A privately owned museum of rural life in North Cornwall from 50 to 100 years ago. Two wagons and a dog cart; sections on agriculture, cidermaking, slate and granite quarrying, blacksmith's and wheelwright's tools, cobbling, the dairy and domestic scene. Pilgrim Trust award 1978.

Open: Apr-Sept Mon-Sat 10-5 closed Sun.

Admission: Fee charged.

Location: Follow signs to museum and TIC.

FALMOUTH

FALMOUTH ART GALLERY AND MUSEUM

(Falmouth Town Council)

Municipal Buildings, The Moor, Falmouth TR11 2RT **Tel:** (01326) 313863

The Gallery holds a collection of over 200 works of art ranging from Maritime prints and paintings 1600-1950 to Victorian and Edwardian landscapes and portraits by British artists such as E. Burne-Jones, G. F. Watts, Alfred Munnings, J. W. Waterhouse and Alfred Parsons. Only part of the collection is displayed but it is rotated every 6 months, Spring to Autumn and always includes the work of Henry Scott Juke (1852-1929). The Gallery also holds 10 temporary exhibitions per year featuring local and international artists.

Open: Mon-Fri 10-4.30 and Sat 10-1 closed Bank Holidays but open two days between Christmas and New Year.

Admission: Free.

Location: In the central square of the town on the upper floor of the Passmore Edwards Building above the library.

Exhibitions/Events: Feb 6-Mar 5 Contemporary Czechoslovakian Textiles. Sep 18-Oct 14 Photography Exhibition.

ISLES OF SCILLY

THE VALHALLA FIGUREHEAD COLLECTION

(Tresco)

Abbey Gardens, Tresco, Isles of Scilly **Tel:** (01720) 22849 **Fax:** 0181-312 6632

Figureheads and ships' carvings from wrecks around the Isles of Scilly. A National Maritime Museum Outstation.

Open: Daily Apr-Oct 10-4.

NEWLYN

NEWLYN ART GALLERY

(Newlyn Orion Galleries Ltd)

Newlyn, Penzance TR18 5PZ **Tel:** (01736) 63715 **Fax:** (01736) 331578

Changing exhibitions of contemporary works by leading regional, national and international artists.

Open: Mon-Sat 10-5.

Admission: Free.

Location: On Newlyn Green overlooking Mounts Bay.

Refreshments: Coffee available.

Full disabled facilities. 1995 is the centennial year of Newlyn Gallery.

PENZANCE

TRINITY HOUSE NATIONAL LIGHTHOUSE CENTRE

Wharf Road, Penzance TR18 4BN **Tel:** (01736) 60077

The world's finest collection of lighthouse equipment. Housed in the old Trinity workshops, the museum traces a 400 year history of lighthouses and marine safety. Exhibits include fog signals, glass optics weighing up to 4 tons and a variety of smaller ex-service apparatus. An audio-visual theatre shows a brief history of the first rock lights on the Eddystone Reef and reconstructed living quarters give a feel of life in a rock tower.

Open: Easter-end Oct (every day inc Bank Hols) 11-5.
Admission: Adults £2.50 OAPs/children/students £1 children accompanied by 2 full paying adults free 10-20% discount for parties.
Location: Opposite the docks on Penzance seafront.
Refreshments: None - cafe adjacent.
Parking 300 yds away.

ST. AUSTELL

CHARLESTOWN SHIPWRECK AND HERITAGE CENTRE

(The Cliff Head Hotel)

Charlestown Harbour, St. Austell PL25 3NJ

History of this unique Georgian village and Port Told in Tableaux. Largest collection of shipwreck artefacts in the United Kingdom. Much, much more to see and do.

Open: Mar 1-Nov 30 daily 10-5 (later in high season) open all Bank Hols.
Admission: Adults £2.95 children/OAPs/students £1.95 family £7.40 school parties and groups over 15 in number.
Location: In Charlestown Harbour, south of St. Austell, just off A390.
Refreshments: 100 seater restaurant and outdoor undercover picnic area.
Car parking and coach parking available. Suitable for disabled persons

ST. IVES

THE BARBARA HEPWORTH MUSEUM

(The Tate Gallery)

Barnoon Hill, St. Ives TR26 1AD **Tel:** (01736) 796226 **Fax:** (01736) 794480

Sculptures in wood stone and bronze can be seen in the late Dame Barbara Hepworths house, studio and sub-tropical garden, where she lived and worked from 1949-75. Photographs, documents, and other memorabilia are also exhibited, as are workshops housing a selection of tools and some unfinished carvings.

Open: Nov-Mar Sun 1-5 closed Mon Tues-Sat 11-5 Apr-Oct Sun 11-5 Mon-Sat 11-7 open Bank Hols 11-5 closed Dec 24 25 26 and Jan 1.
Admission: Same as the Tate Gallery for entry into both the Hepworth Museum and the Tate Gallery.
Location: Barnoon Hill St Ives town centre close to Trewyn Gardens.
Bookshop, parking nearby, disabled access with assistance.

ST. IVES SOCIETY OF ARTISTS

Old Mariners Church, Norway Square, St. Ives TR26 1NA **Tel:** (01736) 795582

The purpose of the Society is to paint in the representational tradition; the emphasis is on discipline of observation and draughtmanship. Every new member should be as good if not better than the best artist already existing in the society.

Open: End Mar-mid Nov and mid Dec-mid Jan Mon-Sat inc. 10-4.30 closed for lunch.
Admission: 20p per person.
Refreshments: Several restaurants nearby.
Exhibitions/Events: Several one-Man Shows during the season in the lower gallery.
Public Car Park adjacent to the Gallery.

TATE GALLERY ST IVES

Porthmeor Beach, St.Ives TR26 1TG **Tel:** (01736) 796226 **Fax:** (01736) 794480

Tate Gallery St. Ives displays changing groups of work from the Tate Gallery collection of St Ives painting and sculpture, dating from about 1925 to 1975. Artists include Wallis, Nicholson, Hepworth, Gabo, Lanyon, Frost, Wynter, Heron and Hilton. There are on going displays of work by invited contemporary artists.

Open: Nov-Mar Sun 1-5 closed Mon Tues 11-9 Wed-Sat 11-5 Apr-Oct Sun 11-5 Mon-Sat 11-7 Tues and Thurs 11-9 open Bank Hols 11-5 closed Dec 24 25 26 and Jan 1.
Admission: Adults £2.50 OAPs/students/children/unemployed £1.50 family ticket (2 adults+2 children valid 2 weeks) £10/£5 adults in pre-booked groups £2 OAPs and children in pre-booked groups £1 (groups - over 10 in number) all tickets also includes entry to the Barbara Hepworth Museum.
Location: Porthmeor Beach St Ives.
Refreshments: Roof top cafe restaurant with spectacular views over the beach.
Bookshop, education room, baby change, disabled access, parking nearby.

SALTASH

COTEHELE QUAY AND SHAMROCK - NATIONAL MARITIME MUSEUM OUTSTATION

(with The National Trust)

Saltash **Tel:** (01579) 50830

Display on shipping and trade of the River Tamar. Home of the NMM/NT restored Tamar sailing barge *Shamrock*.

Open: Daily Apr-Oct 11-4.
Location: Off A388 near St. Dominick. (Follow Cotehele House signs).
Resident NMM staff.

TRURO

ROYAL CORNWALL MUSEUM
(Royal Institution of Cornwall)
River Street, Truro TR1 2SJ **Tel:** (01872) 72205 **Fax:** (01872) 40514
Local antiquities and history. Ceramics and art. World famous collections of Cornish minerals.
Open: Mon-Sat 10-5 closed Sun and Bank Hols.
Admission: Adults £1.50 unaccompanied children 50p OAP's £1 accompanied children free.
Location: Truro.
Refreshments: New cafe.
Shop. Full facilities for disabled.

CUMBRIA

BEETHAM

HERON CORN MILL AND MUSEUM OF PAPERMAKING
(Beetham Trust)
c/o Henry Cooke Makin, Waterhouse Mills, Beetham, nr. Milnthorpe LA7 7AR
Tel: (015395) 63363
Working, 18th century lowder water driven corn mill. Some 18th century machinery in place. Demonstrations of milling. Cereal products, information, phamplets, etc., on sale. Museum of papermaking. Established .1988 to commemorate 500 years of papermaking in England. Displays tell the story of papermaking from early times to present. Changing exhibitions. Housed in renovated Barn on same site.
Open: April/Easter-Sept 30 Tues-Sat Bank Hols.
Admission: £1.25 children/OAPs 80p 10% discount parties over 20+ prebooked teachers with school parties free.
Location: 1 mile S of Milthorpe on A6.
Free car park. Parts of mill not suitable for disabled. Paper museum accessible to disabled. Open to prebooked parties in October. Evening parties welcome by prior arrangement.

GRASMERE

DOVE COTTAGE AND WORDSWORTH MUSEUM
(Wordsworth Trust (reg. charity 214472)
Grasmere LA22 9SH **Tel:** (015394) 35544/35547/35003 **Fax:** (015394) 35748
Combined ticket gives access to Dove Cottage (home of Wordsworth during his most creative years, 1799-1808) and the museum which has an extensive display of verse manuscripts, paintings and special exhibitions providing a context for the poet's life and work.
Open: 9.30-5.30 (last admission 5).
Admission: Reductions for parties.
Location: A591 immediately south of turn-off to Grasmere Village.
Refreshments: Restaurant.
Exhibitions/Events: Bicentennary exhibition on John Keats/3 residential courses. Educational visits welcome. Book and gift shop.

HAWKSHEAD

BEATRIX POTTER GALLERY
(The National Trust)
Main Street, Hawkshead LA22 0NS **Tel:** (015394) 36355

THE NATIONAL TRUST

BEATRIX POTTER GALLERY

A selection of Beatrix Potter's original illustrations of her life as landowner, farmer and determined preserver of her beloved Lake District.

The building was once the office of her husband, solicitor William Heelis.

National Trust Shop nearby.

April-Oct.
Sunday-Thursday 10.30-4.30pm
Last admission 4.00pm

Main Street, Hawkshead

Admission: Charge payable. Parties by pre-arrangement only.
Car parking in village.

KENDAL

ABBOT HALL ART GALLERY
Kendal, Cumbria LA9 5AL **Tel:** (01539) 722464 **Fax:** (01539) 722494

ABBOT HALL ART GALLERY

Kendal, Cumbria Tel: (01539) 722464

Impressive Georgian house with work by Ruskin, Turner, Constable, Romney plus modern art collection. Sutherland, Piper, Schwitters, Ben Nicholson, Barbara Hepworth, Elizabeth Frink. Excellent range of art including new gallery display of Lake District landscapes over past 250 years. Furniture by Gillows displayed in recently restored Georgian rooms. Lively programme of changing exhibitions. Access for disabled throughout the Gallery. Adjacent Museum of Lakeland Life recaptures flavour of everyday social and industrial life in the Lakes. Arthur

Ransome Room and John Cunliffe Room (Postman Pat). Also visit award-winning Kendal Museum of Natural History and Archaeology on Station Road.
Open: Daily (except Dec 25 26 and Jan 1) Mon-Sat 10.30-5 Sun 2-5 reduced hours during winter/spring.
Admission: Charge. Concessions for OAPs families children and students.
Location: Off Kirkland near Kendal Parish Church Leave M6 at J 36.
Refreshments: Coffee Shop.
Exhibitions/Events: Regular exhibitions.
Disabled access. Parking.

MARYPORT

MARITIME MUSEUM
(Allerdale Borough Council)
Senhouse Street, Maryport **Tel:** (01900) 813738
Maritime and local history. Two preserved steamships in nearby harbour.

MILLOM

MILLOM FOLK MUSEUM
(Millom Folk Museum Society)
St. Georges Road, Millom LA18 4DQ **Tel:** (01229) 77233
Unique full-scale model of a Hodbarrow iron mine drift, miner's cottage, smithy and many other items.
Open: 10-5 daily from Easter-mid Sept Bank Holiday Suns only.
Admission: Adults 75p children 35p.
Location: In the town of Millom.

PENRITH

PENRITH MUSEUM
(Eden District Council)
Robinson's School, Middlegate, Penrith CA11 2PT **Tel:** (01768) 64671
Local history, archaeology and geology. The museum building, dating from 1670, was a charity school.
Open: June 1-Sept 30 Mon-Sat 10-6 Sun 1-6 Oct 1-May 31 Mon-Sat 10-5.
Admission: Free.

WHITEHAVEN

WHITEHAVEN MUSEUM AND ART GALLERY
(Copeland Borough Council)
Civic Hall, Lowther Street, Whitehaven CA28 7SH **Tel:** (01946) 592302
Whitehaven Beacon. This purpose built heritage centre is due to open Spring/Sumer 1995. It will re-house the Museums local history collections, together with a 'weather-watch balcony', video shows, interactive displays, special exhibitions etc.
Open: Hours to be determined.
Admission: Price to be determined.
Location: South Beach, Whitehaven Harbour
Exhibitions/Events: Regular exhibitions, leactures; publications list available.
Accessible to disabled. For further details please ring (0946) 69311

WINDERMERE

WINDERMERE STEAMBOAT MUSEUM
Rayrigg Road, Windermere LA23 1BN **Tel:** (015394) 45565 **Fax:** (015394) 45847
A unique and historic collection of Steamboats and Motorboats in the Heart of Lakeland. Elegant and beautiful Victorian and Edwardian steam launches, including the S.L.'Dolly' - the oldest working steamboat in the world - plus many other historic craft. Steam launch trips each day (weather permitting). Museum displays.
Open: Every day from Easter-end Oct 10-5.
Location: On the lakeside, O.S. ref. 402976.
Refreshments: Available.
Shop, picnic area, model boat pool, disabled facilities.

WORKINGTON

HELENA THOMPSON MUSEUM
(Allerdale Borough Council)
Park End Road, Workington CA14 4DE **Tel:** (01900) 62598
Costumes and applied art; local history collection.
Open: Mon-Sat Apr 1-Oct 31 10.30-4 Nov 1-Mar 31 11-3.

DERBYSHIRE

BAKEWELL

THE OLD HOUSE MUSEUM
(An Independent Museum)
Cunningham Place, Bakewell **Tel:** (01629) 813165
An early Tudor house with original wattle and daub interior walls and open-timbered chamber. Victorian kitchen, costumes on models, craftsmen's tools, lace, toys etc.
Open: Apr 1-Oct 31: Daily 2-5.
Admission: £1.80 children 80p (1994 rates).
Parties mornings or evenings by appointment.

CHESTERFIELD

CHESTERFIELD MUSEUM AND ART GALLERY
(Chesterfield Borough Council)
Stephenson's Memorial Hall, St. Mary's Gate, Chesterfield S41 7TX **Tel:** (01246) 559727 **Fax:** (01246) 206667
Gallery depicting the story of Chesterfield from Roman times, also small art gallery.
Open: Mon Tues Thurs Fri Sat 10-4.
Admission: Free.
Location: Town centre.
Exhibitions/Events: Changing programme of exhibitions.

REVOLUTION HOUSE
(Chesterfield Borough Council)
Old Whittington, Chesterfield **Tel:** (01246) 453554 **Fax:** (01246) 206667
Originally an alehouse where three conspirators met to plot the Revolution of 1688.
Temporary exhibition of local material, video available of the events of 1688.
Open: Open Easter-end of Oct daily 10-4 also open over Christmas and New Year.
Admission: Free.
Location: 3 miles north of Chesterfield (off A61).

CRICH

THE NATIONAL TRAMWAY MUSEUM
(The Tramway Museum Society)

Crich, near Matlock DE4 5DP **Tel:** (01773) 852565 **Fax:** (01773) 852326

This 'Museum on the Move' offers a mile long scenic journey with unlimited Tram rides, through Period Street to open countryside and panoramic views. The largest National Collection of vintage electric, horse-drawn and steam trams from home and abroad.
Open: April May Sept Oct daily except some Fris June-Aug daily Nov Sun only.
Admission: 1995 charges...please ring for details.
Location: Crich, Derbyshire.
Refreshments: Cafe.
Exhibitions/Events: Throughout the season.
Classic Vehicle Owners - free adm for driver + 1 passenger for all vehicles over 25 years old, if vehicle parked in Period Street for a minimum of 2 hours.

CROMFORD

ARKWRIGHT'S MILL
Cromford, near Matlock DE4 3RQ **Tel:** (01629) 824297
The world's first successful water powered cotton spinning mill. The Arkwright Society are in the process of restoring the mills.
Open: Mill site open 9.15-5 every day except Christmas Day.
Admission: No charge for access to Mill site. Guided tours £1.50 and £1 concessions.
Location: Off A6 17m N of Derby, 3m S Matlock.
Refreshments: Cromford Mill Restaurant.
Exhibitions/Events: Special attractions most summer weekends.
Exhibitions, audio-visual slide display, craft shops, mill shop. Guided Tours available.

DERBY

DERBY INDUSTRIAL MUSEUM
The Silk Mill, Silk Mill Lane, off Full Street, Derby DE1 3AR **Tel:** (01332) 255308
Displays form an introduction of the industrial history of Derby and Derbyshire. They also include a major collection of Rolls-Royce aero engines ranging from an Eagle of 1915 to an RB211 from the first TriStar airliner. New railway engineering gallery now open.
Open: Mon 11-5 Tues-Sat 10-5 Sun and Bank Hols 2-5.
Admission: Free.
School service: Term-time lessons and holiday activities for children.

DERBY MUSEUMS & ART GALLERY
The Strand, Derby DE1 1BS **Tel:** (01332) 255586
Museum. Archaeology, military history, natural history, geology. **Art Gallery.** Major works by 18th century painter Joseph Wright of Derby, including examples of his unusual scientific and industrial subjects. The art collection also specialises in works by other local artists and topographical views of Derby and Derbyshire. The Derby porcelain gallery displays an unrivalled collection.
Open: Mon 11-5 Tues-Sat 10-5 Suns and Bank Hols 2-5.
Admission: Free.
Museum shop. Temporary exhibitions. School service: term-time lessons and holiday activities for children. **Regimental Museum of the 9th/12th Royal Lancers (Prince of Wales), Derbyshire Yeomanry** and material of the **Sherwood Foresters.**

THE DONINGTON COLLECTION
See Leicestershire Section for full entry details.

PICKFORD'S HOUSE MUSEUM
41 Friar Gate, Derby DE1 1DA **Tel:** (01332) 255363
A Georgian town house opened in late 1988 as a social history museum interpreting domestic life in the late 18th and early 19th centuries, both above and below stairs. Displays of Georgian and later period rooms, and historic costumes.
Open: Mon 11-5 Tues-Sat 10-5 Sun and Bank Hols 2-5.
Admission: Free.
Period garden. School service: Term-time lessons and holiday activities for children.

ROYAL CROWN DERBY MUSEUM
Osmaston Road, Derby **Tel:** (01332) 712800
The only factory allowed to use the words 'Crown' and 'Royal', a double honour granted by George III and Queen Victoria. The museum, opened by the Duchess of Devonshire in 1969, traces the development of the company from 1748 to the present day.
Open: Weekdays 9.30-12.30 1.30-4.
Factory tours, factory shop. Closed factory holidays.

ILKESTON

EREWASH MUSEUM
(Erewash Borough Council)
High Street, Ilkeston DE7 5JA **Tel:** (0115) 9440440 Ext. 331
Eighteenth century town house, set in pleasant gardens, housing local history collections in room settings and galleries.
Open: All year Tues Thurs Fri and Sat 10-4 Bank Holidays 10-4 but closed Jan Christmas and New Year.
Admission: Free.
Location: Close to Ilkeston Market Place.
Refreshments: Thursday and Bank Holidays.

MATLOCK

CAUDWELL'S MILL
Rowsley, Matlock DE4 2EB **Tel:** (01629) 734374
This 19th century water turbine powered flour mill with precision roller mills is still producing quality wholemeal flour for sale. See four floors of machinery and exhibitions. Crafts-people in the Stable Yard.
Open: Daily Mar 1-end Oct 10-6 weekends only in winter 10-4.30.
Admission: Adults £2 chidren 5-16 and OAPs £1.
Location: On A6 in village of Rowsley between Matlock and Bakewell.
Refreshments: Cafe.
Exhibitions/Events: Millery each second Sunday of the month.
Car Park.

DEVON

ASHBURTON

ASHBURTON MUSEUM

1 West Street, Ashburton

Local antiquities, implements, bronze age flints, geology, lace. American Indian antiques.

Open: Mid May-end Sept Tues Thur Fri and Sat 2.30-5.

Admission: Free.

Location: Town centre.

BRIXHAM

BRIXHAM MUSEUM

(The Brixham Museum and History Society)

Bolton Cross, Brixham TQ5 8LZ **Tel:** (01803) 856267

Local and Maritime History.

Open: Easter-end Oct Mon-Sat 10-5.

Admission: Modest admission charges. Concessions Children/OAPs/Families.

Central car park 100 yds.

BUDLEIGH SALTERTON

FAIRLYNCH ARTS CENTRE AND MUSEUM

(Trustees)

27 Fore Street, Budleigh Salterton **Tel:** (01395) 442666

Emphasis on local material, local history, archaeology and geology, natural history. Period costume, especially Victorian. Lace. Lace making demonstrations.

Open: Easter-end Oct 2-4.30 mid July-end Aug additionally 11-1 closed Sun mornings 3 weeks from Boxing Day 2.30-4.30.

Admission: Adults 80p children/OAPs/students 50p.

OTTERTON MILL CENTRE AND WORKING MUSEUM

Budleigh Salterton EX9 7HG **Tel:** (01395) 568521/567041

Water mill museum; wholemeal flour production using water power. Gallery with fine art and craft exhibitions (Easter to Dec). Workshops.

Open: Daily summer 10.30-5.30 winter 11.30-4.30.

Admission: Fee charged.

Location: Otterton (off the A376 between Newton Poppleford and Budleigh Salterton).

Refreshments: Restaurant and bakery, picnic area.

Exhibitions/Events: Summer Exhibition 1995 - 'The Undercliff. A Unique Ecosystem'.

Shop. Christmas holiday activities.

HARTLAND

HARTLAND QUAY MUSEUM

Hartland, near Bideford EX39 6DU **Tel:** (01288) 331353

A museum devoted to the Hartland coastline displaying four centuries of shipwreck, natural history, geology, Harland Quay and coastal trades and activities.

Open: Easter week then Whitsun-Sept 30 daily 11-5.

Admission: Adults 50p children 20p.

HONITON

ALLHALLOWS MUSEUM

High Street (next to St. Paul's Church), Honiton EX14 8PE **Tel:** (01404) 44966

Comprehensive exhibition of Honiton Lace with frequent demonstrations of lace making. Local history.

Open: Easter-end Oct weekdays 10-5 (During Oct 10-4) not Suns.

Admission: Adults 80p children 30p.

KINGSBRIDGE

COOKWORTHY MUSEUM OF RURAL LIFE IN SOUTH DEVON

The Old Grammar School, 108 Fore Street, Kingsbridge TQ7 1AW **Tel:** (01548) 853235

A lively local museum with everything from costumes to carts. Complete walk in Victorian kitchen and Edwardian pharmacy, large farm gallery in a walled garden, toys and dolls-house. Craft demonstrations.

Open: Easter-Sept daily 10-5 (except Sun) Oct Mon-Fri 10.30-4.

Admission: Fee charged. Concession groups all year.

MORWELLHAM QUAY

MORWELLHAM QUAY MUSEUM AND 19TH CENTURY PORT AND COPPER MINE

(Morwellham and Tamar Valley Trust)

Morwellham Quay PL19 8JL **Tel:** (01822) 832766; Information only: (01822) 833808 **Fax:** (01822) 833808

A charming riverside village hidden away in 150 acres of Tamar valley woodland. Founded by Monks 1000 years ago, it grew to become by 1868, 'the greatest copper port in Queen Victoria's empire'. Researched and restored for over 20 years by Morwellham Trust and vividly brought to life. Ride underground into a copper mine and enjoy a heavy horsedrawn wagonette ride along the Duke of Bedford's carriageway. Unspoilt country, riverside and woodland trails, slide shows and other exhibits will help in discovering a thousand years of history.

Open: Daily (except Christmas week) summer 10-5.30 (last adm 3.30) winter 10-4.30 (last adm 2.30).

Admission: All inclusive adm charge.

Location: Off A390 between Tavistock and Gunnislake.

Refreshments: Ship Inn & Pasty House Restaurant.

Exhibitions/Events: Victorian Tavern evenings

Free Teacher's Information Pack on request.

OKEHAMPTON

MUSEUM OF DARTMOOR LIFE

West Street, Okehampton EX20 1HQ **Tel:** (01837) 52295

Award winning displays on the land and people, exhibitions programme, research/education facilities,Tea-rooms, Craft shops, and Visitor Centre.

Open: Mon-Sat (+ Suns June-Sept) 10-5 weekdays only in winter.

Admission: Adults £1.50 OAPs £1.20 children/students 75p family £4 group reductions.

PLYMOUTH

CITY MUSEUM AND ART GALLERY

(Plymouth City Council)

Drake Circus, Plymouth **Tel:** (01752) 264878

Local and natural history; fine ceramics, silver, old master paintings; lively changing exhibitions of contemporary art.

Open: Tues-Fri 10-5.30 Sat & Bank Holiday Mon 10-5.

Admission: Free.

Museum shop.

MERCHANT'S HOUSE

(Plymouth City Council)

33 St. Andrew's Street, Plymouth **Tel:** (01752) 264878

Plymouth's rich history packed into a fine 16th century house.

Open: Apr 1-Sept 30 Tues-Fri 10-5.30 Sat and Bank Holiday Mon 10-5 closed lunchtimes 1-2.

Admission: Small charge.

Victorian schoolroom available for group bookings.

TORQUAY

TORQUAY MUSEUM
(Torquay Natural History Society)
529 Babbacombe Road, Torquay TQ1 1HG **Tel:** (01803) 293975
Exciting archaeology gallery featuring important finds from Kents Cavern, Victorian Doll's House, Local history, Natural history, geology, Agatha Christie and temporary exhibitions. Resources of museum available during visits for National Curriculum work in History and Science for Primary Schools, school room, information packs.
Open: Mon-Fri 10-4.45 also Sats Easter-Oct Sun afternoons from 1.30 closed Good Fri and Christmas.
Admission: Fee charged.

TORRE ABBEY HISTORIC HOUSE AND GALLERY
(Torbay Borough Council)
The Kings Drive, Torquay TQ2 5JX **Tel:** (01803) 293593 **Fax:** (01803) 218085

TORRE ABBEY
Torquay

Torre Abbey was founded in 1196 as a monastery for premonstratensian canons. Following the dissolution in 1539, it was adapted for use as a private residence, and in 1930 was purchased by Torquay Borough Council to house its growing art collection.
Contains historic rooms, including the Cary family chapel, mementoes of Agatha Christie, and an extensive collection of mainly 19th century paintings, sculpture and Torquay terracotta pottery. The medieval monastic remains are the most complete in Devon and Cornwall.
A short stroll from the sea front. Torre Abbey is surrounded by colourful gardens and open park land, and stands adjacent to The Riviera Centre with its restaurants and major conference and sports facilities. Guided tours for parties are available on request, and rooms may be hired for functions.

ADMISSION - See editorial reference

Torbay's most historic building: 12th century monastery, later converted into country house. Twenty historic rooms, important pre-Raphaelite paintings, antiques, Torquay terracotta, memorials of Agatha Christie, gardens, Victorian tearooms, quiz sheet for families.
Open: Apr-Oct daily 9.30-6 (last admissions 5).
Admission: Adults £2.50 students/OAPs £2 children £1.50 (under 8's free) family ticket £6.50. Group concessions available.
Location: On the sea front, by Abbey Sands and next to the Riviera Centre.
Refreshments: Tea-rooms in Victorian kitchens.
Extensive grounds and formal gardens.

TOTNES

TOTNES COSTUME MUSEUM
Bogan House, 43 High Street, Totnes TQ9 5NP **Tel:** (01803) 862827
Exhibitions from the Collection, changed annually, on show in historic house.
Open: Spring Bank Hol-Oct 1 Mon-Fri 11-5 Sun 2-5.
Admission: Fee charged.

TOTNES (ELIZABETHAN) MUSEUM
(Charitable Trust)
70 Fore Street, Totnes **Tel:** (01803) 863821
A museum set in an Elizabethan Merchants house of 1575.
Open: Mon-Sat all day.
Location: Main High Street.
Charity No. 296684.

DORSET

BOURNEMOUTH

RUSSEL-COTES ART GALLERY AND MUSEUM
(Bournemouth Borough Council)
East Cliff, Bournemouth BH1 3AA **Tel:** (01202) 551009
In an extravagant version of an Italianate seaside villa the Russel-Cotes houses a spectacular collection of Victorian and Edwardian paintings. This is complemented by sculpture, decorative art and furniture as well as a modern art collection. Important commissions of contemporary craft and sculpture are sited in the award-winning Display Space, beautifully restored Art Galleries and garden.
Open: Tues-Sun 10-5 closed Christmas Day and Good Friday free admission Sat and Sun.
Admission: Adults £1 children/concessions 50p education groups booked 2 days in advance free.
Location: Central Bournemouth on East cliff.
Refreshments: Small tea-room selling drinks and biscuits.
Exhibitions/Events: Year round programme.
Suitable for disabled. Wheelchairs available.

BOVINGTON

THE TANK MUSEUM
(Royal Armoured Corps and Royal Tank Regiment)
Bovington, Nr Wool BH20 6JG **Tel:** (01929) 463953 **Fax:** (01929) 405360

The world's first Tank Museum, with the largest and most comprehensive collection of armoured fighting vehicles; more than 300 from over 25 countries. Also collections of medals, memorabilia, photographs including Lawrence of Arabia Exhibition and fascinating Costume Collection dedicated to the Army wife. Large reference library, national archive and research facilities.
Open: Daily 10-5 closed Dec 23-26.
Admission: Fee charged.
Refreshments: Large restaurant.
Exhibitions/Events: A number of outside events - phone for details.
Gift shop, free video theatre, picnic area, junior assault course, free car park. Easy access for disabled.

LYME REGIS

DINOSAURLAND
Coombe Street, Lyme Regis, Dorset DT7 3NY **Tel:** (01297) 443541/442844
Fossils, models and live animals. Come and meet Peter Langham featured in Lost Worlds, Vanished Lives and Blue Peter.
Open: All year with limited winter opening please phone.
Location: Central Lyme Regis well signposted.
Refreshments: Light.
Guided Walks. Shop.

POOLE

THE OLD LIFEBOAT HOUSE
East Quay, Poole
Poole's 1938 lifeboat *Thomas Kirk Wright*, veteran of Dunkirk. On loan from the National Maritime Museum.
Open: Times fluctuate Easter-end Sept.
Volunteer staff.

SCAPLEN'S COURT
(Poole Borough Council)
High Street, Poole **Tel:** (01202) 683138 **Fax:** (01202) 660896
One of the finest examples of a 15th century town house to be seen on the south coast. This medieval merchants house provides the setting for displays which include a Victorian Chemist Shop, School Room and Kitchen.

WATERFRONT MUSEUM, POOLE QUAY
(Poole Borough Council)
4 High Street, Poole BH15 1BW **Tel:** (01202) 683138 **Fax:** (01202) 660896
Set in the medieval Town Cellars and 18th century, five floored Oakley's Mill, the museum offers an exciting insight into the history of the town and port.

SHAFTESBURY

LOCAL HISTORY MUSEUM
Gold Hill, Shaftesbury **Tel:** (01747) 852157
Five galleries illustrating local history, archaeology, industry, farming, shopping and schooling, coin and costume displays and 1744 fire engine.
Open: Easter-end Sept Mon-Sun 11-5.
Admission: Adults 80p children 20p.

WAREHAM

A WORLD OF TOYS
Arne House, Arne BH20 5BJ **Tel:** (01929) 552018
A Collection of Antique and Collectors Toys, Victorian Music Boxes and Automata etc.
Open: Apr-June 1.30-5 July-Aug 10.30-5 open every day in Aug and Bank Hol Mon.

WIMBORNE MINSTER

PRIEST'S HOUSE MUSEUM OF EAST DORSET LIFE AND GARDEN
23-27 High Street (opposite the Minster), Wimborne Minster BH21 1HR
Tel: (01202) 882533 **Fax:** (01202) 882533
Award winning museum set in beautiful walled garden. Features a working Victorian kitchen, reconstructed stationers and ironmonger's shops, period rooms and special exhibitions.
Open: Apr 1-Oct 29 Mon-Sat 10.30-5 Bank Holiday Suns 2-5 and Suns June 5-Sept 25 2-5.
Admission: Fee charged.
Location: High Street opposite The Minster.
Refreshments: Garden Tea room summer season only.
Exhibitions/Events: Special Exhibitions at summer and Christmas. Regular cooking demos in authentic Victorian kitchen. Regular children's holiday events - please ring up and ask.
Gift shop, free quizzes.

COUNTY DURHAM

BARNARD CASTLE

THE BOWES MUSEUM
(Durham County Council)
Barnard Castle DL12 8NP **Tel:** (01833) 690606 **Fax:** (01833) 37163
The main collections are representative of European art from the late Medieval period to the 19th century. They comprise paintings, tapestries, furniture, porcelain, glass, jewellery, sculpture and metalwork. Paintings by Italian, Spanish, Flemish, Dutch, French and English artists.
Open: Mon-Sat 10-5.30 (Oct Mar Apr 10-5 Nov-Feb 10-4) Sun 2-5 (winter 2-4).

Admission: Adults £2.50 children/OAPs £1.50 (at time of going to press).
Location: Westwick Road.
Refreshments: Tea-room in the building (Apr to Sept).
Free parking. Good facilities for the disabled. Attractive gardens.

DARLINGTON

DARLINGTON ART COLLECTIONS
(Borough of Darlington)
Tubwell Row, Darlington DL1 1PD **Tel:** (01325) 463795
Picture collection of Darlington Borough Council. Selections on show from time to time in local venues.
Public collection of original works of art, chiefly Victorian and 20th century works. Many by local artists.

DARLINGTON MUSEUM
(Borough of Darlington)
Tubwell Row, Darlington DL1 1PD **Tel:** (01325) 463795 (Curator)
Social history of Darlington. Natural history of Teesdale. Historic fishing tackle. Observation beehive during summer months.
Open: Mon-Fri 10-1 and 2-6 (except Thur 10-1 only) Sat 10-1 and 2-5.30.
Admission: Free.

DURHAM

DURHAM LIGHT INFANTRY MUSEUM AND DURHAM ART GALLERY
(Durham County Council) Arts Libraries & Museums Dept)
Aykky Heads, Durham City DH1 5TU **Tel:** 0191-384 2214 **Fax:** 0191-386 1770
Museum: uniforms, medals, weapons and illustrations tell the story of the County Regiment's 200 years of history. **Art Gallery:** Changing exhibitions of art and craft.
Open: Weekdays (except Mon) 10-5 Sun 2-5 open Bank Holiday Mons closed Christmas Day-New Year's Day.
Admission: Adults 80p children/OAPs 40p (subject to alteration).
Location: Near Railway Station and County Hall.
Refreshments: Coffee Bar.
Exhibitions/Events: Military vehicle rally August Bank Holiday.
Car Park. Suitable for the disabled (including lift and toilet facilities).

DURHAM UNIVERSITY ORIENTAL MUSEUM
Elvet Hill, South Road, Durham DH1 3TH **Tel:** 0191-374 2911 **Fax:** 0191-374 3242
Oriental art & antiquities, Ancient Egypt to Modern Japan
Open: Mon-Fri 9.30-1 and 2-5 Sat and Sun 2-5.
Admission: £1 with concessions.
Location: South side of city centre, off South Road A1050 signposted.

ESSEX

BILLERICAY

BARLEYLANDS FARM MUSEUM
(H.R. Philpot & Son (Barleylands) Ltd.)
Barleylands Farm, Barleylands Road, Billericay **Tel:** (01268) 282090/532253 **Fax:** (01268) 532032
Farm museum, working craft shops, farm trail and narrow gauge railway, small animals.
Open: All year Wed-Sun 11-5.
Admission: Adults £2 students/OAPs/children over 5 £1.
Location: A129 between Billericay & Wickford.
Refreshments: Light refreshments.
Free car park for cars and coaches. Disabled toilet. People in wheelchairs half advertised price. Conducted tours by arrangement.

CHELMSFORD

CHELMSFORD AND ESSEX MUSEUM, ESSEX REGIMENT MUSEUM
Oaklands Park, Moulsham Street, Chelmsford CM2 9AQ **Tel:** (01245) 353066 & 260614
Housed in a charming Victorian Italianate mansion there are rocks, fossils, new 'Story of Chelmsford' galleries, pictures, Victorian living room, Essex Regiment, natural history, temporary exhibition gallery, social history and costume, decorative arts, drinking glasses and coins.
Open: Mon-Sat 10-5 Sun 2-5.
Admission: Free.
Refreshments: No
Exhibitions/Events: Yes
Free parking, museum shop

EPPING

THE SQUADRON

North Weald Airfield, Epping CH16 6AA **Tel:** (01922) 524510

Historic and vintage flying aircraft in a 1940 period setting. Authentic NAAR and RAF mess bar. Historic Battle of Britain airfield with original installations. Period machinery in working order. Aircraft from 1917 to ex-military jets.
Open: 7 days a week 10-6.
Admission: Adults £3 (special events £5) children/OAPs/disabled £1.
Location: M11 J 7 2m on A414 signposted North Weald Airfield.
Refreshments: Restaurant and 1940 RAF mess bar.
Exhibitions/Events: Monthly open days for flying.
Parties by appointment. Free parking.

GRAYS

THURROCK MUSEUM

(Thurrock Council)

Thameside Complex, Orsett Road, Grays RM17 5DX **Tel:** (01375) 382555

Over 50 cases of exhibits demonstrating Thurrock's rich archaeological, social and industrial history.
Open: Mon-Sat 9-8 closed Bank hols.
Admission: Free.

HARWICH

HARWICH REDOUBT

(The Harwich Society)

Main Road, Harwich

180ft diameter circular fort built 1808 to defend port against Napoleonic invasion. Now being restored by Harwich Society, and part is museum. Eleven guns on battlements.
Open: Daily 10-5 all year parties by prior arrangement (with 52 Church St).
Admission: £1 family accompanied child free, no unaccompanied child, schools 50p per person.
Location: Opposite 42A main road.
Refreshments: Light drinks available.
Car parking in Harbour Crescent. Shop. Curator: A. Rutter.

PORT OF HARWICH MARITIME MUSEUM

(The Harwich Society)

Harwich Green, Harwich

Housed in a disused lighthouse on the edge of Harwich Green with specialised displays on RN and commercial shipping.
Open: Daily 10-1 and 2-5 Apr 1-Oct 31 parties by prior arrangement apply to 52 Church St.
Admission: 50p and family accompanied child free no unaccompanied children.
Car parking in Harbour Crescent. Curator: P. Gates.

SAFFRON WALDEN

SAFFRON WALDEN MUSEUM

(Uttlesford District Council/Saffron Walden Museum Society)

Museum Street (near Church), Saffron Walden CB10 1JL **Tel:** (01799) 510333 **Fax:** (01799) 510550

Collections of archaeology, local history, ceramics, glass, costume, furniture, dolls and toys, ethnography, ancient Egyptian room, natural history and geology. Castle ruins in grounds.
Open: Mar-Oct Mon-Sat 10-5 Sun and Bank Holidays 2.30-5 in summer and 2.30-4.30 in winter Nov-Feb Mon-Sat 11-4 closed Dec 24 25.
Admission: Adults £1 discounts 50p children under 18 free.

SOUTHEND-ON-SEA

BEECROFT ART GALLERY

(Southend-on-Sea Borough Council)

Station Road, Westcliff-on-Sea, Southend-on-Sea **Tel:** (01702) 347418

Contains the Municipal, Thorpe Smith and Beecroft Collections. Picture loan scheme. Exhibitions changed monthly.
Open: Tues-Sat 9.30-5 closed Sun Mon and Bank Hols.
Admission: Free.

CENTRAL MUSEUM: SOUTHEND MUSEUMS SERVICE
(Southend-on-Sea Borough Council)
Victoria Avenue, Southend-on-Sea SS2 6EW **Tel:** (01702) 330214

Administrative headquarters. The human and natural history of south-east Essex. The only Planetarium in south-east England, outside London. Temporary exhibitions throughout the year.
Open: Mon 1-5 Tues-Sat 10-5 closed Sun and Bank Hols Planetarium Wed-Sat only.
Admission: Free but charge for Planetarium.
Location: Next to Southend Victoria Railway Station.

PRITTLEWELL PRIORY MUSEUM
(Southend-on-Sea Borough Council)
Priory Park, Southend-on-Sea **Tel:** (01702) 342878
Originally a Cluniac Monastery, now a museum of local history and natural history with a large collection of radios, televisions, gramophones and printing equipment. Temporary exhibitions.
Open: Tues-Sat 10-1 and 2-5 closed Sun Mon and Bank Hols.
Admission: Free.
Parties in the mornings by arrangement, guide-lecturer available (fee payable).

SOUTHCHURCH HALL
(Southend-on-Sea Borough Council)
Southchurch Hall Close, Southend-on-Sea **Tel:** (01702) 467671
Moated, timber-framed manor house, 13th-14th century, with small Tudor wing, the open hall furnished as a Medieval hall; with exhibition room dealing with medieval life, local history, castles and buildings.
Open: Tues-Sat 10-1 and 2-5 closed Sun and Mon and Bank Hols.
Admission: Free with a modest charge for presentations to schools.
Mornings during term time reserved for schools only. Guide-lecturer

WALTHAM ABBEY

EPPING FOREST DISTRICT MUSEUM
39/41 Sun Street, Waltham Abbey EN9 1EL **Tel:** (01992) 716882 **Fax:** (01992) 700427

The Museum is situated in two timber framed houses dating from c1520 -c1760. Permanent displays illustrate the social history of the Epping Forest District from the Stone Age to the 20th century, including magnificent oak panelling carved for the Abbot of Waltham during the reign of Henry VIII and a spectacular display of 19th century life featuring a recreation of Victorian shops. There are also changing temporary exhibitions ranging from historical subjects to contemporary arts and crafts, often complemented by workshops, demonstrations, lectures and other events. Outreach and educational programmes include oral history sessions, holiday activities for children, living history workshops and much more.
Open: Fri Sat Sun Mon 2-5 Tues 12-5 closed Wed and Thurs except for party bookings. Open all Bank Holidays except Christmas Day Boxing Day and New Year's Day.
Admission: General admission free and educational/guided visits £15/£20.
Refreshments: Coffee only.
Pre booked school parties are welcome, please telephone for charges/details. Museum shop sells local history publications, souvenirs and gifts.

GLOUCESTERSHIRE

CHELTENHAM

CHEDWORTH ROMAN VILLA
(The National Trust)
Yanworth, Cheltenham GL54 3LJ **Tel:** (01242) 890256
Remains of a Romano-British villa, excavated 1864, set in beautiful wooded coombe. Includes fine 4th century mosaics, two bath houses, spring with temple. Introductory video.
Open: Mar-end Oct Tues-Sun & Bank Hol Mons 10-5.30 Good Friday last admissions 5 Nov 1-Dec 3 11-4 also Dec 9 10.
Admission: Adults £2.70 children £1.35 family £7.40.
Location: 3m NW of Fossebridge on Cirencester-Northleach Road (A429) approach from A429 via Yanworth.
Shop open as villa. Parties must pre-book in writing. Picnic area in nearby woodland.

CHELTENHAM ART GALLERY AND MUSEUM
(Cheltenham Borough Council)
Clarence Street, Cheltenham GL50 3JT **Tel:** (01242) 237431

Foremost Arts and Crafts collection inspired by William Morris. The story of Edward Wilson, a famous son of Cheltenham, and his explorations with Scott of the Antarctic. Collections of important Dutch 17th c. & 19th c. paintings, rare Oriental porcelain and English ceramics. Social history of Cheltenham, Britain's most complete Regency town. Archaeological treasures of the Cotswolds. Special exhibitions throughout the year.
Open: Mon-Sat 10-5.20 closed Sun & Bank Hols.
Admission: Free.
Refreshments: Cafe.
Museum shop. Access for disabled people.

HOLST BIRTHPLACE MUSEUM
(Trustees: administered by Cheltenham Borough Council)
4 Clarence Road, Pittville, Cheltenham GL52 2AY **Tel:** (01242) 524846
Fax: (01242) 262334
The world of Gustav Holst, composer of *The Planets*. The story of the man and his music; his original piano and manuscripts. Hear his music on compact disc. A Regency terrace house showing the 'upstairs-downstairs' way of life in Victorian and Edwardian times, including working kitchen, elegant drawing room, and children's nursery.
Open: Tues-Sat 10-4.20 closed Sun Mon and Bank Hols.
Admission: Fee charged.
Guided tours, by prior arrangement.

PITTVILLE PUMP ROOM MUSEUM
(Cheltenham Borough Council)
Pittville Park, Cheltenham GL52 3JE **Tel:** (01242) 523852 **Fax:** (01242) 262334
Housed in the magnificent Pump Room, overlooking its own beautiful lake and gardens. Imaginative use of original costumes, bringing to life the history of Cheltenham, from its Regency heyday to the Swinging Sixties. Jewellery showing changing taste and fashion from Regency to Art Nouveau including a spectacular collection of tiaras.
Open: Oct 1 94-Apr 30 95 11-4 May 1-Sept 30 11-4.30 closed Tues.
Admission: Fee charged.
Guided tours, by prior arrangement. Free car park.

GLOUCESTER

CITY EAST GATE
(Gloucester City Council)
Eastgate Street, Gloucester
Roman and medieval gate towers and moat in an underground exhibition chamber.
Open: Tours starting at City Museum adjacent May-Sept Sat 10.15-11.15 and 2.15-4.15.
Admission: Adults 40p Children/OAPs free.

CITY MUSEUM AND ART GALLERY
(Gloucester City Council)
Brunswick Road, Gloucester **Tel:** (01452) 524131
The Marling bequest of 18th century walnut furniture, barometers and domestic silver. Paintings by Richard Wilson, Gainsborough, Turner etc. supplemented by art exhibitions throughout the year. Local archaeology including mosaics and sculptures; natural history including a freshwater aquarium.
Open: Mon-Sat 10-5 Sun (July-Sept only) 10-4 open Bank Holidays.
Admission: Free.

FOLK MUSEUM
(Gloucester City Council)
99-103 Westgate Street, Gloucester GL1 2PG **Tel:** (01452) 526467
A group of half-timbered houses, Tudor and Jacobean, furnished to illustrate local history, domestic life and rural crafts. Civil War armour, Victorian toys. Severn fishing traps, wooden ploughs etc. Reconstructed Double Gloucester dairy, ironmonger's, carpenter's and wheelwright's shops. Pin factory with 18th century forge.
Open: Mon-Sat 10-5 Sun (July-Sept only) 10-4 open Bank Holidays.
Admission: Free.

NATIONAL WATERWAYS MUSEUM
Llanthony Warehouse, The Docks, Gloucester GL1 2EH **Tel:** (01452) 318054
Fax: (01452) 318075

An enthralling collection portraying the history of Britain's canals and inland waterways in the beautiful setting of Gloucester's remarkable inland docks. The Museum itself is centred on the magnificent Victorian Llanthony Warehouse where three floors of innovative displays and fascinating exhibits bring to life 200 years of history on our canals. Voted Best Museum of Industrial or Social History - National Heritage Museum of the Year Awards 1991.
Open: Daily except Christmas Day. Access to all.
Admission: Adults £4.25 OAPs £3.25 family (2+2) £9.95.
Location: Gloucester Docks.
Refreshments: Light refreshments and meals in waterside cafe.
Exhibitions/Events: Easter, waterways traditional arts. July, Women of the Waterways.
Souvenir Shop. Boat rides. Horsebus rides. Car Parking.

NATURE IN ART
(The Centre for International Wildlife Art)
Wallsworth Hall, Twigworth, Gloucester GL2 9PA **Tel:** (01452) 731422
Fax: (01452) 730937

A unique collection of fine and decorative art inspired by nature from all parts of the world, and all historical periods, including porcelain, mosaic, furniture, etc. Displayed in a Georgian building c.1750, with interesting features. Constantly changing exhibits.
Open: Tues-Sun 10-5 Bank holiday Mon 10-5 closed Mon and Dec 24 25 26.
Admission: Adults £2.80 children/OAPs £1.95 family £8.50 under 8s free.
Location: On main A38 northside of Gloucester. 2 miles from city centre.
Refreshments: Licensed coffee shop and restaurant.
Winner of a Special Commendation in the National Heritage Museum of the Year Awards. Parties welcome by arrangement. Free parking. Suitable for disabled people. Artist in residence from Feb-Nov, and art course programme. Art shop, play area, outdoor sculptures.

REGIMENTS OF GLOUCESTERSHIRE MUSEUM
Custom House, Gloucester Docks, Gloucester GL1 2HE **Tel:** (01452) 522682
Fax: (01452) 522682

The story of the Glosters and the Royal Gloucestershire Hussars. Life-size displays with sound effects. Fascinating photographs from the last 100 years. Archive film of the Korean War.
Open: Tues-Sun and Bank Hol Mons 10-5.
Admission: Fee charged.
Shop. Facilities for disabled visitors. Voted the Museum achieving the most with the least - National Heritage Museum of the Year Awards 1991.

TRANSPORT MUSEUM
(Gloucester City Council)
Bearland, Gloucester

Horse-drawn vehicles visible from the road at all times.

NEWENT

THE SHAMBLES MUSEUM
16-24 Church Street, Newent **Tel:** (01531) 822144

A complete Victorian town layout of shops, houses, cobbled streets, and alley ways.
Open: Mid Mar-Dec Tues-Sun and Bank Holiday Mon 10-6 (last admission 5).
Admission: Fee charged.
Refreshments: Available (seasonal).
Parties by arrangement. Gift shops.

NORTHLEACH

KEITH HARDING'S WORLD OF MECHANICAL MUSIC
Oak House, High Street, Northleach, Nr Cheltenham GL54 3ET **Tel:** (01451) 860181 **Fax:** (01451) 861133

The World of Mechanical Music is a living museum of the various kinds of self-playing musical instruments which were the pride and joy of our Great Grandparents and the only kind of 'canned' music available in the home before regular broadcasting started up in 1924. The instruments are maintained in the most perfect possible order in our world famous workshops on the premises and introduced and played by our guides in the form of a live entertainment in a period setting. Musical boxes, barrel organs, polyphons, orchestrions, electric reproducing pianos, musical automata are heard at their best.
Open: Every day except Christmas and Boxing Day 10-6.
Admission: Adults £3.50 students/OAPs £2.75 children £1.50 family (2 adults + 2 children) £8.50 adults in charge of children or caring for disabled free. Every tenth admission free for booked parties. Children welcomed.
Location: High Street corner of A40 and A429 (Fosse Way).
Refreshments: Corner Green restaurant opposite, Red Lion 50 yds, both recommended.
All parts accessible to wheelchairs, toilets for disabled. Ample car parking. Free estimates by our restoration/conservation workshop.

TEWKESBURY

THE JOHN MOORE COUNTRYSIDE MUSEUM
41 Church Street, Tewkesbury

Countryside collections and natural history. Also The Little Museum, restored Medieval merchant's cottage.

THE MUSEUM
(Museum Trustees)
Barton Street, Tewkesbury GL20 5PX
Old half-timbered building. Town history, heritage centre, fairground display, model of Battle of Tewkesbury.
Open: Daily 10-4.30 Apr to mid-Oct.
Admission: Small fee. Special reductions for child/OAP.
Parties by arrangement.

WINCHCOMBE

GLOUCESTERSHIRE WARWICKSHIRE RAILWAY
(Gloucestershire Warwickshire Steam Railway Plc)
The Railway Station, Toddington, Nr. Winchcombe G54 5DT **Tel:** (01242) 621405 **Fax:** (01242) 233845
A five mile long preserved steam railway operating through the scenic Cotswolds from the beautifully restored stations at Toddington and Winchcombe. There is a large collection of locomotives and rolling stock to view at Toddington.
Open: Mar-mid Oct Sat Sun and Bank Hol Mon Dec weekends Easter week Spring Hol weeks and school summer hols Tues-Thur.
Admission: Adults £5 children/OAPs £3 5% discount for parties of 20 or more.
Location: Junction of the B4632 and B4077 3m N of Winchcombe 8m from M5 J9.
Refreshments: Flag and Whistle tea-room open every operating day.
Exhibitions/Events: Thomas the Tank Engine, Teddy Bears Picnic and other enthusiast events throughout the year - SAE for details.
Free parking at Toddington and Winchcombe stations.

HAILES ABBEY MUSEUM
(English Heritage)
Hailes Abbey, Winchcombe **Tel:** (01242) 602398
Medieval sculpture and other architectural fragments found in the ruins of the Abbey. Fine collections of 13th century roof bosses, one depicting Samson and the Lion (selected for the Age of Chivalry exhibition). Also medieval floor tiles, manuscripts, pottery and iron work. Exhibition and site information illustrates the history of the Abbey, and recent excavations.
Open: Apr 1-Oct 31 daily 10-6 Nov 1-March 31 Wed-Sun 10-4 closed Dec 24-26 and Jan 1.
Admission: Adults £1.90 concessions £1.40 children 95p (1993 prices).

WINCHCOMBE FOLK AND POLICE MUSEUM
Old Town Hall, Winchcombe GL54 5LJ **Tel:** (01242) 602925
A comprehensive display of artefacts illustrating the history of Winchcombe, together with a collection of British and international police uniforms.
Open: Apr 1-end Oct Mon-Sat 10-5.
Admission: Adults 50p children/OAPs/students 30p (1994 rates).
Parties - maximum 12. Parking nearby. Not suitable for people in wheelchairs.

HAMPSHIRE

BEAULIEU

BEAULIEU ABBEY & EXHIBITION OF MONASTIC LIFE
Beaulieu
Voted Best Museum Educational Initiative - National Heritage Museum of the Year Awards.

MARITIME MUSEUM
Buckler's Hard, Beaulieu **Tel:** (01590) 616203
Collection of models and exhibits of ships built at Buckler's Hard for Nelson's Fleet. Also the 18th century homes of a master shipbuilder. Shipwright and labourer and an Inn Scene have been re-created in the village in the original cottages. This is open to the public as part of the Buckler's Hard restoration programme.
Open: Daily Easter-May 10-6 June-Sept 10-9 Oct-Easter 10-4.30.
Admission: Fee charged.
Location: 87 miles from London.

NATIONAL MOTOR MUSEUM
Beaulieu **Tel:** (01590) 612345
One of the finest and most comprehensive Museums in the world, the National Motor Museum has grown from the Montagu Motor Museum, founded by Lord Montagu in memory of his father, a motoring pioneer. Many special displays and over 250 historic vehicles present the story of motoring from 1894 right up to modern times, with record breaking cars, commercial vehicles, motorcycles and bicycles. 'Wheels' a major feature in the Museum, takes visitors on a ride in space-age 'pods' from 1895 to way beyond the year 2000, past moving displays showing how motoring has developed in Britain over the last 100 years and how it might be in the future.
Open: Daily 10-6 (10-5 in winter).
Admission: Fee charged.
Location: 85 miles from London.
Refreshments: Licensed restaurant.

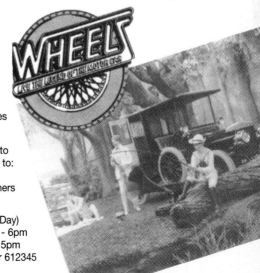

CHAWTON

JANE AUSTEN'S HOUSE
(Jane Austen Memorial Trust)
Chawton **Tel:** (01420) 83262

Jane Austen's home containing many personal relics of herself and her family.
Open: Daily 11-4.30 incl. Sun and Bank Hols closed Mon and Tues Nov Dec Mar and Christmas and Boxing Days Jan and Feb open Sat and Sun only.
Admission: Fee charged.
Location: Road A31, 1 mile S.W. of Alton, signpost 'Chawton'.
Bookshop.

FAREHAM

FORT NELSON
(Royal Armouries Museum of Artillery)
Portsdown Hill, Fareham PO17 6AN **Tel:** (01329) 233734 **Fax:** (01329) 822092
The Royal Armouries museum of artillery, housed in an 1860's Palmerston Fort overlooking Portsmouth Harbour, displays the nation's collection of artillery through the ages, including Tudor cannon, Victorian field guns, a firing Armstrong gun and sections of the Iraqi 'Supergun'.
Open: April-Oct inc weekends and Bank Hols. Firing details and opening times to be confirmed, check for details.
Admission: Supplementary charge on firing and special theme days, check for details.
Location: Down End Road, Portsdown Hill, Fareham.
Refreshments: The Barrack Cafe serves light snacks and beverages.
Group reductions on application. Guided tours only. Education service available by appointment. Curator: N. Hall.

LYNDHURST

NEW FOREST MUSEUM AND VISITOR CENTRE
High Street, Lyndhurst **Tel:** (01703) 283914
Audio-visual show and museum displays telling the story of the New Forest, its history, traditions, characters and wildlife. Includes life-sized models, computer data banks, children's quizzes and the New Forest Embroidery.
Open: 10 daily throughout the year.
Admission: On application. Special reductions.
Parties welcome. Free car parking. Suitable for disabled visitors.

MIDDLE WALLOP

MUSEUM OF ARMY FLYING
Stockbridge, Middle Wallop **Tel:** (01980) 674421

Admission: Adults £3.75 OAPs £2.75 children/students £2.25 (1993 prices) group reductions on application.
Refreshments: Licensed restaurant and coffee shop.
Free cinema, full disabled facilities.

PORTSMOUTH

CITY MUSEUM
(Portsmouth City Council)
Museum Road, Old Portsmouth PO1 2LJ **Tel:** (01705) 827261 **Fax:** (01705) 875276
Permanent displays on the history of Portsmouth. These include domestic life in Portsmouth and a local picture gallery. Also gallery of decorative art, contemporary craft and temporary exhibitions.
Open: Daily 10.30-5.30 closed Christmas Eve Christmas Day and Boxing Day.
Admission: Adults £1 OAPs 75p students/UB40 60p children under 13 free.

D-DAY MUSEUM AND OVERLORD EMBROIDERY
(Portsmouth City Council)
Clarence Esplanade, Portsmouth **Tel:** (01705) 827261
The museum incorporates the Overlord Embroidery, the modern counterpart of the Bayeux Tapestry, depicting the allied invasion of Normandy on June 6 1944. It consists of 34 panels measuring a total of 272ft. in length. Exciting displays and audio-visual. Refreshments available in 50th Anniversary extension.
Open: Daily 10-5.30 closed Christmas Eve Christmas Day and Boxing Day.

CHARLES DICKENS' BIRTHPLACE MUSEUM
(Portsmouth City Council)
393 Old Commercial Road, Portsmouth PO1 4QL **Tel:** (01705) 827261
A house of 1805 in which the famous novelist was born and lived for a short time, now restored and furnished to illustrate the middle class taste of the early 19th century. Small display of items pertaining to his work.
Open: Daily 10.30-5.30 may be subject to alteration.
Admission: Adults £1, concessions.
Readings regularly arranged. Please telephone for details.

HMS VICTORY
(Portsmouth Historic Ships)
HM Naval Base, Portsmouth **Tel:** (01705) 819604 (Group visits: 839766)
Centrepiece of the Naval Heritage Area at Portsmouth is HMS *Victory*, flagship of Vice Admiral Lord Nelson at the Battle of Trafalgar. His cabin, the 'cockpit' where he died and the sombre gundecks where his men lived and fought, can all be visit-

ed in a memorable and moving history tour. Visitors can also see the painstaking and highly skilled work, currently being carried out to restore the splendid old ship to her Trafalgar condition. But the *Victory* is more than just a preserved warship. She is the flagship of the Commander in Chief, Naval Home Command and is manned by officers and ratings of the Royal Navy, so each visit has a unique naval flavour.
Open: March-Oct 10-5.30 Nov-Feb 10-5 with extended opening during the summer Telephone (01705) 839766.
Admission: Entry price includes access to the Royal Naval Museum.
All tours of the ship are guided.

HMS WARRIOR 1860
(Portsmouth Historic Ships)
HM Naval Base, Portsmouth **Tel:** (01705) 291379 Group visits (01705) 839766
During her heyday in the 1860s *HMS Warrior* was the pride of Queen Victoria's Navy, one of the most influential warships in the world. The last survivor of the once 45-strong Black Battlefleet, she takes her place in history as the world's first iron-hulled, armoured battleship. Now beautifully and accurately restored, she is back in Portsmouth for everyone to see and enjoy. There are four vast decks available for visitors to explore, all filled with restored Victorian naval artefacts and the personal possessions of the crew. The restoration recaptures one day in the 1860s when the ship was first commissioned. The officers' table is set for formal dinner; whilst on the mess deck pewter plates and bowls are laid out for the seamen; in case of French attack the cannon are awaiting action; the Colt 45s and rifles are ready to load. The domestic life of the 700-strong crew is also displayed, from the washroom complete with mangles; to the hammocks in which you slept and were buried. It is a living exhibition where visitors can sit at the mess tables, touch the cannon, wander down to the Engine Room, see the prison cells - and even examine a cat-o-nine tails at close quarters.
Open: Every day except Christmas Day Mar-Oct 10-5.30 with extended opening in summer Nov-Feb 10-5.
Admission: Fee charged.

MARY ROSE SHIP HALL AND EXHIBITION
(Portsmouth Historic Ships)
H.M. Naval Base, College Road, Portsmouth PO1 3LX **Tel:** (01705) 750521 (Group visits 839766)
In October 1982, thousands watched as Henry VIII's favourite warship, *Mary Rose*, was recovered from the Solent seabed, where she had lain for 437 years. The ship workshop in No.3 Dry Dock is open to visitors and a new viewing gallery is now open. Nearby, an exhibition features a reconstruction of a section of the gun deck and many of the important objects recovered during the excavations. Clothing, weapons, medical equipment are used to illustrate sixteenth century social and military history, and an audio visual presentation helps the visitor relive the exciting years of underwater exploration and salvage.
Open: Mar-Oct 10-5.30 Nov-Feb 10-5 with extended opening during summer.
Admission: Fee charged.
Refreshments: Available in the Naval Base at the Tradewinds Restaurant Boathouse No.7 (seats 350) and at the Victory Buffet (seats 125) full meals and snacks.
Gift shop adjacent to exhibition features exciting range of souvenir items. No car parking in Naval Base. Historic Ships car park nearby. Suitable for disabled persons. *Wheelchairs are available. *NB. In the Ship Hall, access for wheelchairs is limited to a single gallery.

NATURAL SCIENCE MUSEUM AND BUTTERFLY HOUSE
(Portsmouth City Council)
Eastern Parade, Portsmouth **Tel:** (01705) 827261
Geology and natural history of the Portsmouth area including a full-size reconstruction of the dinosaur Iguanodon, fresh water aquaria and displays of local woodland, chalk downland and marshland, also a Butterfly House where British butterflies can be seen in free flight.
Open: Daily 10.30-5.30 closed Christmas Eve Christmas Day and Boxing Day.
Admission: Fee charged.
Location: Eastern Parade, Portsmouth.

ROYAL MARINES MUSEUM
Southsea (entry via sea front entrance), Portsmouth PO4 9PX **Tel:** (01705) 819385 **Fax:** (01705) 838420
Considered one of the finest military museums in Britain. It is located in spacious grounds adjacent to Southsea beach and outdoor exhibits include a Falklands Landing Craft into which visitors can walk. The museum tells the story of the Royal Marines from 1664 to the present day in a lively and fascinating way. Popular exhibitions include the talking head of Hannah Sneil and a chilled Arctic display. New displays in 1994 include the D Day story with a film telling of the Royal Marines' involvement in D Day. The new exhibition Hall with theatrical settings from Zeebrugge to present day - plus the Jungle Room with sights and sounds of the jungle including a live snake and scorpions. Plus one of the greatest medal collections in the country.
Open: Daily Whitsun-Aug 9.30-5 Sept-May 10-4.30.
Admission: Fee charged.
Location: On the Southsea seafront, at the eastern end of the Esplanade.
Refreshments: Full catering facilities available.
Exhibitions/Events: Phone for annual events programme.
Free car parking and seafront entrance. Well stocked shop offers a wide range of quality goods for all ages. Junior Commando assault course.

THE ROYAL NAVAL MUSEUM, PORTSMOUTH
(Portsmouth Historic Ships)
H.M. Naval Base, Portsmouth **Tel:** (01705) 733060 (Group visits 839766)
YOU'VE SEEN THE SHIPS, NOW MEET THE MEN. Alongside *HMS Victory*, the *Mary Rose* and *HMS Warrior 1860* stands the Royal Naval Museum, the only museum in Britain devoted to the overall history of the Royal Navy. Here the ghosts of past seamen are brought vividly to life in a series of exciting, modern displays that tell the story of our Senior Service from earliest times right up to the present day. Pride of place is given to the possessions of ordinary officers and seamen and the displays concentrate on the social history of the Royal Navy. A new 20th century wing is now open including the 'Vital Link' story of the Wren's role in D-Day.
Open: 10.30-4.30 all year.
Admission: Fee charged.

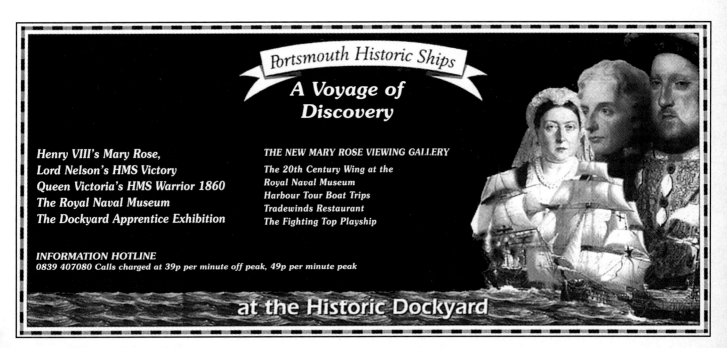

Within the Museum complex there is a buffet and a well-stocked souvenir and book shop.

SOUTHSEA CASTLE AND MUSEUM
(Portsmouth City Council)
Clarence Esplanade, Portsmouth **Tel:** (01705) 827261
Fort built in 1545 by King Henry VIII as part of his national coastal defences. Contains displays illustrating Portsmouth's development as a military fortress, aspects of naval history and local archaeology.
Open: Daily 10.30-5.30 Mar-Oct 10-4.30 closed Christmas Eve Christmas Day and Boxing Day.

SELBORNE

THE OATES MUSEUM AND GILBERT WHITE'S HOUSE
The Wakes, High Street, Selborne, Nr. Alton GU34 3JH **Tel:** (01420) 511275

Fascinating museum on the remarkable Oates family and in particular Capt. Lawrence Oates who accompanied Scott on his illfated Antarctic Expedition in 1912 and Frank Oates, Victorian naturalist and explorer in South America and South Africa. Evocative displays. Also historic house and tranquil garden, home of the famous 18th century naturalist Rev. Gilbert White, author of 'The Natural History of Selborne'.
Open: 11-5 daily from weekend before Easter-end Oct then weekends during winter.
Admission: Adults £2.50 OAPs/students £2 children £1 (first child free) free admission to shop plant sales.
Location: In centre of village.
Refreshments: Stone's throw away along high street picnic area.
Exhibitions/Events: Snowdrop Day in Jan/Feb, Unusual Plants Fair & Jazz on Jun 24 and 25, Mulled wine day in Nov.
Groups at special rates and some evenings by arrangement.

SOUTHAMPTON

SOUTHAMPTON CITY ART GALLERY
(City Council)
Civic Centre, Southampton **Tel:** (01703) 632601 **Fax:** (01703) 832153
Specialising in British painting, particularly 20th century; a good collection of Old Master paintings and Impressionist and Post-Impressionist works.
Open: Tues Wed Fri 10-5 Thurs 10-8 Sat 10-4 Sun 2-5.
Admission: Free.
Refreshments: Tea, coffee, light meals & snacks.

WINCHESTER

WINCHESTER CITY MUSEUM
(Winchester City Council)
The Square, Winchester **Tel:** (01962) 848269
Archaeology and history of Winchester and central Hampshire. 19th century shops.
Open: Mon-Sat 10-5 Sun 2-5 closed Mon in winter.
Admission: Free.

HEREFORD & WORCESTER

BEWDLEY

BEWDLEY MUSEUM
(Wyre Forest District Council)
The Shambles, Load Street, Bewdley **Tel:** (01299) 403573

Housed in the town's 18th century Shambles the museum offers a fascinating insight into the past trades of the Wyre Forest area.
Open: Wed-Fri 10.30-4.30 Sat & Sun 12-5 Easter-early Sept (at other times by appointment).
Admission: Adults £1 OAPs and unaccompanied children 50p accompanied children free.

BROMSGROVE

AVONCROFT MUSEUM OF HISTORIC BUILDINGS
Stoke Heath, Bromsgrove B60 4JR **Tel:** (01527) 831363/831886

See the new additions, visit the gift shop. Also refreshments, picnic area, free coach and car park. Open most days, March to November. For details of events, opening times and party bookings – Telephone (01527) 831886/831363

AVONCROFT MUSEUM OF BUILDINGS
Stoke Heath, Bromsgrove, Worcestershire B60 4JR.
OFF A38 BROMSGROVE BY-PASS – 3½ MILES SOUTH M42 JUNC 1

An open-air museum containing buildings of great interest and variety, from a fully-operational Windmill to a 15th century Merchant's House; from the 18th century, an ice house, earth closet and a cider mill, and also a 19th century toll house. Recent exhibits include the 14th century Guesten Hall Roof from Worcester, a 19th century lock up and now the National Telephone Kiosk Collection.
Open: June-Aug daily 11-5.30 Apr May Sept Oct daily 11-5 (closed Mon) open Bank Hols Mar & Nov Tues Wed Thurs Sat & Sun 11-4.30 closed Mon and Fri and Dec-Feb.
Admission: Adults £3.50 children £1.75 OAPs £2.80 family ticket (2 + 3) £9.40 parties at reduced rates welcome by arrangement.
Refreshments: Available.
Souvenir and book shop. Free car park and picnic site.

BROMSGROVE MUSEUM
(Bromsgrove District Council)
26, Birmingham Road, Bromsgrove B61 0DD **Tel:** (01527) 577983/831809
Local history displays. The Norton Collection of Social and Industrial History.
Open: Mon-Sat 9.30-5 Sun 2-5 closed Christmas Day.
Admission: Adults £1 children/OAPs 50p pre-arranged parties welcome.
Public Car Park opposite.

DROITWICH SPA

DROITWICH HERITAGE CENTRE
Droitwich Spa **Tel:** (01905) 774312 (24 hours)

Droitwich Heritage & Information Centre

St Richard's House, Victoria Square, Droitwich Spa, Worcs. WR9 8DS Telephone: (01905) 774312 (24hrs)

8 excellent reasons to visit us:
* Exciting Local History Exhibition * Tourist Information
* Brass Rubbing Centre * Varied Temporary Displays
* Group Tours & Trails * Souvenirs
* Unique BBC Radio Room

and a very Warm Welcome

Originally the St Andrew's Brine Baths, the building has been carefully converted into a local history museum, exhibition hall and tourist information centre. The town's history display depicts the fascinating development of Droitwich from Iron Age salt town to present day luxury spa resort. Incorporated in the display are finds from some of the most significant archaeological excavations of recent times, including Iron Age salt making containers, skeleton, preserved brain with a reconstruction of the owner's face from the skull, and other Roman artefacts, an Elizabethan salt bushel and many items connected with the salt and spa industries of the town. The centre also has an extensive programme of temporary exhibitions and is also an established brass rubbing centre offering a wide selection of brasses.
Open: Summer Mon-Fri 9.30-5 winter Mon-Fri 9.30-4 Sat 10-4.
Admission: Free.
Location: Victoria Square.
Exhibitions/Events: Jan 14-Feb 25 1995 The Droitwich Art Society. Mar 4-Apr 1 Holiday Information Service (HIS) Hundreds of brochures to choose your UK holiday from. Apr 8-May 13 'The Saltway Quilters' - Exhibition of members work. May 20-June 17 'Worcestershire Nature Conservation Trust'. June 24-Aug 5 'It's Only Rock & Roll'. Aug 12-Sept 9 'Talking Through Your Hat'.
Parties welcome, information sheets and guides available. Free car parking space, suitable for disabled visitors. Museum Shop.

For further details on editorial listings or display advertising contact:

the Editor:
Deborah Valentine
Windsor Court, East Grinstead House
East Grinstead, West Sussex RH9 1XA
Tel: (01342) 335794 Fax: (01342) 335720

HARTLEBURY

HEREFORD AND WORCESTER COUNTY MUSEUM

(Hereford and Worcester County Council)

Hartlebury Castle, Hartlebury, near Kidderminster DY11 7XZ **Tel:** (01299) 250416

A wide ranging collection showing the social history of the country from prehistoric times to the Edwardian era, all housed in a fortified 17th century manor house.

Open: Mar 1-Nov 30 Mon-Thurs 10-5 Fri and Sun 2-5.

Admission: Please phone for current rates.

Location: Signposted from A449 trunk road between Kidderminster and Worcester.

Refreshments: Light lunches and afternoon teas served during summer months.

HEREFORD

CHURCHILL GARDENS MUSEUM

(Hereford City Council)

Venn's Lane, Hereford **Tel:** (01432) 267409

Part of the extensive costume collection is always on show, also fine furniture, choice water-colours and paintings by local artists. Period rooms including Victorian kitchen, Parlour and Nursery. The Brian Hatton Gallery is an extension of the museum and is devoted to the work of this local artist. Also changing exhibitions.

Open: Tues-Sat 2-5 Sun (Apr-Oct) 2-5 closed Mon but open Bank Hol Mons.

Admission: Adults £1 children/OAPs 40p joint adm to The Old House £1.50 children/OAPs 70p. Charges subject to review.

Party visits welcome by appointment.

HEREFORD CITY MUSEUM AND ART GALLERY

(Hereford City Council)

Broad Street, Hereford **Tel:** (01432) 268121 Ext 207 **Fax:** (01432) 342492

Collections of archaeology and natural history and social history. The collection includes pictures by local artists and examples of applied art, silver, pottery and porcelain. Changing exhibitions monthly. Temporary Exhibition Programme.

Open: Tues Wed Fri 10-6 Thurs and Sat 10-5 (winter closes at 4 on Sat) closed Mon but open Bank Hol Mons.

Admission: Free.

Party visits welcome by appointment.

THE OLD HOUSE

(Hereford City Council)

High Town, Hereford **Tel:** (01432) 268121 Ext 207

The Old House is preserved as a Jacobean period museum and is furnished accordingly.

Open: Apr-Sept Mon-Sat 10-1 and 2-5.30 Oct-Mar Mon 10-1 closed pm open Bank Hol Mons Tues-Fri 10-1 and 2-5.30 Sat 10-1 also 2-5.30 summer only.

Admission: Adults £1 children/OAPs 40p joint adm to Churchill Gardens Museum £1.50 children/OAPs 70p charges subject to review.

Parties welcome by appointment. End 1994-Spring 1995 closed for repair work, please phone in advance of visit.

MALVERN

MALVERN MUSEUM

(Malvern Museum Society)

Abbey Gateway, Abbey Road, Malvern WR14 3ES **Tel:** (01684) 567811

A museum of local history, housed in the medieval Priory Gatehouse, sections on geology, the Water Cure, Elgar, Morgan and Santler cars, radar research and medieval and Victorian Malvern.

Open: Easter-Oct except Wed in school terms 10.30-5 daily including Suns and Bank Hols.

Admission: Adults 50p children 10p.

Location: Abbey Gateway.

Refreshments: No but several within 100 yds.

Parties by arrangement. Car Parks nearby.

OMBERSLEY

OMBERSLEY GALLERY

Church Terrace, Ombersley WR9 0EP **Tel:** (01905) 620655

Set in the heart of a picturesque Worcestershire village, a Craft Council Selected Gallery enjoying an enviable reputation for attracting the work of internationally renowned artists and fine crafts people. Regular exhibitions featuring painters, ceramic artists and other crafts.

Open: Tues-Sat 10-5 throughout the year.

Admission: None.

Location: J 6 M5 off the A449 to Kiddeerminster.

Refreshments: Restaurant and tea-room.

Exhibitions/Events: Diary available.

REDDITCH

FORGE MILL NEEDLE MUSEUM AND BORDESLEY ABBEY VISITOR CENTRE

(Redditch Borough Council)

Needle Mill Lane, Riverside, Redditch B97 6RR **Tel:** (01527) 62509

The only needle museum in Britain is sited in a restored 18th century needle mill, complete with a working water-wheel. Regular needlework exhibitions. The newly opened Visitor Centre exhibits some of the unique archaeological finds from the nearby 12th century abbey ruins. Educational information and National curriculum related activities for schools.

Open: Daily except Fri throughout summer season also open at certain times in winter months please ring for details.

Location: Off A441 Birmingham Road near to J 2 of M42.

Refreshments: Pre booked groups only.

Exhibitions/Events: Regular programme of exhibitions.

For details of admission charges and opening times, contact above address.

ROSS-ON-WYE

THE BUTTON MUSEUM

Kyrle Street, Ross-on-Wye HR9 7DB **Tel:** (01989) 566089

Unique award winning museum of dress and uniform buttons through the ages.

Open: Apr 1-Oct 31 10-5 daily.

Admission: Adults £1.50 OAPs/students £1.25 children under 16 free with adult.

WORCESTER

CITY MUSEUM AND ART GALLERY

(Worcester City Council)

Foregate Street, Worcester WR1 1DT **Tel:** (01905) 25371 **Fax:** (01905) 722350

Exciting range of exhibitions/events. 19th century chemists shop, contemporary art/craft, River Severn and Military displays. Cafe, Shop, Lift.

Open: Mon-Wed and Fri 9.30-6 Sat 9.30-5.

HERTFORDSHIRE

HATFIELD

MILL GREEN MUSEUM AND MILL
(Welwyn Hatfield District Council)
Mill Green, Hatfield AL9 5PD **Tel:** (01707) 271362
Working mill producing flour. Adjoining former Miller's house has local history displays and a small temporary exhibition gallery.
Open: Tues to Fri 10-5; weekends and Bank Hols 2-5.
Admission: Free. Donations welcome.
Location: Between Hatfield and W.G.C. at the junction of the A1000 and the A414
Suitable for the disabled. Car parking.

HERTFORD

HERTFORD MUSEUM
(Trust)
18 Bull Plain, Hertford **Tel:** (01992) 582686
Fine collections from Hertford, Hertfordshire and beyond: archaeology, social history, natural history, geology, fine art and photographs. Changing exhibition and events programme. Attractive Jacobean Garden. Activity room for schools.
Open: Tues-Sat 10-5 closed Sun and Mon.
Admission: Free.
Ground floor suitable for disabled. Museum shop.

HITCHIN

HITCHIN MUSEUM AND ART GALLERY
(North Hertfordshire District Council)
Paynes Park, Hitchin SG5 1EQ **Tel:** (01462) 434476
Displays of social history, costume, Hertfordshire Yeomanry Regimental Museum. Pharmaceutical gallery with reconstructed Victorian chemist's shop, complemented by physic garden of medicinal plants adjoining building, open same hours. Art exhibitions changed monthly.
Open: Mon-Sat 10-5 Sun 2-4.30 closed Bank Hols.
Admission: Free.

LETCHWORTH

FIRST GARDEN CITY HERITAGE MUSEUM
(Letchworth Garden City Corporation)
296 Norton Way South, Letchworth SG6 1SU **Tel:** (01462) 482424 482710 (Saturday) **Fax:** (01462) 480253
Exhibition of items relating to the Garden City movement and the development and social history of Letchworth Garden City, displayed in the former office and home of the architect Barry Parker. Temporary exhibitions.
Open: Mon-Fri 2-4.30 Sat 10-1 and 2-4 closed Sun Christmas and Boxing Day.
Admission: Free.

LETCHWORTH MUSEUM AND ART GALLERY
(North Herts. District Council)
Broadway, Letchworth SG6 3PF **Tel:** (01462) 685647
Displays on the archaeology of North Hertfordshire. Major natural history gallery in the county. Monthly art exhibitions.
Open: Mon-Sat 10-5 and some Bank Holidays closed Suns and some Bank Hols.
Admission: Free.

LONDON COLNEY

THE MOSQUITO AIRCRAFT MUSEUM
Salisbury Hall, London Colney, St. Albans, Hertfordshire **Tel:** (01727) 822051
Display of de Havilland Aircraft, aircraft and memorabilia, featuring the de Havilland Mosquito Prototype.
Open: Mar 1-Oct 31 Tues Thurs Sat 2-5.30 Sun and Bank Hols 10.30-5.30.
Admission: Adults £3 children/OAPs £1 parties by appointment.

ROYSTON

MUSEUM
(Royston Town Council)
Lower King Street, Royston SG8 7AL **Tel:** (01763) 242587
Local social history and archaeology, paintings by E.H. Whydale, ceramics and glass. Temporary exhibitions (changing every 4-5 weeks). Postal history collection.
Open: Wed Thurs & Sat 10-5 Sun & Bank Hol Mon 2.30-5 Mar-end of Oct.
Admission: Free.
Location: In historic medieval new town, and opposite King James I Hunting Lodge
Small Shop. Parties by arrangement. Parking at Town Hall, 5 mins walk. Ground floor suitable for disabled.

ST. ALBANS

CLOCKTOWER
(St. Albans District Council)
Market Place, St. Albans
Erected in 1402-11; restored by Sir Gilbert Scott in 1866. The tower stands 77ft. high with five storeys.
Open: Good Friday-Mid Sept Sat Sun and Bank Hols only.
Admission: Adults 25p children 10p.
Location: In centre of St. Albans.

THE MUSEUM OF ST. ALBANS
(St. Albans District Council)
Hatfield Road, St. Albans AL1 3RR **Tel:** (01727) 819340 **Fax:** (01727) 859919
The impressive Salaman collection of craft and trade tools, temporary exhibitions and wildlife garden.
Open: Mon-Sat 10-5 Sun 2-5.
Admission: All admissions free.
Location: In city centre of St. Albans 3 mins. walk from St. Peters Street

ST. ALBANS ORGAN MUSEUM
320 Camp Road, St. Albans **Tel:** (01727) 851557/873896
A permanent working exhibition of mechanical musical instruments. Dance Organs by Decap, Bursens, and Mortier; Mills Violano-Virtuoso; reproducing pianos by Steinway and Weber; musical boxes; Wurlitzer and Rutt theatre organs.
Open: Every Sun except Christmas Day 2.15-4.30.
Admission: Adults £2 children 60p family ticket £5.
Refreshments: Light only.
Parties by arrangement. Souvenirs. Shop.

THE VERULAMIUM MUSEUM
(St. Albans District Council)
St. Michael's, St. Albans AL3 4SW **Tel:** (01727) 819339 Recorded information out of office hours **Fax:** (01727) 859919
The museum has been completely re-displayed. New displays include recreated Roman rooms, 'hands-on' Discovery Areas, excavation videos - the museum of everyday life in Roman Britain. Stands on the site of the Roman City of Verulamium and houses material from the Roman and Belgic cities including several of the finest mosaics in Britain, one of which is preserved *in situ* in the 'Hypocaust annexe'.
Open: Mon-Sat 10-5.30 Sun 2-5.30 last admission 5.
Admission: (incl. Hypocaust) adults £2.50 children/students/OAPs £1.50 family ticket (2 adults + 2 children) £6.60. Residents free.
Location: In 100 acre park close to M25 M1 and A405.

STEVENAGE

STEVENAGE MUSEUM
St. George's Way, New Town Centre, Stevenage SG1 1XX **Tel:** (01438) 354292
A local museum which tells the story of Stevenage through its displays. There is also a natural history and geology display. The temporary exhibition area houses up to six exhibitions each year. A comprehensive education service provides talks and loans material to Hertfordshire schools.
Open: Mon-Sat 10-5 closed Sun.
Admission: Free.
Suitable for disabled. Multi-storey car park 100 yds.

TRING

THE WALTER ROTHSCHILD ZOOLOGICAL MUSEUM, TRING

Akeman Street, Tring HP23 6AP **Tel:** (01442) 824181 **Fax:** (01442) 890693
Mounted specimens of animals from all parts of the world.
Open: Mon-Sat 10-5 Sun 2-5 closed Jan 1, Good Fri & Dec 24-26.
Picnic shelter and garden picnic area.

WATFORD

WATFORD MUSEUM

(Watford Council)
194 High Street, Watford WD1 2HG **Tel:** (01923) 232297 **Fax:** (01923) 249729
Local history with special emphasis on printing, brewing and wartime, plus an art gallery and a temporary exhibition gallery with displays changing monthly.
Open: Mon-Fri 10-5 Sat 10-1 and 2-5 closed Sun and Bank Hols.
Admission: Free.
Location: 200 yards south of High Street Railway Station. In front of Watford Springs Leisure Complex.
Suitable for disabled visitors. Lift to 1st floor; ramped access and full toilet facilities.

WELWYN GARDEN CITY

WELWYN ROMAN BATHS

(Welwyn Hatfield District Council)
Welwyn By-pass, Old Welwyn **Tel:** (01707) 271362
A third century AD bath house, the one visible feature of a villa complex, preserved in a specially constructed vault under the A1 (M).
Open: Thurs to Sun and Bank Holidays 2-5 (or dusk if earlier).
Admission: Fee charged for adults. Children free.
Location: Under the A1(M) at its junction with the A1000 just off central roundabout of the Welwyn by-pass.
Telephone to arrange party visits. Suitable for the disabled. Car parking.

HUMBERSIDE

BARTON-ON-HUMBER

BAYSGARTH HOUSE MUSEUM

(Glanford Borough Council)
Baysgarth Leisure Park, Caistor Road, Barton-on-Humber **Tel:** (01652) 632318
An 18th century town house and park with displays of porcelain, local history, archaeology and geology. Adjacent cottage and stable block house rural craft and industrial displays.
Open: Thurs Fri and most Bank Holidays 10-4 Sat and Sun 10-5.
Admission: Free.
Car park free.

BEVERLEY

SKIDBY WINDMILL AND MUSEUM

(Beverley Borough Council)
Skidby, Beverley HU16 5TF **Tel:** (01482) 882255 **Fax:** (01482) 883913
Restored windmill and museum relating to milling and corn production.
Open: May-Sept Tues-Sat 10-4 Sun and Bank Hols 1.30-4.30 operated alternate Suns commencing first Sun in May Oct-Apr Mon-Fri 10-4.
Admission: Adult £1 children/OAPs 50p family £2 (inflation increase likely by 1/4/95).
Location: Skidby 4m S of Beverly of A164 Beverly-Hessle Road.
Refreshments: Limited refreshments available.
Exhibitions/Events: Series of weeks to be arranged.

BRIDLINGTON

BRIDLINGTON ART GALLERY AND MUSEUM

(Borough of East Yorkshire)
Sewerby Hall, Bridlington YO15 1EA **Tel:** (01262) 677874 **Fax:** (01262) 674265
Wide range of temporary exhibitions. Permanent Amy Johnson exhibition. Local and natural history and archaeology. Old farm implements.
Open: May 1-Oct 1 every day 10-6 also Oct 2-Jan 9 1996 and Mar 4-Apr 30 4 days per week Sat-Tues 11-4.
Admission: Charge applies summer season to estate admission to Hall inclusive.
Location: 2 m north east of Bridlington.
Refreshments: Tea-room and tavern.
Enquiries tel above number.

GOOLE

GOOLE MUSEUM AND ART GALLERY
(Humberside County Council)
Goole Library, Market Square, Goole DN14 5AA **Tel:** (01405) 762187
Collections illustrating the early history of the area and the formation and development of Goole as a port. Maritime paintings. Temporary exhibitions.
Open: Mon and Wed 10-7 Tues Thurs Fri 10-5 Sat 9.30-12.30 and 2-4.
Admission: Free.

GREAT GRIMSBY

BACK O' DOIG'S
(Great Grimsby Borough Council)
Alexander Docks, Great Grimsby DN31 1UF **Tel:** (01472) 242000/344867 ext 1785 **Fax:** (01472) 344887
Local/social history.
Open: Mon-Sat 10-5.
Admission: Free.
Location: Alexander Dock (adjacent to National Fishing Heritage Centre) off A180 Victoria Street.
Refreshments: At N.F.H.C.

HORNSEA

HORNSEA MUSEUM
Burns Farm, 11 Newbegin, Hornsea **Tel:** (01964) 533443
19th century home and village life. Period rooms, local history, farming, rural trades. Occasional craft displays.
Open: May 1-end Sept plus Easter.
Admission: Moderate charge.
Location: Town centre.
Refreshments: Summer holidays.
Large garden. Small gift shop. Parties by arrangement all year.

HULL

FERENS ART GALLERY
(Hull City Council)
Queen Victoria Square, Hull HU1 3RA **Tel:** (01482) 593912 **Fax:** (01482) 593913
The Gallery extended during 1990/1991, has the latest facilities for educational and Live-Art activities with a new cafe-restaurant, La Loggia. The extension houses a busy programme of exhibitions. The old building continues to show the permanent collections of Old Masters, mainly Dutch and Flemish, Portraits, Marine Paintings and Contemporary Art, with an emphasis on British works, and features 'Hull Through the Eyes of the Artist', a fresh look at local views.
Open: Mon-Sat 10-5 Sun 1.30-4.30.
Admission: Free.
Location: City centre

city of hull
MUSEUMS & ART GALLERIES

Welcome to The Old Grammar School

The Old Grammar School on South Church Side is Hull's oldest secular building. The history of the school can be traced back to 1347. The present building, however, was erected 1583-5 and has now achieved the status of an Ancient Monument. This is where both the poet Andrew Marvell and the slavery abolitionist William Wilberforce were educated. The school actually vacated the building in 1878, after which there was period of neglect. The Council took it over and began its renovation in 1985-88 and it now forms the Old Grammar School Museum, Hull's lively Social History Museum.
The visitor enters the museum through one of its many doors on South Church Side, and finds themselves in a reception and sales area.
Directly opposite the entrance is a lift leading to 'The Story of Hull and Its people' exhibition on the first floor. To the right, a staircase leads there also.

Temporary Exhibition Gallery:

The museums temporary exhibition gallery, however, is found on one's left, and visitors are asked to start their visit here.
The current temporary exhibition is 'Faith in the City'. Opened in December 1993, and running until July 1995, 'Faith in the City' explores the religious diversity of the people of Hull.
If the visitor walks through a short corridor they will come to an orientation area, introducing this exhibition. This area also reveals the building's beautiful russet brickwork. The oak 'gothic' doors, spiral staircase and the black and red quarry tiled floor, all date from renovation work which took place in the late 19th century.
The next door way leads into the exhibition gallery itself. This was originally the school hall, and a stage area is still to be seen at its far end.

'Faith in the City'

With objects, photographs, words and sound, 'Faith in the City' looks into the six major religions as found in Hull today: Hinduism, Judaism, Buddhism, Christianity, Islam and Sikhism. The exhibition takes a thematic approach; areas explored included private prayer, public worship, rites of passage, festivals, feasting, fasting and food laws, the role of religion in the community and the idea of pilgrimage. A photographer and a video producer were specially commissioned to record events throughout 1992/93, and people's personal experiences of their own faith can be heard on three sets of headphones.
From the temporary exhibition gallery one is led full circle back into the sales area. If the visitor would then like to take the lift or staircase to the first floor, it will lead them to the Permanent Exhibition Gallery: 'The Story of Hull and Its People'.

The First Floor:

The first floor of the Old Grammar School had originally been used by Hull merchants. They abandoned the building in the early 18th century, and it became Hull's first assembly rooms, for concerts, dances and card parties. However, it was badly neglected during the 19th century, being rented by a fishmonger, an ironmonger and even used as a potato warehouse before being bought by the Vicar of Holy Trinity in 1883, for use as a Clergy House and Mission Hall.
Public toilets, including facilities for wheelchair users can be found at the top of the staircase, or on the left hand side, as one leaves the lift.
Passing through the museum's spacious lecture theatres, which has been a venue for various public events, including plays, meetings and concerts, the visitor arrives at the beginning of 'The Story of Hull and Its People'.

'The Story of Hull and Its People'.

Opened in1990 this gallery, using many recollections from local people, looks at the personal experiences which make up Social History. Themes such as childhood adolescence, education, courtship and marriage are explored, together with home life, health care and work. It is hoped displays will one day continue to include areas like politics, crime, old age and death.
The exhibition's innovatory design includes The Game of Life, where visitors can follow experiences of different fictional characters as they make their way through life. Videos also complement the displays telling about housing in Hull and its docks.
On leaving the exhibition, visitors must make their way back through the lecture theatre, and down once more to the sales area, by stairs or by lift. Please stop and have a look around our shop before leaving the museum. We hope you enjoyed your visit.

Refreshments: Hot and cold freshly prepared.
Exhibitions/Events: Various exhibitions/events - details from the site.
Multi-storey Car park adjacent, Education Room (prior booking essential), cafe, shop and lift

HULL AND EAST RIDING MUSEUM
(Hull City Council)
36 High Street, Hull **Tel:** (01482) 593902
Major new displays on the archaeology and environmental history of Hull and East Riding area open late in 1995/early 1996.
Open: Currently closed.

OLD GRAMMAR SCHOOL
(Hull City Council)
South Church Side, Hull **Tel:** (01482) 593902
Hull's oldest secular building, 1583, shows the first phase of The Story of Hull and its people, with videos, visitor participation etc in displays from childhood to parenthood over 700 years. Ground floor special exhibition.
Open: Mon-Sat 10-5 Sun 1.30-4.30.
Admission: Free.
Lift to first floor, toilets and Education Room available (prior booking essential)

SPURN LIGHTSHIP
(Hull City Council)
Hull Marina, Hull **Tel:** (01482) 593902
Built 1927 and restored 1985/6, visitors can see the master's cabin, crew's quarters and light mechanism etc.
Open: Mon-Sat 10-5 Sun 1.30-4.30 closed Mon and Tues winter months.
Admission: Free.

STREETLIFE - HULL MUSEUM OF TRANSPORT
(Hull City Council)
26 High Street, Hull **Tel:** (01482) 593902
A new museum, opened 1989, showing public transport from horse-drawn vehicles, including the rare Ryde Pier Tram, to the Kitson steam tram and the newly restored Hull Tram. Cycle shop of the 1950's, workshop and garage forecourt and the social history of cycling - boneshaker to BMX. Phase 3 and 4 under construction during 1994/5, opens Autumn 1995.
Open: Mon-Sat 10-5 Sun 1.30-4.30.
Admission: Free.
Refreshments: Cafe, toilets, shop and lift.

TOWN DOCKS MUSEUM
(Hull City Council)
Queen Victoria Square, Hull **Tel:** (01482) 593902
Whales and Whaling with collection of Scrimshaw; Fishing and Trawling; Court Room of the former Docks Board; Hull and the Humber; Ships and Shipping. Temporary exhibitons
Open: Mon-Sat 10-5 Sun 1.30-4.30.
Admission: Free.
Location: City Centre.
Refreshments: Available at nearby Art Gallery.
Exhibitions/Events: Full schedule of temporary exhibitions.
Lift to basement education area (prior bookings for groups essential) and first floor displays. Sales desk.

UNIVERSITY OF HULL ART COLLECTION
(University of Hull)
The Middleton Hall, University of Hull, Cottingham Road, Hull HU6 7RX
Tel: (01482) 465192 **Fax:** (01482) 465192
Specialising in art in Britain 1890-1940. Painting, sculpture and drawings including work by Sickert, Steer, Lucien Pissarro, Augustus John, Stanley Spencer, Gill, Epstein and Moore. Also the Thompson Collection of Chinese Ceramics (chiefly 17th century) and temporary exhibitions.
Open: Mon-Fri 2-4 (Wed 12.30-4) except public holidays.
Admission: Free.
Parties welcome. Limited car parking. Access for disabled persons. Hon. Curator: John G. Bernasconi.

WILBERFORCE HOUSE MUSEUM
(Hull City Council)
23-25 High Street, Hull **Tel:** (01482) 593902
Birthplace of the slave emancipator with slavery collections, 17th and 18th century Merchants' houses with collections of furniture, silver and costume, period rooms.
Open: Mon-Sat 10-5 Sun 1.30-4.30.
Admission: Free.
Toilets, sales area and education room (prior booking essential),walled garden at rear.

POCKLINGTON

PENNY ARCADIA
(Penny Arcadia Ltd)
Ritz Cinema, Market Place, Pocklington YO4 2AR **Tel:** (01759) 303420
Comprehensive collection of coin-operated amusement machines. Presentation included audio-visual on stage and screen on the history of the industry and its importance in pioneering so many developments - cinema, recorded sound etc the machines are demonstrated in guided tours.
Open: May & Sept 12.30-5 June July & Aug 10-5 groups anytime by arrangements.
Admission: Adults £3 children under 15 and senior citizens £2 special reductions for parties adults £2 children under 15 and senior citizens £1.50.
Location: Market Place, Pocklington 12 miles east of York.
Suitable for the disabled.

SCUNTHORPE

MUSEUM AND ART GALLERY
(Scunthorpe Borough Council)
Oswald Road, Scunthorpe DN15 7BD **Tel:** (01724) 843533 **Fax:** (01724) 281705
Regional Museum for South Humberside.
Open: 10-4 Tues-Sat 2-5 Sun.
Admission: Free.

ISLE OF MAN

CASTLETOWN

CASTLE RUSHEN
(Branch of Manx National Heritage)
Castletown **Tel:** (01624) 675522 **Fax:** (01624) 661899
This finely preserved medieval castle, on the site of a Viking stronghold, was developed as a fortress by successive Kings and Lords of Man between the thirteenth and sixteenth centuries. Major redevelopment, completed in 1991, recreates castle life at important phases in its history.
Open: Easter-end of Sept daily 10-5.
Admission: Fee charged.
Location: Castletown, Isle of Man.

THE NAUTICAL MUSEUM
(Branch of Manx National Heritage)
Bridge Street, Castletown **Tel:** (01624) 675522 **Fax:** (01624) 661899
Across the harbour from Castle Rushen, the displays centre on the late 18th century armed yacht 'Peggy' in her contemporary boathouse. Part of the original building is constructed as a Cabin Room of the Nelson period and the museum also displays many nautical exhibits, ship models etc, a fine range of photographs of Manx vessels in the days of sail and a reconstruction of a sailmaker's loft.
Open: Easter-end of Sept daily 10-5.
Admission: Fee charged.
Location: Castletown, Isle of Man

ST. MARY'S CHAPEL, LATER THE GRAMMAR SCHOOL
(Branch of Manx National Heritage)
Castletown **Tel:** (01624) 675522 **Fax:** (01624) 661899
The former capital's first church built around 1200 AD. It was also used as a school from at least 1570 and served exclusively in that capacity from 1702 until its closure in 1930. The interpretive displays include a Victorian school-room.
Open: Easter-end Sept daily 10-5.
Admission: Free.
Location: Castletown, Isle of Man.

DOUGLAS

MANX NATIONAL HERITAGE
Douglas **Tel:** (01624) 675522 **Fax:** (01624) 661899

The headquarters of Manx National Heritage is at the Manx Museum, incorporating the National Museum of the Island with displays of Manx Archaeology, History, Folk Life and Natural Sciences. The building also houses the National Art Gallery with works of Manx interest and the Island's National Archive and Reference Library.
Open: All year round Mon-Sat 10-5.
Admission: Free.
Location: Douglas, Isle of Man.
Refreshments: Bay Room Restaurant.

LAXEY

LAXEY WHEEL AND MINERS
(Branch of Manx National Heritage)
Laxey **Tel:** (01624) 675522 **Fax:** (01624) 661899
The spectacular focus to this historic mining valley is the Great Laxey Wheel. Completed in 1854, the 'Lady Isabella' is the largest wheel of its kind in the world and was built to operate the pumping system which cleared water from the lead mines. Enjoy the mines trail and even venture underground!
Open: Easter-end Sept daily 10-5.
Admission: Fee charged.
Location: Laxey, Isle of Man.

PEEL

ODIN'S RAVEN
(Branch of Manx National Heritage)
Peel **Tel:** (01624) 675522 **Fax:** (01624) 661899
In 1979, in celebration of the Island's Millenium, this two-thirds scale replica Viking ship was sailed by a mixed Norwegian and Manx crew over 1500 miles from Norway to the Isle of Man. The story of the voyage is presented in the boathouse that now preserves this magnificent ship.
Open: Easter-end Sept daily 10-5.
Admission: Fee charged.
Location: Peel, Isle of Man.

PEEL CASTLE
(Branch of Manx National Heritage)
Peel **Tel:** (01624) 675522 **Fax:** (01624) 661899
St. Patricks Isle is surrounded by the imposing walls of Peel Castle which also enclose the eleventh century church of St. Patrick and the round tower, the thirteenth century Cathedral of St. German and the later apartments of the Lords of Man.
Open: Easter-end of Sept daily 10-5.
Admission: Fee charged.
Location: Peel, Isle of Man

PORT ST. MARY

THE CREGNEASH VILLAGE FOLK MUSEUM
(Branch of Manx National Heritage)
Near Port St. Mary **Tel:** (01624) 675522 **Fax:** (01624) 661899
Illustrates, in situ, the life of a typical Manx upland crofting/fishing community at the turn of the century. Many of the buildings are thatched and include a crofter-fisherman's home, a weaver's shed with handloom, a turner's shed with treadle lathe, a thatched farmstead and a smithy. Church Farm is being developed as a traditional working farm, and other demonstrations, including spinning, are given on certain days each week. The property adjoins the Manx National Trust lands of the Spanish Head area.
Open: Apr-Sept daily 10-5.
Admission: Fee charged.
Refreshments: Village restaurant.

RAMSEY

THE GROVE MUSEUM
(Branch of Manx National Heritage)
Near Ramsey **Tel:** (01624) 675522 **Fax:** (01624) 661899
A small, pleasantly-proportioned early Victorian house with associated range of outbuildings. The house displays a series of Victorian period rooms, a costume room and general museum displays. The outbuildings contain early agricultural equipment and vehicles and include a horse-powered threshing mill restored to a working condition. The pleasant garden is being brought back to its Victorian state, with ornamental pool and fish pond, and waterfowl on the duckpond.
Open: Apr-end of Sept daily 10-5.
Admission: Fee charged.
Location: Ramsey, Isle of Man
Refreshments: Restaurant.

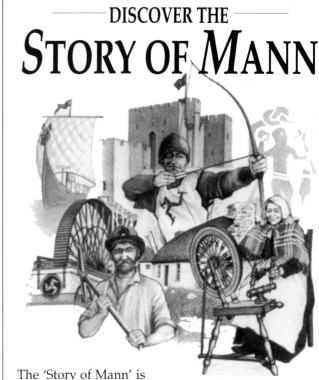

ISLE OF WIGHT

BRADING

ISLE OF WIGHT WAX MUSEUM
Brading PO36 ODQ **Tel:** (01983) 407286 **Fax:** (01983) 402112
Scenes of Island history from Roman times to present day with authentic costume, wax figures and period furniture, cleverly brought to life with sound, light and animation.
Open: All the year May-Sept daily 10-10 Oct-Apr daily 10-5.
Admission: Charged.

LILLIPUT MUSEUM OF ANTIQUE DOLLS AND TOYS
High Street, Brading PO36 0DJ **Tel:** (01983) 407231
Collection with over 2,000 exhibits dating from c.2000 BC to c.1945.
Open: 7 days a week from mid Mar-mid Jan low season 10-5 high season 9.30-9.30.
Admission: Adults £1.35 OAPs/children 95p under 5 yrs Free.

COWES

SIR MAX AITKEN MUSEUM
The Prospect, 83 High Street, Cowes PO31 7AJ **Tel:** (01983) 295144 **Fax:** (01983) 200253
Open: May-Sept Mon-Fri 10-4.
Admission: Adults £1 OAPs and children 50p.

EAST COWES

OSBORNE HOUSE
(English Heritage)
East Cowes **Tel:** (01983) 200022
Queen Victoria's seaside home was built at her own expense in 1845 and designed by Thomas Cubitt. Here, she and Prince Albert sought peace and solitude, away from the affairs of state. At the request of their son, King Edward VII, this wonderful monument to Victorian family life has been preserved almost unchanged. The house itself is an Italianate villa with two tall towers. The apartments and rooms contain mementoes of royal travel abroad, sometimes incorporated into the decor. You will see intricate Indian plaster decoration, furniture made from deer antlers and over 400 works of art, pictures and pieces of furniture. There is even a fascinating glimpse into the early years of the royal children in the newly restored Royal Nursery.
Open: Apr 1-Oct 31 daily 10-5 (last admission one hour before closing).
Admission: Adults £5.50 concessions £4.10 children £2.75 (1994 prices).

NEWPORT

CARISBROOKE CASTLE MUSEUM
(English Heritage)
Newport **Tel:** (01983) 522107
Isle of Wight Museum - collection illustrating the history of the castle and the imprisonment of Charles I together with items relating to Tennyson's home on the island. Various other aspects of island history are also shown.
Open: Apr 1-Oct 31 daily 10-6 Nov 1-Mar 31 daily 10-4 closed Dec 24-26 Jan 1.
Admission: Adults £3.20 concessions £2.40 children £1.60 including admission to Castle (1994 prices).

NATIONAL WIRELESS MUSEUM
(C.E.M. Trust)
'Lynwood', 52 West Hill Road, Ryde PO33 1LN **Tel:** (01983) 567665
Tells the history of wireless communications from its beginning at the end of the last century, when Marceni came to the island and built his first transmitter ar Alum Bay. Marceni birthday exhibition 22 April. Annual Wight Wireless Rally 3 September.
Open: Mon-Fri 10-5 Sun 1-5 closed Sat open all Bank Hols.

KENT

BIRCHINGTON

POWELL-COTTON MUSEUM AND QUEX HOUSE & GARDENS
Quex Park, Birchington **Tel:** (01843) 42168

POWELL-COTTON MUSEUM
(A Registered Charity, No. 307757)
and
QUEX HOUSE AND GARDENS,
Quex Park, Birchington, Kent
Unique collections of African and Asian fauna and native artefacts, firearms, E. Kent archaeological material, superb Oriental Fine Arts, beautifully furnished Regency Mansion, gardens, lawns and Victorian Walled Kitchen Garden under restoration provide something for everyone at Quex Park.

Combine a mornings visit to Canterbury with a never to be forgotten afternoon at Quex, set in 250 acres of beautiful gardens & woodland. The fine Regency house was built in 1808 by John Powell Powell, High Sheriff of Kent and is still the Powell-Cotton family home. Seven of the rooms are on view with superb family collections - fine furniture, porcelain, pictures, silver, clocks etc. Of unique importance is the Museum built adjoining the House by Maj. P.H.G. Powell-Cotton, Naturalist, Explorer, Photographer. Author and Collector Extraordinary. Words cannot do justice to the amazing collections housed in this remarkable private museum of nine large galleries, built between 1895 and 1973. The African and Asian animals in their huge natural landscape dioramas look so alive that visitors have claimed to have seen them move; one of the most important ethnographical collections is housed here together with a very large weapons and cannon collection, African butterflies, local archaeological material, treasures from the Orient, including a unique series of Chinese Imperial and Export porcelains and English and European pottery and porcelain.
Open: Museum House & Gardens Apr-Oct inc Tues Wed Thurs and Sun 2-6 Mar Nov and Dec-3rd Sun inc 2-5 **Museum and Gardens** Sun only. Closed Jan and Feb except to parties by appointment also open Bank Hols and Easter when in Mar.
Admission: House Museum & Gardens (Summer) adults £2.50 children under 16 and OAPs £1.80 **Museum & Gardens (Winter)** adults £2 children under 16 & OAPs £1.30 **Gardens only** adults £1 children/OAPs 60p.
Location: A28 12 miles east of Canterbury; signposted St. Nicholas-at-Wade and Prospect Roundabouts and Birchington Square.
Refreshments: New restaurant opening 1995.
Free parking for cars & coaches.

BROADSTAIRS

DICKENS' HOUSE MUSEUM
(Thanet District Council)
Victoria Parade, Broadstairs CT10 1QS **Tel:** (01843) 862853

Open: Daily Apr-Oct 2.30-5.30.
Admission: Fee charged.

CANTERBURY

CANTERBURY HERITAGE MUSEUM
(Canterbury City Council)
Stour Street, Canterbury **Tel:** (01227) 452747 **Fax:** (01227) 455047
A timewalk from the Romans to Rupert Bear. Includes holograms, video and computers.
Open: Mon-Sat 10.30-5 also June-Oct Suns 1.30-5 closed Good Friday and Christmas.
Admission: Adults £1.50 10% discount for groups of 10+ many other concessions until Mar 31 1995.
Location: On the riverbank in city centre car parks and British Rail within walking distance.
Shop.

THE ROMAN MUSEUM
(Canterbury City Council)
Butchery Lane, Canterbury **Tel:** (01227) 785575 **Fax:** (01227) 455047
A new museum around a Roman site; excavated finds; computer programme; hands-on area.
Open: Mon-Sat 10-5 all year, also Suns Jun-Oct 1.30-5 closed Good Friday and Christmas.
Admission: Adults £1.50 10% discount for groups of 10+ and many other concessions until Mar 31 1995.
Location: City centre within walking distance of car parks and British Rail.
Suitable for disabled. Disabled toilet. Shop.

THE ROYAL MUSEUM & ART GALLERY AND BUFFS REGIMENTAL MUSEUM
(Canterbury City Council)
High Street, Canterbury CT1 2JE **Tel:** (01227) 452747 **Fax:** (01227) 455047
Decorative arts, archaeology, regimental history, special exhibitions gallery.
Open: All year Mon-Sat 10-5 closed Good Friday and Christmas week.
Admission: Free.
Location: In the High Street, car parks and British Rail within walking.

THE WEST GATE MUSEUM
(Canterbury City Council)
St. Peter's Street, Canterbury **Tel:** (01227) 452747 **Fax:** (01227) 455047
Panoramic views from the battlements; prison cells; replica armour to try on.
Open: All year Mon-Sat 11-12.30 and 1.30-3.30 closed Good Friday & Christmas.
Admission: Adults 60p 10% discount for groups of 10+ and many other concessions until Mar 31 1994.
Location: On the riverbank close to car parks and Canterbury West Station.
Shop.

WHITSTABLE MUSEUM & GALLERY
(Canterbury City Council)
Oxford Street, Whitstable CT5 1DB **Tel:** (01227) 276998
Seafaring history featuring oysters, divers and wrecks. Special exhibitions gallery.
Open: All year 10.30-1 and 2-4 closed Wed Sun Good Friday and Christmas week.
Admission: Free.
Location: Within walking distance of car parks and British Rail.
Suitable for disabled. Shop.

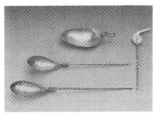

CHATHAM

FORT AMHERST

off Dock Road, Chatham ME4 4UB **Tel:** (01634) 847747
Georgian Fort.
Open: Every day 10.30-5.
Admission: 1994 £3.50 and £2.

THE HISTORIC DOCKYARD, CHATHAM

(Chatham Historic Dockyard Trust)
Chatham ME4 4TE **Tel:** (01634) 812551 **Fax:** (01634) 826918

The most complete Georgian dockyard in the world. Now a living museum. See ropes, flags and sails made here as they have been for over 400 years. Step back in time to 1758 in the award-winning Wooden Walls gallery and relive the building of sail-powered warships. Allow at least 4 hours to visit.
Open: Daily Easter-Oct 29. Feb, Mar, Nov open Weds, Sat and Sun.
Admission: Fee charged, please telephone for details.
Location: Signposted from M2 (J3).
Refreshments: Licensed restaurant, coffee and tea shop.
Open air and undercover picnic facilities. Free on-site car parking, shops, access for the disabled, toilets.

DOVER

DOVER CASTLE

(English Heritage)
Dover **Tel:** (01304) 201628
One of the most powerful medieval fortresses in Western Europe. Included in admission to Dover Castle is Hellfire Corner, the secret war tunnels concealed in the white cliffs from where Vice Admiral Ramsay masterminded the evacuation of Dunkirk in 1940. Also see 'Live and Let's Spy' who was the Real 'Q'? a new display within the castle.
Open: Apr 1-Oct 31 daily 10-6 Nov 1-Mar 31 daily 10-4 closed Dec 24-26 Jan 1.
Admission: Adults £5.25 concessions £3.95 and children £2.60 (1994 prices) Hellfire Corner - extra charge.

FAVERSHAM

FLEUR DE LIS HERITAGE CENTRE

(The Faversham Society)
13, Preston Street, Faversham ME13 8NS **Tel:** (01795) 534542

Audio-visual, bygones and colourful displays on 1,000 years of life in one of Britan's finest Heritage Towns with over 400 listed buildings. Housed in a 15th century inn, where the plot to murder 'Arden of Faversham' was hatched in 1551, this is the first Heritage Centre in the South.
Open: Daily 10-4 closed Suns from Nov-Mar inclusive.
Admission: Adults £1 children/OAPs/other concessions 50p.

FOLKESTONE

FOLKESTONE MUSEUM AND GALLERY

(KCC Arts and Libraries Depertment)
2, Grace Hill, Folkestone CT20 1HD **Tel:** (01303) 850123 **Fax:** (01303) 242907
Important collections of fossils, Natural history and archaeology of the area and town. Programme of exhibitions and 'live' events. Local history linked to Heritage Research Collection.
Open: Mon-Sat 9.30-5 closed Sun and Bank Hols.
Admission: None.
Location: First floor of Folkestone Library.
Exhibitions/Events: Seperate programmes issued throughout the year.
Pay car park nearby.

GILLINGHAM

SMALL EXHIBITS AND LOCOS
(Sittingbourne & Kemsley Light Railway)
Kemsley Down Station, 85 Balmoral Road, Gillingham ME7 4QG **Tel:** (01795) 424899
Exhibition of railways in Kent, including many pictures of former Bowater Industrial Railway (paper mills). Also small exhibits of railways, steam locos on display outdoors, and display of Bowater wagons.
Open: Easter-Oct Sun all Bank Hols and Aug Wed and Sat from 2 access by steam train ride from Milton Halt.
Admission: By steam train ride admission included in fare Adults £2 children 3-13/OAPs £1. Party fare is minimum adult £1.40 Child 70p.
Location: Kemsley Down Station.
Refreshments: Light Refreshments.

GOUDHURST

FINCHCOCKS, LIVING MUSEUM OF MUSIC
Goudhurst **Tel:** (01580) 211702
Magnificent collection of historical keyboard instruments in 18th century manor. Played whenever the house is open. Many musical events.
Open: Season Apr-Oct.
Admission: c. £5.
Location: Finchcocks Museum.
Refreshments: Teas on open days. Full catering by reservation.
Exhibitions/Events: 'The Lost Pleasure Gardens' Exhibition. Festival of concerts. Opera and Lectures September.

GRAVESEND

NEW TAVERN FORT
(Gravesend Borough Council, Leisure Sevices)
Riverside Leisure Area, Gravesend **Tel:** (01474) 337600
A guardian of the Thames against foreign invasion for over 200 years it now welcomes visitors. Many of the emplacements have been re-armed and the underground magazines are open during summer weekends. Details from the Tourist Information Centre on (01474) 337600.

HYTHE

HYTHE LOCAL HISTORY ROOM
(Hythe Town Council and Kent County Council)
Oaklands, Stade Street, Hythe **Tel:** (01303) 266152
Local history.
Open: Mon-Sat when Library is open.

MAIDSTONE

MUSEUM AND ART GALLERY
(Maidstone Borough Council)
St. Faith's Street, Maidstone ME14 1LH **Tel:** (01622) 754497
Housed in 16th century Chillington Manor, the museum (extended considerably in the 19th century) contains outstanding collections, some of national importance. These include ceramics, natural history, costume, furniture, Japanese decorative art, local history and, in the recently refurbished Art Gallery, 17th & 18th century Dutch & Italian oil paintings. Also on display is the museum of the Queen's Own Royal West Kent Regiment.
Open: on-Sat 10-5.30 Sun 2-5 Bank Hol Mon 11-5.30.
Admission: Free.

MUSEUM OF KENT LIFE
Lock Lane, Sandling, Maidstone ME14 3AU **Tel:** (01622) 763936 **Fax:** (01622) 662024
The history of the Kent Countryside explained through displays on farming history, exhibits of agricultural tools and machinery and outside planting of crops important to Kent, including orchard fruits, hops, arable, pasture and market garden crops, and livestock typical to the county, especially Romney Marsh Sheep. New extended display on H.E.Bates & Darling Buds of May.
Open: Easter-end Oct daily.
Admission: Adults £3 children/students/OAPs £1.50.
Location: Off J6 M20.
Refreshments: Licenced tea-rooms.
Gift Shop, concessions on group bookings.

TYRWHITT-DRAKE MUSEUM OF CARRIAGES
(Maidstone Borough Council)
Archbishop's Stables, Mill Street, Maidstone **Tel:** (01622) 663006
Housed in the stable block of the nearby Archbishops Palace, the Carriage Collection is thought to be the finest and most wide-ranging in Britain. Most types of carriages are represented, all in superbly original condition, alongside a number of Royal vehicles.
Open: 10.30-5.30 7 days.
Admission: Adults £1.50 children/OAPs £1.

MARGATE

OLD TOWN HALL MUSEUM
(East Kent Maririme Trust)
Market Place, Margate **Tel:** (01843) 231213 or (01843) 587765
Margate's development as a seaside resort; also old Court Room and Victorian Police cells.
Open: Apr-Sept 10-5 (except Sun) Oct-Mar Mon-Fri 10-4.30.
Admission: Fee charged. Concessions. Groups welcome (booking advisable).
Small selection of souvenirs.

NEW ROMNEY

ROMNEY TOY AND MODEL MUSEUM
(Romney, Hythe & Dymchurch Railway)
New Romney Station, New Romney TN28 8PL **Tel:** (01797) 362353
A fascinating collection of old, and not so old, toys and models. The centrepiece is one of the largest operating model railways in the country with up to 30 trains in operation at any one time. Collection also includes historic photos and displays about the Romney, Hythe and Dymchurch railway.
Open: Mar and Oct weekends Easter-End Sept daily other times by arrangement.
Admission: Adults 70p children 35p (1993) no party reduction.
Location: .5m off A259 at New Romney station.
Refreshments: 60 seat cafeteria.
Parking 25p in station Car Park. Stairlift fitted.

PADDOCK WOOD

WHITBREAD HOP FARM
Beltring, Paddock Wood TN12 6PY **Tel:** (01622) 872068
Award winning tourist attraction set in the heart of beautiful Kent countryside. Largest collection of Victorian Oasthouses in the world, Shire Horse Centre, Hop Story Exhibition, Owl Flying Displays, Working Pottery, Animal Village, Nature Trail, Weekend Special Events.
Open: Daily 10-6.
Admission: Adults £4.95 children £3 OAPs and disabled £3.50.
Refreshments: Restaurant.
Gift Shop.

RAMSGATE

MARITIME MUSEUM COMPLEX
(East Kent Maritime Trust)
Royal Harbour, Ramsgate CT11 8LS **Tel:** (01843) 587765
National and local maritime history Museum with adjacent Dry Dock and historic vessels.
Open: All year winter Mon-Fri summer 7 days.
Admission: Small charge with concessions and groups welcome (booking advisable).

RAMSGATE LIBRARY GALLERY
Guildford Lawn, Ramsgate CT11 9AY **Tel:** (01843) 593532
Opened in 1982, Ramsgate Library Gallery has been constructed to provide a continuous, high quality programme of exhibitions and related events, covering all aspects of the visual arts. The Gallery is funded by Kent County Council, with financial assistance from South East Arts. For a current brochure, please telephone Our Arts Promotion Officer on (01843) 223626
Admission: Free.

RAMSGATE MUSEUM
(Kent County Council)
Ramsgate Library, Guildford Lawn, Ramsgate CT11 9AY **Tel:** (01843) 593532
The story of bygone Ramsgate; watercolours, photos, archaeology, holiday souvenirs.
Open: Mon-Thurs 9.30-6 Fri 9.30-7 Sat 9.30-5 closed on public holidays.
Admission: Free.
Limited car parking nearby. Suitable for disabled persons.

RICHBOROUGH

RICHBOROUGH CASTLE
(English Heritage)
Richborough **Tel:** (01304) 612013
Objects found during excavation of the site, Roman pottery, coins and other small objects.
Open: Apr 1-Oct 31 daily 10-6.
Admission: Adults £1.80 concessions £1.35 children 90p (1994 prices).

ROCHESTER

CHARLES DICKENS CENTRE
(City of Rochester-upon-Medway)
Eastgate House, High Street, Rochester **Tel:** (01634) 844176
'Step back into Dickensian England and experience the reality of Victorian Life'.
Open: All year 10-5.30 last admission 4.45 closed Dec 25 26 but open Jan 1.
Admission: On Application.

GUILDHALL MUSEUM
(City of Rochester-upon-Medway)
Guildhall, High Street, Rochester ME1 1PY **Tel:** (01634) 848717
Local history, archaeology, arms and armour, costumes, Victoriana, models of ships and aircraft. Napoleonic prisoner-of-war work.
Open: Daily 10-5.30 except Christmas Day Boxing Day and Good Friday last admission 5.
Admission: Free.
Exhibitions/Events: Usually two special exhibitions per year

SANDWICH

THE PRECINCT TOY COLLECTION
38 Harnet Street, Sandwich CT13 9ES
Dolls' houses, Noah's Arks, dolls, clockwork toys etc.
Open: Easter-end Sept Mon-Sat 10.30-4.30 Sun 2-4.30 Oct Mon Sat and Sun only 2-4 1st 2 weekends Dec 2-4.
Admission: Adults £1 children/OAPs 50p children under 4 years free.

TENTERDEN

SMALLHYTHE PLACE
(The National Trust)
Smallhythe, Tenterden TN30 7NG **Tel:** (01580) 762334
Small early 16th century timbered house, home of the famous actress, Dame Ellen Terry. Now a superb theatrical and personal museum.
Open: Apr-end Oct daily 2-6 (except Thurs and Fri) or dusk if earlier but open Good Fri. Last admission .5 hr before close. Pre-booked parties Tues 11-12.30 only.
Admission: Fee charged.
Location: 3m S of Tenderden on B2082.
Children must be accompanied. Visitors restricted to 25 at any one time.

TENTERDEN AND DISTRICT MUSEUM
Station Road, Tenterden TN30 6HN **Tel:** (01580) 764310
Townscape and history of Tenterden, Limb of the Cinque Ports. Local trades and industries, building materials; bygones, agricultural implements, hop gardens. The Col. Stephens Railway Collection.
Open: Mar Sat and Sun 2-4.30 Apr-Oct daily 2-4.45 except Fri and in late July/August 11-4.45 except Fri. Special arrangements for groups.
Admission: Adults 75p OAPs 50p children 25p.

TUNBRIDGE WELLS

TUNBRIDGE WELLS MUSEUM AND ART GALLERY
(Tunbridge Wells Borough Council)
Civic Centre, Mount Pleasant, Royal Tunbridge Wells TN1 1JN **Tel:** (01892) 547221
Local history, Tunbridge ware, dolls, toys, bygones, natural history, and regularly changing art exhibitions.
Open: Mon-Sat 9.30-5 closed Sun and Bank Holidays and Easter Sat.
Admission: Free.
Location: In the library and museum building, next to the Town Hall.

AN EXCITING & INTRIGUING JOURNEY BACK THROUGH HISTORY

THE GUILDHALL MUSEUM

The popular Guildhall Museum in Rochester's historic High Street has been re-opened after extensive refurbishment.

Among the many innovations are a new entrance reached by the cobblestoned Bull Lane and adorned with period gates, and the installation of new display cabinets, allowing some exhibits to go on show for the first time in many years.

Exhibits have been arranged chronologically, so visitors can step from Prehistoric through Roman times into the 16th Century and onwards.

There is a special emphasis on "hands-on" features, such as Anglo-Saxon coin minting and audio-visual displays, to make the museum especially enthralling for children.

The centre-piece is a life-size replica of one of the convict hulks once moored on the River Medway. These were a common sight between the 1770s and 1850s, and you can now experience life on board.

The Guildhall Museum's refurbishment was part of an overall programme of improvements which has also seen the acquisition of a new wing for the Museum's Victorian and Edwardian collections.

COME ALONG & VISIT THE GUILDHALL MUSEUM TODAY!

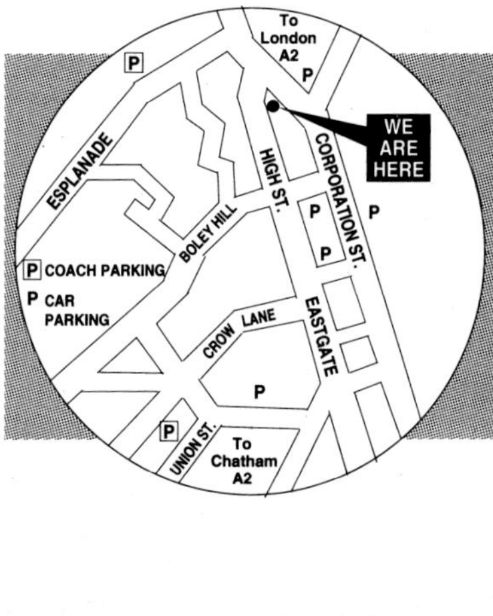

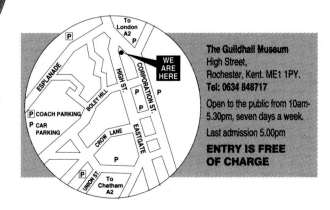

The Guildhall Museum
High Street,
Rochester, Kent. ME1 1PY.
Tel: 0634 848717

Open to the public from 10am-5.30pm, seven days a week.

Last admission 5.00pm

ENTRY IS FREE OF CHARGE

City of ROCHESTER UPON MEDWAY

LANCASHIRE

BLACKBURN

BLACKBURN MUSEUM AND ART GALLERY
(Blackburn Borough Council)
Museum Street, Blackburn BB1 7AJ **Tel:** (01254) 667130
The R.E. Hart collection of coins, illuminated manuscripts, and printed books; Japanese prints, oil paintings, English watercolours, British and Oriental ceramics and decorative art, icons and gallery of South Asian art and culture. Local and social history, East Lancashire Regimental collection.
Open: Tues-Sat 9.45-4.45.
Admission: Free.
Location: Blackburn Town Centre.
Refreshments: Not on site.
Children's activity, questionnaire and colouring sheets are available on request.

LEWIS TEXTILE MUSEUM
(Blackburn Borough Council)
Exchange Street, Blackburn BB1 7JN **Tel:** (01254) 667130
Ground floor display of historic textile machinery and models. The machines can be operated for visiting parties by prior arrangement. Constantly changing art exhibitions in first floor gallery.
Open: Tues-Sat 9.45-4.45.
Admission: Free.
Location: Town centre.
Refreshments: Not on site.

SUNNYHURST WOOD VISITOR CENTRE
(Blackburn Borough Council)
Sunnyhurst Wood, Darwen, Blackburn **Tel:** (01254) 701545
Changing displays on the history of Darwen; a full programme of changing art exhibitions.
Open: Tues Thur Sat Sun and Bank Hol Mons 2-4.30.
Admission: Free.
Location: In Sunnyhurst Wood.
Refreshments: Refreshments adjacent to centre.

WITTON COUNTRY PARK VISITOR CENTRE
(Blackburn Borough Council)
Witton Country Park, Preston Old Road, Blackburn **Tel:** (01254) 55423
Located in the stables with displays of harness and agricultural machinery and a natural history room. A fresh section is the newly opened wildlife centre.
Open: Mon-Sat 1-5 Sun and Bank Hol Mons 11-5 Nov-Mar closed Mon-Wed.
Admission: Free.
Location: in Witton Country Park.
Refreshments: Available.

BURNLEY

TOWNELEY HALL ART GALLERY AND MUSEUMS AND MUSEUM OF LOCAL CRAFTS AND INDUSTRIES
(Burnley Borough Council)
Burnley BB11 3RQ **Tel:** (01282) 424213

TOWNELEY HALL
ART GALLERY & MUSEUMS
Burnley, Lancashire

The former home of the Towneley family, dating originally from the 14th Century, has been an Art Gallery & Museum since 1903. A separate Museum of Local Crafts & Industries is housed in the brew-house, and there is a Natural History Centre with Nature Trails in the grounds.

Fine collection of oil paintings and early English watercolours. Large collections of period furniture, and decorative arts. Major summer exhibitions and temporary loan exhibitions. There is a Natural History Centre with a modern aquarium and nature trails in the ground. A separate museum of local crafts and industries is housed in the brew-house.
Open: Hall and Natural History Centre: Mon-Fri 10-5 Sun 12-5 all year. **Natural History Centre only:** Apr-Sept Sat 10-5.
Admission: Free.
Location: Two miles from Burnley Centre
Refreshments: Cafe in grounds all year.
Exhibitions/Events: Fifteen exhibitions from Easter to Christmas.
Parties by appointment. Educational activities

Blackburn Museums & Art Galleries

Scene in the South Asian Gallery.

Sekiya on the Sumida River, by Hokusai, from the large collection of Japanese prints bequeathed by the late T.B. Lewis.

COLNE

BRITISH IN INDIA MUSEUM
Newtown Street, Colne BB8 0JJ
Paintings, photographs, coins, stamps, medals, diorama, model railway and other items.
Open: Mon-Sat 10-4 except Tucs closcd Jan and Dec July 4-July 13 Sept 5-Sept 11 and all Bank Holidays.

LANCASTER

CITY MUSEUM
(Lancaster City Council)
Market Square, Lancaster LA1 1HT **Tel:** (01524) 64637 **Fax:** (01524) 847663

Prehistoric, Roman and Medieval archaeology and local history. Museum of the King's Own Royal Regiment.
Open: Mon-Sat 10-5.
Admission: Free.
Location: City Centre.
Exhibitions/Events: Regular programme of exhibitions.
Shop.

MARITIME MUSEUM
(Lancaster City Council)
St. George's Quay, Lancaster LA1 1RB **Tel:** (01524) 64637 **Fax:** (01524) 847663
Ship models, the Port of Lancaster, inshore fishing, the Lancaster canal, Morecambe Bay. AV show.
Open: Easter-Oct daily 11-5 Nov-Easter daily 2-5.
Admission: Fee charged.
Location: On riverside close to City Centre.
Refreshments: Cafe.
Exhibitions/Events: Regular programme of exhibitions.
Shop.

PERIOD COTTAGE
(Lancaster City Council)
15 Castle Hill, Lancaster **Tel:** (01524) 64637 **Fax:** (01524) 847663
Dwelling furnished in style of c1820 artisan.
Open: Easter-end Sept daily 2-5.
Admission: Fee charged.
Location: Close to City Centre.
Access difficult for disabled.

LEYLAND

THE BRITISH COMMERCIAL VEHICLE MUSEUM
(The British Commercial Vehicle Museum Trust)
King Street, Leyland PR5 1LE **Tel:** (01772) 451011
Largest commercial vehicle museum in Europe devoted to the history of British Commercial Vehicles. Over 40 restored exhibits dating from 1896 to the present day including steam wagons, buses, fire engines, vans and the famous popemobile. Winner of North West Tourist Board Best Small Attraction for 1992.
Open: Apr-end Sept daily except Mons 10-5 Oct and Nov weekends only open Bank Hol Mons during season.
Admission: Adults £3 children/OAPs £1.50.
Location: 3/4 mile from junction 28 of M6 motorway in centre of Leyland.
Refreshments: Vending machines only.
Free car park. Museum shop. Facilities for the disabled.

SOUTH RIBBLE MUSEUM AND EXHIBITION CENTRE
(South Ribble Borough Council)
The Old Grammar School, Church Road, Leyland PR5 1EJ **Tel:** (01772) 422041
Timber framed Tudor Grammar School housing Borough's Museum collection. Local history and archaeology. Monthly exhibitions by local artists.
Open: Tues 10-4 Thurs 1-4 Fri 10-4 Sat 10-1 closed Bank Hols.
Admission: Free.
Car parking 200m from main town centre car park. Not suitable for disabled persons.

LYTHAM ST. ANNES

TOY AND TEDDY BEAR MUSEUM
373 Clifton Drive North, St. Annes FY8 2PA **Tel:** (01253) 713705
An award winning Museum, displayed in a lovely old period building with over 200 dolls, 35 dolls houses, working train layout, trains and old tinplate toys. 'The Mini Motor Museum'. A must for bear lovers with unusual bear displays, and many old bears to see by Steiff, Bing, Chad-Valley and others.
Open: Whit-Oct 31 daily 11-5 (closed Tues) winter months open Sun and all school and Bank Hols.

PRESTON

HARRIS MUSEUM AND ART GALLERY
(Borough of Preston)
Market Square, Preston PR1 2PP **Tel:** (01772) 258248 Information line: (01772) 257112 **Fax:** (01772) 886764
Magnificent Greek Revival building housing fine collections of British paintings, ceramics, glass and costume. Story of Preston gallery. Lively programme of contemporary art and social history exhibitions with accompanying events and activities.
Open: Mon-Sat 10-5 closed most Bank Holidays.
Admission: Free
Refreshments: Cafe.
Shop.

RIBCHESTER

MUSEUM OF CHILDHOOD
Church Street, Ribchester PR3 3YE **Tel:** (01254) 878520 **Fax:** (01254) 823977
A museum of childhood, toys, models, dolls, miniatures, curios, dolls houses, model fairground and Punch and Judy. Special Period Doll exhibition.
Open: 10.30-5 Tues-Sun inc.
Location: J31 on M6 sign posted on A59.
Museum shop.

ROSSENDALE

ROSSENDALE MUSEUM
(Rossendale Borough Council)
Whitaker Park, Rawtenstall, Rossendale **Tel:** (01706) 217777/226509

Former nineteenth century mill owner's mansion housing displays of fine and decorative arts and furniture, including a reconstruction of a Victorian drawing room. Natural history collections include William Bullock's tiger and python. Local history; temporary exhibitions.
Open: Mon-Fri 1-5 Sat 10-5 (Apr-Oct) 10-4 (Nov-March) Sun 12-5 (Apr-Oct) 12-4 (Nov-March) groups at other times by arrangement.

RUFFORD

RUFFORD OLD HALL
(The National Trust)
Rufford, nr Ormskirk L40 1SG **Tel:** (01704) 821254
A superb example of a medieaval hall - one of the finest in Lancashire - of half-timber and plaster panels. Interesting collection of local bygones in the stable.
Open: April-end Oct.
Location: East side of A50, North end of Rufford village, 7m North of Ormskirk.
Refreshments: Restaurant.
Educational visits welcomed. Especially good for Living History and Tudor period.

LEICESTERSHIRE

ASHBY-DE-LA-ZOUCH

ASHBY-DE-LA-ZOUCH MUSEUM
North Street, Ashby-de-la-Zouch LE6 5HU **Tel:** (01530) 560090
Small museum with local material; including model of Ashby Castle under attack, and early 20th century shop.
Open: Mon-Fri 10-12 and 2-4 Sat 10-4 Sun 2-4 (Easter-Sept) for winter opening ring first.
Admission: Adults 25p OAPs 20p children 15p (no reductions) parties (max. 20) can book for evenings.
Parking. Charity status - voluntarily run.

CASTLE DONINGTON

THE DONINGTON COLLECTION
Donington Park Castle Donington DE74 2RP **Tel:** (01332) 810048 **Fax:** (01332) 812829
The world's largest collection of single seater racing cars consisting of 130 vehicles displayed in 5 modern halls.
Open: 10-5 daily last admission 4.
Admission: Adults £4 children/OAPs £1.50 family £9.50 students £2.50.
Location: Donington Park Derbyshire/Leicestershire border.
Refreshments: Restaurant.

DONINGTON-LE-HEATH

THE MANOR HOUSE
(Leicestershire County Council)
Donington-le-Heath, Nr. Coalville **Tel:** (01530) 831259 **Fax:** (0116) 2473011
Fine medieval manor house of c.1280 with 16th-17th century alterations. Now restored as period house. Fine gardens.
Open: Wed before Easter-Sept 30 Wed-Sun 2-6 inc. Bank Holidays.
Admission: Free.
Refreshments: Tea-shop in adjoining barn.
Access for disabled to ground floor only. Visitor car park.

LEICESTER

BELGRAVE HALL AND GARDENS
(Leicestershire County Council)
Church Road, Belgrave, Leicester LE4 5PE **Tel:** (0116) 266 6590 **Fax:** (0116) 247 3011
Small Queen Anne house of 1709-1713, with period room settings from late 17th to late 19th century. Coaches in stable block. Outstanding period and botanic gardens with over 6,500 species of plants.
Open: Weekdays 10-5.30 Sun 2-5.30 closed Good Friday Christmas Day and Boxing Day
Admission: Free.
Access for disabled to all gardens, but ground floor only of three storey house. Unrestricted street parking outside.

JOHN DORAN GAS MUSEUM
(British Gas East Midlands)
Aylestone Road, Leicester **Tel:** (0116) 253 5506
A GEM of a museum which traces the story of gas from the early days of the small 'gas works' to the discovery of natural gas. An all gas 1920s kitchen is one of the many attractions which appeal to young and old alike.
Open: Tues-Fri 12.30-4.30 closed Sat-Mon Good Friday Bank Hols and Tues following.
Admission: Free.

JEWRY WALL MUSEUM
(Leicestershire County Council)
St. Nicholas Circle, Leicester LE1 4LB **Tel:** (0116) 247 3021 **Fax:** (0116) 247 3023
Museum of Leicestershire Archaeology from earliest times to AD1500 in modern building looking over Roman Baths site and the massive 2nd century Roman Jewry Wall.
Open: Weekdays 10-5.30 Sun 2-5.30 closed Good Friday Christmas Day and Boxing Day.
Admission: Free.
Exhibitions/Events: 2 major outdoor living history events each year.
Access for disabled via rear entrance in Holy Bones; public parking in centre of St. Nicholas Circle by Holiday Inn.

THE LEICESTERSHIRE MUSEUM AND ART GALLERY
(Leicestershire County Council)
New Walk, Leicester **Tel:** (0116) 255 4100 **Fax:** (0116) 247 3011
Rutland Dinosaur and other geology displays in new gallery. Ancient Egypt Gallery; major regional Art Gallery with European art collection from 15th century including German Expressionists and French Impressionists; important decorative arts collection, especially ceramics. New Natural History gallery - Variety of Life.
Open: Weekdays 10-5.30 Sun 2-5.30 closed Good Friday Christmas Day and Boxing Day.
Admission: Free.
Full access for disabled. Very limited car parking. Multi storey car park in East St. 200 yards.

LEICESTERSHIRE RECORD OFFICE

(Leicestershire County Council)

Long Street, Wigston Magna, Leicester LE8 2AH **Tel:** (0116) 257 1080
Fax: (0116) 257 1120

One of the largest County Record Offices, with extensive collections of official and private archives, both urban and rural, relating to Leicestershire. Now combined with the LEICESTERSHIRE COLLECTION, the local studies library, to include large holdings of published local material; including newspapers, maps and sound recordings.

Open: Mon Tues Thurs 9.15-5 Wed 9.15-7.30 Fri 9.15-4.45 Sat 9.15-12.15 closed Bank Hol Weekends Mon-Tues and for annual stocktaking week in October.

Admission: Free.

Refreshments: Limited availability.

Visitors' car park. Full disabled access and toilet. Induction loop in lecture room.

WYGSTON'S HOUSE MUSEUM OF COSTUME

(Leicestershire County Council)

Wygston's House, Applegate, St. Nicholas Circle, Leicester **Tel:** (0116) 247 3056
Fax: (0116) 247 3011

Important late medieval building with ater additions, housing costume from 1750 to present day. Reconstruction of draper's dress shop of 1920's.

Open: Weekdays 10-5.30 Sun 2-5.30 closed Good Friday Christmas Day and Boxing Day.

Admission: Free.

Access for disabled ground floor only.

MUSEUM OF TECHNOLOGY

(Leicestershire County Council)

Corporation Road, Abbey Lane, Leicester LE4 5PX **Tel:** Curatorial enquiries: (01530) 510851

Housed in 1891 Abbey Pumping station formerly used as part of Leicester's sewer and draining system. Original four giant beam engines, built by Gimson of Leicester. New exhibition opening in 1995 devoted to public health and utilities. Extensive transport collection, site narrow gauge railway and rare steam excavator. Regular programme of steam and other special events. Extensive grounds.

Open: Weekdays 10-5.30 Sun 2-5.30 closed Good Friday Christmas Day Boxing Day.

Admission: Free except on Special Event days.

Location: Leicester city bus No. 54.

Access for disabled except to Beam Engines. Visitors' car park.

MUSEUM OF THE ROYAL LEICESTERSHIRE REGIMENT

(Leicestershire County Council)

The Magazine, Oxford Street, Leicester LE2 7BY **Tel:** (0116) 255 5889
Fax: (0116) 243 7011

History of the Royal Leicestershire Regiment (17th Foot) including mementos, battle trophies and relics, housed in late 14th century Newarke Gateway.

Open: Weekdays 10-5.30 Sun 2-5.30 closed Christmas Day Boxing Day and Good Friday.

Admission: Free.

Wheelchair access impossible. Multi-storey car park in Newarke St, 150 yards.

NEWARKE HOUSES MUSEUM

(Leicestershire County Council)

The Newarke, Leicester LE2 7BY **Tel:** (0116) 247 3222 **Fax:** (0116) 247 3011

Social history collections of Leicestershire from late 1485 to present day. Features include 19th century street scene. Fine collection of clocks, and display on Leicester's 19th century giant Daniel Lambert. Quiet period garden leads to Castle Close.

Open: Weekdays 10-5.30 Sun 2-5.30 closed Good Friday Christmas Day and Boxing Day.

Admission: Free.

No disabled access. Multi-storey car park in Newarke St, 200 yards.

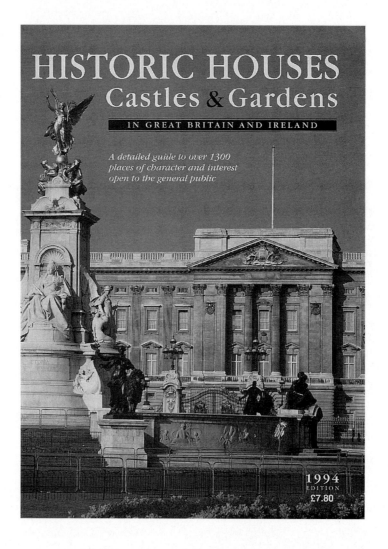

SNIBSTON DISCOVERY PARK

(Leicestershire County Council)

Ashby Road, Coalville, Leicester LE67 3LN **Tel:** (01530) 510851 (01530) 813608 (24hrs) **Fax:** (01530) 813301

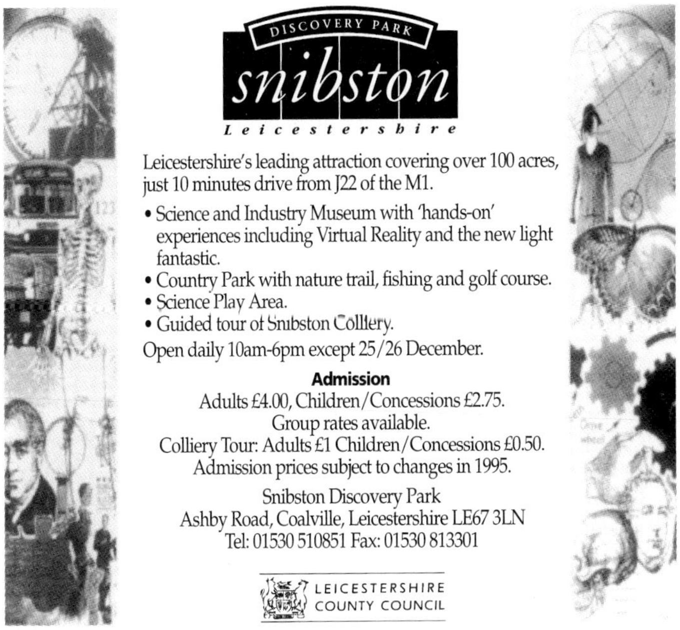

Major new Science and Industry Museum with the emphasis on 'hands on' participation, working wheelwrights workshop dating from 1742. Country park with trails and lakes. New from 1994 - Colliery tours and virtual reality.
Open: 10-6 daily closed Christmas Day and Boxing Day.
Admission: Adults £4 children and OAP's £2.75 reduced rates for groups prices subject to change in 1995.
Location: 10 mins. from J22 off the M1, on A50 in Coalville.
Refreshments: Coffee shop.
Exhibitions/Events: Yera round programme - free brochure available
Free parking. Gift shop and Tourist Information Centre. Telephone for free colour brochure and more details. All areas fully accessible for disabled. Coach park. Special events.

LOUGHBOROUGH

THE BELL FOUNDRY MUSEUM

(John Taylor Bell Founders Ltd)

Freehold Street, Loughborough LE11 1AR **Tel:** (01509) 233414 **Fax:** (01509) 263305

Unique exhibition of the bellfounder's craft. Original material relating to bells, their history and fittings. Industrial archaeology and historic furnace area.
Open: All year Tues-Sat and Bank Hol Mons 9.30-12.30 and 1.30-4.30.
Admission: Museum only adults 75p children 50p pre-booked combined museum visit and bell foundry party visits adults £3 children (under 16) £1.50 school party rate children £1 two supervising teachers free other adults at child rate.
Ample free parking.

LUTTERWORTH

STANFORD HALL MOTORCYCLE MUSEUM

Lutterworth LE17 6DH **Tel:** (01788) 860250 **Fax:** (01788) 860870

Outstanding collection including unique racing and other motorcycles, most in running order, housed in the Stables at Stanford Hall.

Open: Easter-24 Sept Sat Sun 2.30-6 (last admission 5.30) Bank Hol Mons and Tues following and Event days 12-6 (last admission 5.30).

Admission: Adults £2.80 children £1 (1995 charges) including Stanford Hall grounds.

Location: 6 miles NE Rugby near Swinford. M1 exits 18 or 19 (from the North only) M6 Exit at A14/M1 North junction.

MARKET BOSWORTH

BOSWORTH BATTLEFIELD VISITOR CENTRE AND COUNTRY PARK

(Leicestershire County Council)

Battlefield Visitor Centre, Sutton Cheney, Market Bosworth CV13 0AD
Tel: (01455) 290429

Site of the famous Battle of Bosworth Field, 1485, between Richard III and the future Henry VII. Comprehensive interpretation of the Battle with Visitor Centre including exhibitions, models, film theatre. Illustrated Battle Trails around Battle site. Series of Special Medieval attractions during summer months.

Open: Battlefield Visitor Centre Apr 1-Oct 31 Mon-Fri 1-5 Sat Sun and Bank Hol Mon 11-6. Country Park and Battle Trails all year during daylight hours.

Admission: Adults £2 children/OAPs £1.30 pre-booked parties of 20 or more £1.60 and children/OAPs £1. Parties taken throughout the year by appointment.

Refreshments: Cafeteria.

Car parks 50p. Coaches £2.50. Suitable for disabled persons. Special charges apply on main Special Event Days. Book and gift shops. 1995 Opening Times and Charges subject to review.

MARKET HARBOROUGH

THE HARBOROUGH MUSEUM

(Leicestershire County Council)

Council Offices, Adam and Eve Street, Market Harborough LE16 7LT **Tel:** (01858) 432468 **Fax:** (01858) 462766

Museum of the town of Market Harborough and its surrounding area illustrating the Medieval planned town and its role as a market, social and hunting centre and a stagecoach post. Displays from the Symington Collection of Corsetry and a local bootmaker's workshop.

Open: Mon-Sat 10-4.30 Sun 2-5 closed Good Friday Christmas Day and Boxing Day.

Admission: Free.

Access for disabled via lift in Council offices (on Sat, Sun and Bank Hols please contact museum staff). Visitors' car park.

MELTON MOWBRAY

MELTON CARNEGIE MUSEUM

(Leicestershire County Council)

Thorpe End, Melton Mowbray LE13 1RB **Tel:** (01664) 69946

Local museum of the history and environment of the Borough of Melton (which includes the famous Vale of Belvoir); sporting paintings and local exhibitions.

Open: Mon-Sat 10-5 Sun 2-5 Easter Sun-last Sun in Sept closed on Sun Oct-Easter Good Friday Christmas Day and Boxing Day.

Admission: Free.

Full disabled access. Street parking nearby.

OAKHAM

OAKHAM CASTLE
(Leicestershire County Council)
Market Place, Oakham **Tel:** (01572) 723654
12th century Great Hall of Norman Castle in castle grounds with earlier motte. Unique collection of horseshoes presented by visiting Peers of the Realm.
Open: Castle Grounds late Mar-late Oct 10-5.30 daily Late Oct-late Mar 10-4 daily **Great Hall** late Mar-late Oct Tues-Sat and Bank Hol Mon 10-1 and 2-5.30 Sun 2-5.30 late Mar-late Oct Tues-Sat 10-1 2-4 Sun 2-4 closed Mon (except Bank Holdays) Good Friday Christmas Day and Boxing Day.
Admission: Free.
Access for disabled to Great Hall. Parking only for disabled visitors on request. Correspondence and enquiries to Rutland County Museum.

RUTLAND COUNTY MUSEUM
(Leicestershire County Council)
Catmos Street, Oakham LE15 GHW **Tel:** (01572) 723654
The Museum of Rutland Life, including agricultural equipment, implements and wagons, local crafts and domestic items, local archaeology. All housed in a splendid 18th century Cavalry Riding School. Special gallery on the Volunteer Soldier in Leicestershire and Rutland.
Open: Mon-Sat 10-5 Sun (late March-late Oct) 2-5 (late Oct-late March) 2-4 closed Good Friday Christmas Day and Boxing Day.
Admission: Free.
Access for disabled throughout except balcony displays. Stair climber available. Public car park adjacent.

SHACKERSTONE

SHACKERSTONE RAILWAY MUSEUM
(Shackerstone Railway Society Ltd)
Shackerstone Station, Shackerstone CV13 6NW **Tel:** (01827) 880754
Museum of RAILWAYANIA, much of it 19th century with special emphasis on railways of WEST LEICESTERSHIRE.
Admission: Adults 50p children free Sat Sun and Bank Hols no reductions for parties but 10% reduction for 15 or more people on train rides.
Refreshments: Victorian tea-rooms.
Exhibitions/Events: See timetable.
Free car parking.

LINCOLNSHIRE

BOSTON

GUILDHALL MUSEUM
(Boston Borough Council)
South Street, Boston PE21 6HT **Tel:** (01205) 365954

The museum houses the original prison cells in which the early Pilgrim Fathers were imprisoned in 1607 after their abortive attempt to leave England for religious freedom in Holland. Pictures and prints of local interest. Local archaeological material. Collection of firemarks and maritime exhibits. Monthly exhibition programme.
Open: Mon-Sat 10-5 also Sun 1.30-5 Apr-Sept only.
Admission: Charge includes the use of a personal audio guided tour children free.
Shop.

EAST KIRKBY

LINCOLNSHIRE AVIATION HERITAGE
(F. & H. Panton Bros)
Old Airfield, East Kirkby PE23 4DE **Tel:** (01790) 763207
Based on a 1940's Bomber Airfield. Permanent display AVRO Lancaster Bomber, original Control Tower, photograph exhibition, Escape Museum, Wartime Living Room, Military Vehicles. Tour of Airfield approx. 3 miles, extra.NAAFI refreshments all day. Gift shop. Souvenirs. Memorabilia. Aircraft Recovery Group exhibits all weather. Ample free parking. Much, much more.
Open: Mon-Sat summer 10-5 Nov-Easter 10-4 (last admission 1 hour before closing) open Bank Hols. Closed Sun.
Admission: Adults £3 OAPs £2.50 children 5-15 £1.50. Reductions for disabled and parties over 10 in number (price on application).
Refreshments: Tea-room with hot and cold snacks.

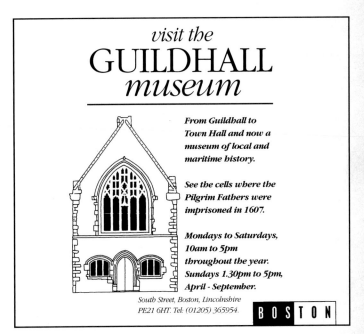

LINCOLN

THE LAWN
(Lincoln City Council)
Union Road, Lincoln LN1 3BL **Tel:** (01522) 560330

Former psychiatric hospital converted into Conference and Visitor Centre with extensive grounds. Various attractions: National Cycle Museum: Sir Joseph Banks Conservatory and aquarium, with shop and information centre; Lincoln Archaeology Centre explains the work of the City's archaeologists with hands-on displays; Charlesworth Centre describing history of the Lawn Hospital and psychiatric treatment in general. Also conference and function rooms.
Open: Daily all year round.
Admission: Free (except Cycle Museum).
Location: Alongside Lincoln Castle
Refreshments: Pub and restaurant.
Exhibitions/Events: Regular programme of indoor and outdoor events.
Shops. Extensive grounds, picnic areas and children's play area.

LINCOLN CATHEDRAL LIBRARY
Lincoln **Tel:** (01522) 544544
Medieval MSS and early printed books. Summer Exhibition in Medieval Library (small charge). Group visits to Wren Library by appointment. Reference collection on church history/architecture (appointment only).

MUSEUM OF LINCOLNSHIRE LIFE
(Lincolnshire County Council)
Newland, Lincoln **Tel:** (01522) 52222
One of the largest social history museums in the region. Extensive agricultural, industrial and domestic collections.
Open: Daily May-Sept 10-5.30. Oct-Mar Mon-Sat 10-5.30. Sun 2-5.30. Closed Good Friday 24-27 Dec inc. New Years Day.

USHER GALLERY
(Lincolnshire County Council)
Lindum Road, Lincoln LN2 1NN **Tel:** (01522) 527980
The major Lincolnshire venue for all aspects of the fine and decorative arts. Usher collection of watches, porcelain and miniatures; Peter de Wint watercolours; local topographical works; Tennyson memorabilia and coin gallery. Continuous programme of temporary exhibitions.
Open: Mon-Sat 10-5.30 Sun 2.30-5 closed New Years Day Good Friday Christmas and Boxing Day.
Admission: Adults £1 children/students 50p Free Fri. Courier free with parties.
Refreshments: Cafe - light refreshments.

NEWLAND

CHURCH FARM MUSEUM
(Lincolnshire County Council)
Newland, Lincoln **Tel:** (01522) 552222
Fully furnished farmhuse, with reconstructed barns, and thatched cottage. Agricultural/domestic and craft collections on site.
Open: Apr-Oct inc. daily 10.30-5.30

SPALDING

AYSCOUGHFEE HALL AND GARDENS
(South Holland District Council)
Churchgate, Spalding **Tel:** (01775) 725468

Displays on land reclaimation, agriculture, horticulture and social history.
Open: Gardens open all year. Museum open daily Mar-Oct and closed weekends Nov-Feb.

THE PINCHBECK ENGINE HOUSE
(South Holland District Council & Welland & Deeping Internal Drainage Board)
West Marsh Road, Spalding **Tel:** (01775) 725468/722444

This restored steam beam engine driving a scoop wheel was erected in 1833 to drain Spalding and Pinchbeck. It ceased operations in 1952 when it was the last of its type working in The Fens. Newly open to the public is this fine example of early 19th Century industrial engineering and architecture. Displays tell the story of the evolution of The Fens through embanking and draining.
Open: Daily Apr-Oct other times by appointment.
Admission: Free.

LONDON (inc Greater London)

LONDON

AGE EXCHANGE REMINISCENCE CENTRE
(Age Exchange Theatre Trust Ltd)
11 Blackheath Village, Blackheath SE3 9LA **Tel:** 0181-318 9105
A 'Hands-On' Museum of everyday objects from the 1920's-40's. Includes regular changing exhibitions on themes.
Open: 10.00-5.30 Mon-Sat not open Bank Hols.
Admission: Free. For parties £1-£1.50 is charged per person.
Location: BR station and local buses are close.
Refreshments: Small cafe-sandwiches, home made cakes-tea/coffee etc.
Disabled access. Museum shop.

APSLEY HOUSE
(A branch of the Victoria and Albert Museum)
The Wellington Museum, Hyde Park Corner W1V 9FA **Tel:** 0171-499 5676
Apsley House, also known as the Wellington Museum, is a magnificent building of architectural and historical significance. The home of the Dukes of Wellington since 1817 it was originally built by Robert Adam between 1771 and 1778 for the second Earl of Bathurst, Baron Apsley. Apsley House is now administered by the Victoria and Albert Museum. Closed since Jan 1992 for extensive renovation, it is planned to re-open the house to the public in June 1995.
Open: Dates to be confirmed.
Admission: Not available yet.
Location: Hyde Park Corner.

THE ASSOCIATION GALLERY
The Association of Photographers, 9-10 Domingo Street EC1Y 0TA **Tel:** 0171-608 1445
The Association Gallery features purely photograhic exhibitions on a variety of topics. It exists to act as a showcase for the work of our members who are professional photographers in the fields of advertising, fashion and editorial photography. Contemporary British photography of the highest professional standards.
Open: Mon-Fri 9.30-6 closed Christmas and New Year and all Bank Hols.

BANKSIDE GALLERY
(Blackfriars tube), 48 Hopton Street, Blackfriars SE1 9JH **Tel:** 0171-928 7521 **Fax:** 0171-928 2820
Royal Watercolour Society and the Royal Society of Painter-Printmakers. Spring and Autumn exhibitions plus open exhibitions and contemporary and historical exhibitions from Britain and abroad.

BARBICAN ART GALLERY
(Corporation of London, Libraries & Art Galleries Dept)
Gallery floor, Barbican Centre, Silk Street EC2Y 8DS **Tel:** 0171-638 4141 Extension 7619 **Fax:** 0171-638 0364

BARBICAN ART GALLERY

Don't miss the different and interesting exhibitions at this leading art gallery. From Cecil Beaton to Van Gogh...... '...large, brilliant and wildly diverse'. Independent on Sunday. Telephone 0171-588 9023 (recorded information) for details of current exhibitions and opening times.
Admission: Charges vary with each exhibition half price for children/students/OAPs/ registered disabled and unemployed reduced rates for pre-booked parties.
Location: In the heart of the City of London.
Refreshments: Available in cafes throughout the centre.
NCP paying car park in Barbican Centre and Aldersgate Street. Details about all the Centre's facilities including free parking for people with disabilities are available from the Information Desk on 0171-638-4141 ext 7538, Minicom 0171-382 7297.

BEN URI ART SOCIETY AND GALLERY
21 Dean Street W1V 6NE **Tel:** 0171-437 2852
The aim of the Society, which is a registered charity founded in 1915, is to promote Jewish art as part of the Jewish cultural heritage. The gallery provides a showcase for exhibitions of contemporary art by Jewish artists, as well as for the society's own permanent collection of over 600 works by artists including Bomberg, Auerbach, Gertler, Epstein and Kitaj.
Open: Mon-Thurs 10-5 some Sun afternoons closed Fri Sat Jewish Hols and Bank Hols.
Admission: Free.
Group visits welcome. NCP car park opposite. Suitable for disabled persons.

BETHNAL GREEN MUSEUM OF CHILDHOOD
(A branch of the Victoria and Albert Museum)
Cambridge Heath Road E2 9PA **Tel:** 0181-980 3204
The National Museum of Childhood has one of the largest displays of toys in the world- a unique collection of toys, dolls, dolls' houses, games and puppets from the 17th century to the present day. Also children's costume, nursery furniture and baby equipment in two displays devoted to the Social History of childhood.
Open: Mon-Thurs and Sat 10-5.50 closed Fri Christmas Eve Christmas Day Boxing Day New Year's Day Good Friday and May Day Bank Holiday.
Admission: Free.
Location: Close to Bethnal Green Underground station on the central line.
Refreshments: Cafe serving salads, dandwiches, cakes, hot and cold drinks (from end Oct 1994).
Exhibitions/Events: Activities for children every school holidays/half-terms. Art workshops every Sat.

BEXLEY MUSEUM

(Bexley London Borough)

Hall Place, Bourne Road, Bexley DA5 1PQ **Tel:** (01322) 526574 **Fax:** (01322) 522921

Historic house, permanent and temporary exhibitions, general and local. Local Studies Centre. Visitor Centre.
Open: Mon-Sat 10-5 (dusk in winter) Sun (in summer) 2-6 beautiful gardens open daily and Visitor Centre open daily in Summer.
Admission: Free.
Location: Close to A2 Black Prince interchange.
Refreshments: Cafe and Restaurant nearby.

BRAMAH TEA AND COFFEE MUSEUM

The Clove Building, Maguire Street SE1 2NQ **Tel:** 0171-378 0222 **Fax:** 0171-378 0219

The two great oriental trades which brought romance to the port of London and a new social life to Europe. Illustrated in a unique colourful collection of pictures, silver and ceramics.
Open: Each day 10-6 closed Christmas and Boxing Day.
Admission: Adult £3 concessions and children £1.50 family (2 adults + up to 4 children) £6 party of over 10 people £2.50 conc. £1.25.
Location: Next to Design Museum by the River Thames.
Refreshments: Tea and coffee house selling tea coffee and cakes.
Exhibitions/Events: On-going interests.
Suitable for disabled persons, wheelchairs available. Car Parking available.

BRITISH DENTAL ASSOCIATION MUSEUM

(Smith Turner Historical Collection)

63-64 Wimpole Street W1M 8AL **Tel:** 0171-935 0875 **Fax:** 0171-487 5232

Collection illustrating the history of dental surgery.
Open: Mon-Fri 10-4 closed Bank Hols.
Admission: Free.
Location: Near Regents Park and Bond Street tubes.

THE BRITISH LIBRARY

Great Russell Street WC1 **Tel:** 0171-636 1544

The British Library is the UK's national library and its exhibitions, lectures and seminars are based on its vast collections, world famous for their richness and variety. Many of the most outstanding items in the Library's collections are on permanent display. They include Magna Carta, the first folio edition of Shakespeare's works (1623), the Lindisfarne Gospels and the Gutenberg Bible, 1455 (the first book printed in movable type).
Open: Mon-Sat 10-5 Sun 2.30-6.

BRITISH MUSEUM

Great Russell Street WC1B 3DG **Tel:** 0171-636 1555

Comprising the national collection of antiquities and Prints and Drawings. The Museum departments are: Greek and Roman, Egyptian, Pre-historic and Romano-British, Western Asiatic, Oriental, Japanese, Coins, Medals and Bank Notes, Medieval and Later, Prints and Drawings and Ethnography (see under Museum of Mankind).
Open: Weekdays 10-5 Sun 2.30-6.
Admission: Free.
Location: Underground stations Tottenham Court Road Holborn Russell Square

BROMLEY MUSEUM

(London Borough of Bromley)

The Priory, Church Hill, Orpington BR6 0HH **Tel:** (01689) 873826

The archaeology of the London Borough of Bromley from earliest times to Domesday, and Sir John Lubbock, 1st Lord Avebury, the man responsible for giving this country its Bank Holidays. New 20th century History room.
Open: 9-5 except Thurs Sun and Bank Holidays.
Admission: Free.
Refreshments: No.
Exhibitions/Events: Yes.

BT MUSEUM - THE STORY OF TELECOMMUNICATIONS

145 Queen Victoria Street EC4V 4AT **Tel:** 0171-248 7444. Information Line:(0800) 289 689 **Fax:** 0171-236 5464

BT's Museum of telecommunications, is a fun way to learn through activities. It follows over 200 years of telecommunications history from the early days of telegraphing to the latest developments in optical fibre. Displays include two working fax machines, videophones and a Button A, Button B telephone kiosk.
Open: Mon-Fri 10-5 except Bank Hols special opening each year on Lord Major's Show day (second Sat in Nov).
Admission: Free.
Location: Near Blackfriars Underground.

BUCKINGHAM PALACE, THE QUEEN'S GALLERY

Buckingham Palace Road SW1 **Tel:** 0171-493 3175

Changing exhibitions of works of art from the Royal Collection. 1995 exhibition 'Faberge'.
Open: Mar-Dec.
Admission: Fee charged.

BUCKINGHAM PALACE, THE ROYAL MEWS

Buckingham Palace Road SW1W 0QH **Tel:** 0171-493 3175

The Royal Mews provides a unique opportunity to see how horse, carriage and tack combine to create the familiar pageantry associated with State Occasions.
Open: Every Wed 12-4 all year with additional days during the Summer.
Admission: Fee charged.

CABARET MECHANICAL THEATRE

33/4 The Market, Covent Garden WC2E 8RE **Tel:** 0171-379 7961

A collection of contemporary automata and mechanical sculpture. Over 60 exhibits can be operated by button, and the majority have their mechanics on view. Features work of Paul Spooner, Tim Hunkin and Keith Newsread among others. Alao shop selling limited editions and cut-outs, videos etc.
Open: Daily 10-6.30.
Admission: Adults £1.95 children/students/OAPs/unemployed £1.20 family £4.95 parties of 10+ 20% discount.
Location: Lower courts of Covent Garden Market.

CABINET WAR ROOMS

Clive Steps, King Charles Street SW1A 2AQ **Tel:** 0171-930 6961

Take a step back to the dark days of the Second World War when Churchill and his Chiefs of Staff masterminded Britain's war effort from a complex of secret underground rooms beneath Whitehall. A fascinating personal sound tour takes you through 21 historic rooms which have been preserved exactly as they were fifty years ago. See the Cabinet Room, the Map Room, Churchill's bedroom and the Transatlantic Telephone Room which allowed Churchill to speak directly to the President in the White House.
Open: Daily 10 last admission 5.15 closed Dec 24-26.
Admission: Fee charged.
Location: Nearest tube station Westminster.
Information: 071-930 6961.

CANADIAN HIGH COMMISSION

(Michael Regan - Visual Arts Officer)

Public entrance on Grosvenor Street W1X 0AB **Tel:** 0171-258 6600 **Fax:** 0171-258 6322

Changing displays of Canadian art, craft and design.
Open: Mon-Fri 10-5 closed Bank Hols.
Admission: Free.
Suitable for disabled persons.

CAREW MANOR AND DOVECOTE

(London Borough of Sutton)

Church Road, Beddington SM6 7NH **Tel:** 0181-770 4781 **Fax:** 0181-770 4777

This building contains a Grade I listed late-medieval Great Hall, with an arch-braced hammer-beam roof. The house is used as a school, but the Hall is now accessible on Sundays and Bank Holiday Mondays from Easter until Nov, together with the restored early 18th century Dovecote, with its 1,288 nesting boxes and potence, which is a scheduled ancient monument. Guided tours available of the Dovecote, the Great Hall and the ancient cellars of the house which contain medieval, Tudor, and later features (cellars accessible on guided tours only). Some tours take in the late 14th century Church of St Mary, Beddington, with its Norman font and 15th century Carew Chapel containing important Carew memorials (the Carews of Beddington were lords of the manor for over four hundred years). Carew Manor and Beddington Church stand on the edge of Beddington Park, the landscaped home park of the Carews, through which a Heritage Trail has been established.
Open: Suns & Bank Holiday Mons from Easter-Nov 1 (telephone Sutton Heritage Service 0181-773 4555 for details).
Admission: Fee charged.
Location: Church Road, Beddington. Off A232 .75m E of junction with A237.
Guide book, trail leaflet and other publications and souvenirs available.

CARLYLE'S HOUSE

(The National Trust)

24 Cheyne Row, Chelsea SW3 **Tel:** 0171-352 7087

Portraits, furniture, prints, 'personal relics' and a small library of books belonging to Thomas Carlyle.

CARSHALTON HOUSE

(Daughters of the Cross)

Pound Street, Carshalton (St. Philomena's) SM5 3PN **Tel:** 0181-770 4781/0181-773 4555 **Fax:** 0181-770 4777

An important listed building, built by about 1707 around the core of an older house and with grounds originally laid out by Charles Bridgeman, Carshalton House is open on a limited number of occasions each year. Its garden buildings include the unique Water Tower, now in the care of the Carshalton Water Tower Trust. The house contains principal rooms with 18th century decoration, including the 'Adam' or Blue Room and the Painted Parlour (attributed to Robert Robinson). Openings are organised by Sutton Heritage Service in conjuction with the Water Tower Trust and the Daughters of the Cross. Tours of the house and grounds and a programme of short talks on the house and its people are given during the day (included in entrance fee); Publications are available. Carshalton House is close to Sutton's Heritage Centre at Honeywood, in the Carshalton conservation area.
Open: Dates for 1995 are Easter Bank Holiday Mon (Apr 17) August Bank Holiday Mon (Aug 28) 10-5 (last adm. 4.15).
Admission: Adults £2.50 children under 16 £1.50.
Location: Pound Street, Carshalton, at junction with Carshalton Road, on A232.
Refreshments: Available.
Gift shop. For further details telephone Sutton Heritage Service on 0181-773 4555.

CHARTERED INSURANCE INSTITUTE MUSEUM

20 Aldermanbury EC2V 7HY **Tel:** 0171-606 3835

Collection of fire marks and other artifacts and documents illustrating the history of insurance.
Open: Mon-Thurs 9-5 Fri 9-4.45.
Admission: Free.
Sometimes in use for private functions. Visitors are advised to telephone in advance (ext 3273).

CHELSEA COLLEGE OF ART AND DESIGN (THE LONDON INSTITUTE)

Tel: 0171-351 3844

Summer Shows. Foundation, B'TEC National Diploma, and BA Degree shows are held in June/early July. MA Degree shows are held in the first week of September. Please telephone college for details. See above.

CHISWICK HOUSE

(English Heritage)

Burlington Lane, Chiswick W4 **Tel:** 0181-995 0508

Villa designed by the Earl of Burlington 1725 and derived from villas by Palladio and Scamozzi. William Kent assisted with the interior decoration. New exhibition covering the development of House and Grounds.
Open: Apr 1-Oct 31 daily 10-6 Nov 1-Mar 31 Wed-Sun 10-4 closed Dec 24 25.
Admission: Adults £2.30 concessions £1.70 children £1.15 (1994 prices) adm price includes a free personal stereo guided tour.

CHURCH FARMHOUSE MUSEUM

(London Borough of Barnet)

Greyhound Hill, Hendon NW4 4JR **Tel:** 0181-203 0130

Local history, furnished rooms in period style. Special exhibitions throughout the year.
Open: Mon-Thurs 10-5 Sat 10-1 and 2-5.30 Sun 2-5.30 closed Fri.
Admission: Free.
Location: Nearest tube - Hendon Central.
Audio guide available.

CITY & GUILDS OF LONDON ART SCHOOL

124 Kennington Park Road SE11 4DJ **Tel:** 0171-735 2306/5210 **Fax:** 0171-582 5361

Degree Show for Restoration & Conservation Studies, Painting, Sculpture, Decorative Arts, Illustrative Arts, Lettering, Stonecarving, Wood Carving & Gilding held annually at the end of the Summer Term.
Open: End June/beginning July.
Location: Kennington Underground.

COMMONWEALTH INSTITUTE

Kensington High Street W8 6NQ **Tel:** 0171-603 4535 **Fax:** 0171-602 7374

Visit the Commonwealth Institute and discover a world under one roof! See and hear the sights and sounds of life in other Commonwealth lands by exploring circular galleries of country exhibitions in this spectacular tent-shaped building. The history, landscapes, wildlife, arts and cultures of the commonwealth countries await you. There are also art and craft exhibitions, cultural events and holiday and weekend activities for all the family.The commonwealth Shop has gifts, crafts, and toys from around the world, and the Commonwealth Brasserie is open for light meals and refreshments.
Open: Closed Christmas Eve Christmas Day Boxing Day New Years Day Good Friday and May Day.
Admission: Adults £1 children 50p under 5's free.
Location: Tube - High Street Kensington, Earl's Court, Olympia, Holland Park. Bus 9,10,27,28,31,49, C1 Hoppa.
Refreshments: Commonwealth Brasserie.

COURTAULD INSTITUTE GALLERIES

Somerset House, Strand WC2R ORN **Tel:** 0171-873 2526 **Fax:** 0171-873 2772
The Galleries of the University of London, including the famous Courtauld Collection of French Impressionist and Post-Impressionists, and other collections of Western European art from the 14th to the 20th centuries.
Open: Weekdays 10-6 Sun 2-6.
Admission: Adults £3 concessions £1.50.

THE CRAFTS COUNCIL

44a Pentonville Road, Islington N1 9BY **Tel:** 0171-278 7700
The national centre for the crafts. Crafts Council gallery with exhibitions throughout the year. Information Centre, Picture Library of 32,000 slides, Reference Library, Gallery Shop with showcase exhibitions, the Crafts Council Collection, cafe.
Open: Tues-Sat 11-6 Sun 2-6 closed Mon.
Admission: Free.
Cafe, gallery shop.

CUMING MUSEUM

(London Borough of Southwark)
155-157 Walworth Road SE17 1RS **Tel:** 0171-701 1342
The Museum of Southwark's History. The worldwide collections of the Cuming family joined with the local history of Southwark, from Roman times to the present. Special displays of Medieval Southwark, Dickens, and George Tinworth's sculpture.
Open: Tues-Sat 10-5 closed Sun and Mon.
Admission: Free.
Exhibitions/Events: Until 22 Apr 1995 - 'Use Your Loaf at the Cuming'. June 1995-Apr 1996 'In the Limelight'.
A 1992 Museum Of The Year Award winner.

CUTTY SARK CLIPPER SHIP

(The Maritime Trust)
King William Walk, Greenwich SE10 9HT **Tel:** 0181-858 3445 **Fax:** 0181-853 3589

Built in 1869, the *Cutty Sark* began life as a clipper on the tea run and later transported wool from Australia. Fully rigged, her raked-back masts carried over 30,000 square feet of sail, which with favourable winds enabled her to cover 360 miles in one day. An informative display on board tells her story, with cabins on the upper deck illustrating life on board a ship in the late 19th century. In the lower hold the 'long John Silver' collection of merchant ships' figureheads on display is the most extensive in this country. Traditional ship building skills can also be seen (weekdays) as part of the current restoration programme.
Open: Mon-Sat 10-6 Sun 12-6 winter close 5 closed Dec 24 25 26.
Admission: Adults £3.25 concessions £2.25 family £8 (from 1/4/94) Wheel chair attendants/helpers free party discount available Mon-Fri if booked. **Gipsy Moth IV** Sir Francis Chichester's Round the World yacht, small charge.
Souvenir Shop on board. Car park and coach parking alongside. Only partly suitable for disabled.

ANTHONY D'OFFAY GALLERY

9, 21 & 23 Dering Street, off New Bond Street W1R 9AA **Tel:** 0171-499 4100 **Fax:** 0171-493 4443
Postwar international art: Carl Andre, Michael Andrews, Georg Baselitz, Joseph Beuys, Fransesco Clemente, Gilbert & George, Richard Hamilton, Howard Hodgkin, Jasper Johns, Ellsworth Kelly, Anselm Kiefer, Willem de Kooning, Jeff Koons, Leon Kossoff, Jannis Kounellis, Richard Long, Bruce Mclean, Mario Merz, Tatsuo Miyajima, Reinhard Mucha, Bruce Nauman, Sigmar Polke, Gerhard Richter, Kiki Smith, James Turrell, Cy Twombly, Bill Viola, Andy Warhol, Boyd Webb, Lawrence Weiner.

DE MORGAN FOUNDATION - OLD BATTERSEA HOUSE

30 Vicarage Crescent, Battersea SW11 3LD **Tel:** 0181-788 1341

DE MORGAN FOUNDATION OLD BATTERSEA HOUSE

The ground floor of this elegantly restored Wren style period building which is a private home houses a substantial part of the De Morgan Foundation Collection which has been here since the early 1930s. Paintings and drawings by Evelyn De Morgan, her uncle Roddam Spencer Stanhope, J.M. Strudwick and Cadogan Cowper are displayed with ceramics by William De Morgan.
Open: By appointment only - usually Wed afternoons.
Admission: £1 optional catalogue £1.50 no special reductions. Parties maximum 30 (split into two groups of 15).
Write in advance to: De Morgan Foundation, 21 St Margaret's Crescent, Putney, London SW15 6HL. Car parking in Vicarage Crescent. No special facilities for disabled but front steps are the only minor obstacle (no wheelchairs available). Visitors often also arrange a visit to Old Battersea Church nearby by contacting the Vicar. Works from the Foundation's collection are also on public display at Cardiff Castle, Cragside House Northumbria, Knightshayes Court, Tiverton, Devon. The St.John portraits are at Lydiard Park, Swindon.

THE DESIGN MUSEUM BY TOWER BRIDGE

Shad Thames SE1 2YD **Tel:** 0171-407 6261 **Fax:** 0171-378 6540

DESIGN MUSEUM

The Design Museum is a museum of everyday things: the first to explain why and how mass-produced consumer objects work and look the way they do, and how design contributes to the quality of our lives.

Directions:	The Design Museum is South of the River Thames, by Tower Bridge.
Tube	Tower Hill (Circle and District Line). London Bridge (Northern Line).
BR	London Bridge.
DLR	Tower Gateway.
Buses	15,78 to Tower Hill, 42,47, P11 to Tooley Street. Ample parking.

Design Museum, Shad Thames, Butlers Wharf, London SE1 2YD.

From cars to cameras, the Design Museum is the first museum in the world to look at how design affects our lives. A number of special temporary exhibitions explore in detail the lives of designers, architects and their work.
Open: 11.30-6 weekdays 12-6 weekends
Admission: Adults £4.50 concessions £3.50.
Location: South of the River Thames by Tower Bridge.
Refreshments: Restaurant, cafe, shop and parking
Cafe, restaurant. Disabled access.

THE DICKENS HOUSE MUSEUM

48 Doughty Street WC1N 2LF **Tel:** 0171-405 2127
A tribute to the novelist, was his home from 1837 to 1839 where he finished 'The Pickwick Papers' and worked on 'Oliver Twist', 'Barnaby Rudge' and 'Nicholas Nickleby'. Displays include manuscripts, first editions, letters, quill pens, original drawings, and the grandfather clock which belonged to Mosses Pickwick.
Open: Mon-Sat 10-5.
Admission: £3 £2 £5 £1.

GEFFRYE MUSEUM

Kingsland Road, Shoreditch E2 8EA Tel: 0171-739 9893

This is one of London's most friendly and enjoyable Museums. Set in elegant 18th century almshouses with delightful gardens, the Museum presents the changing style of the domestic interior.

The displays take you on a walk through time, from the 17th century, with oak furniture and panelling, past the elegance of the Georgian period, the ornate style of the Victorians, to 20th century art deco and post war utility. A personal sound guide offers background information, and the Museum has a comprehensive reference library and furniture trades archive.

The Museum has a lively programme of temporary exhibitions and events, and there are special activities for children and families most weekends and during school holidays. School and adult groups are always welcome, but must book in advance.

Books, guides and souvenirs available from the shop, and refreshments from the coffee bar. Delightful Herb Garden open April to October.

Admission Free.

Hours of Opening: Tuesdays to Saturdays 10.00 - 5.00
Sundays and Bank Holiday Mondays 2.00-5.00

Nearest Stations: Liverpool St, then buses 22A, 22B, 149.
Old st (exit 2), then bus 243, or fifteen minutes walk.

Disabled access, Parking available in nearby streets.

THE GEFFRYE MUSEUM TRUST

DULWICH PICTURE GALLERY

College Road SE21 7AD **Tel:** 0181-693 5254; Recorded information 0181-693 8000 **Fax:** 0181-693 0923

Dulwich Picture Gallery
College Road, London, SE21 0181-693 5254
An outstanding collection of Old Master paintings in England's oldest public gallery surrounded by park and fields

'London's most perfect Gallery' *The Guardian*, England's oldest public art gallery was designed by Sir John Soane especially for the unique collection of Old Masters which includes works by Rembrandt, Rubens, Claude, Poussin, Van Dyck, Reni and a particularly fine Dutch collection.
Open: Tues-Sun.
Admission: Adults £2 concessions £1 children free and free admission on Fris. Free guided tours Sat and Sun 3. Pre-booked group visits with guide; extended tour to include Dulwich College. Idyllic setting for corporate entertaining fifteen minutes from City and West End.

EAST HAM NATURE RESERVE

(Governors of the Passmore Edwards Museum/Newham Leisure Services)

Norman Road E6 4HN **Tel:** 0181-470 4525

EAST HAM
Nature
Reserve

The Churchyard of St Mary Magdalene, East Ham, the largest in London, managed with care to provide a variety of wildlife habitats. Trails with wheelchair access and tapping board. Visitor Centre has displays on the natural sciences and local social history, shop and teaching/activities facilities (including audio-visual equipment for visitors with impaired vision or hearing).
Open: Open daily Mon-Thurs and Sat 10-5 Sun 2-5.
Admission: Free. Party visits must be booked in advance.
Location: At junction of A117 and A13.
Phone for details of special events and seasonal variations on opening times.

ERITH MUSEUM

(Bexley London Borough)

Erith Library, Walnut Tree Road, Erith DA8 1RS **Tel:** (01322) 526574
Local history, including archaeology, industry and famous events.
Open: Mon and Wed 2.15-5.15 Sat 2.15-5.
Admission: Free.

THE FAN MUSEUM

(The Fan Museum Trust)

12 Crooms Hill, Greenwich SE10 8ER **Tel:** 0181-858 7879/0181-305 1441 **Fax:** 0181-293 1889
The world's only museum of fans with its unsurpassed collections housed in beautifully restored listed Georgian houses. Changing exhibitions, shop, workshop, study facilities. Orangery and landscaped garden. Special tours and private functions.
Open: Tues-Sat 11-4.30 Sun 12-4.30 closed Mon.
Admission: Adults £2.50 concessions children/OAPs/disabled £1.50 family rates (as from Jan 1 1995 admission charges will be increased to £3 and £2 respectively).
Location: Opposite Greenwich Theatre.
Refreshments: By prior arrangement and for Group Visits only.
Exhibitions/Events: Three thematic exhibitions a year, **FANS ON THE GRAND TOUR** Jul 1994-Jan 1995, The Worshipful Company of Fan Makers - an exhibition of their collections - Jan-May 1995, Collectors' Choice May 1995-Oct 1995. Events by prior arrangement.
Gold and silver tours on request. Car park adjacent to museum. Lift, ramp, and lavatory for disabled. Fan making classes.

FARADAY'S LABORATORY AND MUSEUM

(The Royal Institution)

The Royal Institution of Great Britain, 21 Albemarle Street W1X 4BS **Tel:** 0171-409 2992 **Fax:** 0171-629 3569
The Laboratory, where many of the most important discoveries were made, has been restored to the form it was known to have in 1845. An adjacent museum houses a unique collection of original apparatus arranged to illustrate the more significant aspects of Faraday's contribution to the advancement of science.
Open: Mon-Fri 10-4 parties at other times by arrangement.
Admission: Adults £1 children 50p.

FENTON HOUSE

(The National Trust)

Hampstead Grove, Hampstead NW3 **Tel:** 0171-435 3471
The Benton-Fletcher collection of early musical instruments and the Binning collection of porcelain and furniture in a William and Mary House.

ALEXANDER FLEMING LABORATORY MUSEUM

(St. Mary's NHS Trust)

St. Mary's Hospital, Praed Street W2 1NY **Tel:** 0171-725 6528
Reconstruction of the laboratory in which Fleming discovered Penicillin in 1928.
Open: Mon-Thurs 10-1 and at other times by appointment Mon-Thurs 1-5 Fri 10-5 closed Public Holidays.
Admission: Adults £2 OAPs/children/students/unemployed/schools £1 parties by appointment.
Location: British Rail/Underground Paddington.

FORTY HALL MUSEUM

(London Borough of Enfield)

Forty Hill, Enfield, Middlesex EN2 9HA **Tel:** 0181-363 8196 **Fax:** 0181-367 9098
Built in 1629 for Sir Nicholas Raynton, Lord Mayor of London. 17th and 18th Century furniture and pictures. Local history. Exhibitions.
Open: 11-5 Thurs-Sun all year.
Admission: Free.
Location: Close to A10/M25 junction.
Refreshments: Cafeteria.

FREUD MUSEUM

20 Maresfield Gardens, Hampstead NW3 5SX **Tel:** 0171-435 2002/435 5167 **Fax:** 0171-431 5452
The museum contains Sigmund Freud's extraordinary collection of antiquities, his library and furniture, including the famous couch. The founder of psychoanalysis came to London as a refugee from Nazi-occupied Vienna. The study where he practised has been preserved exactly as it was in his lifetime. Interpretive displays; archive films; shop.

Open: Wed-Sun 12-5 all year.
Admission: Adults £2.50 OAPs/students £1.50 children under 12 free.
Location: Finchley Road Underground Station.
Group tours booked in advance.

GEFFRYE MUSEUM

Kingsland Road, Shoreditch E2 8EA **Tel:** 0171-739 9893

A unique presentation of the changing style of the English domestic interior, set in elegant 18th century almshouses with delightful gardens. Fine collections of furniturc, paintings and decorative arts. Reference library and furniture trades archive. Full programme of exhibitions, events, weekend and holiday activities. Tranquill walled herb garden.
Open: Tues-Sat 10-5 Sun and Bank Hol Mons 2-5. Herb garden open Apr-Oct.
Admission: Free.
Location: Stations: Liverpool Street, then buses 22A, 22B, 149, or Old Street, then bus 243 or 15 minute walk.
School and adult groups welcome, but please book in advance.

JILL GEORGE GALLERY LTD

38 Lexington Street, Soho W1R 3HR **Tel:** 0171-439 7343/7319 **Fax:** 0171-287 0478

Contemporary Art Gallery specialising in paintings, drawings, small sculpture and limited edition prints by British artists, from the established artist to the recent graduate. Monthly exhibition programme.
Open: 10-6 weekdays 11-4 Sat.

GOETHE-INSTITUT LONDON

50 Princes Gate, Exhibition Road SW7 2PH **Tel:** 0171-411 3400

Exhibitions of German Art.
Open: Mon-Thurs 10-8 Fri 10-4 Sat 9.30-12.30 please check first.
Admission: Free.
Location: Underground South Kensington.
Refreshments: Available.

GREENWICH BOROUGH MUSEUM

(London Borough of Greenwich)

232 Plumstead High Street SE18 1JT **Tel:** 0181-855 3240 **Fax:** 0181-316-5754

Local museum of archaeology, history and natural history. Also temporary exhibitions, children's activities and sales point.
Open: Mon 2-7 Tues Thur Fri & Sat 10-1 and 2-5 closed Wed and Sun.
Admission: Free.
Schools Service, Saturday Club.

MARTYN GREGORY GALLERY

34 Bury Street, St. James's SW1Y 6AU **Tel:** 0171-839 3731 **Fax:** 0171-930 0812

British watercolours and paintings. Pictures relating to China and the Far East.

GUNNERSBURY PARK MUSEUM

(London Boroughs of Ealing and Hounslow)

Gunnersbury Park W3 8LQ **Tel:** 0181-992 1612 (schools tel: 081 992 2247) **Fax:** 0181-752 0686

Local history museum for the London Boroughs of Ealing and Hounslow. Collections cover archaeology, social history, domestic life, toys and dolls, costume gallery, transport (including Rothschild carriages), crafts and industries, especially laundry. Housed in part of an early 19th century former Rothschild country house set in a large park. Programme of temporary exhibitions. Victorian kitchens, open on weekends during the summer.
Open: Nov-Mar daily 1-4 Apr-Oct daily 1-5 (6 weekends and Bank Holidays).
Admission: Free.
Location: Underground: Acton Town. Bus: E3 (daily), 7 (Suns only).
Refreshments: Cafe in park.
Special facilities for schools by arrangement with interpretative officer. Good access: Ground floor displays with ramps. Toilets (including disabled) in nearby car park.

HAMPSTEAD MUSEUM

(Burgh House Trust (Registered Charity))

Burgh House, New End Square NW3 1LT **Tel:** 0171-431 0144

1703 house with original panelling and staircase. A museum of Hampstead history, old photographs and water colours. Constable Room, Allingham collection.
Open: Wed-Sun 12-5 Bank Hols 2-5.

HARINGEY MUSEUM AND ARCHIVES SERVICE

(London Borough of Haringey)

Bruce Castle, Lordship Lane, Tottenham N17 8NU **Tel:** 0181-808 8772 **Fax:** 0181-808 4118

Local history. Postal history. Art Gallery.
Open: Wed-Sun 1-5 closed winter Bank Hols and Good Friday groups at other times by arrangement.
Admission: Free.
Exhibitions/Events: Holiday activities for children temporary exhibition programme.

HARROW MUSEUM AND HERITAGE CENTRE

(Harrow Arts Council)

Headstone Manor, Pinner View, Harrow **Tel:** 0181-861 2626

Based in listed medieval barn and moated house. Purpose to reflect the history of Harrow: 1930's, Victorian, Agriculture and Trades displays, changing exhibitions.
Open: Wed-Fri 12.30-5 Sat Sun and Bank Holidays 10.30-5 closed Mon open Tues afternoons for lectures. Parties by arrangement morning and evening.
Admission: Free.
Car parking. Easy access and toilet for disabled persons. Catering, books and souvenir shop.

HAYWARD GALLERY, SOUTH BANK CENTRE

Belvedere Road, South Bank Centre SE1 **Tel:** 0171-928 3144 Recorded information 0171-261 0127 Advance Bookings 0171-928 8800.

Since 1968 the Hayward has been the originator or host of many of the world's most influential exhibitions. Historical and contemporary exhibitions have included Art in Latin America, Magnum Photographers, Chinese Paintings from the British Museum, Twilight of the Tsars, Doubletake: Collective Memory and

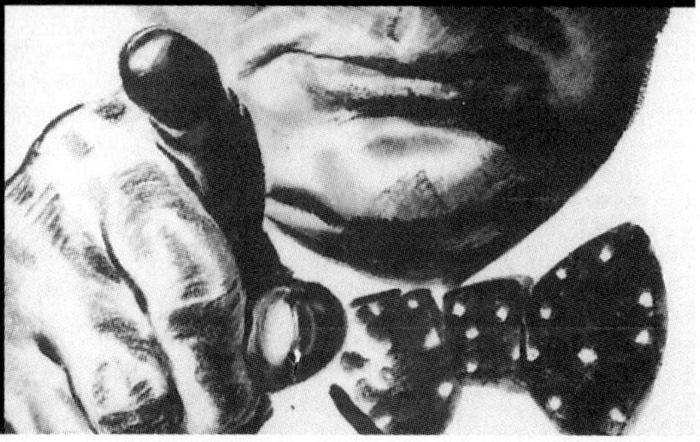

Current Art as well as exhibitions devoted to the work of Leonardo da Vinci, Andy Warhol, Jasper Johns, Richard Long, Georgia O' Keeffe, Magritte and Salvador Dali.
Open: Daily 10-6 late night Tues & Wed until 8 closed between exhibitions.
Admission: Fee charged to all shows.
Location: Underground: Waterloo/Embankment. Buses: Waterloo.
Refreshments: Available at neighbouring Royal Festival Hall.
Exhibitions/Events: Exhibitions for 1995 include Yves Klein, Impressions of France: Landscape in the Paris Salon 1860-90, and Art and Power: Art and Architecture in Europe 1932-45.
We welcome people with disabilities and to ensure that your visit is as straightforward as possible please telephone the Gallery Superintendent on 0171-928-3144.

HERITAGE CENTRE
(London Borough of Sutton)
Honeywood Walk, Carshalton SM5 3NX **Tel:** 0181-773 4555 **Fax:** 0181-770 4777
Discover the fascinating history of the area now within the London Borough of Sutton (which includes Beddington, Carshalton, Cheam, Sutton and Wallington). Based in 'Honeywood', a listed building of 17th century origin; with permanent displays plus a changing programme of exhibitions covering many aspects of local life. Features include a magnificent Edwardian billiard room, a Childhood room with late Victorian and Edwardian toys and games, a Tudor Gallery and an Art Gallery. A wide range of unusual gifts, souvenirs and local history publications are on sale in the shop. 'Honeywood' overlooks Carshalton's picturesque town ponds, in the heart of a conservation area.
Open: Heritage Centre Wed-Fri 10-5 Sat Sun & Bank Holiday Mon 10-5.30. Tea-rooms open Tues-Sun 10-5.15.
Admission: Adults 75p children 40p.
Location: Honeywood Walk, Carshalton. By Carshalton Ponds, opposite Greyhound Inn. Station: Carshalton .25 mile.
Refreshments: Tea-rooms, with separate non-smoking area.
Free entry to the shop and tearooms, which serve a tempting array of hot and cold food. Art Gallery and rooms available for hire. Telephone the Heritage Centre on 0181-773-4555 for further information and details of current exhibitions.

HMS BELFAST
(Imperial War Museum)
Morgans Lane, Tooley Street SE1 2JH **Tel:** 0171-407 6434 **Fax:** 0171-403 0719
Launched in 1938, HMS Belfast is Europe's last surviving warship of the Second World War. Permanently moored close to London Bridge, visitors can explore all seven decks of HMS Belfast, from the bridge to the boiler rooms, and on the way experience what life was like below decks for both officers and crew.
Open: Summer (Mar 1-Oct 31) 10-6 Winter (Nov 1-Feb 28) 10-5 closed Dec 24 25 26.
Admission: Adults £4 children £2 OAPs/students/unemployed £3 parties of 10+ adults £3.20 children £1.60 concessions £2.40.
Location: British Rail - London Bridge. Underground - London Bridge, Tower Hill. Buses to London Bridge. Ferry service across the river.
Refreshments: Corporate hospitality facilities. Cafe onboard serves hot and cold snacks/drinks etc.

HMS BELFAST
Morgans Lane off Tooley Street SE1 2JH **Tel:** 0171-407 6434
Visit Europe's largest preserved Second World War warship and discover how sailors lived, worked and fought aboard this impressive cruiser, which helped sink the *Scharnhorst* and saw action on D-Day and later in the Korean War. She is now permanently moored on the Thames, close to the Tower of London. Visitors can explore all seven decks from the Bridge to the Boiler and Engine Rooms, including the gun turrets, mess decks, galley, punishment cells and more. Special exhibitions and the latest A/V displays recreate the conditions of life on board.
Open: Daily summer Mar 1-Oct 31 10-last adm 5.15 winter 10-last adm 4.15 closed Dec 24-26.
Admission: Charged.
Location: Nearest tube station London Bridge.
Refreshments: Cafe.
Information: 0171-407 6434.

HOGARTH'S HOUSE
(London Borough of Hounslow)
Hogarth Lane, Great West Road, Chiswick W4 **Tel:** 0181-994 6757

Open: Mon-Sat 11-6 (Oct-March 11-4) Sun 2-6 (Oct-March 2-4) closed Tues all year also for first two full weeks of Sept and last three weeks in Dec for staff holidays (due to refurbishment of house-may be closed for short periods - to check telephone first).
Admission: Free.
Use Chiswick House Grounds' car park or named spaces in Axis Business Centre adjacent to the house.

HORNIMAN MUSEUM AND GARDENS
100, London Road, Forest Hill SE23 EPQ **Tel:** 0181-699 1872/2339
Museum dealing with the study of man and his environment. Ethnographical, natural history collections and aquarium. The Music Room Gallery houses a large collection of musical instruments from all parts of the world. Special exhibitions throughout the year. Library by appointment only. Education centre for schools and children's leisure activities. Free lectures and concerts (autumn and spring).
Open: Weekdays 10.30-5.30 Sun 2-5.30 open Good Friday closed Christmas Eve Christmas Day and Boxing Day cafe open Mon-Fri 11-4.30 Sat 11-5.30 Sun 2.30-5.30.
Admission: Free.
Location: Forest Hill London.
Refreshments: Café.
Exhibitions/Events: New exhibition sacred lands, devoted lives until Jan 1996.
Pleasantly located with gardens, picnic area, nature trails and animal enclosures. Free parking in Sydenham Rise (opp. museum) please park across from the built up side of the road

IMPERIAL WAR MUSEUM
(A National Museum)
Lambeth Road SE1 6HZ **Tel:** 0171-416 5000 **Fax:** 0171-416 5374
See thousands of imaginatively displayed exhibits from art to aircraft, from Utility clothes to a U-boat, in this award winning museum. Special features include: interactive videos, the walk through Trench Experience with soldiers going over the top, the dramatic Blitz Experience - complete with sound, smells and other effects, and 'Operation Jericho' - a chance to find out what it was like to fly with the RAF on a daring bombing raid over Occupied Europe.
Open: Daily 10-6 closed Dec 24-26
Admission: Fee Charged.
Location: Nearest tube station Lambeth North.
Refreshments: Cafe shop
Exhibitions/Events: Special 50th Anniversary exhibitions throughout 1995: D-Day to Victory until Jun 25; London at War mid Mar to end Nov. Please ring for further information.
Information: 0171-416 5000 or 0171-820 1683 (recorded information).

THE JEWISH MUSEUM
Raymond Burton House, 129, Albert Street NW1 7LB **Tel:** 0171-284 1997
Collection of antiquities illustrating Judaism and Jewish history. National collection of Jewish ceremonial art. A new museum opening in 1995.
Open: From Jan 1995 Sun-Thurs 10-4 closed Fri Sat Bank and Jewish Hols.

KEATS HOUSE (WENTWORTH PLACE)

(Camden Borough Council)

Keats Grove, Hampstead NW3 2RR **Tel:** 0171-435 2062 **Fax:** 0171-431 9293

Keats's Regency home where he spent the greater part of his five creative years. Relics and manuscripts of the famous poet.

Open: Apr-Oct Mon-Fri 10-1 and 2-6 Sat 10-1 and 2-5 Sun and Bank Hols 2-5 Nov 1-Mar 31 Mon-Fri 1-5 Sat 10-1 and 2-5 Sun 2-5 closed Christmas Eve Christmas Day Boxing Day New Year's Day Good Friday Easter Eve and May 3.

Admission: Free.

Audio tours, English, French, German and Japanese, conducted tours for parties by prior arrangement. Shop.

KENWOOD - THE IVEAGH BEQUEST

(English Heritage)

Hampstead Lane NW3 **Tel:** 0181-348 1286

The paintings include a fine Rembrandt self-portrait, Vermeer's 'Guitar Player' and works by Van Dyck, Hals and Cuyp, as well as English 18th century paintings by Reynolds, Gainsborough and Romney. Important collection of English neo-classical furniture, housed in Robert Adam mansion.

Open: Apr 1-Oct 31 daily 10-6 1 Nov-31 Mar daily 10-4 closed Dec 24 25.

Admission: Free.

KEW BRIDGE STEAM MUSEUM

(Kew Bridge Engines Trust)

Green Dragon Lane, Brentford TW8 OEN **Tel:** 0181-568 4757

Working forge, steam railway, models.

Open: Daily 11-5 engines work weekends only.

Admission: Fee charged family and party rates.

Refreshments: Cafe at weekends.

Exhibitions/Events: For an annual programme send a S.A.E. for list.

Suitable for the disabled.

KINGSTON MUSEUM

Wheatfield Way, Kingston upon Thames KT1 2PS **Tel:** 0181-546 5386 **Fax:** 0181-547 6747

Local history displays telling the story of Kingston from pre-history to today; Martinware pottery, Eadweard Muybridge showcase; Kingston Families gallery; temporary exhibitions in the art gallery. Local History room now located at the North Kingston Centre, Richmond Road, Kingston upon Thames KT2 5PE tel: 0181-547-6738

Open: Daily 10-5 closed Wed and Sun Local History room open daily 10-5 (closed Sat and Sun with a late evening Tues until 7).

Admission: Free.

Location: Kingston town centre. Next door to the library.

LEIGHTON HOUSE ART GALLERY AND MUSEUM
(The Royal Borough of Kensington and Chelsea Libraries and Arts Service)
12 Holland Park Road, Kensington W14 8LZ **Tel:** 0171-602 3316 **Fax:** 0171-371 2467
Leighton House, the home of Frederic Lord Leighton P.R.A. designed for him 1864-66 by George Aitchison R.A. Leighton lived here until his death in 1896. His unique collection of Islamic tiles is displayed in the walls of the Arab Hall and the Victorian interiors, now restored to their original appearance, are hung with paintings by Leighton, Millais, Watts and Burne-Jones. Fine 'New Sculpture' by Leighton, Brock, Thorneycroft in the house and garden. Study collection of Leighton drawings may be seen by appointment. Temporary exhibitions of modern and historic art throughout the year.
Open: Mon-Sat 11-5.30 garden open Apr-Sept closed Bank Hols.
Admission: Free.
Child under 16 to be accompanied by an adult. All parties and tours of the house by arrangement with the Curator.

LINLEY SAMBOURNE HOUSE
(The Victorian Society)
18 Stafford Terrace W8 7BH **Tel:** 0181-994 1019

Open: Mar 1-Oct 31 Wed 10-4 Sun 2-5 parties admitted at other times by prior arrangement apply to The Victorian Society, 1 Priory Gardens, London W4 1TT. 081-742 3438.
Admission: Adults £3 OAPs £2.50 children £1.50.

LITTLE HOLLAND HOUSE
(London Borough of Sutton)
40 Beeches Avenue, Carshalton SM5 3LW **Tel:** 0181-770 4781 **Fax:** 0181-770 4777
The home of Frank Dickinson (1874-1961), follower of William Morris and of the Arts and Crafts movement; artist, designer and craftsman in wood and metal, who built the house himself to his own design and in pursuance of his philosophy and theories. Features his interior design, paintings, hand-made furniture and other craft objects.
Open: Feb-Dec first Sun in month plus Sun and Mon of Bank Hol weekends 1.30-5.30 closed Christmas Eve-Jan 2.
Admission: Free.
Location: On B278, a few minutes from Carshalton Beeches B.R. Station.
Further information from Sutton Heritage Service on 0181 773 4555 or 0181 770 4781. Guided tours for groups available.

LIVESEY MUSEUM
(London Borough of Southwark)
682 Old Kent Road SE15 1JR **Tel:** 0171-639 5604
Southwark's family museum holds a lively programme of hands-on exhibitions for children up to 12 years, their schools, families and carers.
Open: Mon-Sat 10-5.
Admission: Free.
Exhibitions/Events: Until Aug 19 'Air Aware'.

THE LONDON GAS MUSEUM
Bromley-By-Bow **Tel:** 0171-987 2000 ext 3344
The London Gas Museum, Bromley-By-Bow, is a small museum illustrating the history of the gas industry with particular emphasis on London. It contains many examples of gas memorabilia and items of interest are constantly being discovered and sent to the museum for classification and display. The Museum was created by British Gas in 1982, 170 years after the establishment of a gas supply in London. On this large site a gasworks was constructed in 1870 by the Imperial Gas Light Company in an attempt to maintain its commercial position against the competition from an even larger gasworks at Beckton, established by the Gas Light and Coke Company which commenced gas production the same year.
Parking available. Organised parties are welcome by arrangement with the museum.

THE LONDON MUSEUM OF JEWISH LIFE
(The Sternberg Centre)
80 East End Road N3 2SY **Tel:** 0181-349 1143
Permanent display on Jewish immigration and settlement in London with reconstruction of tailoring workshop and immigrant home. Travelling displays, walking tours and educational programmes.
Open: Mon-Thurs 10.30-5 Sun (except in Aug and on Bank Holiday weekends) 10.30-4.30 closed Fri and Sat Jewish Festivals Public Holidays and Dec 25- Jan 4.

MALL GALLERIES
(Federation of British Artists)
The Mall SW1Y 5BD **Tel:** 0171-930 6844
The Federation of British Artists is a long-established registered charity and the umbrella organisation for nine of the country's leading art societies. The gallery shows a lively programme of events for professional and amateur artists, schools, colleges, the local community and gallery visitors.
Exhibitions/Events: Varied with works for sale.

MARBLE HILL HOUSE
(English Heritage)
Richmond Road, Twickenham **Tel:** 0181-892 5115
A perfect example of an English Palladian villa. Early Georgian paintings and furniture.
Open: Apr 1-Oct 31 daily 10-6 Nov 1-Mar 31 Wed-Sun 10-4 closed Dec 24 25.
Admission: Free admission.

MARKFIELD BEAM ENGINE AND MUSEUM
(Markfield Beam Engine and Museum Ltd, Charitable Company, Limited by Guarantee)
Markfield Road, South Tottenham N15 4RB **Tel:** 0181-800 7061 or (01763) 287331

Open: Apr-Nov. Parties by arrangement only can include special steaming on weekdays.
Admission: Fee charged and concessions.
Location: Trains and buses, Tottenham Hale and Seven Sisters stations 5 min. walk
Car parking not on site. Suitable for disabled persons. Technical Director: A.J. Spackman, MSc, DIC, CEng, FRSA.

MARTINWARE POTTERY COLLECTION
(London Borough of Ealing)

Southall Public Library, Osterley Park Road, Southall **Tel:** 0181-574 3412

Martinware Pottery was made by the Martin brothers at their factory in Southall from 1877-1915. The display is open on request during Library hours, Tues-Sat.

Admission: Free.

Please telephone for an appointment.

MATTHIESEN FINE ART LTD

7-8 Mason's Yard, Duke Street, St. James's SW1Y 6BU **Tel:** 0171-930 2437 **Fax:** 0171-930 1387

Specialising in Italian, Spanish and French Old Master paintings, 19th century paintings and sculpture.

Open: 10-5 by appointment.

MCC MUSEUM
(Marylebone Cricket Club)

Lord's Ground NW8 8QN **Tel:** 0171-289 1611 **Fax:** 0171-289 9100

Contains new displays illustrating the history of cricket.

Open: All match days Mon-Sat 10.30-5 open match days on Sun 12-5.

Admission: Fee charged, ground adm also payable on most match days.

For details of Gestetner tour of Lords, on match days and on other occasions, telephone 0171-266 3825.

MEDICI GALLERIES

7 Grafton Street W1X 3LA **Tel:** 0171-629 5675 **Fax:** 0171-495 2997

Exhibitions throughout the year, original paintings, ceramics and sculpture by contemporary artists; original prints, limited editions and reproduction prints. Greeting cards, Christmas cards and calendars.

Open: Mon-Fri 9-5.30 closed Bank Holidays.

Admission: Free.

Disabled access available by arrangement.

WILLIAM MORRIS GALLERY
(London Borough of Waltham Forest)

Lloyd Park, Forest Road E17 4PP **Tel:** 0181-527 3782

Newly re-designed and expanded displays tell the life story of William Morris (1834-1896), the designer-craftsman, poet and socialist, with numerous examples of his textiles, wallpapers, stained glass, furniture, books etc. and work by his associates in the Arts & Crafts Movement. Also pictures by the Pre-Raphaelites and their contemporaries. Located in Morris's boyhood home (built c1750) with its own attractive gardens.

Open: Tues-Sat and 1st Sun each month 10-1 and 2-5.

Admission: Free.

Location: Nearest tube station: Walthamstow Central (Victoria Line).

Group visits by prior arrangement, Guided tours available (charge) by prior arrangement. Educational activities by arrangement. Access for disabled to ground floor and grounds. Shop.

MUSEUM OF GARDEN HISTORY
(The Tradescant Trust)
Lambeth Palace Road SE1 7LB **Tel:** 0171-401 8865 **Fax:** 0171-401 8869

Permanent exhibition of aspects of garden history including a collection of antique garden tools. Lectures; Concerts; Exhibitions; Tombs of the Tradescants and Admiral Bligh of the *Bounty* in the replica 17th century garden.
Open: Daily Mon-Fri 11-3 Sun 10.30-5 closed Sat and closed from the second Sun in Dec-first Sun in Mar.
Location: Nearest underground: Victoria or Waterloo, then 507 or C10 buses.
Refreshments: Available.
Exhibitions/Events: Regular exhibitions, lectures, fairs and courses.
Gift shop. Groups welcomed, but prior arrangement essential.

THE MUSEUM OF LONDON
London Wall EC2Y 5HN **Tel:** 0171-600 0807

museum of LONDON

Opened in December 1976 (Museum of the Year - 1978) - presents the visual biography of the London area from 250,000 years ago. Exhibits (based on collections of former Guildhall and London Museums) arranged chronologically include the Lord Mayor's Coach, models and room reconstructions, everyday tools and rich men's extravagances, Mithraic treasure, the Great Fire experience, 18th century prison cells, 19th century shops, Selfridge's lifts. Education Department, Print Room, Library, by appointment.
Open: Tues-Sat 10-5.50 Sun 12-5.50 closed Mons (except Bank Hols) Dec 24-26 incl and New Year's Day.
Admission: Adults £3 concessions £1.50 family ticket £7.50. All valid for 3 months.
Location: City of London, 5 min. from St. Paul's.
Refreshments: Restaurant and tea shop.
Parties must book in advance.

MUSEUM OF MANKIND
6 Burlington Gardens W1X 2EX **Tel:** 0171-437 2224
(Ethnography Department of the British Museum).
Open: Weekdays 10-5 Sun 2.30-6.
Admission: Free.
Location: Underground stations: Piccadilly Circus, Green Park.

MUSEUM OF RICHMOND
Old Town Hall, Whittaker Avenue **Tel:** 0181-332 1141
This new independent museum deals with Richmond's rich and colourful history in a lively and informative way. Varied collection, models, dioramas and audio visual displays.
Open: Tues-Sat 11-5 also Suns May-Oct 2-5 closed Bank Hols.
Admission: Adults £1 annual pass £3 children/OAPs/unemployed 50p annual pass £1.50 pre-booked school parties admitted free and parties welcome weekday mornings by arrangement.
Public car park nearby. Suitable for disabled persons, no wheelchairs available.

MUSEUM OF THE MOVING IMAGE (MOMI)
South Bank, Waterloo SE1 8XT **Tel:** 0171-401 2636 24hr recorded information
Fax: 0171-633 9323 (Administration)
The award-winning Museum of the Moving Image (MOMI) vividly brings to life the history and magic of cinema and TV.Fourty four exhibit areas take the visitor on a journey from the earliest pre-cinema experiments to the technical wizardry of a modern TV studio. In between there are hundreds of film and TV clips, a fine collection of movie props and memorabilia and a cast of actor-guides. There is even the opportunity to read the 'News at Ten', be interviewed by Barry Norman, or animate a cartoon.
Open: Daily 10-6 (except Dec 24-26) last admission 5.
Admission: Adults £5.50 children(5-16)/concessions £4 students £4.70 family ticket (up to 2 adults and 4 children) £16. Prices are subject to review Jan 1995.
Location: Under Waterloo Bridge next to Royal National Theatre.
Refreshments: At adjacent National Film Theatre.
Exhibitions/Events: Various special exhibitions and displays throughout the year.
Gift and book shops. Information Telephone above.

MUSEUM OF THE ROYAL PHARMACEUTICAL SOCIETY OF GREAT BRITAIN
1 Lambeth High Street SE1 7JN **Tel:** 0171-735 9141 **Fax:** 0171-735 7629
Fine and decorative art, including an important collection of English tin glazed drug jars, crude drug specimens retail and dispensing equipment, advertising material and other ephemera, photographs, satrical, topographical and botanical prints and drawings. The linked archive and library contain an important collection of pharmacopoeias and other rare books.
Open: By appointment.
Admission: Free.
Location: as address.
By appointment only.

THE MUSICAL MUSEUM
(A Charitable Trust)
368 High Street, Brentford KT10 8HF **Tel:** 0181-560 8108

THE MUSICAL MUSEUM
BRENTFORD

A LIVE DEMONSTRATION OF THE MILLS "VIOLANO VIRTUOSO" WHICH PLAYS AUTOMATICALLY A VIOLIN AND PIANO.

Alive with the sound of music, a museum which takes you back to a bygone age to hear and see a marvellous working collection of automatic musical instruments. From small musical boxes, reproducing grand pianos, and orchestrions to a mighty Wurlitzer theatre organ, this museum will appeal to both those old enough to remember the age of the pianola and those young enough to learn that modern computer techniques played instruments in 1913!

Open: Working demonstrations every Sat and Sun 2-5 Apr-Oct inclusive additional days during the summer holidays.
Admission: Adults £3.20 concessions £2.80 family tickets. Party visits by arrangement.
Location: Near Kew Gardens and Kew Bridge Engines.

NARWHAL INUIT ART GALLERY

(Ken & Tija Mantel)

55 Linden Gardens, Chiswick W4 2EH **Tel:** 0181-747 1575 **Fax:** 0181-742 1268

Narwhal Inuit Art Gallery - a permanent exhibition of Canadian, Russian and Greenlandic contemporary Inuit (Eskimo) art. Carvings in stone, bone and horn plus graphics. 1955 to present.
Open: By appointment 7 days a week.

NATIONAL ARMY MUSEUM

(A National Museum)

Royal Hospital Road, Chelsea SW3 4HT **Tel:** 0171-730 0717 **Fax:** 0171-823 6573

NATIONAL ARMY MUSEUM
CHELSEA

The story of the British soldier in peace and war from Tudor times to the present day. Exhibits include weapons, equipment, paintings, personal relics and one of the world's finest collections of uniforms. Dramatic reconstructions show the soldier in conditions ranging from the jungles of Burma to the deserts of Sudan.
Open: Daily 10-5.30 closed Jan 1 Good Fri May Bank Holiday and Dec 24-26.
Admission: Free.
Location: Nearest Tube: Sloane Square.
Refreshments: Available.
Regular Special Exhibitions. (See Press or telephone Museum for details). Free coach parking for pre-booked groups. All Galleries accessible to visitors in wheelchairs.

THE NATIONAL GALLERY

Trafalgar Square WC2N 5DN **Tel:** 0171-839 3321 National Gallery Info 0171-747 2465 (Gallery hours) Recorded Info 0171-839 3526 (24 hours)

The Nation's outstanding permanent collection of Western painting from c.1260-1920, including works by Leonardo, Rembrandt, Constable and Cézanne. Exhibitions centred on specific aspects of the Collection, plus an excellent Education service offering quizzes, audio-visual shows and lectures for adults. The Sainsbury Wing opened in July 1991 and provides galleries for the Early Renaissance collection, together with galleries for temporary exhibitions, a large auditorium for lectures, the Micro Gallery computer information room, a restaurant and shop.
Open: Mon-Sat 10-6; Sun 2-6. Closed Jan 1, Good Friday, May Day and Dec 24, 25, 26. Shops: Mon-Sat 10-5.40 Sun, 2-5.40.
Admission: Free. (Charges for some major exhibitions in the Sainsbury Wing).
Refreshments: Restaurants open Mon-Sat 10-5 (last orders 4.30) Sun 2-5.
Shops and restaurant.

NATIONAL MARITIME MUSEUM

(A National Museum)

Romney Road, Greenwich SE10 9NF **Tel:** 0181-858 4422 **Fax:** 0181-312 6632

Galleries here and in the Old Royal Observatory in Greenwich Park, part of the Museum, show many aspects of maritime history in paintings and prints, ships models, relics of distinguished sailors and events, navigational instruments and charts, history of astronomy, medals, a large library with a reference section, information service and a fine collection of manuscripts. A new Nelson exhibition (opens June 95) is the latest of many new developments in this huge museum of Britain's maritime history, housing an exceptional collection of oil paintings, ship models and relics of naval heroes and explorers. Also see the Old Royal Observatory on Longtitudinal 0° with its displays on space and time and the beautiful restored 17th century Queen's House all included on the same ticket.

Open: Mon-Sat 10-5 Sun 12-5 closed Christmas Eve Christmas Day and 26 December. Queen's House closed Jan 4-31.
Admission: (until Apr 95) includes all 3 sites - adult £4.95 children £2.95 OAPs/students/disabled £3.95 family £14.95.
Location: Greenwich. Station: Maze Hill (BR); Island Gardens (Docklands Light Railway); River services from London piers.
Refreshments: Licensed Restaurant.
For NMM Outstations see Saltash and Tresco (Isles of Scilly).

NATIONAL PORTRAIT GALLERY

St. Martin's Place WC2H 0HE **Tel:** 0171-306 0055 **Fax:** 0171-306 0056

VIRGINIA WOOLF BY GC BERESFORD

Portraits of famous men and women in British history and culture: poets and princesses, statesmen and sportsmen, artists and actresses, explorers and astronomers, on display in paintings, sculpture, drawings, miniatures and photographs. The Gallery has constantly changing displays, with a programme of special exhibitions, acquisitions, commissions and four outstations; Montacute House, Beningbrough Hall, Gawthorpe Hall and Bodelwyddan Caste (see separate entries).
Open: Closed Dec 24-26 Jan 1 Good Friday May Day Bank Holiday open Mon-Sat 10-6 Sun 12-6.
Admission: Free.
Location: Nearest tube Charing Cross Leicester Square.

NATIONAL POSTAL MUSEUM

King Edward Building, King Edward Street EC1A 1LP **Tel:** 0171-239 5420
Fax: 0171-600 3021

Reginald M. Phillips and Post Office Collections of British postage stamps, and related material. Frank Staff collections of postal history. UPU collection of world stamps since 1878. Special exhibitions each year. Philatelic correspondence archives of Thos. de la Rue and Co., covering postage and/or revenue stamps of 200 countries or states 1855-1965 on microfilm. Research facility available by prior arrangements.
Open: Mon-Fri 9.30-4.30.
Admission: Free.
Exhibitions/Events: Adressing postcodes-until end of April 1995

THE NATURAL HISTORY MUSEUM

Cromwell Road, South Kensington SW7 5BD **Tel:** 0171-938 9123
Fax: 0171-938 9290

Exciting exhibitions on Dinosaurs, Ecology and Creepy Crawlies in one of London's finest landmarks. Hands-on displays, public events, vast collections of gemstones and meteorites, and treasures from the natural world.
Open: Every day (except 23-26 Dec) Mon- Sat 10-5.50 pm; Sun 11-5.50pm.
Admission: Standard admission charge, concessions & free periods.
Refreshments: Restaurant, snack bar, cafe, picnic area.
Facilities for the disabled, wheelchairs available.

Vincent van Gogh: Wheatfield, with Cypresses (detail)

NATIONAL MARITIME MUSEUM
THE QUEEN'S HOUSE ◆ OLD ROYAL OBSERVATORY
GREENWICH

THE STORY OF BRITAIN & THE SEA ◆ A ROYAL PALACE FROM THE TIME OF CHARLES I
THE CENTRE OF TIME & SPACE
Outstanding collections & magnificent buildings within a Royal Park.

0181-858 4422

NORTH WOOLWICH OLD STATION MUSEUM
(Governors of the Passmore Edwards Museum/Newham Leisure Services)
Pier Road E16 2JJ **Tel:** 0171-474 7244

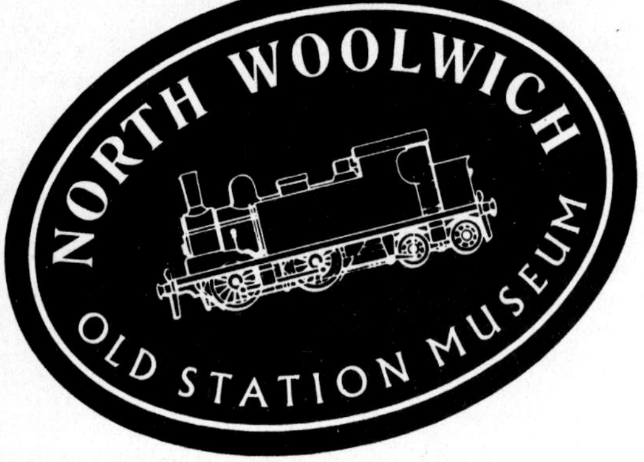

Discover the history
of the Eastern Counties Railway
the Great Eastern LNER
and BR Eastern Region

Photos, tickets and posters, railway models, equipment, 1876 Coffee Pot locomotive and aspects of Newham social and industrial heritage in a dignified Victorian station. Education Service, holiday activities. Engines in steam first Sunday of summer months and special events (phone for details). Summer opening may be extended.
Open: Mon-Thurs and Sat 10-5 Sun and Bank Hol 2-5 phone to confirm opening hours.
Admission: Free.
Shop.

OLD SPEECH ROOM GALLERY, HARROW SCHOOL
(Governors of Harrow School)
High Street, Harrow-on-the-Hill, Middlesex **Tel:** 0181-869 1205 or 0181-422 2196
Situated in the Old Schools at Harrow School, Old Speech Room Gallery was designed by Alan Irvine in 1976. It houses the School's collections: Egyptian and Greek antiquities, watercolours, some Modern British pictures, printed books, Harroviana, natural history. Exhibitions average 3 a year.
Open: Term time daily (except Wed) 2.30-5 School holidays Mon-Fri 2.30-5 other closures during school exeats. Enquiries - telephone the above number.
Admission: Free.
Tour parties can be arranged. Curator: Carolyn Leder MA.

ORLEANS HOUSE GALLERY
(London Borough of Richmond upon Thames)
Riverside, Twickenham TW1 3DJ **Tel:** 0181-892 0221 **Fax:** 0181-744 0501

ORLEANS HOUSE GALLERY
RIVERSIDE, TWICKENHAM

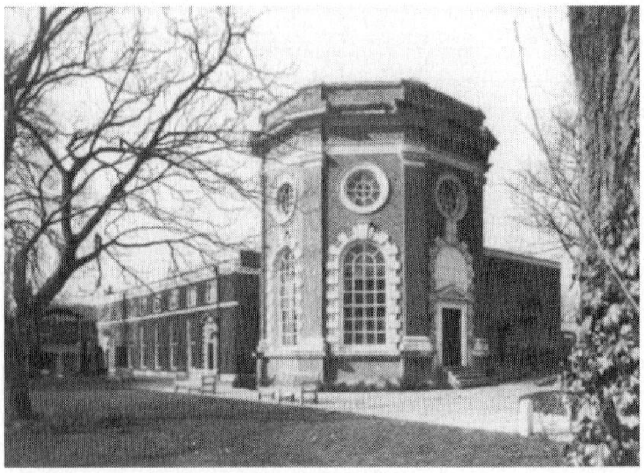

In this beautiful riverside setting by the Thames stands the remains of Orleans House, James Gibbs' splendid baroque Octagon Room. c.1720. The adjacent Gallery shows temporary exhibitions.

Remains of Orleans House, James Gibbs' baroque Octagon Room c. 1720 in a beautiful riverside setting. The adjacent gallery shows temporary exhibitions on a range of subjects, and houses the Ionides Collection, 18th and 19th century oil paintings, water-colours and prints of Richmond and Twickenham (this collection is not on permanent display).
Open: Tues-Sat 1-5.30 (Oct-Mar 1-4.30) Sun 2-5.30 (Oct-Mar 2-4.30) Bank Hols 2-5.30 New Year's Day 2-4.30 closed Mon (except Hols) and Dec 24-26 and Good Friday.
Admission: Free.
Free parking. WCs. Access for disabled: W,S.

OSTERLEY PARK HOUSE
(The National Trust)
near Osterley Station **Tel:** 0181-560 3918

An 18th century villa set in a landscaped park. Elegant neo-classical interior decoration and furnishings designed by Robert Adam for the Child family.
Location: Isleworth, 0.5 m North of Great West Road, near Osterley Station.

PERCIVAL DAVID FOUNDATION OF CHINESE ART
(University of London, School of Oriental and African Studies)
53 Gordon Square WC1H 0PD **Tel:** 0171-387 3909 **Fax:** 0171-383 5163

UNIVERSITY OF LONDON
PERCIVAL DAVID FOUNDATION OF CHINESE ART

53 Gordon Square, London WC1H 0PD

The Collection comprises some 1,700 items consisting of ceramics of the Song. Yuan, Ming and Qing dynasties, and a Reference Library of some 5,000 books and periodicals dealing with the art and culture of the Far East. it was presented to the University of London in 1950 by Sir Percival David and the Foundation is administered and financed on behalf of the University by the School of Oriental and African Studies.

OPENING HOURS:
MONDAY TO FRIDAY
10.30am – 5pm
CLOSED WEEKENDS
& BANK HOLIDAYS

Blue and white Temple Vase inscribed and dated 1351

The First and Second Floor Galleries house permanent displays. Special exhibitions are sometimes held in the Ground Floor Gallery. Evening lectures and other events are periodically held for members of the Friends Society, which was established in July 1991.
Open: 10.30-5 Mon-Fri.
Admission: Free - donations welcome.
Location: Bloomsbury, London.
Refreshments: None.
Exhibitions/Events: Occasional special exhibitions.

PITSHANGER MANOR MUSEUM
(London Borough of Ealing)
Mattock Lane, Ealing **Tel:** 0181-567 1227 **Fax:** 0181-567 0595

PITSHANGER MANOR MUSEUM
MATTOCK LANE, EALING

Built 1800-04 by the architect Sir John Soane, Pitshanger Manor is set in an attractive park. A Victorian room holds a changing and extensive display of Martinware Pottery including a unique chimney-piece of 1891.

The Breakfast Room, Pitshanger Manor Museum

Set in an attractive park, Pitshanger Manor was built 1800-04 by the architect Sir John Soane (1753-1837) as his family home. The house incorporates a wing of the late 1760s by George Dance. The interiors are being restored. All rooms are open to the public every afternoon. If viewing required mornings, please enquire in advance. A Victorian room holds a changing and extensive display of Martinware pottery including a unique chimney-piece of 1891. Extensive exhibition and cultural programme. **Martinware Pottery Collection at Southall Public Library** *see under M.*
Open: Tues-Sat 10-5 (Times may vary) closed Sun Mon Easter Christmas and New Year.
Admission: Free (parties by arrangement in advance).
Refreshments: Tea and coffee vending machine.
Partial access for the disabled. **Martinware Pottery Collection at Southall Public Library** *see under M.*

SPENCER HOUSE
No. 27 St James's Place SW1

London's most magnificent private palace

Spencer House, built in 1756-66 for the first Earl Spencer, an ancestor of HRH The Princess of Wales, is London's finest surviving eighteenth-century town house. This magnificent private palace has regained the full splendour of its late-eighteenth-century appearance, after a painstaking ten-year restoration.

Eight state rooms containing eighteenth-century furniture and paintings, including loans from the Royal Collection and the V&A, are open to the public for viewing on Sundays, and are available for private and corporate entertaining during the rest of the week.

Advance bookings for group tours. Telephone: 0171-499 8620, Tues-Fri 10am-1pm

Information on private and corporate entertaining: Telephone: 0171-409 0526

QUEEN ELIZABETH'S HUNTING LODGE

(Corporation of London)

Ranger's Road, Chingford E4 7QH **Tel:** 0181-529 6681

The royal hunting grandstand was built for Henry VIII in 1543. It is one of the finest examples of timber framed architecture in the U.K. It has recently re-opened with new displays after major conservation work.

Open: Wed-Sun 2 closes 5 or dusk if earlier.

Admission: Adults 50p accompanied children free.

Cafe nearby.

RANGER'S HOUSE

(English Heritage)

Chesterfield Walk, Blackheath SE10 **Tel:** 0181-853 0035

A long Gallery of English Portraits from the Elizabethan to the Georgian period in the famous 4th Earl of Chesterfield's house at Blackheath, including the Suffolk collection of paintings. Dolmetsch collection of musical instruments on the first floor.

Open: Apr 1-Oct 31 daily 10-6 Nov 1-Mar 31 Wed-Sun 10-4 closed Dec 24 25.

Admission: Adults £2 concessions £1.50 children £1 (1994 prices). Admission price includes a free Personal Stereo Guided Tour.

ROYAL ACADEMY OF ARTS

Piccadilly W1V 0DS **Tel:** 0171-439 7438 **Fax:** 0171-434 0837

The Royal Academy is internationally renowned for its major loan exhibitions, held in some of Europe's most beautiful galleries. 1995 highlights include **Nicolas Poussin, Odilon Redon (1840-1916), The Revival of the Palladian Style, From Manet to Gauguin, Africa: The Art of a Continent** and **David Hockney**, as well as the celebrated **Summer Exhibition** (see national press for details).

Open: Daily including weekends 10-6 last admission 5.30.

Admission: Fee charged.

Location: Underground - Piccadilly Circus/Green Park. Bus 9, 14, 19, 22, 38.

ROYAL AIR FORCE MUSEUM

(A National Museum)

Grahame Park Way, Hendon NW9 5LL **Tel:** 0181-205 2266 24 hr info line 0181-205 9191 **Fax:** 0181-200 1751

Britain's only National Museum of aviation, telling the story of flight from the early days to the present time. Some 70 aircraft are now on show, with galleries depicting aviation history from the Royal Engineers of the 1870s up to the RAF of the 1990s.

Open: From Apr 10-6.

Admission: Adults £5.20 children/OAPs £2.60 family ticket £12.60.

Location: North London.

Refreshments: Licensed family restaurant.

Exhibitions/Events: 17th May onwards: 'Wings over Water'. 17th May-31st Oct: 'Flying for Invasion'.

ROYAL ARMOURIES

(The National Museum of Arms and Armour)

HM Tower of London EC3N 4AB **Tel:** 0171-480 6358

Britain's oldest national museum, the Royal Armouries, still in its original home at the Tower of London, houses one of the finest collections of arms and armour in the world. The White Tower houses European armours and weapons from the Dark Ages including the armours of Henry VIII, Charles I, and Charles II. The basement of the White Tower houses the block and axe and other instruments of torture and punishment. The New Armouries houses the British Military Armoury, and a display which brings the story of arms and armour up to the present century.

Open: Summer(BST) - Mon-Sat 9-6 Sun Peak 10-6 Jun-Aug Mon-Sat 9-6.30 Sun 10-6.30 Winter(GMT) - Mon-Sat 9.30-5 Sun 10-5 last admission 5(BST) and 4(GMT).

Admission: Tel 0171-709 0765 concessions for OAPs/unemployed/students/disabled family ticket (2 adults 3 children) discount for groups of 15 or more.

Location: Underground: Circle and District lines to Tower Hill. Bus routes: 15, 42, 78. Riverboat: to Tower Pier.

VICTORIA AND ALBERT MUSEUM

THE WORLD'S FINEST MUSEUM OF THE DECORATIVE ARTS

The V&A is the world's finest museum of the decorative arts. It's collections, housed in magnificent Victorian buildings, span 2,000 years and include sculpture, furniture, fashion and textiles, paintings, silver, ceramics and glass, jewellery, books, prints, and photographs from Britain and all over the world.

Opening times: Monday 12.00-17.50. Tuesday to Sunday 10.00-17.50. Open every day except January 1, December 24, 25, 26. Good Friday and May Day Bank Holiday. **Tel: 0171 938 8500.**

Visitors are asked to make a voluntary donation at the entrance. Four free guided tours a day. Groups are welcome. Good access for disabled visitors. Restaurant. Shop.

Highlights of 1995 exhibition programme:

Warworks: Women, photography and the art of war (11 January - 19 March 1995) Images, themes and iconography of war are explored by eleven women photographers.

Japanese Studio Crafts (24 May - 3 September 1995) An exhibition of contemporary Japanese crafts drawn from the V&A's own collection and studios in Japan.

Wedgwood (8 June - 17 September 1995) A major exhibition to celebrate the bicentenary of the death of Josiah Wedgwood.

The Peaceful Liberators: Jain Art from India (22 November - 18 February 1996) The first large-scale presentation in the West of Jain art.

Botanical Illustrations: The Walter Florilegium Plates (10 May -24 September 1995) A display of botanical illustrations from the V&A's rich and varied collection.

ROYAL COLLEGE OF MUSIC DEPARTMENT OF PORTRAITS AND PERFORMANCE HISTORY

Prince Consort Road, South Kensington SW7 2BS **Tel:** 0171-589 3643

An extensive collection of portraits of musicians, comprising some 320 original portraits and many thousands of prints and photographs. Also houses the College's important collection of concert programmes.

Open: During termtime Mon-Fri by appointment parties by arrangement.

Admission: Free.

ROYAL COLLEGE OF MUSIC MUSEUM OF INSTRUMENTS

Prince Consort Road, South Kensington SW7 2BS **Tel:** 0171-589 3643

Internationally renowned collection of musical instruments. Over 600 keyboard, stringed and wind instruments from c. 1480 to the present, including the Donaldson, Tagore, Hipkins, Ridley and Hartley collections.

Open: Wed during term-time 2-4.30 (subject to review).

Admission: Fee charged.

Parties and special visits by appointment with the Curator.

ROYAL HOSPITAL MUSEUM

(Commissioners Royal Hospital)

Royal Hospital Road, Chelsea SW3 4SR

Pictures, plans and maps, medals and uniforms, connected with Royal Hospital.

Open: Mar-Sept only Mon-Sat 10-12 and 2-4 also Sun 2-4 closed Bank Hol weekends

SCIENCE MUSEUM

Exhibition Road, South Kensington SW7 **Tel:** 0171-938 8000/8080/8008

The outstanding collections at the Science Museum form an unparalleled record of mankind's greatest inventions and achievements. There are nearly a thousand working exhibits. Carry out your very own experiments in 'Launch Pad'; test your skill at flying a model jump jet in 'Flight Lab'; and discover how health is measured using state-of-the-art interactive exhibits in Health Matters. From Stevenson's Rocket to the Apollo 10 space capsule you can discover what technology is, how it works and what it can do for you. Discover them for yourself seven days a week at the Science Museum, South Kensington.

Open: 10-6 Mon-Sat 11-6 Sun.

Admission: Fee charged.

SHERLOCK HOLMES MUSEUM

221b Baker Street NW1 **Tel:** 0171-935 8866

The Sherlock Holmes Museum

The World famous lodging house of the great detective Sherlock Holmes is open to the public as a Museum of unique interest.

Sherlock Holmes' autograph & exclusive souvenirs are available. Bring your camera!

Open daily 10.00am – 6.00pm
Adults £5.00 Children £3.00
Group rates on request.

221b BAKER ST. LONDON
Telephone 0171 935 8866
Fax 0171 738 1269

The 1991 Historic Houses Association Annual General

Sherlock Holmes and Doctor Watson are believed to have resided in lodgings at 221b Baker Street from about 1881-1904. The rooms at this address have been faithfully maintained to preserve their Victorian atmosphere and are open to the public as a museum. Seventeen steps lead up to the familiar 1st floor study overlooking Baker Street and convey visitors back a hundred years into the world of Sherlock Holmes. Memorabilia from the stories and personal possessions of the great detective are on display and visitors can also read some of the letters written to Mr Holmes by admirers from around the world. His autograph is given free to every visitor and exlusive souvenirs are available from the gift shop. The Museum is run by the Sherlock Holmes International Society and is a member of the Historic Houses Association.

Open: Every day 10-6.

Admission: Adults £5 children £3.

Location: Underground station Baker Street.

SIR JOHN SOANE'S MUSEUM

13 Lincoln's Inn Fields WC2A 3BP **Tel:** 0171-405 2107 Information line 0171-430 0175

The museum was built by Sir John Soane, R.A., in 1812-13 as his private residence and contains his collection of antiquities and works of art. Gallery with changing exhibitions.

Open: Tues-Sat 10-5 (Lecture tours Sat 2.30 maximum 25 people no groups) late evening opening on the first Tues of each month 6-9. Groups welcome but please book. Closed Bank Hols.

Admission: Free.

SOUTH LONDON GALLERY

(London Borough of Southwark)

65 Peckham Road SE5 8UH **Tel:** 0171-703 6120

Annual programme of 6/7 temporary exhibitions, mainly of contemporary British art. Permanent collection, including reference collection of 20th century prints shown in special exhibitions.

Open: Tues Wed Fri 10-5 Thurs 10-7 Sun 2-5 closed Sat Mon and Bank Hol weekends.

Admission: Free.

Exhibitions/Events: Please contact gallery for details of 1995 exhibitions.

SPENCER HOUSE

27 St. James's Place SW1 **Tel:** 0171-409 0526

Spencer House, built 1756-66 for the first Earl Spencer, an ancestor of HRH The Princess of Wales, is London's finest surviving private palace.

Open: Its eight state rooms are open to the public on Sun (except during Jan and Aug) from 11.30-5.30 access is by guided tour (last tour 4.45) tickets may be purchased on the door from 10.30 to avoid disappointment visitors are advised to purchase tickets early in the day or use the advance reservation system (tel 0171-499 8620 Tues-Fri 10-1 only).

Admission: Adults £6 concessions (Students with cards/Friends of the V&A/ Friends of the Tate Gallery/Friends of the Royal Academy with cards/children under 16 - no children under 10 admitted) £5 prices are valid until end March 1995.

Location: Underground Green Park

Also available for private and corporate entertaining. Access for disabled visitors.

ST. JOHN'S GATE, THE MUSEUM OF THE ORDER OF ST. JOHN

(The Headquarters of the Order of St. John)

St. John's Lane, Clerkenwell EC1M 4DA **Tel:** 0171-253 6644 **Fax:** 0171-490 8835

Open: Mon-Fri 10-5 Sat 10-4 with tours at 11 and 2.30 on Tues Fri and Sat.

Admission: Free (donation requested).

TATE GALLERY

Millbank SW1P 4RG **Tel:** 0171-887 8000 Recorded Information: 071 887 8008 **Fax:** 0171-887 8007

The Tate Gallery houses the National collections of British art from the 16th century to the present day including the Turner Collection in the Clore Gallery and of International 20th-century painting and sculpture.

Open: Mon-Sat 10.00-5.50 Sun 2.00-5.50 closed New Year's Day Good Friday May Day bank holiday Christmas Eve Christmas Day Boxing Day.

Admission: Free to the Gallery except for major loan exhibitions of which there are three a year with concessions to paying exhibitions for OAP's UB40 holders and students in full time education (group booking is for schools only).

Refreshments: Restaurant; Mon-Sat 12-3 Closed Sun. Coffee shop; Mon-Sat 10.30-5.30 Sun 2-5.15 self-service cold buffet.

Museum shop. Suitable for disabled. For wheelchairs please telephone the Gallery in advance tel: 0171-887 8814 (Warders office). Metered parking in Atterbury Street beside the Gallery.

THAMES BARRIER VISITORS' CENTRE

Unity Way, Woolwich SE18 5NJ **Tel:** 0181-854 1373

A multi-media show and exhibition of photographs, models, video film and information display tubes about the history of the Thames Barrier.

Open: Daily except Christmas.

Admission: Fee charged.

Location: A206 Woolwich Road between Blackwall Tunnel and Woolwich ferry

Refreshments: Self-service cafeteria. Function room and evening carvery for prebooked groups.

Exhibitions/Events: Gates raised monthly for experiments and tests

Car park. Free coach park. Evening booking by arrangement. Disabled access.

THEATRE MUSEUM

(Victoria & Albert Museum)

Russell Street, Covent Garden WC2E 7PA **Tel:** 0171-836 7891

Theatre Museum, national museum of the performing arts, exhibits from Shakespeare to the present day, include costumes, models, paintings and other theatrical memorabilia.

Open: Tues-Sun 11-7 last admission 6.30 closed all public holidays.

Admission: Adults £3 children 5-16/unemployed/students/disabled £1.50 groups - adult and education £2 and £1. Corporate hire available.

Location: Covent Garden.

Exhibitions/Events: 'Wind in the Willows; From Page to Stage'. 'Slap! A Celebration of Stage Make-up'.

THOMAS CORAM FOUNDATION FOR CHILDREN

(Foundling Hospital Art Treasures)

40 Brunswick Square WC1N 1AZ **Tel:** 0171-278 2424 **Fax:** 0171-837 8084

About 150 paintings, prints etc., including works by Hogarth, Gainsborough and Reynolds; historical records; musical scores by Handel; furniture and clocks; mementoes from the Foundling Hospital (founded 1739).

Open: Mon and Fri 1.30-4.30. Groups at other times by appointment. Closed at weekends Public Hols and when the rooms are in use for conferences. Please phone before visiting to ensure the rooms are open.

Admission: Adults £1 OAPs/registered art students and children 50p.

Location: Underground stations: Russell Square, King's Cross. Buses to Russell Square.

TOWER BRIDGE

(Corporation of London)

SE1 2UP **Tel:** 0171-403 3761 **Fax:** 0171-357 7935

The interior of this world renowned lifting bridge can be explored almost in its entirety. Panoramic high level views, the original Victorian steam machinery and a new state-of-the-art exhibition.

Open: The bridge is open daily Apr 1-Oct 31 10-6.30 Nov 1-Mar 31 10-5.15 Last ticket 75 mins before closing closed Dec 24 25 26 and Jan 1.

Admission: Adults £5 children(5-15)/OAPs £3.50 parties of 20 or more 20% off normal rates Jan-June Sept-Dec.

UNIVERSITY COLLEGE MUSEUM OF ZOOLOGY AND COMPARATIVE ANATOMY

Gower Street WC1E 6BT **Tel:** 0171-387 7050 Ext 3564

Specialised teaching collection of Zoological material. By arrangement only.

VALENCE HOUSE MUSEUM AND ART GALLERY

(London Borough of Barking and Dagenham)

Becontree Avenue, Dagenham RM8 3HT **Tel:** 0181-592 4500 Ext 4293 0181 595 8404 **Fax:** 0181-595 8307

A partly moated, 17th century manor house devoted to local history and art, featuring the Fanshawe portraits. In the grounds is a period style herb garden.

Open: Tues-Fri 9.30-1 and 2-4.30 and Sat 10-4.

Refreshments: On Saturdays only.
Exhibitions/Events: Temporary exhibitions in the O'Leary Gallery.

VESTRY HOUSE MUSEUM
(London Borough of Waltham Forest)
Vestry Road, Walthamstow E17 9NH **Tel:** 0181-509 1917
A local history museum housed in an early eighteenth century workhouse in the Walthamstow Village Conservation Area. The permanent displays illustrate aspects of past life in Waltham Forest and include displays of costume and local domestic life, a reconstructed Victorian parlour, a nineteenth century police cell, the Bremer Car, c.1894, etc. Temporary exhibition programme throughout the year. Vestry House also serves as the base for Waltham Forest's Archives and Local History Library.
Open: Mon-Fri 10-1 and 2-5.30 Sat 10-1 and 2-5 group visits by prior appointment.
Admission: Free.
Location: Nearest station: Walthamstow Central (Victoria Line).
Special facilities for schools by arrangement.

VICTORIA AND ALBERT MUSEUM
(Department of National Heritage)
Cromwell Road, South Kensington SW7 2RL **Tel:** 0171-938 8500 Recorded information on 0171-938 8441 (general) 0171-938 8349 (exhibitions)
The greatest museum of Decorative Arts in the world. Its collections, housed in magnificent Victorian buildings, span 2000 years of art and design from around the world.
Open: Tues-Sun 10-5.50 Mon 12-5.50 closed Dec 24 25 26 Jan 1 May Day Bank Hol and Good Fri.
Admission: Visitors are asked to make a voluntary donation at the entrance - For guidance - adults £4.50 concessions £1 children under 12/V&A Patrons/Friends of V&A are asked not to contribute.
Location: South Kensington.
Refreshments: Restaurant serving hot and cold meals, drinks, snacks, salads and sandwiches. Music played some weekdays and Jazz Brunch on Sun 11-3. Closes at 5 every day. During the summer months there is a garden cafe in the Pirelli Gardens.
Exhibitions/Events: Jan 11-Mar 19 'Warworks: Women, photography and the art of war'. May 24-Sept 3 'Japanese Studio Crafts: Tradition and the Avant-Garde'. June 8-Sept 17 'Wedgwood'. Nov22-Feb 18 'The Peaceful Liberators: Jain Art from India'. May 10-Sept 24 'Botanical Illustrations: The Walter Florilegium Plates'.
Free guided tours daily. 80% accessibility to disabled visitors and wheelchairs available. A number of new packages for groups (see groups leaflet for details of prices etc.).

THE WALLACE COLLECTION
Hertford House, Manchester Square W1M 6BN **Tel:** 0171-935 0687
This unique collection of superb paintings, beautiful French eighteenth century furniture, porcelain, clocks and objects d'art, plus the largest array of arms and armour outside the Tower of London, is displayed in the luxurious setting of the original family home which was left to the nation by Lady Wallace at the end of the last century.
Open: Weekdays 10-5 Sun 2-5.
Admission: Free.
Location: Tube: Bond Street. Buses: Selfridges, Oxford Street.
Contact: Bunty King.

THE WANDLE INDUSTRIAL MUSEUM
The Vestry Hall Annexe, London Road, Mitcham, Surrey CR4 3UD **Tel:** 0181-648 0127
Reflects the life and industries of the River Wandle. Special exhibits on Arthur Liberty, William Morris, Merton Priory, Lord Nelson, Surrey Iron Railway, snuff and tobacco.
Open: Every Wed 1-4 and first Sun of month 2-5.
Admission: Adults 20p concessions 10p no special reductions.

WANDSWORTH MUSEUM
(London Borough of Wandsworth)
The Courthouse, Garratt Lane, Wandsworth SW18 2PU **Tel:** 0181-871 6369 for latest information on the new museum

The story of Wandsworth will be told in a new and exiting way at the new Wandsworth Museum opening in September 1995.
Open: From Sept 1995.
Admission: Free.

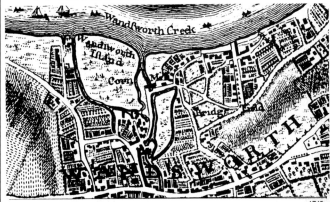

WESLEY'S CHAPEL
49, City Road EC1Y 1AU **Tel:** 0171-253 2262 **Fax:** 0171-608 3825
The Museum of Methodism is situated in crypt of Chapel built by Wesley. Adjacent is 18th century house where he died. House closed for refurbishment Sep 94 to Feb 95.
Open: Mon-Sat 10-4 Sun 12-2.

WESTMINSTER ABBEY MUSEUM
(Dean and Chapter of Westminster)
SW1P 3PA **Tel:** 0171-222 5152 0171-233-0019 **Fax:** 0171-233 2072

Museum housed in magnificent Norman Undercroft. The Abbey's famous collection of Royal and other effigies forms centrepiece of the exhibition. Other items on display include replicas of Coronation regalia and surviving panels of medieval glass.
Open: Daily 10.30-4.
Admission: Fee charged (includes adm to Chapter House and Treasurey).

WHITECHAPEL ART GALLERY
80-82 Whitechapel High Street E1 7QX **Tel:** 0171-522 7888 **Fax:** 0171-377 1685
A purpose-built gallery opened 1901 in the heart of the East End. Organises major exhibitions, generally of modern and contemporary art; no permanent collection. An extensive community education programme for adults and children - public tours, lectures, workshops, audio-visual programmes and studio visits.
Open: Tues-Sun 11-5 (Wed to 8) closed Mon and Bank Hols.
Admission: Most exhibitions are free.
Location: Adjacent to Aldgate East Tube Station.
Refreshments: Cafe.
Bookshop. Full access for people with disabilities.Lecture theatre fitted with induction loop.

WHITEHALL
(London Borough of Sutton)
1 Malden Road, Cheam SM3 8QD **Tel:** 0181-643 1236 **Fax:** 0181-770 4777
Timber-framed house built c.1500. Features revealed sections of original fabric and displays including medieval Cheam pottery, Nonsuch Palace, timber-framed buildings and Cheam School. Changing exhibition programme, and variety of events throughout the year.
Open: Apr-Sept Tues-Fri & Sun 2-5.30 Sat 10-5.30 Oct-Mar Wed Thurs and Sun 2-5.30 Sat 10-5.30 open Bank Holiday Mons 2-5.30 closed Christmas Eve-Jan 2 (incl).
Admission: Adults 75p children 40p.
Location: On A2043 just N of junction with A232. Station: Cheam (.25m).
Refreshments: Tea-room.
Exhibitions/Events: Changing programme. Ring 0181-643 1236 for details.
Further information from Sutton Heritage Service on 0181-770 4781. Party bookings, guided tour facilities available. Please ring in advance. Gift shop. Exhibition space and rooms available for hire.

THE WIMBLEDON LAWN TENNIS MUSEUM
All England Club, Church Road, Wimbledon SW19 5AE **Tel:** 0181-946 6131
Fax: 0181-944 6497

Admission: 10% reduction for parties of 20 or more booked in advance.
Curator Miss Valerie Warren.

WIMBLEDON SOCIETY'S MUSEUM
Village Club, Ridgway, Wimbledon SW19 4QD **Tel:** 0181-946 9398
History and natural history of Wimbledon. Photographic survey mostly 1900-14 containing 2000 prints. Good collection of watercolours and prints.
Open: Sat 2.30-5.
Admission: Free.
Location: At junction of Ridgeway and Lingfield Road.

WIMBLEDON WINDMILL MUSEUM
(Wimbledon Windmill Museum Trust)
Windmill Road, Wimbledon Common SW19 **Tel:** 0181-947 2825

The history of windmills and windmilling told in pictures, models and the machinery and tools of the trade.
Open: Easter-Oct Sat Sun and Public Hols 2-5.
Admission: Adults £1 Children 50p group visits by arrangement.
Refreshments: Available.
Free parking for cars and coaches.

WOODLANDS ART GALLERY

90, Mycenae Road, Blackheath SE3 7SE **Tel:** 0181-858 5847

Gallery on the ground floor of John Julius Angerstein's country villa built in 1774, surrounded by pleasant garden. The gallery is leased from the London Borough of Greenwich and staffed by volunteers. Ten contemporary art exhibitions per year by invitation and selection of British, International and Local Artists. Friends Society, childrens workshop, disabled access, gardens, parking.

Open: Daily 11-5 Sun 2-5 closed Wed Bank Hols and Dec 20-Jan 7 1995.

Location: By Westcombe Park Station; Bus 53, 54, 75, 108, 286 to Blackheath Standard, A2 to Maze Hill.

Refreshments: Tea and coffee available.

Exhibitions/Events: 10 exhibitions per year.

Contemporary Art of all fields. Parties welcome. Car Parking available.

ZELLA NINE GALLERY

2 Park Walk SW10 0AD **Tel:** 0171-351 0588 **Fax:** 0171-352 4752

Over 5,000 watercolours, etchings, lithographs and other works on paper by major and new British artists.

Open: Daily including Sun and Bank Hols 10-9.

Admission: Free.

Not suitable for disabled persons.

GREATER MANCHESTER

ASHTON-UNDER-LYNE

THE MUSEUM OF THE MANCHESTERS: A SOCIAL AND REGIMENTAL HISTORY

(Tameside Metropolitan Borough)

Ashton Town Hall, The Market Place, Ashton-under-Lyne **Tel:** 0161-342 3078/342 3710

The history of the Manchester Regiment, displayed with the social history of the community in which it was based.

Open: Mon-Sat 10-4 open Bank Hols.

Admission: Free.

Full access and facilities for disabled.

PORTLAND BASIN INDUSTRIAL HERITAGE CENTRE

(Tameside Metropolitan Borough)

Portland Place, Portland Street South, Ashton-under-Lyne **Tel:** 0161-308 3374

200 years of Tameside's social and industrial history displayed in a former canal warehouse with a waterwheel on the wharf.

Open: Oct-Mar Tues-Sat 10-4 Sun 12-4 Apr-Sept Tues-Sat 10-6 and Sun 10-6 closed Mon but open Bank Holiday Mon.

Admission: Free.

Refreshments: Available.

Full access and facilities for disabled.

BOLTON

BOLTON MUSEUM AND ART GALLERY

(Bolton Metropolitan Borough Council)

Le Mans Crescent, Bolton **Tel:** (01204) 22311, Ext. 2191 **Fax:** (01204) 391352

Collections of archaeology, local and industrial history, natural history, geology and Egyptology. Art gallery containing collection of 18th century watercolours; sculpture, ceramics; temporary exhibitions gallery.

Open: Mon Tues Thurs and Fri 9.30-5.30 Sat 10-5 closed Wed Sun and Bank Hols.

Admission: Free.

Location: Bolton town centre adjacent to the Town Hall.

HALL I'TH' WOOD MUSEUM

Green Way, off Crompton Way, Bolton **Tel:** (01204) 301159

Open: Apr-Sept Tues-Sat 11-5 Sun 2-5 closed Mons except Bank Hols 11-5 Oct-Mar (inclusive) closed to the general public.

Admission: Adults £1.55 concessions 75p.

Location: Bus 546 from Town Centre.

Open to pre-booked educational parties and evening party tours.

SMITHILLS HALL MUSEUM

off Smithills Dean Road, Bolton **Tel:** (01204) 841265

Open: As for Hall i'th' Wood Museum.

Admission: As for Hall i'th' Wood Museum.

Location: Bus 526 from Town Centre.

LEIGH

TURNPIKE GALLERY

(Wigan Metropolitan Borough)

Leigh Library, Civic Square, Leigh WN7 1EB **Tel:** (01942) 604131 ext 211 **Fax:** (01942) 262451

Contemporary art works, changing exhibition programme including major touring exhibitions.

Open: Mon-Fri 10-5.30 Wed 10-5 Sat 10-3.

Admission: Free.

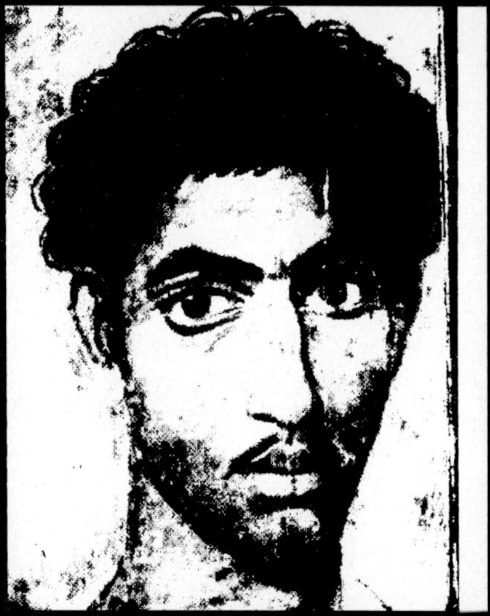

MANCHESTER

GREATER MANCHESTER POLICE MUSEUM

(Greater Manchester Police)

Newton Street, Manchester **Tel:** 0161-856 3287

Set in a Victorian Police Station, the Police Museum features a reconstructed Charge Office of the 1920's, the station cells and in three other rooms collections of uniforms, equipment, forgery exhibits and photographic displays.
Open: By appointment only throughout the year closed weekends Public and Bank Hols.
Admission: All visits free of charge.
Parties - no minimum number, but a maximum size of 20 persons only per visit.
Curator: Mr Duncan Broady. Assistant: Mrs Christine Watkins.

MANCHESTER JEWISH MUSEUM

(Trustees of Manchester Jewish Museum)

190 Cheetham Hill Road, Manchester M8 8LW **Tel:** 0161-834 9879 or 832 7353

The museum is in a former Spanish and Portuguese synagogue built in 1874. Downstairs the synagogue has been restored to its original condition whilst upstairs, in the former ladies gallery, there is an exhibition on the history of Manchester's Jewish community over the last two and hundred and fifty years.
Open: Mon-Thurs 10.30-4 Sun 10.30-5 closed Fri Sat and Jewish holidays.
Admission: Adults £2 concessions £1.25 family ticket £6.50 no charge for teachers with school parties or on preliminary visits Booking Fee £5 per group.
Location: On A665 .5m from Manchester City Centre metrolink to Victoria Station.
Exhibitions/Events: Calendar of events available on request.
Temporary exhibition area and programme of trails, talks and concerts. Car parking on street nearby. Suitable for disabled persons on ground floor only. All parties **must** be booked in advance with the Administrator, Don Rainger.

MANCHESTER MUSEUM

The University, Oxford Road, Manchester M13 9PL **Tel:** 0161-275 2634

The Manchester Museum is fascinating place to visit and houses internationally important collections. Situated in splendid Victorian gothic buildings, the museum is a rich storehouse of treasures with innovative and exciting displays. There are displays of natural history - mammels, birds, butterflies, shells, plants, fossils and minerals - and human history - the archaeology of ancient Egypt, of the Meditteranean, the art of the Pacific and Far East, coins and the world's finest collection of archery. There is also a small display of live animals including fish, crocodiles and snakes.
Open: Mon-Sat 10-5 closed a few days at Christmas and on Good Friday.
Museum shop. Frequent bus services from Albert Square and Piccadilly stopping near the front entrance of the Museum. Car parking. **Museum of the Year 1987.**

Oldham Art Galleries and Museums

Oldham Art Gallery – contemporary art, photography and historical thematic exhibitions.
Also arts-related events and activities and a community loan exhibition service.
New contemporary Craft and Design Gallery opens 1993.

Museum: The Green Room.

Husband and Wife by Howard Hodgkin

Bellizona – The Bridge over the Ticino c. 1843 by J.M.W. Turner.

Oldham Museum – Going up Town – Shopping in Oldham – a major exhibition on the history and development of Oldham town centre. Includes videos, activity guide, worksheets.

Also natural history displays in The Green Room. The New Education Service Phone 633 2392. Art Gallery 0161-911 4653. Museum 0161-911 4657.

THE MUSEUM OF SCIENCE AND INDUSTRY IN MANCHESTER

Liverpool Road, Castlefield, Manchester M3 4FP **Tel:** 0161-832 1830 (24 hour info. line) **Fax:** 0161-833 2184

Located in the buildings of the world's oldest passenger railway station (1830), the Museum of Science and Industry has fifteen galleries that amuse, amaze and entertain. Visit 'Underground Manchester' where you can walk through a reconstructed Victorian sewer and discover the sights and smells of the city beneath your feet. Reach for the stars with a journey through the Galaxy in the 'Out of this World' space gallery. Xperiment! in the hands-on science centre where you can shake hands with yourself and walk away from your own shadow.

Open: Daily 10-5 except 23 24 25 Dec 1994.

Admission: Adults £3.50 concessions £1.50 under 5s free. Group rates (minimum 10 people) adults £2.50 concessions £1.20 prices valid until 31 Mar 1995.

Location: Liverpool Road just off Deansgate, Manchester.

Refreshments: Xpression coffee shop/Kites cafe.

Mosaics gift shop.

MUSEUM OF TRANSPORT

Boyle Street, Cheetham, Manchester M8 8UW **Tel:** 0161-205 2122

A working museum, specialising in preserved buses with a collection of over 60 large vehicles.

Open: Wed Sat Sun and Bank Holidays (except Christmas) 10-5.

Admission: Adults £1.60 children/OAPs £1 family £4.

Location: Situated behind Queen's Road bus garage; near junction of A6010/A665, 3m S of M62, junction 17, and 1m N of city centre. Nearest Metrolink Woodlands Road.

Parties by arrangement. Vintage bus services, special events, annual rally in September. Education Talks service. Visits, disabled persons weekend. Contact 0161-205 2122.

PUMP HOUSE PEOPLE'S HISTORY MUSEUM

(Funded by Association of Greater Manchester Authorities)

Left Bank, Bridge Street, Manchester M3 3ER **Tel:** 0161-228 7212

The museum celebrates the lives of people over the last 200 years and offers visitors the opportunity to disvover how working people lived whether they were Victorian cotton workers or today's footballers.

Open: Tues-Sun 11-4.30 and Bank Hols.

Admission: £1 and concessions free (no admission charge on a Fri) parties welcome.

Refreshments: Clarion cafe offers lunches, refreshments, fine wines and continental beers.

The Museum Shop has a wide range of books, T-shirts, postcards and greetings cards. Suitable for disabled people. Parking at Gartside Street Car Park.

SALFORD MUSEUMS AND ART GALLERIES

Endless Chain Haulage, 'Buile Hill No. 1 Drift Mine' – Salford Mining Museum

SALFORD MUSEUM AND ART GALLERY: Chief features: L. S. Lowry collection of paintings and drawings; temporary art exhibitions; 'Lark Hill Place', a 19th century 'street' of shops and period rooms; Gallery of Victorian Art.

SALFORD MINING MUSEUM: History and technology of Coalmining; reproduction of underground mine and drift mine.

ORDSALL HALL MUSEUM: Manor House with fine 16th century spere truss in Great Hall; collections of furniture, kitchen equipment and local history items.

VIEWPOINT PHOTOGRAPHIC GALLERY (City of Salford) The Old Fire Station, Crescent, Salford (just across the road from the Museum and Art Gallery).

The Gallery shows a wide range of exhibitions including major national and international shows in addition to thematic exhibitions which use archival material and the work of regionally based photographers.

THE WHITWORTH ART GALLERY
(University of Manchester)

Oxford Road, Manchester M15 6ER **Tel:** 0161-273 4865 information line 0161-273 5958 **Fax:** 0161-274 4543

Major centre for the study and display of art and design. Innovative displays drawn from outstanding collections of British watercolours; drawings; prints; textiles (from Coptic weaves to modern fabrics); wallpapers and modern art. Temporary exhibitions.
Open: Mon-Sat 10-5 Thurs 10-9 closed Sun Christmas to New Year and Good Friday.
Admission: Free.
Location: Opposite the Manchester Royal Infirmary frequent bus service to Gallery.
Exhibitions/Events: Yes.

Award winning Bistro, and Shop. Car parking. Disabled access.

OLDHAM

OLDHAM ART GALLERY
(Oldham Leisure Services)

Union Street, Oldham OL1 1DN **Tel:** 0161-678 4653 **Fax:** 0161-627 1025

Frequently changed exhibitions of contemporary art and photography. Collections comprising early English watercolours, British 19th and 20th century paintings, modern prints, English ceramics and glass, plus small Oriental collection. New contemporary Craft and Design Gallery.
Open: Wed Thurs and Fri 10-5 Tues 10-1 Sat 10-5 Sun 1-5 closed Mon.
Admission: Free.
Refreshments: Cafe.
Exhibitions/Events: Full programme of exhibitions and events available on request.

OLDHAM MUSEUM
(Oldham Leisure Services)

Greaves Street, Oldham OL1 1DN **Tel:** 0161-678 4657 **Fax:** 0161-627 1025

Two floors devoted to changing exhibitions of local interest.
Open: Wed Thurs and Fri 10-5 Tues 10-1 Sat 10-5 Sun 1-5 closed Mon.
Admission: Free.
Exhibitions/Events: Full programme of exhibitions and events available on request.
Local studies library in adjacent building.

SADDLEWORTH MUSEUM & ART GALLERY

High Street, Uppermill, Oldham OL3 6HS **Tel:** (01457) 874093 or 870336

An independent museum alongside the Huddersfield canal. Woollen textile machinery (regular working), Victorian Rooms, Transport, Art Gallery.
Open: Daily throughout year also Shop and Tourist Information Centre.

ROCHDALE

ROCHDALE ART GALLERY

Esplanade, Rochdale OL16 1AQ **Tel:** (01706) 342154

Public Art Gallery showing contemporary and historic art.
Open: Tues-Sun 10-4 (1995 opening times not confirmed please ring first).
Admission: Free.
Location: Central Rochdale, opposite Rochdale Town Hall.
Refreshments: Cafe-bar

ROCHDALE PIONEERS CO-OPERATIVE MUSEUM

Toad Lane, Rochdale OL12 ONU **Tel:** 0161-832 4300 **Fax:** 0161-831 7684

Houses the original store of the Rochdale Co-operative Pioneers containing documents, pictures and other material of British and international co-operative interest.
Open: 10-4 Sun 2-4 closed Mon.
Admission: Adults 50p children 10p OAPs free.

SALFORD

LANCASHIRE MINING MUSEUM, SALFORD
(City of Salford)

Buile Hill Park, Eccles Old Road, Salford M6 8GL **Tel:** 0161-736 1832

The museum is devoted to the history and technology of coal-mining and reproductions of an underground mine and a drift mine illustrate this theme.
Open: Mon-Fri 10-12.30 and 1.30-5 Sun 2-5.
Admission: Free.

MUSEUM AND ART GALLERY
(City of Salford)

Peel Park, The Crescent, Salford M5 4WU **Tel:** 0161-736 2649

The main museum exhibit is that of a period street typical of a northern industrial town at the time of the turn of the century. The Art Gallery permanently displays a comprehensive collection of the works of L.S. Lowry and holds frequently exhibitions by artists of this region. There is a gallery of Victorian Art and a 20th century gallery.
Open: Mon-Fri 10-4.45 Sun 2-5.
Admission: Free.
Location: On A6.
Refreshments: The Gallery Coffee Shop.

ORDSALL HALL MUSEUM
(City of Salford)

Taylorson Street, Salford M5 3EX **Tel:** 0161-872 0251

The building reflects 600 years of architecture and social history, with Tudor Great Hall and medieval 'Star Chamber' bedroom. There is a farmhouse kitchen and regular temporary exhibitions and activities.
Open: Mon-Fri 10-12.30 and 1.30-5 Sun 2-5.
Admission: Free.
Location: Close to Salford Quays.

VIEWPOINT PHOTOGRAPHIC GALLERY
(City of Salford)

The Old Fire Station, Crescent, Salford M5 4NZ **Tel:** 0161-737 1040

The Gallery shows a wide range of exhibitions including major national and international shows in addition to thematic exhibitions which use archival material and the work of regionally based photographers.

Open: Mon-Fri 9.30-5 Sun 2-5 closed Sat.
Admission: Free.
Location: Opposite Museum & Art Gallery.
Refreshments: Available.

STALYBRIDGE

THE ASTLEY CHEETHAM ART GALLERY
(Tameside Metropolitan Borough)

Trinity Street, Stalybridge **Tel:** 0161-338 2708/3831

The Cheetham Collection of paintings; 14th century Italian paintings to Burne-Jones. Monthly exhibition programme covering fine art, craft and photography.

Open: Mon Tues Wed and Fri 1-7.30 Sat 9-4 closed Sun and Thurs.
Admission: Free.

STOCKPORT

BRAMALL HALL
(Stockport Heritage Services)

Bramhall, Stockport SKY 3NX **Tel:** 0161-485 3708 **Fax:** 0161-486 6959

Fine 14th to 16th century half-timbered Hall originally the home of the Davenport family.

Open: Apr-Sept daily 1-5 Sun 11-5 Oct-Dec 1-4 closed Mon Jan-Mar weekends only 1-4 closed Dec 25 & 26 but open Jan 1. Group visits welcome at any time but by prior arrangement please.
Admission: Adults £2.75 children/OAPs £2 family ticket (2 adults+2 children) £8 (subject to revision) group rates on request.
Location: 4m from town centre signposted on major roads.
Refreshments: Cafe and tea-room providing full range of hot and cold catering.
Exhibitions/Events: Family activities arranged for summer, Christmas and Easter periods.
Schools and organised parties all year, by appointment.

LYME HALL AND PARK
(The National Trust)

Disley, Stockport SK12 2NX **Tel:** (01663) 762023 **Fax:** (01663) 765035

Fine house dating from the 16th century, remodelled in early 18th century in Palladian style.

Open: House Apr 1-Oct 31 Sat-Wed 1.30-5 (Bank Hol Mon 11-5) **Garden** Apr 1-Oct 31 daily 11-5 Nov 6-Dec 7 Sats and Suns 12-4 **Park** daily 8.30-8.30 or dusk if earlier. Tours of house outside opening hours by arrangement. Tours of Park or Gardens by arrangement.
Admission: House and Garden £3 family £7 Garden only £1 Park only £3 per car.
Location: Entrance on A6. 6.5 miles SE of Stockport, 9 miles NW of Buxton.
Refreshments: Tea-room open Apr 1- Oct 31. Light lunches and teas in the Servants Hall Sat-Wed 12-5. Lakeside Coffee Shop. For winter opening Tel (01663) 766492. Highchair available.
Extensive gardens and 1,320 acre park. Tea-room and Shop accessible for disabled and limited access to parts of Hall and Garden: prior arrangement advisable. Extensive education opportunities in House and Park. Children's Playground. No dogs in Garden and to be kept under close control in Park.

STOCKPORT ART GALLERY

War Memorial Building, Wellington Road South, Stockport SK3 8AB
Tel: 0161-474 4453 **Fax:** 0161-480 4960

Changing exhibitions of contemporary art, photography and craft with emphasis on complementary events - practical workshops for children and adults, lectures etc. 'Artlink' scheme for purchasing or borrowing contemporary works of art including paintings, sculpture, photographs and craft work. Small permanent collection of 19th and 20th century British paintings.

Open: Mon-Fri 11-5 (Wed 11-7) Sat 10-5 closed Sun. Schools and organised parties all year by appointment.
Admission: Free.
Location: 5 mins walk from Stockport railway and bus station.
Exhibitions/Events: Family events throughout year, especially summer period.

STOCKPORT MUSEUM
(Metropolitan Borough of Stockport)

Vernon Park, Turncroft Lane, Stockport SK1 4AR **Tel:** 0161-474 4460 **Fax:** 0161-474 4449

Displays on the history of Stockport from Pre-historic times to the present, and the 'Green Gallery' - a display on the local environment.

Open: Apr-Oct daily 1-5 Nov-Mar Sat and Sun only 1-5 open Bank Holiday Mons.
Admission: Free.
Location: 1m from town centre -follow signposts.
Refreshments: Tea-room providing light snacks and refreshments.
Exhibitions/Events: Family activities arranged for summer, Christmas and Easter.
Schools and organised parties all year, by appointment. Tours of Stockport's unique system of underground World War II air raid shelters by arrangement. Telephone for details.

WIGAN

WIGAN PIER
(Wigan Metropolitan Borough Council)
Wigan Pier, Wigan WN3 4EU **Tel:** (01942) 323666 **Fax:** (01942) 323666
Step back in time and live the life of 1900. Experience live theatre through the actors bringing history to life. Shop in the market, work down the mine, drink in the pub, go to school, journey to Blackpool - all without leaving Wigan! At Trencherfield Mill marvel at what is probably the largest working mill steam engine in the world. See the working mill, colliery and ropemaking machinery.
Open: Phone for details.
Admission: Generous group discounts.
Location: Close to M6, M61 and two mainline railways.
Refreshments: Cafe, pub, restaurant.
Exhibitions/Events: Phone for details.
Other attractions include gift shop, concert, conference and exhibition hall, water-buses. Full education service and new this year is the 'Palace of Varieties' Victorian Music Hall. Magic Lantern Show featuring 'The Wigan Pier Story'. Free parking. Accessible to disabled persons. Phone for further information.

MERSEYSIDE

BIRKENHEAD

BIRKENHEAD PRIORY
(Wirral Metropolitan Borough Council)
Priory Street, Birkenhead LH41 5JH **Tel:** 0151-666 1249
Remains of Benedictine Monastery established 1150 AD.
Open: Tues-Sat 10.30-1.30 and 2-5 Sun 2-5 open Bank Holidays.
Admission: Free.
Newly restored refectory available as a conference facility.

HISTORIC WARSHIPS
Birkenhead L41 1DJ **Tel:** 0151-650 1573 **Fax:** 0151-650 1473
The Submarine ONYX and Frigate PLYMOUTH are both Falklands Veteran Warships, now on public display for you to explore -whatever the weather! It's unique!
Open: From 10 seven days a week throughout the year.
Admission: Fee charged.
Location: Close by first motorway exit from Mersey (Wallasey) Tunnel from Liverpool 200 yards. AA signs.
Refreshments: Available.

HISTORIC WARSHIPS AT BIRKENHEAD
(Wirral Metropolitan Borough Council)
West Quay Dock, Dock Road, Birkenhead **Tel:** 0151-650 1573 **Fax:** 0151-650 1473
Floating museum comprising two historic Falklands veterans, the frigate HMS Plymouth. the ship that led the battle fleet into San Carlos waters, and the hunter-killer submarine, HMS Onyx, the only conventional sumarine to serve in the South Atlantic, built at the famous Cammell Larid shipyard in Birkenhead.
Open: Sept-Mar 10-4 (last entry) Apr-June 10-5 (last entry) July-Aug 10-6 (last entry).
Admission: Adults £4 children/OAPs £2 family ticket £10 Sat/Sun children/OAPs £2.50 also includes former Mersey Bar Lightship.
Refreshments: Available.
Car parking. Parties welcome by prior arrangement.

SHORE ROAD PUMPING STATION
(Wirral Metropolitan Borough Council)
Shore Road near Woodside, Birkenhead L41 6DN **Tel:** 0151-650 1182
Home of the giant restored steam engine - 'The Giant Grasshopper' and Victorian street scene.
Open: Tues-Sat 10.30-1.30 2-5 Sun 2-5 open Bank Holidays.
Admission: Fee charged.

ST. MARY'S TOWER
Priory Street, Birkenhead **Tel:** 0151-666 1249
Tower of the 1st Parish Church of Birkenhead restored with original Knox bell and clock.
Open: Tues-Sun 2-5 open Bank Holidays.

WILLIAMSON ART GALLERY & MUSEUM
(Wirral Metropolitan Borough Council)
Slatey Road, Birkenhead L43 4UE **Tel:** 0151-652 4177 **Fax:** 0151-670 0253
Fourteen galleries display valuable collections of British watercolours, British oil paintings including artists of the Liverpool School, Liverpool porcelain, Birkenhead Della Robbia Pottery. Museum displays include maritime and local history. Temporary exhibition programme presents constantly changing displays of all types.
Open: Tues 10-5 Sun 2-5 closed Good Fri and Christmas Day.
Admission: Free.
Car parking. Suitable for disabled persons. One wheelchair available.

WOODSIDE VISITOR CENTRE
(Wirral Metropolitan Borough Council)
Woodside, Birkenhead L41 6DU **Tel:** 0151-647 6780 **Fax:** 0151-666 2448
Open: Mon-Sun 11-5.
Refreshments: Available.
Information Office. Metropolitan Borough of Wirral, Department of Leisure Services and Tourism, Tel: 0151-647 2366.

LIVERPOOL

LIVERPOOL MUSEUM
(National Museums and Galleries on Merseyside)
William Brown Street, Liverpool L3 8EN **Tel:** 0151-207 0001 **Fax:** 0151-478 4390
One of Britain's finest museums with collections from all over the World, from the wonders of the Amazonian rain forests to outer space. Located in the centre of the city, the Liverpool Museum contains over a million specimens. Outstanding items on display include Egyptian mummies, masks, weapons, classical sculpture and land transport exhibits. The Museum also contains a Planetarium, Aquarium, Vivarium and an award-winning Natural History Centre. Major exhibitions are shown on the ground floor.
Open: Mon-Sat 10-5 Sun 12-5 closed Christmas Eve Christmas Day Boxing Day New Year's Day and Good Friday.
Admission: Free - a small charge is made for the Planetarium and major exhibitions.
Refreshments: A coffee bar serving hot and cold snacks, is open 7 days a week, and special facilities are available for educational groups.

MERSEYSIDE MARITIME MUSEUM
(National Museums and Galleries on Merseyside)
Albert Dock, Liverpool L3 4AA **Tel:** 0151-207 0001 **Fax:** 0151-478 4590
Award-winning museum combining craft demonstrations, working displays and permanent galleries. The museum traces the history of the port and includes permanent displays on the Battle of the Atlantic Gallery, World of Models, Emigrants to a new World and the Titanic and Lusitania. Situated within the museum is Anything to Declare? HM Customs and Excise National Museum. Visitors experience through interactive hands-on displays the activities of Customs Officers today, including concealed goods, drug smuggling, control of endangered species, VAT and the collection of duties.
Open: Daily 10.30-5.30 (last ticket sold at 4.30) closed Dec 24 25 26 Jan 1 and Good Friday.
Admission: Fee charged joint ticket allows admission into Museum of Liverpool Life.
Refreshments: The Museum has a restaurant and Waterfront Cafe.
Gift shop and car parking facilities.

MUSEUM OF LIVERPOOL LIFE
(National Museums and Galleries on Merseyside)
Mann Island, Liverpool L3 4AQ **Tel:** 0151-207 0001
Exploring the history of Liverpool, its people and their contribution to national life, the museum focuses on three themes - Mersey Culture, Making a Living and Demanding a Voice.
Open: Daily 10.30-5.30 (last ticket 4.30) closed Dec 24 25 26 Jan 1 and Good Fri.
Admission: Joint ticket with Merseyside Maritime Museum.

SUDLEY HOUSE
(National Museums and Galleries on Merseyside)
Mossley Hill Road, Liverpool L18 5BX **Tel:** 0151-724 3245
Sudley, a fine house overlooking the Mersey, was formerly the home of a wealthy 19th century shipowner who bought paintings of the taste of that period. On display is a fine collection of late 18th and 19th century British paintings including Turner, Bonnington, Cox, Copley, Fielding and Landseer.
Open: Mon-Sat 10-5 Sun 12-5 Sudley Tea-rooms open Sat and Bank Hols 10-4.30 Sun 12-4.30 closed Dec 24 25 26 Jan 1 and Good Friday.
Admission: Free.

TATE GALLERY LIVERPOOL

Albert Dock, Liverpool L3 4BB **Tel:** 0151-709 3223 Information line 0151-709 0507 **Fax:** 0151-709 3122

Opened in May 1988 by His Royal Highness The Prince of Wales, Tate Gallery Liverpool offers a unique opportunity to see the best of the National Collection of twentieth century art. The Gallery, a converted Victorian warehouse, has a changing programme of displays, providing visitors with a rare opportunity to see international exhibitions not previously seen outside London.
Open: Tues-Sun 10-6 closed Mon but open Bank Holidays.
Admission: Free except for special loan exhibitions adults £2.50 concessions £1.
Location: Albert Dock.
Refreshments: Licenced coffee shop, serving hot and cold food.

UNIVERSITY OF LIVERPOOL ART GALLERY

3 Abercromby Square, Liverpool L69 3BX **Tel:** 0151-794 2347/8 **Fax:** 0151-708 6502

The Gallery contains a selection from the University's collections: sculpture; paintings, including works by Audubon and Wright of Derby; watercolours, including works by Turner; contemporary prints; furniture; porcelain and silver.
Open: Mon Tues and Thurs 12-2 Wed and Fri 12-4 or by appointment closed Public Hols and Aug.
Admission: Free.
Refreshments: Available in University Precinct.

WALKER ART GALLERY

(National Museums and Galleries on Merseyside)

William Brown Street, Liverpool L3 8EL **Tel:** 0151-207 0001 **Fax:** 0151-478 4190

One of the finest galleries in Europe with outstanding collections of European art from 1300 to the present day. The gallery is especially rich in European old masters by Rubens, Rembrandt and Poussin. The French impressionists include Monet, Seurat and Degas. Recent refurbishment's include the Eighteenth Century and High Victorian Galleries.
Open: Mon-Sat 10-5 Sun 12-5 closed Dec 24 25 26 Jan 1 and Good Fri.
Refreshments: Tea-room.
Baby change facilities. Disabled access.

PORT SUNLIGHT

LADY LEVER ART GALLERY

(National Museums and Galleries on Merseyside)

Port Sunlight Village, Wirral L62 5EQ **Tel:** 0151-645 3623 **Fax:** 0151-643 1694

An outstanding collection of English 18th century paintings and furniture, Chinese porcelain, Wedgwood pottery and Victorian paintings, formed by the first Viscount Leverhulme at the turn of the century as the centrepiece of his model village, Port Sunlight. Of special note is the series of superb carved and inlaid cabinets, some by Chippendale, and paintings by Reynolds, Wilson, Sargent, Burne-Jones and Leighton.
Open: Mon-Sat 10-5 Sun 12-5 closed Dec 24 25 26 Jan 1 and Good Friday.
Refreshments: Restaurant.

PRESCOT

PRESCOT MUSEUM OF CLOCK AND WATCH-MAKING

(Knowsley Borough Council in conjunction with National Museums & Galleries Merseyside)

34 Church Street, Prescot L34 3LA **Tel:** 0151-430 7787 **Fax:** 0151-430 7219

Open: Tue-Sat 10-5 Sun 2-5 open Bank Holiday Mon 10-5 closed Christmas Day Boxing Day New Year's Day and Good Friday.
Admission: Free.

ST. HELENS

PILKINGTON GLASS MUSEUM

(Pilkington P.L.C.)

Prescot Road, St. Helens WA10 3TT **Tel:** (01744) 692014 **Fax:** (01744) 692080

Evolution of glassmaking techniques. A rare vessel glass collection. Glass in buildings, transport, optics and science.
Open: Mon-Fri 10-5 evenings for groups by appointment Sat Sun and Bank Hols 2-4.30 closed Christmas to New Year.
Admission: Free.
Location: A58 one mile from town centre.
Exhibitions/Events: Full exhibition programme.
Schools and organised parties by prior arrangement with the Curator.

SOUTHPORT

ATKINSON ART GALLERY

(Merseyside-Sefton Borough Council)

Lord Street, Southport **Tel:** (01704) 533133 Ext 2110

Permanent collections include British art of the 18th, 19th and 20th centuries. Oils, watercolours and sculpture. Contemporary prints. Old English glass and Chinese porcelain. Continuous programme of temporary exhibitions.
Open: Mon Tues Wed and Fri 10-5 Thurs and Sat 10-1.
Admission: Free.

BOTANIC GARDENS MUSEUM

(Merseyside-Sefton Borough Council)

Churchtown, Southport **Tel:** (01704) 27547

A small museum with interesting displays of local history (The Growth of Southport), natural history, Victoriana, dolls and Liverpool porcelain.
Open: All year Tues-Fri 11-3 Sat and Sun 2-5 closed Mon (open Bank Hol Mons but closed Fri following).
Admission: Free.

NORFOLK

BRESSINGHAM

BRESSINGHAM STEAM MUSEUM AND GARDENS

(Bressingham Steam Preservation Co. Ltd)

Bressingham, Diss Norfolk IP22 2AB **Tel:** (01379 88) 386 and 382 (24 hr recorded info line) **Fax:** (01379 88) 8085

Live Steam Museum. Hundreds of steam related exhibits including the world famous 'Royal Scot' locomotive. Fire Museum, Victorian steam roundabout, daily train rides, beautiful 6 acre Dell garden, adjacent plant centre.
Open: 1 April-31 Oct 10-5.30 services vary according to programme.
Admission: On application.
Location: 2.5 miles west of Diss on the A1066.
Refreshments: Bressingham Butler restaurant and Bressingham Picnic Pantry.
Exhibitions/Events: The Museum operates a varied week-end events programme during its main open season. Provisionally Registered Museum.

CROMER

THE CROMER MUSEUM

(Norfolk Museums Service)

East Cottages, Tucker Street, Cromer NR27 9HB **Tel:** (01263) 513543

Row of cottages with displays about the people, natural history and geology of the area. Furnished 1890's home of local fishing people.
Open: Mon-Sat 10-5 Sun 2-5 closed Mon 1-2.
Admission: Adults £1 special concessions 60p children 50p.

FAKENHAM

THE THURSFORD COLLECTION

(J.R. Cushing)

Thursford Fakenham NR21 0AS **Tel:** (01328) 878477 **Fax:** (01328) 878415

Live musical shows each day from nine mechanical organs and one Wurlitzer cinema organ; there are road rollers, showmen's engines, traction engines, barn/oil engines, and a Savage Venetian Gondola switchback ride.
Open: Apr 1-Oct 31 1-5 June July and Aug 11-5 Christmas as per programme during Dec.
Admission: Adults £4.35 children £1.95 OAPs £3.95.
Location: One mile off A148 Fakenham/Holt.
Refreshments: Self-service hot meals and light snacks.
Free car parking. Suitable for disabled persons. Small Norfolk village of gift shops.

GREAT YARMOUTH

ELIZABETHAN HOUSE MUSEUM
(Norfolk Museums Service)
4 South Quay, Great Yarmouth NR30 2QH **Tel:** (01493) 855746
16th century merchant's house with period rooms including Victorian kitchen and scullery.
Open: Easter fortnight Mon-Fri 10-5 Sun 2-5 closed Good Friday. Sun before Whit-end Sept Sun-Fri 10-5
Admission: Joint ticket allows free admission to Tolhouse and Maritime Museum adult £1 concession 60p children 50p
Location: Soull Quay

EXHIBITION GALLERIES
(Norfolk Museums Service)
Central Library, Tolhouse Street, Great Yarmouth NR30 2SH **Tel:** (01493) 858900
Travelling and local exhibitions.
Open: During exhibitions enquire for details.
Admission: Free.
Location: Central library, Tolhouse Street.

MARITIME MUSEUM FOR EAST ANGLIA
(Norfolk Museums Service)
Marine Parade, Great Yarmouth NR30 2EN **Tel:** (01493) 842267
Once a home for shipwrecked sailors, now a museum with displays which include wrecks and rescues, herring fishing and artefacts associated with Nelson.
Open: Easter fortnight Mon-Fri 10-5 Sun 2-5 closed Good Friday. Sun before Whit-end Sept Sun-Fri 10-5.
Admission: Joint tickets allow free admission to Elizabethan House and Tolhouse adults £1 concessions 60p children 50p.
Location: Marine parade.

NELSON'S MONUMENT
(Norfolk Museums Service)
South Beach Parade, Great Yarmouth **Tel:** (01493) 858900
217 steps to the top of 144ft. Monument erected in 1819 as a memorial to Nelson.
Open: July 2-Aug 27 Sun only 2-5 Oct 21 2-5.
Admission: Adults 50p concessions 40p children 30p.
Location: South Bead Parade, Great Yarmouth.
Refreshments: No.
Panoramic views of Great Yarmouth from top.

OLD MERCHANT'S HOUSE, ROW 111 HOUSES AND GREYFRIARS' CLOISTERS
(English Heritage)
Great Yarmouth **Tel:** (01493) 857900
Two 17th Century town houses of a type unique to Great Yarmouth, containing original fixtures and displays of local architectural fittings salvaged from bombing in 1942-43.
Open: (Entry by tour only) Apr 1-Sept 30 daily 10-6.
Admission: Adults £1.25 concessions 95p children 60p (1994 prices).

THE TOLHOUSE MUSEUM AND BRASS RUBBING CENTRE
(Norfolk Museums Service)
Tolhouse Street, Great Yarmouth NR30 2SQ **Tel:** (01493) 858900
Yarmouth's oldest civic building which once served as courtroom and town gaol. Dungeons with their originals cells. Local history museum and brass rubbing centre.
Open: Easter fortnight Mon-Fri 10-5 Sun 2-5 closed Good Friday. Sun before Whit-end Sept Sun-Fri 10-5.
Admission: Adult 50p concession 40p child 30p or joint ticket which allows free admission to Maritime Museum and Elizabethan House adult £1 concession 60p children 50p.

GRESSENHALL

NORFOLK RURAL LIFE MUSEUM AND UNION FARM
(Norfolk Museums Service)
Beech House, Gressenhall, Dereham NR20 4DR **Tel:** (01362) 860563
Displays illustrating history of the County of Norfolk over the past 200 years housed in 1777 Union Workhouse. Reconstructed village shop, saddlers, wheelwrights and basket makers' workshops; farmworker's home and garden. Union Farm is a working 1920s farm.
Open: Sun before Easter-last Sun in Oct.
Admission: Adults £3.50 concessions £2.50 children £1.50.
Location: 2m NW of Deneham off B1145.
Refreshments: Tea-room.
Exhibitions/Events: Programme available.

KING'S LYNN

THE LYNN MUSEUM
(Norfolk Museums Service)
Old Market Street, King's Lynn PE30 1NL **Tel:** (01553) 775001
Natural history, archaeology and local history relating to NW Norfolk.
Open: Mon-Sat 10-5 closed Sun & Bank Hols.
Admission: Adults 60p concessions 40p children 30p.

THE TOWN HOUSE - MUSEUM OF LYNN LIFE
46 Queen Street, King's Lynn PE30 5DQ **Tel:** (01553) 773450
Museum opened in 1992 which illustrates the history of King's Lynn. Historic room displays including costume, toys, a working Victorian kitchen and a 1950s living room.
Open: Summer Tues-Sat 10-6 Sun 2-5 Winter Tue-Sat 10-5.
Admission: Adults £1 concessions 60p children 50p.

NORWICH

BRIDEWELL MUSEUM OF LOCAL INDUSTRIES
(Norfolk Museums Service)
Bridewell Alley, Norwich NR2 1AQ **Tel:** (01603) 667228 **Fax:** (01603) 765651
Exhibits illustrating Norwich Trades, industries and aspects of city life.
Open: 10-5 Mon-Sat.
Admission: Adults £1.40 children 70p concessions £1.20.
Location: Norwich City Centre.

NORWICH CASTLE MUSEUM
(Norfolk Museums Service)
Norwich **Tel:** (01603) 223624 **Fax:** (01603) 765651

Large collections of art (particularly of the Norwich School), local archaeology and natural history (Norfolk Room dioramas), social history and ceramic display. Important loan exhibitions.

ROYAL NORFOLK REGIMENTAL MUSEUM

(Norfolk Museums Service)

Shirehall, Market Ave, Norwich NR1 3JQ **Tel:** (01603) 223649 **Fax:** (01603) 765651

A museum displaying the history of the Royal Norfolk Regiment since 1685.
Open: Mon-Sat 10-5 Sun 2-5.
Admission: Adults £1.40 children 70p concessions £1.20.
Location: Norwich City Centre.

SAINSBURY CENTRE FOR VISUAL ARTS

University of East Anglia, Watton Road, Norwich NR4 7TJ **Tel:** (01603) 592470 (office hours) (01603) 56060 (24 hrs) **Fax:** (01603) 259401

The Robert and Lisa Sainsbury Collection is wide-ranging, remarkable and of international importance. With the recent addition of Sir Norman Foster and Partners' superb new Crescent Wing seven hundred paintings, sculptures and ceramics are on permanent display with Picasso, Moore, Bacon and Giacometti shown alongside art from Africa, the Pacific and the Americas. The Centre also houses the Anderson Collection of Art Nouveau. Three special exhibitions a year.
Open: Galleries open daily (except Mon) 12-5.
Admission: Adults £1 concessions 50p.
Refreshments: Restaurant buffet and coffee bar.
Accessible to disabled people.

ST. PETER HUNGATE CHURCH MUSEUM

(Norfolk Museums Service)

Princes Street, Norwich NR3 1AE **Tel:** (01603) 667231 **Fax:** (01603) 765651

15th century church used for display of ecclesiastical art and parish life in Norfolk.
Open: 10-5 Mon-Sat.
Admission: Adults 50p children 30p concessions 40p.
Location: Norwich City Centre.

STRANGERS' HALL

(Norfolk Museums Service)

Charing Cross, Norwich NR2 4AL **Tel:** (01603) 667229 **Fax:** (01603) 765651

Late medieval mansion furnished as a museum of urban domestic life 16th-19th centuries.
Open: Mon-Sat 10-5.
Admission: Adults £1.40 children 70p concessions £1.20.
Location: Norwich City Centre.

THETFORD

THE ANCIENT HOUSE MUSEUM

(Norfolk Museums Service)

White Hart Street, Thetford IP24 1AA **Tel:** (01842) 752599

Early Tudor half-timbered house with collections illustrating Thetford and Breckland life, history and natural history.
Open: 10-5 Mon-Sat all year 2-5 Sun 28 May-24 Sept.
Admission: Free except Aug adults 60p children 30p OAPs 40p.
Location: White Hart Street, Thetford, Norfolk.
Refreshments: Not available in Museum (coffee shops/hotels nearby).
Exhibitions/Events: Temporary exhibitions about locality; holiday activity days for families.

WALSINGHAM

SHIREHALL MUSEUM

(Norfolk Museums Service)

Common Place, Little Walsingham NR22 6BP **Tel:** (01263) 513543 or (01328) 820510

The principal exhibit is the Georgian court room which may be seen with its original fittings including the prisoners' lock-up. The museum contains many items illustrating the history of Walsingham including a display on the history of pilgrimage.
Open: 10-5 Mon-Sat 2-5 Sun closed (lunch) Mon 1-2

WELLS-NEXT-THE-SEA

BYGONES AT HOLKHAM

Holkham Park, Wells-next-the-Sea **Tel:** (01328) 710806/710277

BYGONES
AT HOLKHAM
A unique and comprehensive collection of Victorian and Edwardian agricultural and domestic items displayed in the restored 19th century stables adjacent to Holkham Hall in Holkham Park.
EXHIBITIONS INCLUDE: Craft Tools, Cars, Carriages, Fire Engines, Sewing Machines, a Working Pump Room. Laundry, Victorian Cottage Kitchen, Brewery, Dairy, Harness Room, Engineerium, New History of Farming Display.
ALSO: Holkham Hall, Holkham Pottery, Holkham Garden Centre, Teas in a modern complex adjoining the Bygones Collection, Lake Cruises, Gift Shops.
Holkham Park, Wells next the Sea, Norfolk.
On the A149: Fakenham 8 miles, King's Lynn 30 miles, Norwich 34 miles.

A unique and comprehensive collection of the Victorian and Edwardian era. Housed in the magnificent 19th century stable buildings in Holkham Park the exhibition includes: Fire Engines, Vintage Cars, Craft Tools, Victorian Kitchen, Laundry, Dairy, Gramophones & Television, Cobblers shop, Engineerium, Carriages, Steam Engines & Models, Medical & Veterinary items.
Open: May 30-Sept 30 daily except Fri and Sat 1.30-5 during Easter May Spring and Summer Bank Holidays Sun & Mon 11.30-5.
Admission: Adults £3 children £1.50 pre-paid parties 20+ 10% reduction.
Location: On the A149: Fakenham 10 miles, King's Lynn 30 miles, Norwich 34 miles.
Refreshments: Tea-rooms.
Also visit Holkham Hall, Holkham Pottery and Holkham Garden Centre.

WELLS AND WALSINGHAM LIGHT RAILWAY

Wells-next-the-Sea NR23 1QB

The longest 10 1/4' gauge narrow gauge steam railway in the world. Unique Garratt steam loco. Daily timetable service between Wells-next-the-Sea and the historic town of Walsingham Pilgrimage Centre and shrine of'Our Lady of Walsingham'.
Open: Good Fri-end Sept every day and Norfolk school holiday in Oct.
Admission: Adult return £4 child return £3 family return (2 adults+4 children) £12. 10% reduction for parties of 15 or over.
Location: Wells-next-the-Sea.
Refreshments: Light refreshments.
Adequate free parking. Souvenirs. Talking timetable and info (0328) 856506.

NORTHAMPTONSHIRE

KETTERING

ALFRED EAST GALLERY

Sheep Street, Kettering **Tel:** (01536) 410333 Ext 381

An exciting programme of temporary exhibitions of fine art, craft and photography. Permanent collection of works by Sir Alfred East RA and Thomas Cooper Gotch on view by appointment.
Open: Mon-Sat 9.30-5.
Admission: Free.

MANOR HOUSE MUSEUM
Sheep Street, Kettering **Tel:** (01536) 410333 Ext 381
Displays reflecting the growth of the town and borough of Kettering. Regular series of temporary exhibitions with related events.
Open: Mon-Sat 9.30-5.
Admission: Free.

NORTHAMPTON

CENTRAL MUSEUM & ART GALLERY
(Northampton Borough Council)
Guildhall Road, Northampton NN1 1DP **Tel:** (01604) 39415

The largest collection of footwear in the United Kingdom! Northampton's History: Objects, sound and film combined to tell the history of the town from the Stone Age to the present. Decorative arts - outstanding Chinese and English ceramics. The Art Gallery - a fine collection of Italian 15th-18th century paintings, and British art. Special temporary exhibitions.
Open: 10-5 Mon-Sat 2-5 Sun please phone to confirm.
Admission: Free.
Refreshments: In adjacent Visitor Centre.

STOKE BRUERNE

THE CANAL MUSEUM
Stoke Bruerne **Tel:** (01604) 862229
Visit Stoke Bruerne with its famous Canal Museum and discover 200 years of colourful canal history and traditions. There are traditional 'Roses and Castles' painting demonstrations, a shop, Blisworth Tunnel, flight of seven locks, boat trips and countryside walks.
Open: Easter-Oct daily 10-6 Oct-Easter daily (except Mon) 10-4.
Admission: Fee charged.
Location: 4 miles south of J15 M1 motorway.
Refreshments: Pub, restaurants, tea rooms.

NORTHUMBERLAND

ALNWICK

ALNWICK CASTLE MUSEUM
(Duke of Northumberland)
Alnwick Castle, Alnwick NE66 1NQ **Tel:** (01665) 510777
This is one of the oldest private museums in England, open to public viewing since 1826. Prehistoric, Roman, Celtic and Viking artefacts collected by the Third and Fourth Dukes, 1817-65. Items from Pompeii and items of Percyana.
Admission: Charge for museum is included in charge for admission to Alnwick Castle. Organised party rates by arrangement.
Location: On the A1068 northern outskirts of the town.
Refreshments: Tearoom.
Free car parking at castle.

BERWICK-UPON-TWEED

BERWICK BOROUGH MUSEUM & ART GALLERY
(Berwick-upon-Tweed Borough Council)
The Clock Block, Berwick Barracks, Berwick-upon-Tweed TD15 1DQ
Tel: (01289) 330933

Situated in the first ever purpose built Barracks, come and peer through a Window on Berwick, or enter the dragon and step into Cairo Bazaar where some of the 800 pieces donated to Berwick by Sir William Burrell are displayed. The art treasures comprise 42 important paintings, including a Degas and many fine items of porcelain, glass and metalware. With a changing programme of art exhibitions, this is a most unconventional museum.
Open: Easter-Oct Mon-Sat 10-12.30 and 1.30-6 Sun 10-1 and 2-6 Oct-Easter Tues-Sat 10-12.30 and 1.30-4 Sun 10-1 and 2-4 closed Mon.
Admission: English Heritage Standard Charge and fee is for the whole Barracks complex and includes two other museums, the Kings Own Scottish Borderers Regimental museum and By Beat of Drum of which English Heritage are custodians.
Car parking. Suitable for disabled on ground floor only (no wheelchairs available).

THE CELL BLOCK MUSEUM
(Berwick-upon-Tweed Corporation (Freemen) Trustees)
The Town Hall, Marygate, Berwick-upon-Tweed **Tel:** (01289) 330900
A Georgian town hall and former town jail situated in the town centre, this magnificent building with its 150ft spire now houses the Cell Block Museum, Guild Hall, Council Chamber and Mayor's Parlour. Learn of bygone Berwick, see civic artefacts and cells in their original state and also ring out tunes on the town hall bells, the only town hall in England where this is possible. Learn the history that makes Berwick-upon-Tweed unique, sign the visitors book and find out who spent a night locked in the cells.

Open: Weekdays only Easter-end Sept closed Bank Holidays.
Admission: Adults £1 children 30p special reductions for school groups parties by arrangement.
Car parking nearby. Guided tours only at 10.30 and 2, several flights of stairs are involved.

CHESTERS

CHESTERS MUSEUM

(English Heritage)

Hadrian's Wall near Chollerford, Chesters **Tel:** (01434) 681379

Roman inscriptions, sculpture, weapons, tools and ornaments from the forts at Chesters, Carrawburgh, Housesteads, Greatchesters and Carvoran.
Open: Apr 1-Oct 1 daily 10-6 Nov 1-Mar 31 daily 10-4 closed Dec 24-26 Jan 1.
Admission: Adults £2 concessions £1.50 children £1 (1994 prices).

CORBRIDGE

CORBRIDGE ROMAN STATION

(English Heritage)

Corbridge **Tel:** (01434) 632349

Roman pottery, sculpture, inscribed stones and small objects.
Open: Apr 1-Oct 31 daily 10-6 Nov 1-Mar 31 Wed-Sun 10-4 closed Dec 24-26 Jan 1.
Admission: Adults £2 concessions £1.50 children £1 (1994 prices).

FORD & ETAL ESTATES

HEATHERSLAW CORN MILL

Cornhill-on-Tweed, Ford & Etal Estates **Tel:** (01890) 820338

A rare chance to visit a restored and working 19th Century water powered corn mill

LADY WATERFORD HALL AND MURALS

Ford Village, Berwick-upon-Tweed, Ford & Etal Estates **Tel:** (01890) 820224

A beautiful Hall and Murals by Louisa, Marchioness of Waterford.

HEXHAM

BORDER HISTORY MUSEUM

(Tynedale Council)

The Old Gaol, Hallgate, Hexham NE46 3NH **Tel:** (01434) 652349 **Fax:** (01434) 652423

Open: Every day Easter-end Oct 10-4.30 Nov & Feb Sat Sun Mon Tues 10-4.30.
Admission: Adults £1.30 children/students/OAPs/unemployed 60p.
Linked with the Border Library, Moothall.

HOUSESTEADS

HOUSESTEADS MUSEUM

(English Heritage)

Bardon Mill, Hexham, Housesteads **Tel:** (01434) 344363

Roman pottery, inscribed stones, sculpture and small objects.
Open: Apr 1-Oct 31 daily 10-6 Nov 1-Mar 31 daily 10-4 closed Dec 24-26 Jan 1.
Admission: Adults £2.20 concessions £1.65 children £1.10 (1994 prices).

LINDISFARNE

LINDISFARNE PRIORY

(English Heritage)

Holy Island, Lindisfarne **Tel:** (0128 989) 200

The fascinating story of Lindisfarne is told in an exhibition which gives an impression of life for the monks, including a reconstruction of a monk's cell. (Tide times restrict access to island).
Open: Apr 1-Oct 31 daily 10-6 Nov 1-Mar 31 daily 10-4 closed Dec 24-26 Jan 1.
Admission: Adults £2.20 concessions £1.65 children £1.10 (1994 prices).

MORPETH

MORPETH CHANTRY BAGPIPE MUSEUM

The Chantry, Bridge Street, Morpeth NE61 1PJ **Tel:** (01670) 519466

Set in a restored 13th century church building, the museum has one of the largest and best collections of its kind in the world. The infra red sound system allows each visitor (including the deaf) a unique musical experience.
Open: Mon-Sat Jan-Feb 10-4 Mar-Dec 9.30-5.30 closed Bank Holidays and between Christmas and New Year.
Admission: Adults £1 children/OAPs 50p parties £3 inc. MA free.
Location: Off A1.
Free disc parking in Morpeth.

NOTTINGHAMSHIRE

MANSFIELD

MANSFIELD MUSEUM AND ART GALLERY

(Mansfield District Council)

Leeming Street, Mansfield NG18 1NG **Tel:** (01623) 663088

Exhibitions; Images of Mansfield Past and Present; The Nature of Mansfield; William Billingsley Porcelain; Watercolours of Old Mansfield.
Open: Mon-Sat 10-5 closed Sun and Bank Hols.
Admission: Free.
Refreshments: Available in Theatre next door.

NEWARK-ON-TRENT

VINA COOKE MUSEUM OF DOLLS & BYGONE CHILDHOOD

The Old Rectory, Cromwell, Nr Newark-on-Trent NG23 6JE **Tel:** (01636) 821364

Old dolls, toys and costumes. Handmade portrait dolls.
Open: 10.30-5 daily groups by appointment.
Admission: Adults £2 children £1.
Refreshments: Shop.
Picnic area and interesting gardens. Souvenirs and crafts for sale. Car parking free. Unsuitable for disabled persons.

NOTTINGHAM

DJANOGLY ART GALLERY

The Arts Centre, University Park, University of Nottingham NG7 2RD **Tel:** (0115) 9513192 **Fax:** (0115) 9513194

The Gallery mounts temporary exhibitions of contemporary and historical art throughout the year. There is a programme of educational activities run in conjunction with the exhibitions as well as musical events, poetry readings and small-scale drama performances.
Open: Mon-Fri 10-6 Sat 11-6 Sun 2-5.
Admission: Free.
Location: South entrance of the university campus, off A6005 University Boulevard.
Refreshments: Cafe.
Bookshop. Car park, access for disabled.

THE LACE CENTRE

(The Nottingham Lace Centre Ltd)

Severns Building, Castle Road, Nottingham NG1 6AA **Tel:** (0115) 9413539

All types of lace made in the Nottingham area are displayed and may be purchased for the benefit of Tourists.
Open: Jan & Feb 10-4 Sun-Fri 10-5 Sat Mar-Dec 10-5 every day except Christmas Day and Boxing Day.
Admission: Free. Parties of up to 30 including coach parties.
Location: Castle Road at the side Nottingham Castle opposite the Robin Hoos Statue.
Refreshments: Available next door.
Disabled are catered for one at a time.

RETFORD

THE BASSETLAW MUSEUM
(Bassetlaw District Council)
Amcott House, Grove Street, Retford **Tel:** (01777) 706741
Archaeology, local history, bygones, decorative arts. Opened Dec 1986.
Open: Mon-Sat 10-5 closed Sun see also Worksop Nottinghamshire.
Admission: Free.

WORKSOP

THE HARLEY GALLERY
(The Harley Foundation)
Welbeck, Nr. Worksop S80 3LW **Tel:** (01909) 501700
A unique gallery situated in the heart of the Dukeries, built on the site of the former Welbeck Estate Gasworks, and set in a landscaped water garden. Exhibitions of contemporary arts and crafts and historic fine and decorative art.
Open: May-Oct 12-5 Fri Sat Sun and Bank Hol Mon.
Admission: £1 (subject to shange) under 5's free.
Location: 4m south of Worksop on A60.
Refreshments: Restaurant in Dukeries Garden Centre next door.
Free car parking. Suitable for disabled persons.

WORKSOP MUSEUM
(Bassetlaw District Council)
Memorial Avenue, Worksop
Items of local interest. Pilgrim Fathers' exhibition. Part of the Bassetlaw Museum (see Retford, Nottinghamshire).
Open: Mon-Wed Fri 10-5 Thurs Sat 10-1 closed Sun.
Admission: Free.

OXFORDSHIRE

ABINGDON

ABINGDON MUSEUM
(Oxfordshire County Council with Abingdon Town Council)
The County Hall, Market Place, Abdingdon **Tel:** (01235) 523703
The museum is housed in the Old County Hall, built in 1677 (to designs by Sir Christopher Kempster) when Abingdon was the county town of Berkshire. The display combines contemporary crafts with traditional craftsmanship from the town.
Open: Tues-Sun 11-5 summer 11-4 winter.
Admission: Free.
Location: Centre of town.
Shop/car park nearby.

BANBURY

BANBURY MUSEUM
(Oxfordshire County Council with Cherwell District Council)
8 Horsefair, Banbury OX16 0AA **Tel:** (01295) 259855 **Fax:** (01295) 270556
The museum overlooks Banbury Cross, and is housed in the old boardroom of the Poor Law Guardians. There is an exciting programme for the temporary exhibition gallery. The comprehensive collection of photographs and glass plate negatives of the region can be viewed on microfiche by appointment with the Senior Museum Officer, who welcomes enquiries and the opportunity to identify local finds.
Open: Apr-Sept Mon-Sat 10-5 Oct-Mar Tues-Sat 10-4.30.
Admission: Free.
Refreshments: Available.
Shop, guided tours by arrangement. Tourist Information Centre, toilets, car park nearby. Access for the disabled.

DIDCOT

DIDCOT RAILWAY CENTRE
(Great Western Society Ltd)
Didcot OX11 7NJ **Tel:** (01235) 817200
Re-creating the Golden Age of the Great Western Railway. Steam trains in the engine shed, reconstructed station, Brunel broadgauge demonstration. Train rides on steaming days. Small exhibits museum.
Open: All year Sat Sun and Bank Hols (not Christmas or Boxing Day) 11-5 also daily Easter-end Sept. Steaming Days first and last Sun each month from Mar, Bank Hols and all Suns June-Aug also Weds during Aug.
Admission: £3-£5 depending on event.
Location: Didcot Parkway BR Station (Signed from M4 junc.13 & A34).
Refreshments: Meals, snacks and drinks.
Car parking. Souvenir shop. General Manager: M. Dean.

OXFORD

THE ASHMOLEAN MUSEUM OF ART AND ARCHAEOLOGY
Beaumont Street, Oxford OX1 2PH **Tel:** (01865) 278000 **Fax:** (01865) 278018
British, European, Mediterranean, Egyptian and Near Eastern archaeology. Italian, Dutch, Flemish, French and English oil paintings; Old Master and modern drawings, watercolours and prints; miniatures; European ceramics; sculpture and bronzes; English silver; objects of applied art. Coins and medals of all countries and periods. Casts from the antique. Chinese and Japanese porcelain, painting and lacquer. Chinese bronzes, Tibetan art, Indian sculpture and painting, Islamic pottery and metalwork.

Open: Tues-Sat 10-4 Sun 2-4 closed Mons, St.Giles Fair in Sept and a period over Christmas the New Year and Easter. Open Bank Hol Mons and Easter-late summer 2-5.
Admission: Free.
Location: Oxford City Centre.
Exhibitions/Events: Wood engraving here and now (May-Aug 1995); Dutch and Flemish drawings from Windsor Castle (Aug-Oct 1995)
Guided tours available. Education Service, temporary exhibition programme. School and adult party advanced bookings (0865) 278015. Gift shop.

CHRIST CHURCH LIBRARY
Peckwater Quadrangle, Oxford OX1 1DP **Tel:** (01865) 276169 **Fax:** (01865) 276276
Statuary, Carrolliana, manuscripts and printed books.
Open: Mon-Fri (by special appointment only).

CHRIST CHURCH PICTURE GALLERY
Oxford 0X1 1DP **Tel:** (01865) 276172 and 286320 **Fax:** (01865) 202429
Important Old Master paintings and drawings.
Open: Mon-Sat 10.30-1 and 2-4.30 or 5.30 Easter-end Sept Sun 2-4.30 or 5.30 Easter-end Sept closed for one week at Christmas and Easter.
Admission: Adults £1 children 50p reduced rates for parties by arrangement.
Location: Enter by Canterbury Gate.
Free guided tours of the collections each Thurs 2.15-3.

MUSEUM OF OXFORD
(Oxfordshire County Council)
St. Aldates, Oxford **Tel:** (01865) 815559

The museum tells the story of the City and the University: history, archaeology, architecture and environment, and is the starting point for anyone who wants to learn more about Oxford. Situated opposite the Information Centre, it is housed in the historic Town Hall, also the meeting point for Oxford Walking Tours. In addition to ancient, medieval and later objects, there are maps, plans, many excellent models and reconstructed Oxford interiors from the 16th century to the present day.
Open: Tues-Sat 10-5.
Admission: Free.
Shop/guided tours of Castle Mound.

THE OXFORD STORY
(Heritage Projects Oxford Ltd)
Broad Street, Oxford OX1 3AJ **Tel:** (01865) 728822 **Fax:** (01865) 791716

The Oxford Story - a brilliantly imaginative presentation of key aspects of The University's story, devised in partnership with the University. The Oxford Story skillfully blends scholarship, technology and audio-visual techniques to bring the University's past to life. From your moving scholar's desk you experience eight centuries of the sights, sounds and personalities encountered by Oxford students. Witness great events, the Martyrdom of Cranmer in Broad Street, the University as a seat of the Royalist cause during the Civil War and the creation of *Alice's Adventures* by Oxford Don, Lewis Carroll. Above all you encounter great men and women who shaped both the University and the world.
Open: Daily (except Christmas Day).
Admission: Adults £4.50 children £3.25 OAPs/students/family and group reductions available all year.
Location: Central Oxford.
Exhibitions/Events: Please contact for details.
Parties are advised to book in advance. Gift shop.

OXFORD UNIVERSITY MUSEUM
Parks Road, Oxford OX1 3PW **Tel:** (01865) 272950 information line (01865) 270949 **Fax:** (01865) 272970
The museum in its high-Victorian Gothic building makes freely available to the public the University's very extensive natural history collections which inlude the remains of the Dodo, fossil dinosaur material and the historic collections donated by scientists such as Darwin, Burchall and Hope. The collections are displayed in the vast glass-roofed Museum Court whose wrought-iron arches forming branches and leaves, and carved stone capitals depicting birds, animals and plants, show the influence of John Ruskin.
Open: Mon-Sat 12-5 (opening times change at Easter and Christmas).
Admission: Free (donations box to provide facilities for people with disabilities)
Exhibitions/Events: 16 Feb-30 March - Bats.
New enfomological displays now open.

THE PITT RIVERS MUSEUM
Parks Road (entrance through University Museum), Oxford OX1 3PP **Tel:** (01865) 270949 Information line **Fax:** (01865) 270943
World famous museum of anthropology with a unique Victorian atmosphere. Audio tour provided by Sir David Attenborough. At the Balfour Building, 60 Banbury Road, displays on music making and hunter-gatherer societies.
Open: Mon-Sat 1-4.30 closed for a period over Christmas the New Year and Easter.
Admission: Free.
Education Service (0865) 270927. Temporary exhibition programme. Gift shop.

SWALCLIFFE

SWALCLIFFE BARN
(Oxfordshire County Council)
Swalcliffe, nr Banbury **Tel:** (01295) 788278 or 78562 Schools Contact Sibford Gower School (01295) 78270
Known locally as the Tythe Barn, Swalcliffe Barn was built for the Rectorial Manor of Swalcliffe by New College, who owned the manor. Constructed between 1400 and 1409, it is one of the dozen best barns in the country, with much of its medieval timber half-cruck roof intact. The Oxfordshire Building Trust owns it and repaired it with a grant from English Heritage. Oxfordshire County Museums lease the barn as 'display storage' and visitors may see some of the collection of agricultural and trade vehicles.
Open: Easter Sun & Mon 2-5 Suns in May & Sept 2-5 Sat & Sun in June July & Aug Bank Hol Mons May & Aug 2-5. Other times and from Oct-Mar by arrangement in advance with the Swalcliffe Society (see above) or Oxfordshire County Museum (0993) 811456.
Admission: Free.
Disabled access; toilet.

WANTAGE

VALE AND DOWNLAND MUSEUM CENTRE
(Oxfordshire County Council with the Vale and Downland Museum Trust)
The Old Surgery, Church Street, Wantage OX12 8BL **Tel:** (01235) 771447 **Fax:** (01235) 74316
Housed in a converted 16/17th century cloth merchant's house with modern extensions and a reconstructed barn, the museum has permanent displays showing the geology, local history and archaeology of Wantage and the Vale of the White Horse, and a programme of temporary exhibitions. Local community groups are invited to exhibit on local issues. As a branch museum of the County service, schools are warmly invited to use the museum and education room.
Open: Tues-Sat 10.30-4.30 Sun 2.30-5.
Admission: Free.
Location: Town Centre.
Refreshments: Available.
Contact the curator or the education officer, County Museum, Woodstock. Car park nearby. Shop, access for the disabled, picnic area, guided tours on request, toilets .

WITNEY

COGGES MANOR FARM MUSEUM
(Oxfordshire County Council)
Church Lane, Cogges, Witney **Tel:** (01993) 772602
The manor house and farm buildings close to the church and the river are an open-air museum of farming and the history of Cogges over 1,000 years. The house, dairy, farm buildings, walled garden and orchard show life at the turn of the century, with daily demonstrations. New exhibition on Witney Blanket Industry.
Open: Apr-Oct Tues-Fri Bank Hol Mon 10.30-5.30 Sat and Sun 12-5.30 closes at 4.30 from Oct.
Admission: Fee charged.
Location: Just off A40 Oxford - Burford Road.
Refreshments: Available.
Exhibitions/Events: Farming and demonstrations throughout the season.
Special rates for parties. Season tickets. Shop, car park.

COMBE MILL BEAM ENGINE AND WORKING MUSEUM
(An Independent Museum)
Witney, Nr. Long Handborough OX8 8JZ **Tel:** (01993) 891785
19th century sawmill, featuring: a restored beam and two smaller steam engines, a working forge and a display of 19th century artifacts.
Open: In steam third Sun in May (15) Aug (21) and Oct (16) 10-5.
Admission: Adults £1 children/OAPs 50p.
Free parking, riverside picnic area.

WOODSTOCK

OXFORDSHIRE COUNTY MUSEUM
(Oxfordshire County Council, Department of Leisure and Arts)
Fletcher's House, Woodstock OX20 1SN **Tel:** (01993) 811456 **Fax:** (01993) 813239
The County Museum, in a fine town house with a pleasant garden, has permanent display galleries which tell the story of Oxfordshire - its people, buildings and landscapes, from early times to the present day, and a changing programme of temporary exhibitions.
Open: May-Sept Tues-Fri 10-5 Sat 10-5 Sun 2-5 Oct-Apr Tues-Fri 10-4 Sat 10-5 Sun 2-5.
Admission: Free.
Location: In the centre of the town opposite the Church.
Refreshments: Available.
Car park nearby. Shop, picnic area, guided tours by arrangement, toilets.

SHROPSHIRE

ACTON SCOTT

ACTON SCOTT HISTORIC WORKING FARM
(Shropshire County Council)
Wenlock Lodge, Acton Scott, Nr Church Stretton SY6 6QN **Tel:** (01694) 781306/7
A working farm museum using heavy horses and machinery to demonstrate agriculture as it was at about the turn of the century. Crafts demonstrated regularly, programmes available on application. New Education room available, changing exhibition programme.
Open: Apr-Nov daily except Mons but open Bank Holiday Mons.
Admission: Fee charged.
Refreshments: Cafe.
Car park, picnic area, shops. Suitable for disabled visitors.

BRIDGNORTH

DANIEL'S MILL
Eardington, Bridgnorth WV16 5JL **Tel:** (01746) 762753
A picturesque working cornmill with impressive 38 foot cast iron waterwheel millstones producing traditional 100% wholemeal flour. Family owned for over 200 years. Lovingly restored. Guided tours for all visitors.
Open: Easter-end Sept Wed Sat Sun 2-6 Bank Hol Mons 11-6. Groups at all other times by prior arrangement.

MUCH WENLOCK

MUCH WENLOCK MUSEUM
(Shropshire County Council)
High Street, Much Wenlock **Tel:** (01952) 727773
Displays on local history including the Wenlock Olympics, home of the modern Olympic movement. New display 'On Wenlock Edge' features the geology, natural history and industrial history of this important local landscape.
Open: Apr-end Sept Mon-Sat June-Aug daily.
Admission: 50p entrance (adults only).
Exhibitions/Events: Geology 'hands on' sesions can be arranged by appointment.
Suitable for disabled visitors.

SHIFNAL

THE AEROSPACE MUSEUM
(Mr J Francis)
Cosford, Shifnal TF11 8UP **Tel:** (01902) 374112/374872 **Fax:** (01902) 374813
Aviation Museum 1) The Missile Collection 2) The Warplane Collection 3) The Transport Aircraft Collection 4) The Research and Development Aircraft Collection 5) The Aero Engine Exhibition One of the most important aviation

museums in Europe with over 70 aircraft and associated memorabilia on display.
Open: Daily 10-5 (last admission 4).
Admission: Adults £4.20 OAPs £3.10 children £2.40 family £11 special rates for groups.
Location: On A41 less than 1 mile from Junction 3 on the M54.
Refreshments: Light refreshments served in café.
Exhibitions/Events: Royal Air Force Open Day June 18 Large Model Aircraft Rally July 15 and 16.

SHREWSBURY

THE RADBROOK CULINARY MUSEUM

Radbrook College, Radbrook Road, Shrewsbury SY3 9BL **Tel:** (01743) 232686 **Fax:** (01743) 271563

A unique collection of domestic utensils and examples of household crafts covering the late Victorian and Edwardian era and tracing the early years in the formation of Shropshire Technical School for Girls.
Open: Visitors welcome by appointment. Parties welcomed.
Admission: Free.
Location: 3 miles from Shrewsbury on the A488, Bishops Centre Road.
Refreshments: Available 10-2 during College terms
Ample car parking. Suitable for disabled persons.

THE SHREWSBURY MUSEUMS

(Shrewsbury & Atcham Borough Council)

Rowleys House Museum, Barker Street, Shrewsbury SY1 1QH **Tel:** (01743) 361196

Rowley's House, Clive House, Coleham Pumping Station and Shrewsbury Castle. Regionally and nationally important collections in fine, historic buildings. Temporary exhibitions and events. April 1995 - re-opening of Shropshire Regimental Museum at Shrewsbury Castle.
Open: Various times but includes Bank Hols and Summer Suns. Museums leaflets available from regional T.I.C's and Tourist sites.

TELFORD

BLISTS HILL OPEN AIR MUSEUM

(Ironbridge Gorge Museum)

Telford **Tel:** (01952) 433522 **Fax:** (01952) 432204

A working Victorian industrial community set at the turn of the century. Exhibits incl. fully operational Foundry, Candle Factory, Saw Mill, Printing Shop, Pit Head Winding Engine and the only wrought iron works in the world. Also many shops, cottages and Hay Inclined Plane. 42 acre site. Various catering outlets including the 'New Inn', and the 'Forest Glen'.
Open: 10-5 daily.
Admission: Adults £6 or by Passport ticket (1994 prices).
Location: 5 miles south of Telford Town Centre.
Refreshments: A cafe, Victorian pub and Victorian Pavilion.
Exhibitions/Events: Regular programme of special events and street drama.

COALPORT CHINA MUSEUM

(Ironbridge Gorge Museum)

Telford **Tel:** (01952) 580650

Magnificent display of Coalport and Caughley china. Displays on the history of the Works and its people. Housed in the original Coalport factory buildings, and used until 1926. Slide-and-tape show. Working demonstrations and pottery workshops.
Open: 10-5 daily.
Admission: Adults £3 or passport ticket entry (1994 prices).
Location: East from Iron Bridge follow signs.

IRON BRIDGE AND INFORMATION CENTRE

(The Iron Bridge is in the care of English Heritage)

Telford **Tel:** (01952) 433522

The world's first iron bridge. A small exhibition in the adjacent Tollhouse tells its history, and tells visitors more about the whole museum.
Open: Bridge open all the time tollhouse closed Nov-Feb.
Admission: Free.
Location: 5 miles south of Telford Centre.
Refreshments: Various cafés and pubs nearby.

IRONBRIDGE GORGE MUSEUM

(Ironbridge Gorge Museum Trust)

Telford **Tel:** (01952) 433522 **Fax:** (01952) 432204

A major museum based on a unique series of industrial monuments in the Ironbridge Gorge, now a World Heritage Site.
Open: Daily 10-5 (10-6 in July Aug) some small sites close in winter - please ring first.
Admission: Admission to all the museum sites is by 'Passport' ticket valid until all sites have been visited once. Adult passport £8 child £5 family ticket £25 OAP £7 student £5 (1994 rates) ticket admits to all sites.
Location: 5 miles south of Telford Centre.
Refreshments: Forest Glen Pavilion, The New Inn, & Coffee Shop.
Exhibitions/Events: VE DAY 1995 street party and fireworks at Blists Hill Open Air Museum. 'The Willow Pattern Story' Coalport China Museum - exhibition summer 1995. 'The Works' - New exhibition opens 1995 as 'The Arts of Industry'. For further information and party bookings write to: Ironbridge Gorge Museum Trust, Ironbridge, Telford, Shropshire TF8 7AW telephone number above or 432166

JACKFIELD TILE MUSEUM

(Ironbridge Gorge Museum)

Telford **Tel:** (01952) 882030

Housed in the former Craven Dunnill Tileworks, this is the Trust's latest addition. Beautiful display of tiles. Buildings in the process of being restored. Tile manufacture may be seen. Geology Gallery.
Open: 10-5.
Admission: Adults £3 or on passport ticket (1994 price).
Location: On south side of river Severn.
Refreshments: No.

MUSEUM OF IRON AND FURNACE SITE

Telford **Tel:** (01952) 433522

This museum is close to Abraham Darby's blast furnace and tells the story of iron and steel and the history of Coalbrookdale. 'The Works' will open in Spring 1995 as a completely new and redisplayed museum. The Darby Furnace has multi-lingual panels.
Open: 10-5 daily.
Admission: Adults £3 or by passport ticket (1994 prices).
Refreshments: Coffee Shop.

MUSEUM OF THE RIVER

(Ironbridge Gorge Museum)

Telford **Tel:** (01952) 433522

Housed in the restored Severn Warehouse the centre outlines the story of the Gorge in the words and pictures of people who visited it over two centuries. Slide-and-tape show in a special auditorium. Special emphasis on the use of water.
Open: 10-5.
Admission: Adults £2 or on Passport ticket (1994 prices).
Location: 100yds upstream from the Iron Bridge.

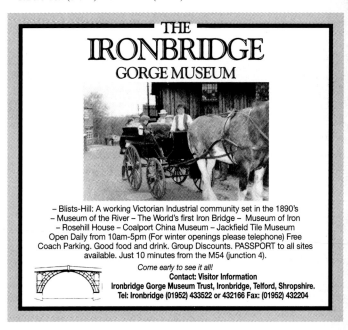

ROSEHILL HOUSE
(Ironbridge Gorge Museum)
Telford **Tel:** (01952) 433522/432551
A restored ironmaster's home, set in the early 19th century, typical of the Darby family houses.
Open: 10-5 closed winter months except by appointment.
Admission: Adults £3 (1994 price).
Location: 100yds walk uphill from Museum of Iron.
Refreshments: Tea-room.

TAR TUNNEL
(Ironbridge Gorge Museum)
Telford **Tel:** (01952) 882030 **Fax:** (01952) 432204
An 18th century mining tunnel from which natural bitumen was extracted and where visitors may go underground wearing hard hats.
Open: Daily 10-5 closed Nov-Mid Feb.
Admission: Adults 80p or by Passport ticket (1994 price).
Location: Close to Coalport China Museum.

WROXETER

WROXETER ROMAN CITY
(English Heritage)
Wroxeter **Tel:** (01743) 761330
The excavated centre of the forth largest city in Roman Britain, with impressive remains of the 2nd century municipal baths. The museum has pottery, coins and other objects from the town.
Open: Apr 1-Oct 31 daily 10-6 Nov 1-Mar 31 Wed-Sun 10-4 closed Dec 24-26 and Jan 1.
Admission: Adults £1.80 concessions £1.35 children 90p (1994 prices).

SOMERSET

AXBRIDGE

AXBRIDGE MUSEUM: KING JOHN'S HUNTING LODGE
(The National Trust administered by Sedgemoor District Council
The Square, Axbridge BS26 2AR **Tel:** (01934) 732012
Built c. 1500. Museum of local history, archaeology, geology, ceramics and glass.
Open: Daily Apr-Sept 2-5.
Admission: Adults £1 children 50p families £2.50.
Location: Centre of Axbridge.

BRIDGWATER

ADMIRAL BLAKE MUSEUM
Blake Street, Bridgwater **Tel:** (01278) 456127
The birthplace of Admiral Blake, containing Blake relics, exhibits relating to the Battle of Sedgemoor. Archaeology and local history.
Open: Mon-Sat 11-5 Sun 2-5 including Bank Holidays.
Admission: Free parties by arrangement.

WESTONZOYLAND PUMPING STATION
(Westonzoyland Engine Trust)
Hoopers Lane, Westonzoyland, Bridgwater **Tel:** (01823) 412713
Earliest land drainage station on Somerset levels. Steam and drainage exhibits, plus working forge and narrow gauge railway.
Open: In steam first Sun in month Apr-Oct plus Bank Hol Suns and Mons 2-5 Static other Suns Apr to Oct.
Admission: Adults £2 OAPs £1.50 children £1.
Car park free. Suitable for disabled but no special toilet, no wheelchairs available.

CHARD

CHARD AND DISTRICT MUSEUM
High Street, Chard TA20 1QL **Tel:** (01460) 65091
Displays on the History of Chard, John Stringfellow pioneer of powered flight, early artificial limbs made in Chard, cider making and agriculture, with a complete blacksmith's forge, carpenter's and plumber's workshop, kitchen, laundry, childhood and costume galleries and barn with agricultural machinery, garage and wagons, lace-making machinery.
Open: April 29-Oct 28 Mon-Sat 10.30-4.30 (also Sun in July and Aug).

GLASTONBURY

SOMERSET RURAL LIFE MUSEUM
(Somerset County Council)
Abbey Farm, Chilkwell Street, Glastonbury **Tel:** (01458) 831197
Museum interpreting Somerset's rural history with award winning permanent exhibitions and a lively programme of events and demonstrations throughout the summer. Temporary exhibitions and magnificent 14th century Abbey Barn.
Open: Easter-Oct 31 weekdays 10-5 weekends 2-6 Nov 1-Easter weekdays 10-5 Sat 11-4 closed Good Friday Christmas Day and Boxing Day.
Admission: Fee charged.
Refreshments: Tea-room (summer only).
Large car park.

STREET

THE SHOE MUSEUM
C. & J. Clark, High Street, Street BA16 OYA **Tel:** (01458) 43131 **Fax:** (01458) 841894

Old shoe machines and hand tools, 19th century documents.

TAUNTON

SOMERSET COUNTY MUSEUM
(Somerset County Council)
Taunton Castle, Taunton **Tel:** (01823) 255504
Set in the medieval castle where Judge Jeffreys held the 'Bloody Assize', the museum displays collections relevant to the county of Somerset, including archaeology, geology and palaeontology, natural history, ceramics, costume, dolls and military gallery. Temporary exhibitions.
Open: Mon-Sat 10-5.
Admission: Fee charged.

YEOVIL

THE MUSEUM OF SOUTH SOMERSET

(South Somerset District Council)

Hendford, Yeovil **Tel:** (01935) 24774 **Fax:** (01935) 75281

The Museum was completely refurbished in 1991, and now has exiting new gallery displays. Friendly Societies and Petters-Westland story on the gound floor. Upstairs are artefacts from the Westland, Lufton and Ilchester Mead sites, displayed within a Roman villa, as well as samples from the 'Stiby' gun collection. Items from the museum's costume and social history collection are also on dislpay and changed regularly in a period room setting.

Open: Tues-Sat 10-4 Mon school parties and appointments only.

Admission: Free - donations welcome.

YEOVILTON

FLEET AIR ARM MUSEUM AND CONCORDE EXHIBITION

R.N.A.S Yeovilton, Ilchester BA22 8HT **Tel:** (01935) 840565 **Fax:** (01935) 840181

The Fleet Air Arm Museum is one of the world's leading aviation museums. The Museum holds the Royal Navy's definitive collections and displays of its airborne strategies and actions. It houses the equipment, records and documents of the Fleet Air Arm's history. There are 89 aircraft in the coloection, and over 40 are on display.

Open: All year except for 24 25 26 Dec 10-5.30 (4.30 Nov-Mar).

Admission: One price includes entrance to all exhibitions. Group rates available on application.

Location: On B3151 just off the A37 and A303 at Ilchester.

Exhibitions/Events: Many exhibitions illustrate the history of Naval aviation in graphical and dramatic form: World Wars I and II Wrens, Kamikaze, Korean War, Falklands Conflict, Gulf War, Harrier 'Jump' Jet (the history of vstol) Concorde 002 (the British prototype). In addition there are displays of weapons, medals and memorabilia, which bring to life the exciting history of naval aviaiton, and the men and women who were part of that history. A major new exhibition is the 'Ultimate Carrier Experience'. A Flight Deck built on land, with steam catapult, deck landing sight, and 11 carrier-borne aircraft parked on the flight deck. Also included are the Island, Flyco, Goofers Deck, Operations Room, Control Centre, Workshops, Living Quarters (wardroom and mess-decks) and a large scissor lift. Visitors join the ship via a helicopter simulation, as it proceeds on a mission of mercy. They see the entire operation unfold, using the latest in audio-visual and interactive technology.

The facilities at the Museum are superb: Free car parking, licenced restaurant, gift shop, baby care room, children's playground, access for the disabled, dog exercise area. Watch the modern Navy train, from our airfield viewing galleries.

MUSEUMS & GALLERIES
IN GREAT BRITAIN AND IRELAND

STAFFORDSHIRE

BURTON-UPON-TRENT

BASS MUSEUM, VISITOR CENTRE AND SHIRE HORSE STABLES

Horninglow Street, Burton-upon-Trent **Tel:** (01283) 511000

The Museum adjoins the Bass Burton Brewery complex and is housed in a range of attractive mid-19th century buildings which formed part of the brewery engineer department. The displays and exhibits cover the History of brewing, the story of brewery transport and the story of bass. Notable exhibits include a detailed working railway model of Burton in 1921, the glass and ceramics associated with beer drinking, reconstructed period bars and working water pumps. Outside in the yard the stables of the famous Bass Shire Horses, a collection of horse-drawn vehicles and several vintage vehicles including the well-Worthington Bottle car of 1923. A 1920's experimental brew house is used for special brews several times a year and the 1905 Robey horizontal tandem compound steam engine is steamed on most Sundays in the summer. A reconstructed Bass Ale dock and steam loco recall the days of the brewery railway system.
Open: 7 days a week Mon-Fri 10 Sat & Sun 10.30 last admission 4 closed Dec 25 26 Jan 1.
Admission: Fee charged.
Location: A50.
Refreshments: Bar and restaurant
Free parking. Brewery tours and/or Education Service by arrangement.
Conference and function rooms available.

LEEK

BRINDLEY WATER MILL AND MUSEUM

(Brindley Mill Preservation Trust)
Mill Street, Leek
Operational corn mill built by James Brindley.
Open: Information on opening times and private visits (0538) 381000.
Admission: Adults £1.20 children/OAPs 60p.
Location: Junction Mill Street, Abbey Green Road, Leek.

CHEDDLETON FLINT MILL

(Cheddleton Flint Mill Industrial Heritage Trust)
Leek Road, Cheddleton, Nr Leek ST13 7HL

Twin water-wheels on the River Churnet operate flint grinding pans. The South Mill foundations date back to the 13th century when it ground corn and was a fulling mill. Converted to grinding flint in about 1800 after it was joined by The North Mill which was built specially in the late 18th century to grind flint. The Museum collection includes a Robey 100hp steam engine, model Newcomen engine, rare 1770 haystack boiler, and the narrow boat 'Vienna' moored on the Caldon Canal. The miller's cottage is furnished as it would have looked in the 19th century.
Open: Buildings open Sat and Sun afternoons throughout the year and on most weekdays.
Admission: Free. Donations welcome.
Location: Between Stoke-on-Trent and Leek on A520.
Books, postcards and wallchart on sale; also guides to the Mill in English, French, German and Italian.

NEWCASTLE-UNDER-LYME

BOROUGH MUSEUM AND ART GALLERY

Brampton Park, Newcastle-under-Lyme **Tel:** (01782) 619705

The Museum & Art Gallery has permanent displays of Staffordshire pottery and glass, weapons, toys and social history, including a recreated Victorian street scene. There is also a frequently changing temporary exhibition programme of fine art and crafts, drawn both from the gallery's permanent collection and touring exhibitions. Set in the 8 acres of Brampton Park, there is an aviary and wildlife garden adjacent to the Museum and a safe children's play area.
Open: Mon-Sat 10-5.30 Sun 2-5.30 closed Bank Holidays and May Day Mon.
Admission: Free.
Free car and coach parking, access for the disabled.

SHUGBOROUGH

MANSION HOUSE, SERVANTS' QUARTERS, MUSEUM OF STAFFORDSHIRE LIFE AND PARK FARM.

(National Trust property administered by Staffordshire County Council)

Milford, Shugborough, Nr. Stafford **Tel:** (01889) 881388

Mansion:18th century ancestral home of the Earls of Lichfield, containing furniture, paintings, porcelain, silver etc. Museumof Staffordshire: housed in the servants' quarters with estate interiors (working brew-house, laundry, kitchen, Victorian School room, coach houses) displays of domestic costume and craft material. Fine collection of horse drawn vehicles. **Working Farm Museum and restored Corn Mill:** Georgian farmstead with agricultural galleries, mill, rare breeds of livestock and traditional farm activities. **Parkland and Gardens:** with neoclassical monuments, beautiful Victorian terraces and rose garden.
Open: Walks and Trails Mar 25-Oct 27 daily including Bank Holiday Mon 11-5 Site open all year to booked parties from 10.30.
Admission: Reduced rates for children/OAPs/registered unemployed and coach parties. Special rates and activities for schools/colleges. Site access for parking, picnic area, park and garden £1.50 per vehicle.
Refreshments: Cafe.
Coach and School parties welcome. National Trust Shop. Visitor Centre. Special events throughout the year, programme available. For further information, including admission charges, please telephone as above.

STAFFORD

ANCIENT HIGH HOUSE

(Stafford Borough Council)

Greengate Street, Stafford **Tel:** (01785) 223181 ext 352 or 40204 **Fax:** (01785) 223156

England's largest timber framed town house, built in 1595. Now has period room settings, shops, video theatre and the Museum of the Staffordshire Yeomanry.
Open: Mon-Fri 9-5 Sat 10-4 in Apr-Oct and 10-3 Nov-Mar.
Admission: Adults £1.35 concessions 70p.
Location: Centre of Stafford.
Exhibitions/Events: Series of temporary exhibitions plus special events and exhibitions to mark the 400th anniversary.

SHIRE HALL GALLERY AND CRAFT SHOP

(Staffordshire County Council)

Market Square, Stafford ST16 2LD **Tel:** (01785) 278345 **Fax:** (01785) 278327

Magnificent 18thC Shire Hall now an Art Gallery with exhibitions of contemporary British art. Craft Shop selected for quality by the Crafts Council and tours of historic court rooms.
Open: Tues-Sat 10-5.
Admission: Free.
Location: Town Centre Location.
Refreshments: Coffee Area.

STAFFORD CASTLE AND VISITOR CENTRE

(Stafford Borough Council)

Newport Road, Stafford **Tel:** (01785) 57698 **Fax:** (01785) 223156
The site of a Norman timber fortress, now covered by the ruins of a 19th century, Gothic Revival building. The Visitor centre contains an audio-visual display, model reconstructions and shop.
Open: Tues-Sun 10-5 Apr-Oct 10-4 Nov-Mar.
Admission: Adults £1.15 concessions 60p.
Location: Off the A518 Newport Road, south-west of Stafford.
Exhibitions/Events: Annual events programme on the Castle site. Temporary exhibitions in the Visitor Centre.

IZAAK WALTON'S COTTAGE

(Stafford Borough Council)

Worston Lane, Shallowford, Stafford **Tel:** (01785) 760278 **Fax:** (01785) 223156
Thatched, timber-framed cottage bequethed to Stafford by Izaak Walton, author of the 'Compleat Angler'. Now has period room settings and a small fishing museum.
Open: Tues-Sun 11-4.30 Apr-Oct.
Admission: Adults £1.15 concessions 60p.
Location: Shallowford, off the A5013 five miles north of Stafford.
Exhibitions/Events: Annual programme of events.

STOKE-ON-TRENT

CITY MUSEUM AND ART GALLERY

(Stoke-on-Trent City Council)

Bethesda Street, Hanley, Stoke-on-Trent ST1 3DW **Tel:** (01782) 202173
Fax: (01782) 205033

An award winning purpose built museum all about 'the Potteries'. Archaeology, Community History and Natural History displays celebrate the unique nature of the area and are complimented by other galleries and exhibits which range from costume to a LF XVI Spitfire (the latter the centre-piece of a display about its designer -

Reginald Mitchell, born locally). In addition the museum is internationally renowned for housing one of the largest and most important collections of English pottery and porcelain (primarily from Staffordshire) in the world. Regular exhibitions range across the whole spectrum from Art to Community History.
Open: Mon-Sat 10-5 Sun 2-5 closed Christmas-New Year.
Admission: Free.
Location: Hanley, Stoke-on-Trent, Staffs.
Refreshments: café/bar
Exhibitions/Events: Ask for a free copy of our quarterly listings.
Guided tour of ceramics gallery available Mon-Fri for pre-booked parties.

THE SIR HENRY DOULTON GALLERY

Nile Street, Burslem, Stoke-on-Trent **Tel:** (01782) 292292

Sir Henry Doulton was recognised by his contemporaries as the greatest potter of his time. This gallery traces the story of Royal Doulton from its foundation in 1815 and includes the world famous collection of over 300 rare figures.
Open: Weekdays 9-4.15 closed factory holidays.
Factory tours, factory shop.

ETRURIA INDUSTRIAL MUSEUM

(Stoke-on-Trent City Council)

Lower Bedford Street, Etruria, Stoke-on-Trent **Tel:** (01782) 287557

Britain's sole surviving steam-powered Potters Mill, 'Jesse Shirley's Etruscan Bone and Flint Mill' was built to grind materials for the agricultural and pottery industries. The mill contains a gear room, grinding pans, boiler and 1820s Beam Engine, 'Princess'. There is also a working forge.
Open: Wed-Sun 10-4 closed Chrismas-New Year.
Admission: Free.
Location: Junction of Trent and Mersey and Caldon Canals.
Exhibitions/Events: 'Princess' in steam. Weekend of first Sunday of the month. April-Nov
Facilities for school parties/groups.

FORD GREEN HALL

(Stoke-on-Trent City Council)

Ford Green Road, Smallthorne, Stoke-on-Trent ST6 1NG **Tel:** (01782) 534771

A timber-framed yeoman's farmhouse built c. 1624 with eighteenth century brick additions. Contains appropriate period furnishings. Regular events including performances of Early Music
Open: Sun-Thurs 1-5 closed Christmas-New Year.
Admission: Free.
Location: Smallthorne, Stoke-on-Trent.
Refreshments: Small tea-room.
Exhibitions/Events: Early Music on the second Sunday of each month.
Shop. Facilities for school parties/small groups.

GLADSTONE POTTERY MUSEUM

Uttoxeter Road, Longton, Stoke-on-Trent **Tel:** (01782) 319232

Gladstone Working Pottery Museum has undergone a major programme of restoration and re-organisation. Visitors now benefit in a number of ways including a new interpretation scheme, new introductory gallery, a Video Room (30 min) and a Bottle Oven Sight, Sound and Smell presentation. There are more demonstrations and presentations of traditional pottery skills, 'Hands-On' opportunities, and a flexible schools support service - please ask for details.
Open: Every day 10-5 (incl. Bank Hols) please phone for Christmas opening times. Evening visits are available by prior arrangement - please ask for details.
Admission: Adults £3 students/OAPs £2.30 children £1.50.
Location: On A50, signposted from A500 link with M6 at Junction 15.
Refreshments: Available.
Roving Gladstone hosts. 'Access for all' - much improved access and services - please ask for details. Group bookings: please enquire.

MINTON MUSEUM

London Road, Stoke-on-Trent **Tel:** (01782) 292292

Minton was founded in 1793 and the museum features the many aspects of the company's world famous artistry - parian, majolica, acid gold, pate-sur pate and fine bone china.
Open: Weekdays 10-12.15 2-3.30 at other times by appointment closed factory holidays.
Factory shop.

WEDGWOOD MUSEUM
(Josiah Wedgwood and Sons Limited, Barlaston)
Barlaston, Stoke-on-Trent ST12 9ES **Tel:** (01782) 204218/204141

A 'Living Museum' displaying the most comprehensive collection of Wedgwood ceramics and art over two centuries, with craft manufacturing centre adjacent.
Open: Mon-Fri 9-5 Sat 10-4 all year and Summer Suns (Easter-Oct) 10-4.
Admission: Adults £2.95 children £1.50 special reductions OAPs and Students.
Refreshments: Available.
Parties welcome. Factory connoisseur tours. Car Parking. Suitable for disabled persons. Curator: Gaye Blake Roberts.

TAMWORTH

TAMWORTH CASTLE AND MUSEUM SERVICE
The Holloway, Tamworth B79 7LR **Tel:** (01827) 63563 **Fax:** (01827) 52769

Norman motte-and-bailey castle with fifteen rooms including a dungeon, haunted bedroom and Norman Exhibition.
Open: Mon-Sat 10-5.30 Sun 2-5.30 last admission 4.30.
Admission: Adults £3 various concessions.
Location: Town centre location in Castle Pleasure Grounds.
Refreshments: Not available in Castle.
Exhibitions/Events: 14 Jan-5 March: Area Museum Service touring exhibition on hats

WALL

WALL ROMAN SITE (LETOCETUM)
(English Heritage/National Trust)
Wall **Tel:** (01543) 480768
Finds from the excavated Roman station called Letocetum.
Open: Apr 1-Oct 31 daily 10-6.
Admission: Adults £1.25 concessions 95p children 60p (1994 prices).

SUFFOLK

CAVENDISH

THE SUE RYDER FOUNDATION MUSEUM
(The Sue Ryder Foundation)
Sue Ryder Home, Cavendish, Sudbury CO10 8AY **Tel:** (01787) 280252
Fax: (01787) 280548

Open: Daily (except Christmas Day) 10-5.30.
Admission: Adults 80p children 12 & under/OAPs 40p.
Location: On A1092 between Long Melford and Clare.
Refreshments: Available.
Gift shop.

DUNWICH

DUNWICH MUSEUM
St. James's Street, Dunwich IP17 3EW **Tel:** (01728) 648796
History of the lost Medieval town and local wild life.
Open: Easter-Sept 11.30-4.30 Oct 12-4 Mar Sat & Sun 2-4.30.
Admission: Donations only.

IPSWICH

CHRISTCHURCH MANSION AND WOLSEY ART GALLERY

(Ipswich Borough Council)

Christchurch Park, Ipswich **Tel:** (01473) 253246

Country house collection of furniture, pictures and ceramics. Works by Gainsborough, Constable and other Suffolk artists. Lively temporary exhibition programme in the Wolsey Art Gallery.

Open: Tues-Sat 10-5 Sun 2.30-4.30 (closing at dusk in winter) open Bank Holiday Mons

Admission: Free

Refreshments: No

All written enquiries to: The Curator, Ipswich Museum, High Street, Ipswich, IP1 3QH

IPSWICH MUSEUM AND HIGH STREET EXHIBITION GALLERY

(Ipswich Borough Council)

High Street, Ipswich IP1 3QH **Tel:** (01473) 213761 **Fax:** (01473) 281274

Geology , natural history, archaeology of Suffolk from earlier times to the medieval period, including the Roman Villa gallery and Mankind Gallery - Africa, Asia, Pacific and the Americas.

Open: Tues-Sat 10-5 (Gallery 4.45).

Admission: Free.

Refreshments: No.

Exhibitions/Events: Horsepower - a two year local history exhibition.

All written enquiries to: The Curator as above.

NEWMARKET

THE NATIONAL HORSERACING MUSEUM

99 High Street, Newmarket CB8 8JL **Tel:** (01638) 667333

400 years of racing history in five galleries of paintings, bronzes, displays and memorabilia supported by video and computer information. Two galleries of works from the British Sporting Art Trust.

Open: Mar-Dec Tues-Sat 10-5 Sun 12-4

Admission: Fee charged reductions for groups of 20 or more.

Location: Newmarket High Street, adjacent to The Jockey Club.

Refreshments: Licensed coffee shop.

Exhibitions/Events: Equing Tours to Racing establishments by arrangement.

Gift Shop, Full facilities for disabled.

STOWMARKET

MUSEUM OF EAST ANGLIAN LIFE

Stowmarket IP14 1DL **Tel:** (01449) 612229

Large open air museum on attractive riverside site in centre of Stowmarket. Reconstructed buildings including Smithy, Watermill and Windpump. Boby Building houses steam gallery, craft workshops and East Anglian industrial heritage display. Working Suffolk Punch horse 'Remus' and local breeds of farm animals. Displays on domestic, agricultural and industrial life. Steam traction engines. Programme of special events and craft demonstrations (send s.a.e.).

Open: Apr-Oct.

Admission: Fee charged. Party reductions tel (01449) 612229.

Location: Two minutes walk from Stowmarket market place.

Refreshments: Available.

Museum gift shop. Charity no. 310322.

SUDBURY

GAINSBOROUGH'S HOUSE

46 Gainsborough Street, Sudbury CO10 6EU **Tel:** (01787) 372958

Gainsborough's House is the birthplace of Thomas Gainsborough RA (1727-88). The Georgian fronted town house, with an attractive walled garden, displays more of the artists's work than any other gallery. The collection is shown together with eighteenth-century furniture and memorabilia. Commitment to contemporary art is reflected in a varied programme of exhibitions throughout the year. These include fine art, craft, photography, printmaking, sculpture and highlights the work of East Anglian artists.

Open: Easter-Oct 31 Tues-Sat 10-5 Suns Bank Hol Mons 2-5 Nov-Maundy Thurs close 4 closed Mon except Bank Hols Good Fri and Christmas to New Year.

Admission: Adults £2.50 OAPs £2 students/children £1.50.

Parties by arrangement.

WOODBRIDGE

SUFFOLK HORSE MUSEUM

(Suffolk Horse Society)

Market Hill, Woodbridge 1P12 4LU **Tel:** (01394) 380083

An exhibition devoted to the Suffolk Punch breed of heavy working horse. Displays, paintings and photographs illustrate its history and future. Shoeing, harness work, showing and the way these horses were kept. The life of the horseman is described as is the relationship of the Suffolk to the social history of East Anglia.

Open: Easter to end of September daily 2-5

Admission: £1.50

Location: Market Hill in centre of Woodbridge

SURREY

CAMBERLEY

SURREY HEATH MUSEUM
(Surrey Heath Borough Council)
Surrey Heath House, Knoll Road, Camberley GU15 3HD **Tel:** (01276) 686252 Ext 284 **Fax:** (01276) 22277
An attractive museum combining permanent displays on local history and environment with a lively programme of temporary displays of local and regional interest.
Open: Tues-Sat 11-5 or by appointment.
Admission: Free.
Location: BR Camberley.
Refreshments: Available 12-2.
Exhibitions/Events: 'The Poulter Drawings' & 'Trading Locally'/further details from museum.
Education Service; please contact for details.

CARSHALTON

HERITAGE CENTRE
(London Borough of Sutton)
Honeywood Walk, Carshalton
see entry under Greater London.

CATERHAM

EAST SURREY MUSEUM
1 Stafford Road, Caterham CR3 6JG **Tel:** (01883) 340275
Changing displays of local history, archaeology, natural history, crafts and local artists.
Open: Wed & Sat 10-5 Sun 2-5.

CHERTSEY

CHERTSEY MUSEUM
(Runnymede Borough Council)
The Cedars, 33 Windsor Street, Chertsey KT16 8AT **Tel:** (01932) 565764 **Fax:** (01932) 571118
Situated in an attractive Regency Town House, Chertsey Museum offers a stimulating variety of displays, including the local history and archaeology of the Borough of Runnymede, the Matthews Collection of 18th and 19th century costume, clocks ceramics and glass. It also has a lively and varied temporary exhibition and events programme.
Open: Tues-Fri 12.30-4.30 Sat 11-4.
Admission: Free
Exhibitions/Events: World War II exhibition, Exhibition of Victorian costume.

EGHAM

THE EGHAM MUSEUM
(The Egham Museum Trust)
Literary Institute, High Street, Egham TW20 9EW **Tel:** (01344) 843047
Local history and archaeology exhibits from Egham, Englefield Green, Thorpe and Virginia Water.
Open: Tues Thurs 10-12.30 and 2-4.30 Sats 10.30-12.30 and 2.30-4.30.
Admission: Free.

EWELL

BOURNE HALL MUSEUM
(Epsom & Ewell Borough Council)
Spring Street, Ewell KT17 1UF **Tel:** 0181-394 1734
A museum for Epsom & Ewell, with relics of Henry VIII's Nonsuch Palace, the Epsom Spa visited by Samuel Pepys, and Surrey's largest Roman town.
Open: Mon-Sat 10-5 closed Christmas and Bank Holidays.
Admission: Free.
Location: Nearest station Ewell West.
Refreshments: Available.
Car parking for 100 cars. Museum shop.

FARNHAM

MUSEUM OF FARNHAM
(Waverley Borough Council)
Willmer House, 38 West Street, Farnham GU9 7DX **Tel:** (01252) 715094 **Fax:** (01252) 715094
Early Georgian (1718) front of cut and moulded brick; fine carvings and panelling. Local history. William Cobbett, decorative arts. Walled garden.
Open: Tues-Sat 10-5.
Admission: Free.
Shop.

RURAL LIFE CENTRE
Reeds Road, Tilford, Farnham GU10 2DL **Tel:** (01252) 795571/792300
Collection includes wagons, farm implements, hand tools, Dairy, Kitchen, Forge, Wheelwright's shop and Arboretum.
Open: Apr-Sept Wed-Sun and Bank Hols 11-6.
Suitable for disabled visitors. Rustic Sunday July 30, 1995.

GODALMING

GODALMING MUSEUM
(Godalming Museum Trust/Waverley Borough Council)
109A High Street, Godalming **Tel:** (01483) 426510
Medieval Building; Local history and people; Lutyens-Jekyll room; Garden; shop; Exhibitions.
Open: Summer Tues-Sat 10-5 winter Tues-Sat 10-4.

GUILDFORD

BRITISH RED CROSS MUSEUM AND ARCHIVES
(British Red Cross)
Barnett Hill, Wonersh, Guildford GU5 0RF **Tel:** (01483) 898595 **Fax:** (01483) 892836
History of the Red Cross movement, particularly British Red Cross from 1870. Features uniform, medals and badges, nursing equipment and other material depicting work of the Society in peace and war. Reference and photograph library and research facilities available.
Open: Appointment only.
Admission: Free.
Parties maximum 20 people. Car parking available.

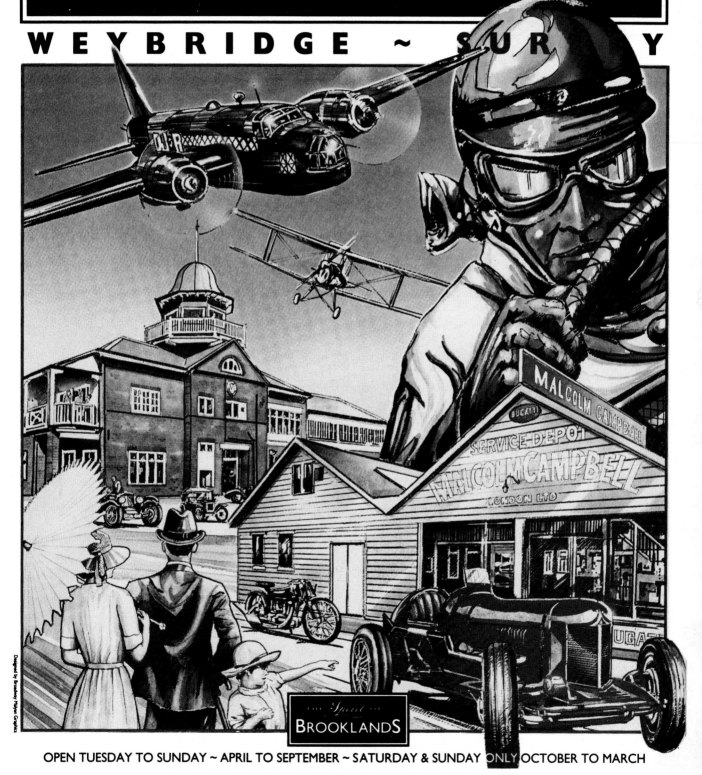

GUILDFORD HOUSE GALLERY
(Guildford Borough Council)
155 High Street, Guildford GU1 3AJ **Tel:** (01483) 44740

Historic house dating from 1660 with fine plaster ceilings and carved staircase. The Borough's Art Collection includes topographical paintings and drawings. Contemporary craftwork and pastel portraits by Guildford born John Russell RA (1745-1806).
Open: Tues-Sat 10-4.45 closed Bank Hols.
Admission: Free.
Location: Centre of Guildford High Street.
Refreshments: Tea-Room serving light meals in old kitchen and courtyard.Open 10-4.30.
Exhibitions/Events: Varied temporary exhibiti0on programme.
Gallery shop selling cratfwork, books and cards.

GUILDFORD MUSEUM
(Guildford Borough Council)
Castle Arch, Guildford **Tel:** (01483) 444750
Archaeological and historical museum for the county, especially West Surrey and Guildford Borough. Needlework collection of general interest.
Open: Mon-Sat 11-5.
Admission: Free.

WESTCOTT

THE WESTCOTT GALLERY
(Anthony and Barbara Wakefield)
4 Guildford Road, Westcott RH4 3NR **Tel:** (01306) 876261
Specialise in contemporary Surrey artists. At least two major exhibitions per year. Browsers welcome.
Open: Mon-Fri 9-5 Sat 10-5 closed Bank holidays.
Admission: Free.
Exhibitions/Events: March 1995 exhibition paintings Gillian Shilson and Leslie Shelton Nov 1995 exhibition of paintings by Susie Hunt and ceramics by Stephanie Wright.
Car parking around Village Green opposite Gallery. Suitable for disabled persons (no wheelchairs available). Framing, restorations, valuations, fine art insurance.

WEYBRIDGE

BROOKLANDS MUSEUM
(Directors and Trustees of Brooklands Museum)
Brooklands Road, Weybridge KT13 0QN **Tel:** (01932) 857381 **Fax:** (01932) 855465
Brooklands museum, the birthplace of British motorsport and aviation. Discover the world's first banked race track; visit Malcolm Campbell's workshop; see the Brooklands racing car collection, the Wellington Bomber rescued from Loch Ness and the unique aircraft collection spanning 85 years.
Open: Tues-Sun and Bank Hols throughout the year summer 10-5 and winter 10-4.
Admission: Adults £4.50 students/OAPs £3.50 children under 16 £2.50 under 5's free family (2+3) £12.50 groups of 20+ £4 per person.
Location: 10 mins from M25 J. 10 and 11, 5 mins from A3.
Refreshments: Sunbeam tea-rooms, club members bar, conference and corporate entertainment.
Exhibitions/Events: Events most weekends.
Good disabled facilities, with wheelchairs provided. The museum also has an extensive picture library featuring aviation, motorsport and social scene prints and slides from the 1900's.

ELMBRIDGE MUSEUM
Church Street, Weybridge **Tel:** (01932) 843573 **Fax:** (01932) 846552
Changing displays of local archaeology, social history, natural history and costume. Current exhibition from Summer 1994, 'A Look Back at Leisure'.
Open: Mon Tues Thurs Fri 2-5 Sat 10-1 2-5 closed Wed and Sun.
Admission: Free.
Special exhibitions throughout the year. Telephone for details.

EAST SUSSEX

BRIGHTON

THE BOOTH MUSEUM OF NATURAL HISTORY
(Brighton Borough Council)
Dyke Road, Brighton **Tel:** (01273) 552586 **Fax:** (01273) 779108
A comprehensive display of British birds, mounted in settings that re-create their natural habitats. Galleries on vertebrate evolution, butterflies of the World and Sussex geology. Frequent temporary exhibitions. Reference collections of insects, osteology, palaeontology, bird and mammal skins, eggs and herbaria.
Open: Mon-Sat 10-5 Sun 2-5 closed Thurs Christmas Day Boxing Day Jan 1 and Good Friday.
Admission: Free.
Location: Dyke Road Brighton.
Exhibitions/Events: Special exhibition programme.
Shop.

BRIGHTON MUSEUM AND ART GALLERY
(Brighton Borough Council)
Church Street, Brighton **Tel:** (01273) 603005 **Fax:** (01273) 779108
The collections include the Willett Collection of English pottery and porcelain; fine and applied art of the Art Nouveau and Art Deco periods; old master paintings, watercolours, furniture, fashion, musical instruments, ethnography, archaeology and Brighton history. Frequent special exhibitions.
Open: Mon Tues Thurs-Sat 10-5 Sun 2-5 closed Wed Good Friday Christmas Day Boxing Day.
Admission: Free.
Refreshments: Café open Mon to Sat. Closed Weds and Sun.
Exhibitions/Events: 1995 exhibitions programme Sussex open Jan-Feb 'Fetishism' Apr-June 'Perfume' and Ethnography gallery.
New Archaeology Gallery opening Oct 94.

PRESTON MANOR

(Brighton Borough Council)

Preston Drove, Brighton BN1 6SD **Tel:** (01273) 603005 Ext 3239

Preston Manor was rebuilt in 1738, with further additions in 1905, and houses a collection of English and Continental furniture and decorative art from the 16th to the 19th century, including the Macquoid bequest. Servants' quarters and Edwardian Day Nursery now open. New 'attic rooms' opening autumn '94.

Open: Tues-Sat 10-5 Sun 2-5 Mon 1-5 (Bank Hols 10-5) closed Good Friday Christmas Day and Boxing Day. Please telephone for details.

Admission: Fee charged.

Location: Preston Park.

Exhibitions/Events: Special schools events.

Walled garden with pets cemetery and 13thC parish church.

THE ROYAL PAVILION

(Brighton Borough Council)

Brighton BN1 1UE **Tel:** (01273) 603005 **Fax:** (01273) 779108

The seaside palace of the Prince Regent (King George IV), containing some of the most dazzling and magnificent interiors in the world. Decorations in a fantastic version of 'The Chinese taste', Regency and other contemporary furniture and works of art, including many original pieces returned on loan from H.M. The Queen. Gardens recently restored to original Regency plans.

Open: Daily 10-5 (June-Sept 10-6) closed Christmas Day and Boxing Day.

Admission: Fee charged reduced for children/OAPs/students and parties.

Refreshments: Queen Adelaide tea-room.

Exhibitions/Events: Final suite of rooms opened - Yellow Bow Rooms now open - Bedroom suite of the Royal Dukes. Plus winter programme of events.

Guided tours by appointment. Pavilion Shop. £10 million structural restoration now complete. For further information on guided tours , special events and room hire, please call Public services on (01273) 603005.

EASTBOURNE

TOWNER ART GALLERY AND LOCAL MUSEUM

Manor Gardens, High Street, Old Town, Eastbourne

Elegant 18th century Manor House in public gardens. **Gallery:** Collection of mainly 19th and 20th century British art, a selection from which is on show at any one time. Houses the South East Arts Collection of Contemporary Art. Lively programme of temporary exhibitions, workshops, talks, concerts and other events. **Local Museum:** The Eastbourne area from Prehistoric times. Also reconstructed Victorian kitchen. Photographic archives.

Open: Wed-Sat 10-5 Sun and Bank Holidays 2-5.
Admission: Adults £2 concessions £1.40 (free to residents/students/children & unemployed) Annual card £6 (£4).
Refreshments: On Sun afternoons.

HASTINGS

MUSEUM AND ART GALLERY
(Hastings Borough)
Cambridge Road, Hastings TN34 1ET **Tel:** (01424) 721202
Paintings, ceramics, Sussex ironwork, new wildlife and dinosaur displays, Oriental, Pacific and American Indian Art, The Durbar Hall (Indian Palace). Temporary exhibitions.
Open: Mon-Fri 10-5 Sat 10-1 and 2-5 Sun 3-5.
Admission: Free.

MUSEUM OF LOCAL HISTORY
(Hastings Borough)
Old Town Hall, High Street, Hastings **Tel:** (01424) 721209
Displays on maritime history, the Cinque Ports, smuggling, fishing, local personalities such as John Logie Baird.
Open: Easter-end Sept Tues-Sun 10-1 and 2-5 Oct-Dec Tues-Sun 2-4 Jan-Easter Sun 3-5.
Admission: Free.

SHIPWRECK HERITAGE CENTRE,
Rock-a-Nore Road, Hastings TN34 3DW **Tel:** (01424) 437452
Enter the hidden world of seafaring history. 3,000 years of treasures from shipwrecks (with videos). An audio-visual show "A SHIPWRECK ADVENTURE". The last Rye Barge "Primrose" under restoration. Live RADAR and SATELLITE pictures of Europe.
Open: Easter-end Sept Tues-Sun 10-1 and 2-5 Oct-Dec Tues-Sun 2-4 Jan-Easter Sun 3-5.
Admission: Free.

HOVE

THE BRITISH ENGINEERIUM
Nevill Road, Hove **Tel:** (01273) 559583 **Fax:** (01273) 566403

The majestic Eastons & Anderson Beam Engine of 1876.

at the
BRITISH ENGINEERIUM
Off Nevill Road
Hove BN3 7QA.

Telephone:
01273-559583

A unique working steam museum telling the story of Britain's engineering heritage within the building of the fully restored Goldstone Pumping Station. See the huge Eastons & Anderson beam engine of 1876, plus hundreds of models and full size engines depicting the history of steam power on land, sea road and rail. Conservation and restoration projects of industrial archaeological material for national and private collections worldwide, can be seen under way in the period workshops.
Open: Daily 10-5 engines in steam first Sun in month and Bank Holidays.
Admission: Adults £3 conc £2 family £8.
Refreshments: Sun.
Exhibitions/Events: Telephone for details.
Access for disabled. Please ask for help on arrival.

HASTINGS MUSEUMS

OLD TOWN HALL MUSEUM
OF LOCAL HISTORY

HASTINGS MUSEUM
& ART GALLERY

HOVE MUSEUM AND ART GALLERY
(Hove Borough Council)

19 New Church Road, Hove BN3 4AB **Tel:** (01273) 779410

Twentieth century paintings and drawings. Eighteenth century pictures, furniture and decorative arts, dolls, toys and dolls houses. New display of Hove history incorporating Hove's pioneer film-makers. Special exhibitions of historic and contemporary art and crafts, housed in one of the town's most impressive Victorian Villas.

Open: Tues-Fri 10-5 Sat 10-4.30 Sun 2-5.
Admission: Free.

WEST BLATCHINGTON WINDMILL
(Hove Borough Council)

Holmes Avenue, Hove

19th century hexagonal and timber windmill on top of flint barns. Complete with rotating cap, sails, grindiing stones, sack hoists and machinery. Museum of local history, agriculture and milling. Souvenir shop. Six floors.

Open: Sun and Bank Holiday May-Sept inc. only 2.30-5.
Admission: Adults 70p children/OAPs/unemployed 30p parties by arrangement anytime.
Location: Holmes Avenue, Hove, East Sussex.
Disabled toilet. Parking adjacent, on street.

RYE

RYE MUSEUM

Rye Castle, Rye TN31 7HH **Tel:** (01797) 226728

Local history collections housed in a 13th century tower. Medieval and other pottery from the Rye kilns. Cinque Ports material, ship building. Romney Marsh.

Open: Easter-late Oct every day 10.30-5.30 (last entry 5) during winter open weekends 11-3.30.
Admission: Fee charged.

SHEFFIELD PARK

BLUEBELL RAILWAY
(Bluebell Railway)

Sheffield Park Station, Sheffield Park, Nr Uckfield TN22 3QL **Tel:** (01825) 722370 (talking timetable) (01825) 723777 (enquiries) **Fax:** (01825) 724139

The Bluebell Railway - Living Museum. Operates vintage steam trains between Sheffield Park, Horsted Keynes and Kingscote (9m) in Sussex. No parking at Kingscote, bus link from East Grinstead stn., train connection by NSC from and to London.

Open: Every weekend daily May-Sept Santa Specials in Dec open for limited viewing other dates brochure timetable available.
Location: A275 East Grinstead and Lewes.
Refreshments: Restaurant and buffet available Pullman dining train.
Museum and shop. Car parking. Special events held annually.

WEST SUSSEX

ARUNDEL

MUSEUM AND HERITAGE CENTRE

61 High Street, Arundel BN18 9AJ **Tel:** (01903) 882344

Old Arundel on view in nine galleries.

Open: Easter-Oct open every weekend and Bank Hols also open Mon-Fri 11-5 in high season.
Admission: Adults £1 children 50p concessions for OAP's & students.
Parties any time by arrangement.

CHICHESTER

CHICHESTER DISTRICT MUSEUM
(Chichester District Council)

29 Little London, Chichester PO19 1PB **Tel:** (01243) 784683

Discover the life and work of the people of Chichester and the local countryside. Temporary exhibitions.

Open: Tues-Sat 10-5.30 closed Sun and Mon.
Admission: Free.
Shop, quiz sheets.

GUILDHALL MUSEUM
(Chichester District Council)

Priory Park, Chichester **Tel:** (01243) 784683

13th century church, later the Town Hall and Law Court. Now a branch of Chichester District Museum.

Open: By prior arrangement with Chichester District Museum.
Admission: Free.

PALLANT HOUSE
(Pallant House Gallery Trust)

9 North Pallant, Chichester PO19 1TJ **Tel:** (01243) 774557 **Fax:** (01243) 536038

British Art at Home - excellent collections of Modern British Art (Moore, Sutherland, Piper, Hitchens, etc.) in the setting of a meticulously restored Queen Anne townhouse. Added attractions include the Geoffrey Freeman Collection of Bow Porcelain (the finest in the world), the lively programme of loan exhibitions, and the peaceful walled formal garden.

Open: All year Tues-Sat 10-5.30 closed Sun Mon and Bank Hols last admissions 4.30.
Admission: Fee charged.
Location: Town Centre.

WEALD AND DOWNLAND OPEN AIR MUSEUM

Singleton, Chichester **Tel:** (01243) 811348 **Fax:** (01243) 811475

A Museum of historic buildings rescued from destruction and re-built on a beautiful 40 acre site in the South Downs. The re-created Bayleaf medieval farmstead, a working watermill, rural craft workshops and timber framed houses are just some of nearly 40 buildings to be explored. A new 'Hands On' gallery explores building materials and techniques.

Open: Mar 1-Oct 31 daily 11-5 Nov 1-Feb 28 Wed Sat and Sun only 11-4 Dec 26-Jan 1 daily 11-4.
Admission: Adults £4.20 OAPs £3.70 children £2.10 family ticket £11 (2 adults + children).
Location: West Sussex.
Refreshments: Light only available Mar-Oct.
Parties by arrangement. Museum shop.

DITCHLING

DITCHLING MUSEUM

Church Lane, Ditchling BN6 8TB **Tel:** (01273) 844744

History comes alive with dioramas and costume tableaux. Country crafts; work by famous local artists; wide-ranging special exhibitions.

Open: Easter-late Oct weekdays 11-5 Sun 2-5 winter weekends only to 4.30.
Admission: Adults £2 first accompanied child free OAPs £1.50 groups larger than 10 - 10% reduction.
Free parking nearby (disabled drivers on-site). Wheelchairs welcome.

HENFIELD

HENFIELD MUSEUM
(Henfield Parish Council)

Village Hall, High Street, Henfield BN5 9DB **Tel:** (01273) 492546
Local history including domestic objects, costume, agricultural tools, archaeology and geology. Local paintings and photographs.
Open: Mon Tues Thurs Sat 10-12 Wed and Sat 2.30-4.30 other times by appointment.
Admission: Free.

HORSHAM

HORSHAM MUSEUM
9 The Causeway, Horsham RH12 1HE **Tel:** (01403) 254959
'Charming, informative, entertaining, attractive; It's a lot larger than we thought'. See why visitors say that. Set in the Historic Causeway, the Tudor timber framed Horsham Museum has a great deal to offer the visitor. With displays on the Wealdon Farmer, bicycles, exotica, domestic bygones, costume, ceramics, furniture, fossils (including a rare dragonfly) etc. Plus two attractively laid out gardens. Horsham is the place to bring the family, or to come on your own and discover a gem of a museum.
Open: Tues-Sat 10-5.
Admission: Free.
Exhibitions/Events: Five temporary exhibitions a year on a variety of themes.

LITTLEHAMPTON

LITTLEHAMPTON MUSEUM
(Littlehampton Town Council)

Manor House, Church Street, Littlehampton BN17 5EP **Tel:** (01903) 715149

LITTLEHAMPTON MUSEUM
WEST SUSSEX

⋆ Fine ship paintings
⋆ Local history & archaeology
⋆ Temporary exhibitions ⋆ Free entry

Maritime paintings, bygones, photographs of the district, local archaeology and history and temporary exhibitions.
Open: Tues-Sat 10.30-4.30 and Aug Bank Hol Mon.
Admission: Free.

STEYNING

STEYNING MUSEUM
Church Street, Steyning BN44 3YB **Tel:** (01903) 813333
Steyning from the Romans to the railway, from Saxon Saint to 400 year old school; its traditions, industry and artistic vitality. Plus regular special exhibitions.
Open: Tues Wed Fri Sat 10.30-12.30 and 2.30-4.30 Sun 2.30-4.30 all year.
Admission: Free.

TANGMERE

TANGMERE MILITARY AVIATION MUSEUM TRUST
Tangmere Airfield, Tangmere PO20 6ES **Tel:** (01243) 775223
The Museum, 1982, tells the story of Military Flying from the earliest days to the present time with the emphasis on this famous 'Battle of Britain' Airfield. Divided into four halls it has a unique collection of exhibits and working displays to fascinate all age groups. Hangar extension housing the actual air speed record breaking aircraft, Meteor and Hunter.
Open: Daily Feb-end Nov 10-5.30 or 4.30 during Nov and Feb.
Admission: Adults £3 OAPs £2.50 children £1 parties by arrangement.
Refreshments: Available - bus service from Chichester.
Free parking, souvenir shop, picnic area, suitable for the disabled.

WORTHING

WORTHING MUSEUM AND ART GALLERY
(Worthing Borough Council)

Chapel Road, Worthing BN11 1HP **Tel:** (01903) 239999 Ext 2528 (Sats (01903) 204229)

'Best Museum of Archaeological or Historical Interest' – Museum of the Year Awards 1987
Shepherding on the South Downs is one of the themes with which the museum deals. Others are the archaeology of the area and the history of the town of Worthing itself, with its seaside life. Other popular features include the Costume Galleries and displays of toys and dolls. The art collections comprise English paintings, pottery and glass. There are frequent exhibitions – current programme on request.
Open daily except Sundays 10 a.m.-6 p.m. April-September: 10a.m.-5 p.m. October-March.
Admission Free. Parties by arrangement. Tel. Worthing 239999 Ext. 2528 (Sats 204229).

Collections include regional archaeology and local history, Sussex bygones, dolls and toys, English paintings, pottery and glass, and costume.
Open: Mon-Sat Apr-Sept 10-6 Oct-Mar 10-5 closed Sun and some Bank Hols.
Admission: Free.
Easy access and toilet for disabled visitors. New Museum Garden for display of outdoor sculpture.

TYNE & WEAR

JARROW

BEDES WORLD

(Jarrow 700 AD Ltd)

Church Bank, Jarrow NE32 3DY **Tel:** 0191-489 2106 **Fax:** 0191-428 2361

Bedes World

The Museum of Early Medieval Northumbria at Jarrow

New Evans and Shalev-designed Museum and 1-acre Farm with 'Anglo-Saxon' landscape, agriculture and experimental constructions of timber buildings from the 7th and 8th centuries now complement exhibitions in 18th -century Jarrow Hall, ruins of a monastic site and 7th-century church of St Paul. Permanent exhibition of material from archaeological excavations includes Anglo-Saxon coloured window-glass, stone sculpture, and model of monastery in Bede's day. AV display based on the life of a monk. Award-winning education programme (contact Education department for school bookings). Herb garden, gift shop, café.
Open: Apr-Oct Tues-Sat 10-5.30 Sun 2.30-5.30 Nov-Mar Tues-Sat 11-4.30 Sun 2.30-5.30 closed Mon (except Bank Hols) between Christmas and the New Year and Good Friday.
Admission: Adults £2.50 children/concessions £1.25 family ticket £5.
Location: Off A185 near south entrance to Tyne Tunnel.
Refreshments: Café serving lunches, teas and light refreshments
Exhibitions/Events: Continuous programme of visiting exhibitions, Living History displays, re-enactment and activity weekends.
Project Director: Dr Chris Grocock; Curator: Miss Susan Mills. Fundraising trust - the Bede Foundation, Director: Dr David Sayers.

NEWCASTLE UPON TYNE

THE CASTLE KEEP MUSEUM

St. Nicholas Street, Newcastle upon Tyne

The keep of the 'New Castle' built by Henry II in 1170. Interpretation of the history of the Castle site.
Open: Apr-Sept Tues-Sun 9.30-5 Oct-Mar Tues-Sun 9.30-4 closed Christmas Day Boxing Day New Year's Day and Good Friday.

HANCOCK MUSEUM

(Tyne & Wear Museums for the University of Newcastle upon Tyne

Barras Bridge, Newcastle upon Tyne NE2 4PT **Tel:** 0191-222 7418 **Fax:** 0191-222 6753

Natural History and Ancient Egypt. Magic of Birds, Yesterday's World as well as changing exhibitions. 1995 exhibitions include Claws!, Creepy Crawly Roadshow, Megabugs. Regular events.
Open: Mon-Sat 10-5 Sun 2-5.
Admission: Adult £1.80 concessions £1 family ticket £5.50.
Refreshments: Café.
Museum shop.

HATTON GALLERY

The Quadrangle, The University of Newcastle upon Tyne NE1 7RU **Tel:** 0191-222 6057 **Fax:** 0191-261 1182

Hosts a programme of temporary exhibitions of contemporary and historical art. The gallery frequently displays items from its own Permanent Collection including British and European paintings, drawings, sculptures and prints from the 16th-17th centuries. On permanent display are the 'Elterwater Merzbarn' a large installation by Dada Artist Kurt Schwitters and the Uhlman Collection of African Sculpture.
Open: The Gallery is open during exhibition periods Mon-Fri 10-5.30 and Sat (term time) 10-4.30.
Admission: Free.
Location: University Quadrangle.

MUSEUM OF ANTIQUITIES
(jointly with the Society of Antiquaries)
The Quadrangle The University of Newcastle upon Tyne, Newcastle upon Tyne NE1 7RU **Tel:** 0191-222 6000 Ext 7844
Prehistoric, Roman, Anglo-Saxon and Medieval antiquities, chiefly from Northumberland. Scale models of Hadrian's Wall and reconstructions of Roman arms and armour and of a temple of Mithras.
Open: Weekdays 10-5 closed Dec 24 25 26 New Year's Day and Good Friday.
Admission: Free.
Museum shop.

THE SHEFTON MUSEUM OF GREEK ART AND ARCHAEOLOGY
Armstrong Building, The Quadrangle, The University of Newcastle upon Tyne NE1 7RU **Tel:** 0191-222 6000 Ext 7966
Collection of ancient Greek and Etruscan art ranging from Minoan to Hellenistic times; vases, terracottas, bronzes, gems and armour.
Open: Normally Mon-Fri 9-1 and 2-4.30 and by appointment.
Admission: Free.

WARWICKSHIRE

GAYDON

HERITAGE MOTOR CENTRE
(The British Motor Industry Heritage Trust)
Banbury Road, Gaydon, nr Warwick CV35 OBJ **Tel:** (01926) 641188 **Fax:** (01926) 641555
The finest collection of uniquely British Cars. 250 vehicles representing the history of the British Motor Industry.
Open: Daily (except Christmas & Boxing Day) Apr-Oct 10-6 Nov-Mar 10-4.30.
Admission: Fee charged with discounts for group bookings.
Location: 2 mins from J12 on M40.
Refreshments: Available.
Suitable for disabled persons. Conference Centre, Education Centre.

LEAMINGTON SPA

LEAMINGTON SPA ART GALLERY AND MUSEUM
(Warwick District Council)
Avenue Road, Leamington Spa **Tel:** (01926) 426559
Paintings by Dutch and Flemish masters; 19th and 20th century oils and watercolours, mainly English. Sixteenth-nineteenth century pottery and porcelain; 18th century English glass. Local history displays.
Open: Mon Tues Thurs-Sat 10-1 2-5 (also Thurs evening 6-8) closed Wed and Sun.
Exhibitions/Events: Changing temporary exhibitions throughout the year

NUNEATON

NUNEATON MUSEUM AND ART GALLERY
Riversley Park, Nuneaton **Tel:** (01203) 376158
Local history, major display on local authoress George Eliot, Art Exhibitions.
Open: Tues-Sat 10.30-4.30 Sun 2-4.30 Tea-room only Mon 10.30-4.30.
Refreshments: Tea-room.
Toilets. Disabled access/lift.

RUGBY

RUGBY LIBRARY AND EXHIBITION GALLERY
St. Mathew's Street, Rugby CV21 3BZ **Tel:** (01788) 542687 or 571813 **Fax:** (01778) 573289
Exhibitions by local artists and societies.
Open: Mon & Thurs 9.30-8 Tues & Fri 9.30-5 Wed 9.30-1 Sat 9.30-4.

STRATFORD-UPON-AVON

THE SHAKESPEARE BIRTHPLACE TRUST'S PROPERTIES
The Shakespeare Centre, Henley Street, Stratford-upon-Avon CV37 6QW **Tel:** (01789) 204016 **Fax:** (01789) 296083
Shakespeare's Birthplace, Anne Hathaway's Cottage, New Place/Nash's House, Hall's Croft and the Shakespeare Countryside Museum at Mary Arden's House; the five beautifully preserved Tudor houses in and around Stratford connected with the dramatist and his family. Outstanding period furniture, museum and folk-life collections and delightful gardens.
Admission: Separate properties from adult £1.80 and inclusive ticket adult £7.50 (1994 prices).
Location: All in or near Stratford and well signed.
Refreshments: Hall's Croft Anne Hathaway's cottage Mary Arden's House.
Send sae for adm details to the Director.

WARWICK

DOLL MUSEUM
(Warwickshire County Council)
Oken's House, Castle Street, Warwick **Tel:** (01926) 495546
Displays on dolls and their houses, puzzles and games.
Open: Easter-end Sept Mon-Sat 10-5 Sun 1-5 plus Sats throughout the year.

ST. JOHN'S HOUSE
(Warwickshire County Council)
St. John's, Warwick **Tel:** (01926) 412132
Warwickshire bygones and period costume. Victorian classroom, kitchen and parlour.
Open: Tues-Sat 10-12.30 1.30-5.30 closed Mon (except Bank Hols) Sun (May-Sept) 2.30-5.

WARWICKSHIRE MUSEUM
(Warwickshire County Council)
Market Place, Warwick **Tel:** (01926) 412500 Sat 412501
Wildlife, geology, archaeology and history of Warwickshire including the famous Sheldon tapestry map and giant fossil plesiosaur.
Open: Mon-Sat 10-5.30 Sun (May-Sept) 2-5.

WEST MIDLANDS

BICKENHILL

NATIONAL MOTORCYCLE MUSEUM

Coventry Road, Bickenhill **Tel:** (01675) 443311

Visit Britain's Motorcycling Heritage
A unique display of hundreds of British motorcycles spanning from your Great-Grand father's era right up to the present day. Alongside stunning machine displays is a wealth of historic documentation and photographs. The visitor is able to capture the full flavour of historic motorcycling.
The museum is on the A45/M42 junction, there's ample parking, a restaurant for a snack or full meal, and a well stocked souvenir shop.
NATIONAL MOTORCYCLE MUSEUM
Coventry Road, Bickenhill, Solihull.
Tel: Hampton-in-Arden (01675) 443311
Open 7 days a week, 10am-6pm.
Near Birmingham Airport
and close to the National Exhibition Centre.

Hundreds of beautifully restored motorcycles create a colourful evocation of the history of British motorcycling. Vintage motorcycles, racing machines, many unusual exhibits. Giant poster boards. Historic documentation of the machines and their riders.
Open: Daily 10-6 (except Christmas Eve Christmas Day and Boxing Day).
Admission: Adults £4.25 children/OAPs £3.25 reduction for parties on application.
Refreshments: Restaurant and snack bar.
Gift and book shop. Conference facilities available. Free coach and car park.

BIRMINGHAM

THE BARBER INSTITUTE OF FINE ARTS

(The University of Birmingham)
Edgbaston, Birmingham B15 2TS **Tel:** 0121-472 0962

An outstanding collection of Old Master and Modern paintings including major works by Bellini, Rubens, Poussin, Murillo, Gainsborough, Rossetti and Whistler. French Impressionist paintings include masterpieces by Monet, Degas, Pissarro, Van Gogh and Gauguin. Among the twentieth century artists represented are Gwen John, Sickert, Léger and Magritte. Also houses an extensive collection of Byzantine and Roman coins. Active schools liaison programme, also concerts, lectures and recitals.
Open: Mon-Sat 10-5 Sun 2-5 closed New Year's Day Good Friday Easter Sunday Christmas Day and Boxing Day.
Admission: Free. Parties by special arrangement if guided tour required.
Location: Edgbaston Park Road, Edgbaston, Birmingham.
Parking facilities, several public and University car parks nearby. Museum shop. Facilities for the disabled.

BIRMINGHAM MUSEUM AND ART GALLERY

Chamberlain Square, Birmingham B3 3DH **Tel:** 0121-235 2834

One of the Best. A spectacular Victorian building housing the world's finest collection of Pre-Raphaelites. The collection includes Fine and Applied Art, archaeology, ethnography, and social history. Other collections are housed at Aston Hall, 17th Century Jacobean House and The Museum of Science and Industry.
Open: Mon-Sat 10-5 Sun 12.30-5.
Admission: Free except Gas Hall.
Location: Birmingham city centre.
Refreshments: Edwardian tea-room.
Exhibitions/Events: Feb 25-June 4 'China: Cradle of Knowledge'(7,000 years of invention and discovery, live craft displays - only British showing). July 22-Oct 1 'Treasures from the Indian Courts' (from V&A collections: textiles, weaponry, metalwork - only British showing).
Lift to all floors.

JEWELLERY QUARTER DISCOVERY CENTRE

(Birmingham City Council)

77-79 Vyse Street, Hockley, Birmingham B18 6HA **Tel:** 0121-554 3598 **Fax:** 0121-236 1766

An exciting living museum which combines a visitor centre with an authentic working jewellery factory which is little changed since the beginning of the century. Video presentations and displays tell the 200 year story of Birmingham's unique jewellery industry and a team of guides and jewellers show how the adjoining Smith and Pepper jewellery works operated before closure in 1981. The entire factory was left totally undisturbed by the departing jewellers and has been preserved to provide an insight into the City's famous industries. Museum of the Year Award winner - Best Industrial Museum 1993.
Open: Mon-Fri 10-4 Sat 11-5.
Admission: Adults £2 concessions £1.50.
Location: Close to Birmingham City Centre.
Refreshments: Coffee and tea available.
Exhibitions/Events: New exhibition Gallery opening 1995.
Full access to all areas of the museum for disabled visitors. Audio guides in French, German, Italian, Spanish, Japanese and Hindi.

SAREHOLE MILL

(Birmingham City Council)

Colebank Road, Hall Green, Birmingham B13 0BD **Tel:** 0121-777 6612

Birmingham's last surviving working watermill. Eighteenth century mill restored to working order during the 1960s. Find out how corn was ground into flour and how Birmingham's early industries were driven by waterpower. Displays about milling, farming and the history of the site. Home to Matthew Boulton from 17 to 1761. Inspiration to JRR Tolkein author of 'The Hobbit'.
Open: Apr 1- Oct 29 during season Mon-Sun 2-5.

COVENTRY

HERBERT ART GALLERY AND MUSEUM

Jordan Well, Coventry CV1 5QP **Tel:** (01203) 832381 **Fax:** (01203) 832410

Archaeology, natural and local history, visual and decorative arts.
Open: Mon-Sat 10-5.30 Sun 2-5 closed part of Christmas period.
Admission: Free.
Refreshments: Coffee shop.
Full access fro disabled people. Baby changing room.

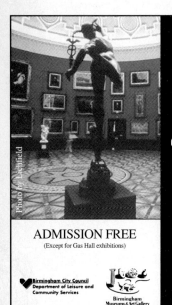

LUNT ROMAN FORT (RECONSTRUCTION)

Baginton, near Coventry **Tel:** (01203) 832381/832433 **Fax:** (01203) 832410
Rampart, gateway, gyrus and granary displaying finds from the site and the life of the soldiers in the fort.
Open: Sat Sun Bank Hols April-Oct every day mid July-August Bank Hol 10-5.
Admission: Adults £2.50 children £1.25.
Refreshments: Picnic Area.
Full access fo disabled people including W.C.

MIDLAND AIR MUSEUM

Coventry Airport, Baginton, Coventry **Tel:** (01203) 301033 **Fax:** (01203) 301033
Over 30 aircraft from diminutive Gnat jet fighter to giant Vulcan bomber and Argosy freighter. Sir Frank Whittle Jet Heritage Centre - exhibition building contains display on work of Coventry born jet pioneer.
Open: Mon-Sat 10.30-5 Sun 10.30-6.
Admission: Adults £2.50 children £1.50 OAP's £1.75 family ticket £7 reductions for parties.
Location: Coventry Airport, Bagington.
Refreshments: Available.
Free car parking. Suitable for disabled persons. Souvenir shop, picnic area.

MUSEUM OF BRITISH ROAD TRANSPORT

(Coventy City Council)
St Agnes Lane, Hales Street, Coventry CV1 1PN **Tel:** (01203) 832425
Fax: (01203) 832465
Take a tour through Britain's road transport heritage at the home of the nation's motor industry. Coventry's Museum of British Road Transport displays the largest collection of its kind - from the earliest cysles to the fastest car on earth. Visitors can step back in time to the elegance of Edwardian motoring and the glamour of the 30's. See how royalty rode in style and reflect on family cars of the 50's and 60's. Experience the wartime bombing of Coventry in the Blitz experience. Our vehicles are not just full sized, Tiatsa Model World displays the history of road transport in miniature.
Open: 7 days a week 10-4.30 (last admission) closed Christmas Day Christmas Eve and Boxing Day.
Admission: Adults £2.95 children/OAPs £1.95 parties of 20+ adults £2 children/OAPs £1.
Location: Coventry City centre.
Refreshments: Cafeteria - range of hot and cold snacks available.
Suitable for disabled persons, wheelchairs available. Local authority car parks nearby.

DUDLEY

BLACK COUNTRY MUSEUM

Tipton Road, Dudley **Tel:** 0121-557 9643

On a 26 acre site in the heart of the Industrial West Midlands buildings and machines from throughout the area create a living tribute to the skills and enterprise of the people of the Black Country. An electric tramcar carries visitors past a unique underground coal mining display 'Into the Thick' and a working replica of the world's first steam engine to the village where carefully reconstructed shops and houses cluster around a chapel and pub next to ironworks and manufactories. Nailmaking and chainmaking, glass cutting, baking, boatbuilding and ironworking are demonstrated regularly providing an educational and entertaining glimpse of times past.
Open: Daily 10-5 Mar 1-Oct 31 Wed-Sun 10-4 Nov-Feb closed Dec 18-25.
Admission: (1995) adults £5.50 OAPs £4.75 children £4.
Location: 3 miles from Junction 2 on M5.
Refreshments: Available.
Museum shop.

WILTSHIRE

DEVIZES

DEVIZES MUSEUM

(Wiltshire Archaeological and Natural History Society)
41, Long Street, Devizes SN10 1NS **Tel:** (01380) 727369
Prehistoric collections of international standing, weapons, exotic ornaments and personal finery. Henge monument room, galleries for Roman, Saxon and Medieval periods. Art Gallery; natural history displays. Local History gallery. New Bronze Age Callery. Library for study of local history.
Open: All year Mon-Sat 10-5 (excluding public holidays).
Admission: Adults £1.75 students/OAPs £1.25 children 40p reduction in admission charge for pre-arranged parties.
Exhibitions/Events: Changing programme of events.

LACOCK

LACKHAM COUNTRY ATTRACTIONS - GARDENS, MUSEUM AND RARE ANIMAL BREEDS

Lacock SN15 2NY **Tel:** (01249) 443111 **Fax:** (01249) 444474
Agricultural implements, machinery, wagons and tools housed in reconstructed farm buildings.
Open: Apr-Oct 11-5.
Admission: Adults £3 children £1 OAPs/concessions £2 membership tickets and party rates available.
Location: 3 miles South of Chippenham on A350 and 1 mile from National Trust village of Lacock.
Refreshments: Coffee shop for light refreshments.
Exhibitions/Events: As well as the museum, the gardens are of particular interest and include an Italian garden of balustrades and rose terraces plus long mixed herbaceous borders and collections of vegetables, fruit and flowers. Also a collection of rare animal breeds.

SALISBURY

SALISBURY AND SOUTH WILTSHIRE MUSEUM

The King's House, 65 The Close, Salisbury SP1 2EN **Tel:** (01722) 332151
Home of the Stonehenge gallery and winner of 6 awards for excellence. Early Man, Pitt Rivers collection, Salisbury history, Wedgwood, ceramics, costume, lace, embroidery. Gift shop. Café (Apr-Oct). Wheelchair facilities.
Open: Mon-Sat 10-5 Suns in Jul Aug and Salisbury Festival 2-5.
Admission: Adults £2.50 children 50p concessions £1.75 valid all calendar year.
Location: Located in the Cathedral Close opposite the west front (Station: Salisbury)

SWINDON

GREAT WESTERN RAILWAY MUSEUM

(Thamesdown Borough Council)
Faringdon Road, Swindon **Tel:** (01793) 493189
Historic G.W.R. locomotives, wide range of name-plates, models, illustrations, posters, tickets etc.

Open: Mon-Sat 10-5 Sun 2-5.
Admission: Adults £2.10 children £1 (admits also to Railway Village Museum) party rates.
Location: Junction 15 on M4 (follow the brown tourist signs).

RICHARD JEFFERIES MUSEUM
(Thamesdown Borough Council)
Coate, Swindon **Tel:** (01793) 493188
Reconstruction of Jefferies' study and cheese room, with personal items, manuscripts, first editions, and historical photographs relating to Richard Jefferies and Alfred Williams.
Open: Restricted usually first and third Sun May-Sept 2-5 telephone to confirm.
Admission: Free.

LYDIARD PARK
(Thamesdown Borough Council)
Lydiard Tregoze, Swindon **Tel:** (01793) 770401
18th Century house, former home of St John family, set in parkland. Fine furniture, portrait collections, original wallpaper and fascinating painted window. Adjacent Parish Church contains exceptional monuments to the St John Family.
Open: Mon-Sat 10-1 and 2-5.30 Sun 2-5.30 early closing Nov-Feb inclusive.
Location: Just off Junction 16 on M4 (follow the brown tourist signs).
Refreshments: Cafe in grounds.
Group tours by appointment. Wheelchair access. Gift shop.

RAILWAY VILLAGE MUSEUM
(Thamesdown Borough Council)
34 Faringdon Road, Swindon **Tel:** (01793) 526161 Ext 4527
A foreman's house in the original G.W.R. Village refurbished as it was at the turn of the century.
Open: Mon-Sat 10-1 and 2-5 Sun 2-5.
Admission: Adults 80p concessions 40p.

SWINDON MUSEUM AND ART GALLERY
(Thamesdown Borough Council)
Bath Road, Swindon **Tel:** (01793) 493188
Archaeology, geology and social history of Swindon and N.E. Wiltshire. Permanent 20th century British art and ceramic collection.
Open: Mon-Sat 10-5.30 Sun 2-5.30.
Admission: Free.

WROUGHTON

SCIENCE MUSEUM
Wroughton Airfield, Wroughton **Tel:** (01793) 814466
Open: Selected days throughout the summer period, for further details telephone as above.
Location: Nr. Swindon, Wiltshire.

NORTH YORKSHIRE

ALDBOROUGH

THE ALDBOROUGH ROMAN MUSEUM
(English Heritage)
Aldborough **Tel:** (01423) 322768
The museum contains Roman finds, including pottery, glass, metalwork and coins from the Roman town.
Open: Apr 1-Sept 30 daily 10-6.
Admission: Adults £1.25 concessions 95p children 60p (1994 prices).

HARROGATE

HARLOW CARR MUSEUM OF GARDENING
(Northern Horticultural Society)
Crag Lane, Harrogate HG3 1QB **Tel:** (01423) 565418
Small museum of gardening implements and history, set within 68 acres of beautiful gardens and woodland.
Open: Daily 9.30-4.
Admission: Fee charge to gardens includes museum.
Location: 2 miles West of Harrogate on B6162 (Otley Road).
Refreshments: Restaurant all year. Also in summer, kiosk with snacks.
Plant sales, shop, access for disabled.

NIDDERDALE MUSEUM
Council Offices, King Street, Pateley Bridge, Harrogate HG3 5LE **Tel:** (01423) 711225
Housed in a Victorian Workhouse, their are nine rooms featuring all aspects of life in Nidderdale.
Open: Daily Easter-end Sept 2-5 winter Suns only parties by arrangement ring (0423) 711743 limited disabled acccss
Admission: From 1.1.94 adults £1 children/OAPs 50p.
Location: Pateley Bridge N. Yorkshire

HAWES

DALES COUNTRYSIDE MUSEUM
Station Yard, Hawes DL8 3NT **Tel:** (01969) 667494/50
Museum about people and landscape of the Pennine Dales.
Open: Apr-Oct Inc. 10-5.
Admission: Adults £1.50 concessions 75p.

MALTON

EDEN CAMP - MODERN HISTORY THEME MUSEUM
Eden Camp, Malton YO17 0SD **Tel:** (01653) 697777
A visit to our unique museum at Eden Camp will transort you back to Wartime Britain. This is no ordinary museum - it is a series of reconstructed scenes, telling the story of civilian life during World War II.
Open: Daily Feb 14-Dec 23 10-5.
Location: Junction of A64 York to Scarborough Rd and A160 Malton to Pickering.
Refreshments: Full catering facilities & bar.
'Yorkshire & Humberside visitor attraction of The Year 1992' England for Excellence, Tourism for All Silver Award.

PICKERING

BECK ISLE MUSEUM OF RURAL LIFE
Pickering **Tel:** (01751) 473653
Regency residence of William Marshall, a noted agriculturist of the late 18th and early 19th centuries. Situated in the centre of an historic town, the many rooms house a considerable collection illustrating the work, social life and customs of the rural community during the past 200 years. Of educational interest to all ages.
Open: 28 Mar-Oct 31 daily 10-5.
Admission: Fee charged.
Parties by arrangement. Phone (01751) 473548.

NORTH YORKSHIRE MOORS RAILWAY
(The North York Moors Historical Railway Trust Ltd)
Pickering Station, Pickering YO18 7AJ **Tel:** (01751) 472508
18 miles journey from Pickering to Grosmont near Whitby. Trains pulled by steam engines. Engine sheds at Grosmont, carriage and wagon works at Pickering. Take a steam hauled journey into railway heritage on the line between Pickering and Grosmont. Originally built by George Stephenson in the 1830's the route offers spectacular scenery.
Open: Easter-end Oct 7 days a week 10-5.
Admission: Standard adult return £8.50 child £4.30 OAP £6.40 10% discount for groups of 20 or more 1 teacher free with each 10 children.
Location: Pickering Stn (South of line) through Levisham Stn, Newtondale Halt, Goathland Stn, Grosmont Stn (North).
Refreshments: Tea-rooms at Pickering Stn and Grosmont Stn.
Exhibitions/Events: All year round see timetable for details.
Dining services on board, evening meals and Sunday lunch. Suitable for disabled persons. Car Parking at Pickering, Levisham and Grosmont.

REETH

SWALEDALE FOLK MUSEUM
Reeth, ncar Richmond DL11 6TX **Tel:** (01748) 884373
Depicts how leadmining and sheep farming shaped life in this remote and beautiful Dale.
Open: Easter-Oct 31 daily and other months by arrangement.
Admission: Fee charged.

RICHMOND

GEORGIAN THEATRE ROYAL
(Bill Sellars)
Victoria Road, Richmond DL10 4DW **Tel:** (01748) 823710
Built in 1788. The country's oldest theatre in original form; also Theatre Museum.
Open: Easter Sat-Oct 31 Mon-Sat 11-4.45 Sun 2.30-4.45.
Admission: Fee charged.
Location: Victoria Road, Richmond, N. Yorks.
Refreshments: Coffee bar.
Parties all year round on application to the Manager.

THE GREEN HOWARDS MUSEUM
Trinity Church Square, Richmond DL10 4QN **Tel:** (01748) 822133 **Fax:** (01748) 826561
Uniforms, medals, campaign relics, contemporary MSS, pictures and prints, headdress, buttons, badges and embellishments from 17th century onwards.
Open: Apr-Oct Weekdays 9.30-4.30 Sun 2-4.30 Nov Feb and Mar weekdays 10-4.30 closed Feb Sat and Sun Mar and Nov Sun and throughout Dec and Jan.
Admission: Fee charged.
Location: In the converted church of the Holy Trinity.

THE RICHMONDSHIRE MUSEUM
(The Richmondshire Museum Trust)
Ryders Wynd, Richmond DL10 4JA **Tel:** (01748) 825611
The history and development of Richmondshire. Lead mining, local crafts, agriculture, cruck house, model of Richmond railway complex, costume and needlecraft, toys, archaeology. Vet's surgery set from Herriot TV series. Barker's chemist set and Grinton Post Office.
Open: Daily Good Friday-late Oct 11-5.
Admission: Adults 80p children/students 60p family groups £2.
Parties by appointment. Disabled access.

RIPON

RIPON PRISON AND POLICE MUSEUM
St. Marygate, Ripon **Tel:** (01765) 690799
A former Victorian prison with cells converted to museum use. the displays deal with crime, punishment, imprisonment and law enforcement over recent centuries.
Open: Easter-Oct weekdays (except July & Aug) 1-5 July Aug 11-5 Sun 1-5.
Admission: Adults £1 OAPs & students 60p children 5-16yrs 50p.
Parties by arrangement at any time, Tel 01765-603006. Car park opposite

SCARBOROUGH

ROTUNDA MUSEUM
(Scarborough Borough Council)
Vernon Road, Scarborough **Tel:** (01723) 374839 **Fax:** (01723) 376941
Fine example of Georgian purpose-built museum opened 1829. The Upper Galleries are lined with original display cabinets and the 'Moveable Stage', as seen on television's 'Cabinet of Curiosities'. Exhibitions illustrate life and activities of people living in the area from the early prehistoric to the development of the seaside spa resort.
Admission: Free.
Books and cards for sale.

SCARBOROUGH ART GALLERY
(Scarborough Borough Council)
The Cresent, Scarborough YO11 2PW **Tel:** (01723) 374753 **Fax:** (01723) 376941
Victorian villa, built 1835 in Italianate style, houses the Laughton Collection, fine works of art from leading artists from 17th to 20th centuries and an extensive local collection of watercolours by Scarborough artists. Monthly exhibitions show a varied range of contemporary and art historical works, crafts, ceramice, sculpture and photography.
Admission: Free.
Refreshments: New coffee room.
Books, cards and prints for sale.

WOOD END MUSEUM
(Scarborough Borough Council)

The Cresent, Scarborough YO11 2PW **Tel:** (01723) 367326 **Fax:** (01723) 376941

Built 1835 and former home of the Sitwells, contains an almost complete collection of their published works, together with portraits and paintings connected with their writings, in the restored West Wing. A double-stored Victorian conservatory, housing tropical plants and aquarium, links with the Main Building where there are displays on local geology and natural history.

Open: Winter mid Oct-Spring bank hol (except easter Tue-Sun 11-4) Fri-Sun 11-4 Summer Spring bank hol-Mid Oct Tue-Sun 10-5 closed Mon but open bank hol Mons.

Admission: Free.

Books, cards, replicas for sale in Museum shop.

SKIPTON

CRAVEN MUSEUM

1st Floor, Town Hall, High Street, Skipton **Tel:** (01756) 794079 **Fax:** (01756) 794079

Folk history, archaeology, geology, costumes, leadmining - a small museum crammed full of curios, guaranteed to have something of interest for everyone.

Open: Apr-Sept weekdays 10-5 closed Tues Sat 10-12 and 1-5 Sun 2-5 Oct-Mar weekdays 1.30-5 closed Tues Sat 10-12 and 1.30-4.30.

Admission: Free.

THIRSK

THIRSK MUSEUM

14-16 Kirkgate, Thirsk YO7 1PQ **Tel:** (01845) 522755

Folk museum, local history, cricket memorabilia. See infamous 'death chair'. Birthplace of Thomas Lord, founder of Lord's Cricket Ground.

Open: Daily Easter-end of Oct.

Admission: Fee charged.

Free car parking nearby.

WHITBY

WHITBY MUSEUM
(Whitby Literary and Philosophical Society)

Pannett Park, Whitby YO21 1RE **Tel:** (01947) 602908

Nationally-important collections of fossils, Whitby jet jewellery, model ships. Fine ethnographic collection. Local archaeology, geology, natural history. Bygones, costumes, dolls and toys.

Open: May-Sept Weekdays 9.30-5.30 Sun 2-5 Oct-Apr Mon Tues 10.30-1 Wed-Sat 10.30-4 Sun 2-4 open Easter Mon 10.30-4 closed Xmas and New Year's hols last admission 30 minutes before closing.

Admission: Fee charged.

Location: Pannett Park.

Bookstall.

YORK

THE ARC
(York Archaeological Trust)

Archaeological Resource Centre, St. Saviourgate, York YO1 2NN **Tel:** (01904) 654324 **Fax:** (01904) 640029

The ARC is 'state of the art' for visitor involvement in archaeology. Whether handling actual artefacts such as pottery sherds, bone, sieved soil samples or experimenting with ancient craft technologies in stitching a Roman shoe, or weaving on a Viking loom, visitors will find themselves in touch with the past. Excavation can be explored with the use of interactive videos, and computers can be used, just as the modern archaeologist does, to record and process details. Visitors can also watch archaeologists at work examining objects and entering data. The ARC dispels the 'backroom' image of archaeological research in an innovative and absorbing way.

Open: Mon-Fri 10-5 Sat and Sun 1-5 closed Good Friday and Dec 18-Jan 2.

Admission: Fee charged.

Location: York City Centre.

National Heritage Museum of the Year Awards - voted 'Best Museum of Archaeological and Historical Interest', sponsored by BBC.

FAIRFAX HOUSE

(York Civic Trust)

Castlegate, York YO1 1RN **Tel:** (01904) 655543 **Fax:** (01904) 652262

An 18th century house designed by John Carr of York and described as a classic architectural masterpiece of its age. Certainly one of the finest townhouses in England and saved from near collapse by the York Civic Trust who restored it to its former glory during 1982/84. In addition to the superbly decorated plasterwork, wood and wrought iron, the house is now home for an outstanding collection of 18th century Furniture and Clocks, formed by the late Noel Terry. Described by Christie's as one of the finest private collections of this century, it enhances and complements the house and helps to create a very special 'lived in' feeling. The gift of the entire collection by Noel Terry's Trustees to the Civic Trust has enabled it to fill the house with the appropriate pieces of the period and has provided the basis for what can now be considered a fully furnished Georgian Townhouse. Annual exhibitions on aspects of 18th century life.

Open: Feb 20-Jan 6 Mon-Thurs and Sat 11-5 Sun 1.30-5 (last adm 4.30) closed Fri except in Aug.

Admission: Adults £3 children £1.50 OAPs £2.50 parties adults (prebooked 15 or more) £2.50 children £1.25.

Public car park within 50 yards. Suitable for disabled persons only with assistance (by telephoning beforehand staff can be available to help). A small gift shop offers selected antiques, publications and gifts. Opening times are the same as the house.

Visit the Jorvik Viking Centre in York and a time car will glide you back 1000 years to a reconstruction of an actual street in Viking Age Jorvik. Complete with sounds and smells, it's an unforgettabe experience.
JORVIK VIKING CENTRE

(York Archaeological Trust)

Coppergate, York YO1 1NT **Tel:** (01904) 643211 **Fax:** (01904) 627097

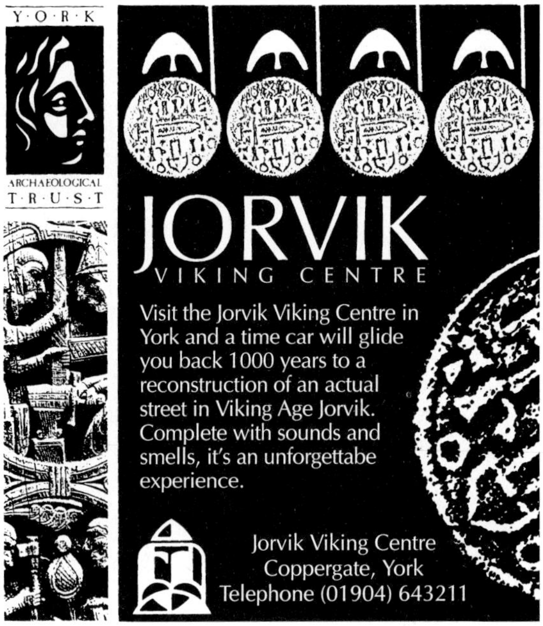

Uncovered by archaeologists Jorvik is the Viking city untouched since the Vikings lived in York a thousand years ago. Cooking-ware, shoes, fragments of clothing, a market, busy wharf and houses have been re-created in accurate detail. The Viking Dig is reconstructed where it took place, with the preserved 10th century buildings replaced where they were found.

Open: Apr-Oct daily 9-7 Nov-Mar daily 9-5.30.

Admission: Fee charged.

Location: York City Centre.

NATIONAL RAILWAY MUSEUM

(Science Museum)

Leeman Road, York YO2 4XJ **Tel:** (01904) 621261 **Fax:** (01904) 611112

Experience nearly 200 years of technical and social history on the railways and see the way they shaped the world.

Open: Mon-Sat 10-6 Sun 11-6 (last adm 5) closed December 24 25 26.

Admission: Adult £4.20 children £2.10 concessions £2.80 (as at 15/7/94 subject to change).

Location: Five minutes walk from main railway station.

Refreshments: Restaurant.

Education service, reference library, conference facilities, corporate hire. Museum shop, car park, free coach parking for pre-booked parties. Facilities for the disabled.

RYEDALE FOLK MUSEUM

(The Crosland Foundation)

Hutton le Hole, York YO6 6UA **Tel:** (01751) 417367

In the heart of the North Yorkshire Moors. Sandford Award winning Museum. Outstanding collection of rescued buildings; including cruck houses, and unique photographic studio. Extensive collections of craft tools, farming equipment and domestic artefacts. Village shop and P.O. Archaeological and industrial displays.

Open: Mar-Oct everyday 10-5.30 last admission 4.30.

Admission: Adults £2.50 OAPs/students £2 children £1.25 family (2+2) £6.50 special rates for disabled and handicapped under 5 yrs old free. For parties adults £2 OAPs/students £1.60 children £1.

Location: 3 miles north of Kirkbymoorside, 20 miles north of York.

YORK CASTLE MUSEUM

(York City Council)

Eye of York, York YO1 1RY **Tel:** (01904) 653611

Featuring complete Victorian and Edwardian streets with fully stocked shops and a pub typical of the period, the museum is a fascinating social history of Brtain over the last 400 years. Founded on a collection by Dr Kirk it includes whole rooms from an 1850's Yorkshire Moorland Cottage to a family home at the time of the 1953 Coronation. Among the thousands of everyday objects are toys and games, televisions and radios as well as fire engines, a hansom cab, vintage cars, even a water driven corn mill which can be seen in summertime. A new exhibition for 1994 is 'Seeing it Through' describing the experiences of York people during the Second World War. The museum is housed in 18th Century debtor and women's prisons and includes the condemned cell where Dick Turpin spent his last night.

Open: Apr-Oct Mon-Sats from 9.30 last admission 5.30 Suns from 10 Nov-Mar last admission 4.

Admission: Fee charged.

Refreshments: Cafe.

Shop.

YORK CITY ART GALLERY

(York City Council)

Exhibition Square, York **Tel:** (01904) 551861

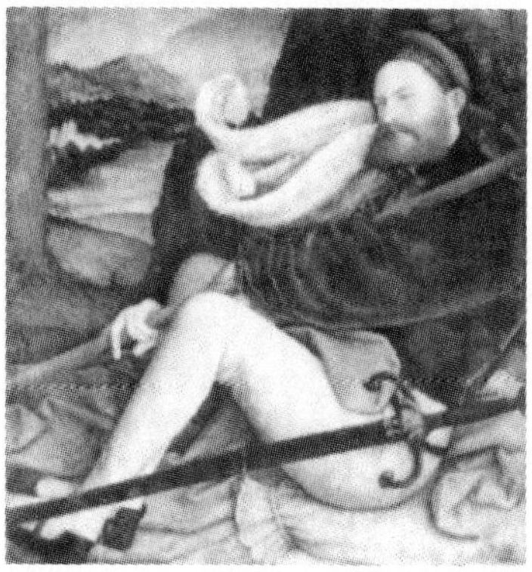

Strigel *Sleeping Soldier*

Outstanding collections of Western European paintings including the Lycett Green collection of Old Masters and works by York artists, notably William Etty; water-colours, drawings and prints mostly devoted to the topography of York; unrivalled collection of pioneer studio pottery. Lively and varied programme of changing exhibitions and events.

Open: Mon-Sat 10-5 Sun 2.30-5 last adm 4.30 closed Dec 25 26 Jan 1 and Good Friday.

Admission: Free (except for some special exhibitions).

Gallery News leaflet available on request. Gallery shop. Facilities for the disabled.

YORK STORY

(York City Council)

The Heritage Centre, Castlegate, York **Tel:** (01904) 628632

Britain's finest Heritage Centre, set up in 1975 to interpret the social and architectural history of the City of York. The exhibitions, which include many notable pieces by modern artists and craftsmen, is equipped with a new audio-visual presentation which shows the history of York, highlighting the surviving buildings and objects. Models and dioramas.

Open: Mon-Sat 10-5 Sun 1-5.

Admission: Adults £1.50 children/OAPs/students/unemployed £1 (prices apply to Mar 1995).

Shop.

YORKSHIRE AIR MUSEUM

(The Trustees of the YAM)

Halifax Way, Elvington, York YO4 5AU **Tel:** (01904) 608595 **Fax:** (01904) 608246

The Yorkshire Air Museum is on a 4 Group RAF station of WW2. It has an interesting collection of aircraft including the only Halifax re-build in the world. It retains an authentic WW2 control tower; it houses the Barnes Wallis collection.

Open: End March-Remembrance Day weekdays 10.30-4 Sats Suns Bank Hols 10.30-5.

Admission: Adults £3 children/senior citizens £2.

Location: On the B1228, 5 miles from York (off the A1079 Hull Road); signposted at Grimson roundabout.

Refreshments: Restaurant.

Car parking. Facilities for the disabled, one wheelchair is available. Shop.

THE YORKSHIRE MUSEUM

(North Yorkshire County Council)

Museum Gardens, York YO1 2DR **Tel:** (01904) 629745 **Fax:** (01904) 651221

Our rare collections illustrate the culture of Roman, Anglo-Saxon, Viking and Medieval life in Yorkshire. Admission charge includes entrance to temporary exhibitions and the new geology gallery 'Time Climb'.

Open: 1 Apr-31 Oct open daily 10-5 from 1 Nov Mon-Sat 10-5 Sun 1-5 last admission 4.30.

Admission: Adults £3 children/OAPs/unemployed £1.75 family ticket £7.

Location: Set in 10 acres of botanical gardens next to St. Mary's Abbey. City centre five minutes walk from York Minster.
Refreshments: Catering can be arranged on request.

SOUTH YORKSHIRE

BARNSLEY

CANNON HALL MUSEUM

(Barnsley Metropolitan Council)
Cawthorne, Barnsley S75 4AT **Tel:** (01226) 790270

Cannon Hall is a late 17th century house remodelled by John Carr of York in the 1760s. The museum has a fine collection of furniture, paintings, glassware and pottery, some of which is displayed in period rooms. It also houses the Regimental Museum of the 13th/18th Royal Hussars (Queen Mary's Own). The museum is situated in Cannon Hall Country Park which with its landscaped grounds provides an ideal setting for a family day out.
Open: Tues Wed Thurs Fri Sat 10.30-5 Sun 12-5 closed Mon.
Admission: By donation.
Location: Off the A635 between Huddersfield and Barnsley

COOPER GALLERY

(Barnsley Metropolitan Borough Council)
Church Street, Barnsley S70 2AH **Tel:** (01226) 242905
The Cooper Gallery presents a continuous programme of temporary exhibitions and related activities, focusing on contemporary art and craft and including thematic exhibitions from the permanent collection. The Cooper Gallery Collections include 17th Century Dutch, 18th and 19th Century French and European paintings and a fine collection of English drawings and watercolours from the Michael Sadler Bequest. Specific examples from the permanent collection may be viewed by prior appointment with the Curator.
Open: Tues-Fri 12.30-4.30 Sat 10-1.30 closed Sun and Mon.
Admission: Free.
Location: Barnsley Town Centre.

WORSBROUGH MILL MUSEUM

(Barnsley Metropolitan Borough Council)
Worsbrough Bridge, Barnsley S70 5LJ **Tel:** (01266) 774527
17th century corn mill restored to working condition. Daily demonstrations of water-powered machinery. Programme of milling days and craft weekends. Various stoneground flours produced for sale. Set in 200 acre country park. Including Open Farm.
Open: Wed-Sun 10-5 summer and 10-4 winter closed Mon and Tues.
Admission: By donation groups £10.
Location: off A61 2 miles north M1 Junction 36.

DONCASTER

DONCASTER MUSEUM AND ART GALLERY

(Doncaster Metropolitan Borough Council)
Chequer Road, Doncaster DN1 2AE **Tel:** (01302) 734293 **Fax:** (01302) 735409
Natural history, prehistoric, Roman and medieval archaeology and local history, militaria, costume, paintings, sculpture, silver, ceramics and glass. The Regimental Collection of the King's Own Yorkshire Light Infantry. Temporary exhibitions of fine art, craft and photography.
Open: Mon-Sat 10-5 Sun 2-5.
Admission: Free.
Location: Off inner ring road/Waterdale.
Full disabled access.

MUSEUM OF SOUTH YORKSHIRE LIFE, CUSWORTH HALL

(Doncaster Metropolitan Borough Council)
Cusworth Park, Cusworth, Doncaster DN5 7TU **Tel:** (01302) 782342 **Fax:** (01302) 782342
Social history collections, agriculture, industry, costume and toys. Temporary exhibitions.
Open: Mon-Sat 11-5 Sun 1-5.
Admission: Free.
Location: off A635 Doncaster - Barnsley road.
Refreshments: Cafe.
Disabled access to ground floor, car parking, large park & shop.

ROTHERHAM

ART GALLERY
(Rotherham Metropolitan Borough Council)
Brian O'Malley Library and Arts Centre, Walker Place, Rotherham S65 1JM
Tel: (01709) 382121 Ext 3624/3635
Continuous programme of temporary exhibitions including, at times, 19th and 20th century paintings from the museum collections.
Open: Tues-Sat 10-5 closed Sun Mon and Bank Hols.

CLIFTON PARK MUSEUM
(Rotherham Metropolitan Borough Council)
Clifton Park, Rotherham S65 2AA **Tel:** (01709) 382121 Ext 3628/3635

CLIFTON PARK MUSEUM
ROTHERHAM, SOUTH YORKSHIRE

The museum is housed in an elegant 18th century mansion, reputedly by John Carr of York. It contains furnished rooms, family portraits, period kitchen, displays of Victoriana, local history, local Roman antiquities, glass and glassmaking, 19th and 20th century paintings, British ceramics including an internationally renowned collection of Rockingham pottery and porcelain, local geology and natural history. There are *regular* temporary exhibitions.

Open: Apr-Sept Weekdays (excluding Fri) 10-5 Sun 2.30-5 Oct-Mar Weekdays (excluding Fri) 10-5 Sun 2.30-4.30.
Admission: Free.
Activities for Schools and other Educational Groups. Free parking.

THE YORK AND LANCASTER REGIMENT MUSEUM
Brian O'Malley Library and Arts Centre, Walker Place, Rotherham S65 1JH
Tel: (01709) 382121 Ext 3625
Uniforms, medals (including V.C.'s), campaign relics and insignia covering the history of the Regiment and its forebears, the 65th, and 84th. Foot, from 1758 to 1968.
Open: For times see Art Gallery entry.
Admission: Free.

SHEFFIELD

ABBEYDALE INDUSTRIAL HAMLET
(Sheffield Metropolitan District Council)
Abbeydale Road South, Sheffield S7 2QW **Tel:** (0114) 2367731
Restored 18th century water-powered scythe works.
Open: Admission charge.
Admission: Free.

BISHOPS' HOUSE
(Sheffield City Council)
Norton Lees Lane, Sheffield S8 9BE **Tel:** (0114) 2557701
Fine timber-framed yeoman farmhouse, built around 1500.
Open: All year Wed-Sun 10-4.30 (Sun from 11) and Bank Hol Mons.
Admission: Adults £1 children 50p.
Location: South side of Sheffield off A61 eastwards at Woodseats.

CITY MUSEUM AND MAPPIN ART GALLERY
(Sheffield Metropolitan District Council)
Weston Park, Sheffield **Tel:** (0114) 272 6281/276 8588
Includes cutlery, Sheffield plate, and Peak District archaeology. British and European art from the 18th century to the present day.
Open: Closed Mon.
Admission: Admission free.

GRAVES ART GALLERY
(Sheffield Metropolitan District Council)
Surrey Street, Sheffield **Tel:** (01702) 735158
British art from the 16th century to the present day, Old Masters and non-European art.
Open: Closed Sun.
Admission: Admission free.

KELHAM ISLAND MUSEUM
Alma Street, Sheffield S3 8RY **Tel:** (0114) 2722106
The industrial and social history of Sheffield since the 19th century.
Open: Closed Fri and Sat.
Admission: Admission charge.

RUSKIN GALLERY
(Sheffield Metropolitan District Council)
101 Norfolk Street, Sheffield S1 2JE **Tel:** (0114) 2735299
Houses the collection of the Guild of St. George. Founded by John Ruskin (1819-1900).
Open: Closed Sun.
Admission: Admission free.

SHEPHERD WHEEL
(Sheffield Metropolitan District Council)
Whiteley Wood, Hangingwater Road, Sheffield **Tel:** (0114) 2367731
Water-powered cutlery grinding wheel and workshops.
Open: Closed Mon and Tues.
Admission: Free.

WEST YORKSHIRE

BATLEY

BAGSHAW MUSEUM
(Kirklees Metrolitan Council)
Wilton Park, Batley **Tel:** (01924) 472514
Exotic Victorian building housing local collections, natural history, ethnography, egyptology and Oriental arts.

BATLEY ART GALLERY
(Kirklees Metropolitan Council)
Market Place, Batley **Tel:** (01924) 435521
Temporary exhibitions.

BIRSTALL

OAKWELL HALL AND COUNTRY PARK
(Kirklees Metropolitan Council)
Nutter Lane, Birstall **Tel:** (01924) 474926
17th century working manor house furnished as the Batt house of the 1690's. Regular events and activities. Set in extensive Country Park. Bronte connections.

BRADFORD

COLOUR MUSEUM
(The Society of Dyers and Colourists)
82 Grattan Road, off Westgate, Bradford BD1 2JB **Tel:** (01274) 390955
Fax: (01274) 392888
Step into the world of colour. This award winning museum has many interactive exhibits which allow you to experience colour, see how we react to it and to discover some of its many uses. You can even use some of the latest technology to take charge of a modern dye making factory and to test the colour of any material.

Open: Tues-Fri 2-5 Sat 10-4 school and other parties can visit on Tues-Fri mornings by prior arrangement.
Admission: Small fee charged.
Exhibitions/Events: Special exhibitons held. Please phone for details.
Gift shop, toilets, disabled access.

NATIONAL MUSEUM OF PHOTOGRAPHY, FILM AND TELEVISION

Pictureville, Bradford BD1 1NQ **Tel:** (01274) 727488 Box Office (01274) 723377 **Fax:** (01274) 723155

Opened in 1983, NMPFT is now the most popular national museum outside London. Affiliated to the National Museum of Science and Industry in London, it has six floors of interactive displays, special exhibitions, theatre and education which attract around 800.000 visitors annually. Permanent displays include: **The Story of Popular Photography (the Kodak Museum)**. Relocated from Kodak Limited in Harrow, this important collection of over 50,000 objects and images has been theatrically re-interpreted to tell the history of photography from the point of view of the man and woman in the street. **Photography is news** explores the techniques and history of photojournalism and includes a 1930s news cinema and displays from the Daily Herald Archive, 1.3 million images from this newpaper's history, now held by the NMPTF. **Television Galleries:** two floors devoted to the history and practice of the craft of television. Visitors can read the news, operate a camera or fly our chromakey magic carpet. In **The IMAX Cinema** is the UK's largest cinema screen, projector and film format. **Pictureville Cinema**, alongside the main building, shows the best in world cinema, old and new. **Special Exhibitions:** two floors of temporary exhibitions showing both still and moving pictures.
Open: Tues-Sun 10.30-6 special exhibitions open until 8 closed Mons except Bank Holidays.
Admission: Free, booking details for cinema on (01274) 732277.
Location: Bradford city centre next to the Alhambra Theatre.
Refreshments: Wine and coffee bars open daily 10.30-5.
Disabled access.

CASTLEFORD

CASTLEFORD MUSEUM

(Wakefield Metropolitan District Council)

Castleford Library Carlton Street, Castleford **Tel:** (01977) 559552

Displays of pottery made in the Castleford area over the last 200 years. During 1995 these will be replaced by displays on Victorian everyday life.
Open: Mon-Fri 2-5 closed weekends and Bank Holidays.
Admission: Free.
Location: Upstairs room in Castleford library.
Refreshments: Available in cafés nearby.
Exhibitions/Events: Tel: (01924) 295351 for details.
Castleford Museum Room is not accessible to wheelchair users.

CLECKHEATON

RED HOUSE

(Kirklees Metropolitan Council)

Oxford Road, Gomersal, Cleckheaton BD19 4JP **Tel:** (01274) 872165

Regency house with strong associations with the Brontes. Completely re-furbished as the Taylor home of the 1830s. Annual events and exhibitions programme.

DEWSBURY

DEWSBURY MUSEUM

(Kirklees Metropolitan Council)

Crow Nest Park, Heckmondwike Road, Dewsbury **Tel:** (01924) 468171

Devoted to the theme of 'Childhood'. Temporary exhibitions throughout the year. Regular art exhibitions.

HALIFAX

BANKFIELD MUSEUM

(Calderdale Metropolitan Borough Council)

Akroyd Park, Halifax HX3 6HG **Tel:** (01422) 354823/352334 **Fax:** (01422) 349020

Textiles, costume, art and military history. The Duke of Wellington's Regimental Museum is also at Bankfield. Lively programme of temporary exhibitions, education activities and family workshops.
Open: Tues-Sat 10-5 Sun 2-5 open Bank Hols.
Admission: Free.
Location: 1 mile from Halifax town centre on the A647 Queensbury/Bradford road.

CALDERDALE INDUSTRIAL MUSEUM

(Calderdale Metropolitan Borough Council)

Entrances Piece Hall and Winding Road, Halifax **Tel:** (01422) 358087

150 years of Calderdale's Industrial history with working machinery, workshops, demonstrations and educational programme.
Open: Tues-Sat 10-5 Sun 2-5.
Admission: Adults £1 children/OAPs/unwaged 50p.
Location: Centre of Halifax adjacent to the Rèce Hall.
Temporary Exhibitions.

EUREKA! THE MUSEUM FOR CHILDREN

Discovery Road, Halifax HX1 2NE **Tel:** (01422) 330069 Information line (01426) 983191 **Fax:** (01422) 330275

Eureka! is the first museum in Britain designed especially for children up to the age of 12. Wherever you go in Eureka! you can touch, listen and smell as well as look.

Open: Telephone the recorded information line for details of opening hours and admission charges.

Location: Next to Halifax Railway Station. Within a few minutes walk of the Town Centre.

Refreshments: Cafe.

Eureka! also offers a programme of events throughout the year. Tel 01422 330069 for details. Museum shop. Facilities for the disabled. English Tourist Board Visitor Attraction of the Year 1993 and Tommy's Parent Friendly Campaign Most Parent Friendly Museum 1994.

THE PIECE HALL

(Calderdale Metropolitan Borough Council)

Halifax HX1 1RE **Tel:** (01422) 358087 **Fax:** (01422) 349310

A handsome 18th century Italian Piazza style building surrounding an open courtyard, Art Gallery, New History of Calderdale. Gallery (opens early 1994). A varied programme of exhibitions and entertainment. All forms of cultural entertainment.

Open: Mon-Sun 10-5 also open Bank Hols.

Admission: Free.

Location: Central Halifax.

Refreshments: Cafe/Restaurant.

50 speciality shops. Outdoor market (Thurs, Fri, Sat)

SHIBDEN HALL

(Calderdale Metropolitan Borough Council)

Shibden Park, Halifax HX3 6XG **Tel:** (01422) 352246 **Fax:** (01422) 348440

1420 half-timbered hall with 17th century furniture; a 17th century barn; early

agricultural implements; coaches and harness; craft workshops.
Open: Mar-Nov Mon-Sat 10-5 Sun 12-5 Feb Sun 2-5 closed Dec Jan and Feb.
Admission: Adults £1.50 children/OAPs/unwaged 75p family ticket £4.50.
Location: One mile from Halifax town centre off A58 Leeds/Bradford road.
Refreshments: Cafe.

SMITH ART GALLERY
(Calderdale Borough Council)
Halifax Road, Brighouse, Halifax **Tel:** (01484) 719222
Permanent collection of 19th century Genre pictures, oils and water-colours - and a changing programme of temporary exhibitions.
Open: Mon Tues Thurs Fri 10-6 closed for lunch 12.30-1 Sat 10-4 closed for lunch 12.30-1 closed Wed Sun and Bank Hols.
Admission: Free.
Location: .5 miles from Brighouse Town Centre on A647 Bradford road.

HEPTONSTALL

HEPTONSTALL
(Calderdale Metropolitan Borough Council)
Heptonstall **Tel:** (01422) 843738
17th century stone school building with local history display and old grammar school furniture.
Open: Weekends and Bank Hols 1-5 mid-week visits by appointment.
Admission: Adults 50p children/OAPs/unwaged 25p.

HOLMFIRTH

HOLMFIRTH POSTCARD MUSEUM
(Kirklees Metropolitan Council)
Huddersfield Road, Holmfirth **Tel:** (01484) 682231
Britain's first Postcard Museum entertains and tells the story of the local firm Bamforth and Co. through their saucy and sentimental postcards, lantern slides and pioneering silent films.

HUDDERSFIELD

HUDDERSFIELD ART GALLERY
(Kirklees Metropolitan Council)
Princess Alexandra Walk, Huddersfield **Tel:** (01484) 513808
Houses a changing collection of British Twentieth-Century art, featuring Bacon, Hockney, Lowry and Riley.
Open: Mon-Fri 10-5 Sat 10-4.
Admission: Free.
Major art exhibitions.

TOLSON MUSEUM
(Kirklees Metropolitan Council)
Ravensknowle Park, Wakefield Road, Huddersfield **Tel:** (01484) 530591
Natural sciences, archaeology, social history farming and transport particularly relating to Huddersfield area.

KEIGHLEY

VINTAGE RAILWAY CARRIAGE MUSEUM
(Vintage Carriages Trust)
The Railway Station, Haworth, Keighley BD22 8NJ **Tel:** (01535) 646472/680425
A collection of historic railway coaches plus three elderly industrial steam locomotives. A sound presentation 'Travellers Tales' tells the history of ordinary passenger travel on our railways. Restoration work can be seen in progress. Also a collection of railway posters including London Transport and Frank Newbould.
Open: 11.30-5 every Sat and Sun throughout the year also Easter May Day Spring Bank Holiday week and mid June-early Sept every day.
Admission: Adults £1 children/OAPs/unemployed/students 50p.
Location: By road: 1 mile from Keighley town centre on the A629 Halifax road. By rail: B.R. to Keighley Station-K.W.V.R. to Ingrow.
Free car parking. Some parts of the museum are suitable for disabled. Museum shop.

LEEDS

ARMLEY MILLS
Canal Road, Armley, Leeds **Tel:** (0113) 263 7861
Once the world's largest woollen mills, this museum is housed in a unique fire-proof building of 1806 on an impressive island site in the River Aire.
Open: Tues-Sat 10-5 Sun 2-5 last entries 1 hr before closing.
Admission: Adults £2 children £1.
Location: Canal Road Armley Leeds.
Refreshments: Drinks by vending machines.
Exhibitions/Events: Series of changing exhibitions..

KIRKSTALL ABBEY
Kirstall, Leeds **Tel:** (0113) 275 5821
Britain's finest early monastic ruin, founded by Cistercian monks in 1152.
Open: Daily dawn-dusk.
Admission: Free.
Location: Kirkstall Leeds.
Refreshments: Opening 1996.

LEEDS CITY ART GALLERY
The Headrow, Leeds LS1 3AA **Tel:** (0113) 247 8248 **Fax:** (0113) 244 9689
Collection Victorian Paintings, early English Watercolours, 20th century British paintings and sculpture; Henry Moore Study Centre. Temp exhibition programme.
Open: Mon-Fri 10-5.30 (Wed until 9) Sat 10-4 closed Sun.
Admission: Free.
Location: Leeds City Centre.
Refreshments: Restaurant 10.30-3.30 (closes Sun).

LEEDS CITY MUSEUM
(City of Leeds)
Municipal Buildings, Leeds LS1 3AA **Tel:** (0113) 247 8275
Collections illustrating nearly every aspect of natural history, ethnography and archaeology. Although their scope is worldwide, they particularly concern the Yorkshire region.
Open: Tues-Fri 9.30-5.30 Sat 9.30-4 closed Suns Mons and Bank hols.
Admission: Free.
Location: Municipal buildings, The Headrow, Leeds.
Refreshments: Available close by.
Exhibitions/Events: Series of changing exhibitions.

MUSEUM OF LEEDS WATERFRONT HERITAGE TRAIL
(City of Leeds)
Leeds
Industrial Museum of the Year 1983. This canalside footpath trail follows eight miles of the Aire Valley from the centre of Leeds to the Village of Rodley, linking the museum with over 120 historical sites.
Admission: Free.
Location: Along 8 miles of Waterfront through Leeds.
Refreshments: Available at Rodley Kirkstall and Leeds.
Guidebook available from local museums and bookshops. See entries for Armley Mills, Kirstall Abbey, Abbey House and Thwaite Mills.

TETLEY'S BREWERY WHARF
The Waterfront, Leeds LS1 1QE **Tel:** (0113) 242 0666
Tetley's Brewery Wharf brings to life the story of the English pub: home of the famous Tetley shire horses, working Farrier, Cooper, glass Engraver and Pub Sign Artist. Experience the exciting Pub Through the Ages tour, from Medieval Kirkstall to the 'Star & Crater'. Visit Tetley's brewery, the Gift Shop and Keel's Maritime themed restaurant. Plus special events.
Open: Mar-Oct every day 10-4 Oct-Mar Wed-Sun 10-4 (last admission).
Admission: Adults £4.50 concessions £3.60 children £2.50 family ticket £12. 10% discount for groups of 10+.
Location: Leeds city centre, opposite Tetley's brewery.
Refreshments: Keels Restaurant with food available all day.
Special Events programme. Horse displays. Boat Trips. Suitable for disabled.

PONTEFRACT

PONTEFRACT CASTLE
(Wakefield Metropolitan District Council)
Castle Chain, Pontefract **Tel:** (01977) 600208/797289 minicom (01924) 375402
Ruins of important castle dating back to the 11th century. Scene of Richard II's death and Royalist stronghold in the Civil War. Visitor Centre houses an exhibition on the castle's history.

Open: Mon-Fri 8.30-7 (dusk) Sat/Sun 10.30-7 (dusk) open all Bank Holidays except Christmas and New Year.
Admission: Free.
Location: Off A645 to the east of the town centre.
Refreshments: Available nearby.
Exhibitions/Events: Pomfret 60 Archery Tournament 2nd Sept 1995.
There is access for wheelchair users to most of the site.

PONTEFRACT MUSEUM
(Wakefield Metropolitan District Council)
Salter Row, Pontefract **Tel:** (01977) 797289 minicom (01924) 375402
Displays on the history of Pontefract, including the fine early 17th century painting of Pontefract Castle. Temporary exhibition programme.
Open: Mon-Sat 10.30-5 Sun 2.30-5 open all Bank Holidays except Christmas and New Year.
Admission: Free.
Location: In the Town Centre next to the library.
Refreshments: Available from cafés nearby.
Exhibitions/Events: 4 Feb-Mar 1995 Dolls and Dolls Houses exhibition, June 1995 Embroiderers Guild, July-Aug 1995 Woodhall Excavations.
Access is limited by two steps at entrance.

SHIPLEY

FUREVER FELINE
(Patsy B Marketing Ltd)
Windhill Manor, Leeds Road, Shipley BD18 1BP **Tel:** (01274) 592955
Fax: (01274) 531359

A theatrical themed display of animated cat characters.
Open: Oct-Mar inc. daily 10-6 Apr-Sept inc. daily 9.30-7 last admission 1.25 hrs before closing time closed Christmas Day only.
Admission: Adults £3.75 children(under 13)/students £2.50 pensioners/disabled £3 family (2+2) £11.
Location: On the A657 out of Shipley, West Yorks.
Refreshments: Coffee bar.
Ample parking space for cars and coaches with easy access to entrance. Full access and facilities for the disabled (including lift). Coffee bar/cinema to seat 96. Gift/souvenir shop.

WAKEFIELD

ELIZABETHAN EXHIBITION GALLERY
(Wakefield Metropolitan District Council)
Brook Street, Wakefield **Tel:** (01924) 295797 minicom (01924) 375402
An attractive Elizabethan building converted to a spacious gallery. A changing and varied programme of temporary exhibitions covers all arts and crafts, as well as history and archaeology.
Open: Mon-Sat 10.30-5 Sun 2.30-5 and Spring/Summer Bank Holidays during exhibitions only.
Admission: Free.
Location: In the City Centre, between the bus station and the open market.
Refreshments: Available from cafés nearby.
Exhibitions/Events: 28 Jan-13 Mar 95 Women's Art, 27 Mar-21 May 95 Giles Cartoons, 17 July-3 Sept Clive Head, 9 Sept-5 Nov Contraband. Access for wheelchair users with assistance.

SANDAL CASTLE
(Wakefield Metropolitan District Council)
Manygates Lane, Sandal, Wakefield **Tel:** (01924) 295351 minicom (01924) 375402
Ruins of 13th century stone castle of the Warennes. Finds from excavations on display in Wakefield Museum.
Open: Daily.
Admission: Free.
Location: To the south of Wakefield off the A61.
There is access for wheelchair users to the main route around the site.

WAKEFIELD ART GALLERY
(Wakefield Metropolitan District Council)
Wentworth Terrace, Wakefield **Tel:** (01924) 375402 also minicom or 295796

Significant early sculptures by Henry Moore and Barbara Hepworth and important work by other major British modern artists form the core of this collection. Paintings from other periods and European schools are also on display. There is a changing programme of temporary exhibitions and displays from the permanent collections.
Open: Mon-Sat 10.30-5 Sun 2.30-5 open all Bank Holidays except Christmas and New Year.
Admission: Free.
Location: To the north of the City Centre, near to Wakefield College.
Refreshments: Available nearby.
Exhibitions/Events: 21 Jan-5 Mar Rembrant-etchings, 18 Mar-30 Apr Wakefield Art Club, 13 May-25 June Rugs, 8 July-3 Sept Gyorgy Gordon paintings, 9 Sept-22 Oct Stephen Court landscape Paintings.
Six steps at the entrance make the building inaccessible to wheelchair users. Sales point.

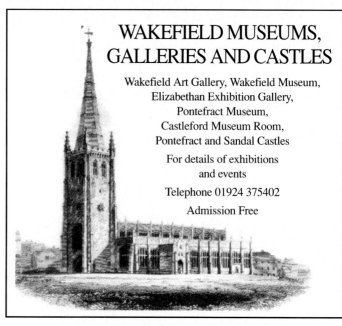

WAKEFIELD MUSEUM
(Wakefield Metropolitan District Council)
Wood Street, Wakefield **Tel:** (01924) 295351 minicom (01924) 375402
Wakefield Museum is full of objects and images which depict Wakefield's long and complex history. Visitors will find everything from flint axes and Roman pottery to model locomotives and plastic tea cups! We also house the exotic and eccentric natural history collections of the Victorian explorer, Charles Waterton. You will see nothing like these anywhere else in Yorkshire! There are also about six temporary exhibitions each year, on topics as diverse as fine china, cartoons, costumes and dolls.
Open: Mon-Sat 10.30-5 Sun 2.30-5 open all Bank Holidays except Christmas and New Year
Admission: Free.
Location: Next to Wakefield Town Hall, Wood Street.
Refreshments: Available from cafés nearby
Exhibitions/Events: Telephone (01924) 295351 for details.
Front steps at the entrance make Wakefield Museum inaccessible to wheelchair users

YORKSHIRE MINING MUSEUM
Caphouse Colliery, New Road, Overton, Wakefield WF4 4RH **Tel:** (01924) 848806 **Fax:** (01924) 840694
Award-winning museum of the Yorkshire coalfield includes an exciting guided tour 450 feet underground. An experienced miner takes visitors through authentic workings where methods and conditions of mining from 1820 to the present day have been reconstructed. On the surface there are indoor and outdoor displays, train rides, genuine pit ponies, steam winder, nature trail and adventure playground.
Open: 10-5 except Dec 24 25 26 and Jan 1.
Admission: Adults £5.50 children 5-16 £4.
Location: On A642 halfway between Wakefield and Huddersfield.
Refreshments: Licensed cafeteria.
Film show, shop. Access for disabled and ample free parking.

YORKSHIRE SCULPTURE PARK
(The Trustees of Yorkshire Sculpture Park)
Bretton Hall, West Bretton, Wakefield WF4 4LG **Tel:** (01924) 830579 administration (01924) 830302 information
Yorkshire Sculpture Park, one of Europes leading open-air art galleries, has pioneered the exhibition of sculpture in the landscape. The park provides opportunities for the making and understanding of sculpture for all members of the community within a magnificent environment. Each year a number of important international and national exhibitions are organised together with a comprehensive education and outreach programme. Major exhibitions from 1994-95 include Henry Moore in Bretton Country Park, Henry Moore: The Late Carvings, Kan Yasuda: Monumental Marbles and Bronzes, Elisabeth Frink: Memorial Exhibition, 70th birthday survey exhibition by Eduardo Paolozzi and the Trojan War Sculpture by Anthony Caro.
Open: Daily winter 10-4 summer 10-dusk.
Admission: Free. For party bookings call (01924) 830302.
Location: 1 mile from junction 38 off the M1.
Refreshments: Cafe serving delicious home-made food.
Free Booster Scooters, Audio Guides and Design and Book Shop. Information Tel: 01924 830302. Education: Tel: 01924 830642.

WALES

CLWYD

CHIRK

CHIRK CASTLE
(The National Trust)
Chirk LL14 5AF **Tel:** (01691) 777701
The castle is an outstanding example of a Marcher Fortress, built 1295-1310 and is still inhabited. The interior provides examples of 16th, 17th, 18th and 19th century decorations. The park was landscaped by Emes in the mid 18th century. Extensive gardens with fine views.
Open: Apr-Oct daily except Mon & Tues (open Bank Hol Mon).
Admission: Fee charged.
Refreshments: Tea-room on site.

RUTHIN

RUTHIN CRAFT CENTRE
Park Road, Ruthin LL15 1BB **Tel:** (01824) 704774

A Crafts Council Selected Gallery housed within a purpose-built Craft Centre in the picturesque Vale of Clwyd. The gallery shows the best of fine crafts by contemporary designer-makers from all over the British Isles. We run an exciting programme of regularly changing exhibitions which aim to show the breadth of excellence in the field of applied arts. There are 11 independant studios where craftsmen work on a daily basis, situated around a landscaped courtyard, a restaurant, ample parking and facilities for the disabled.
Open: 10-5 seven days a week Sun 12-5 in the winter.
Admission: Free.
Refreshments: Licensed restaurant.
Parking. Advanced notice for parties. Suitable for disabled persons - all areas have level accesss for wheelchairs.

ST. ASAPH

BODELWYDDAN CASTLE
(Bodelwyddan Castle Trust)

Bodelwyddan, St. Asaph LL18 5YA **Tel:** (01745) 583539 **Fax:** (01745) 584563
Bodelwyddan Castle has been authentically restored as a Victorian Country House and contains a major collection of portraits and photography on permanent loan from the National Portrait Gallery. The portraits are complemented by furniture from the Victorian & Albert Museum and sculptures from the Royal Academy.
Open: Open throughout the year - please telephone for details.
Admission: Fee charged. Discount rates available for groups of 20 or more.
Location: Just off the A55 near St. Asaph (opposite the Marble Church).
Refreshments: Tea-room. Additional catering service available at the Warner Hotel on the site.
Exhibitions/Events: Programme of temporary exhibitions, concerts and events throughout the year.
Winner of the Museum of the Year Award.

WREXHAM

ERDDIG
(The National Trust)

Wrexham LL13 0YT **Tel:** (01978) 355314
A late 17th century house with 18th century additions that contains much of the original furniture. The outbuildings, including laundry, bakehouse, sawmill and smithy, are in working order. The garden has been restored to its 18th century design and contains varieties of fruit known to have been grown there during that period.
Open: Apr-Oct daily except Thurs and Fri.
Admission: Fee charged.
Refreshments: Tea-room.

KING'S MILL VISITOR CENTRE
(Wrexham Maelor Borough Council)

King's Mill Road, Wrexham LL13 0NT **Tel:** (01978) 362967
Restored mill housing 'The Miller's Tale' - what it was like to live and work in an 18th century mill. Also waterwheel, video presentation and interactive displays.
Open: Easter-Sept Tues-Sun 10-5 also Bank Holiday Mondays.
Admission: Fee charged.

MINERA LEAD MINES
(Wrexham Maelor Borough Council)

Minera, Nr. Wrexham LL11 3DU **Tel:** (01978) 753400
Surface remains of a 19th Century lead mine including a Beam Engine House and Interpretative displays set in a country park.
Open: Easter-Sept Tues-Sun 10-5 also Bank Hol Mons.
Admission: Fee charged.

WREXHAM MAELOR HERITAGE CENTRE
(Wrexham Maelor Borough Council)

47/49 King Street, Wrexham LL11 1HR **Tel:** (01978) 290048

Permanent exhibition on the local, social and industrial history of the Wrexham area especially the brick, tile and terracota industry. Changing temporary exhibition programme.
Open: Mon-Sat 10-5.
Admission: Free.
Location: By Bus Station.

DYFED

ABERYSTWYTH

ABERYSTWYTH ARTS CENTRE EXHIBITIONS

University College of Wales, Aberystwyth SY23 3DE **Tel:** (01970) 622887/2
Fax: (01970) 622883

The Arts Centre is situated on the university campus and has panoramic views over Cardigan Bay. Purpose built in 1972 it has steadily gained recognition as a major arts venue in Wales consisting of four galleries, concert hall, theatre and studio. The Arts Centre has an extensive exhibition programme which includes the work of (mainly contemporary) artists, makers and photographers. There are approximately forty shows a year in all, some of which originate here and tour U.K. An education service for adults and children includes talks, residential courses, workshops, demonstrations etc. The Arts Centre also hosts a Bi-annual International Potters' Festival. Part of the College Ceramics Collection (numbering approx 1,500 pieces) is always on display in the Ceramics Gallery with regular 'Ceramic Series' contemporary ceramics exhibitions opposite. To view the whole collection it is necessary to make an appointment. Tel: (01970) 622467.
Open: Daily Mon-Sat 10-5 and during evening performances 7-9 also Sun 2-5 closed mid May-end June for university exams.
Admission: Free.
Location: On University Campus.
Refreshments: Cafe.
Bookshop and craftshop. (Crafts Council listed). 'Collectorplan' no interest credit scheme available for purchasing art works. Disabled access to lower gallery and cafe. Toilet for disabled.

THE CATHERINE LEWIS PRINT ROOM
(The Library, The University of Wales)
Aberystwyth **Tel:** (01970) 622460 **Fax:** (01970) 622461

Permanent collection of graphic art from 15th-20th century particularly 1860's illustration, 1920's/30's and contemporary prints, 20th century Italian and British photography. Changing exhibitions from the collection and special exhibitions of graphic art (see posters or telephone). Reference available by appointment.
Open: Mon-Fri 9.30-5 Sat (College Term only) 9.30-12.30 (except for Christmas Easter and Bank Hols)
Admission: Free.
Parties by arrangement. Car parking. Suitable for disabled persons.

CEREDIGION MUSEUM
(Ceredigion District Council)
Coliseum, Terrace Road, Aberystwyth SY23 2AQ **Tel:** (01970) 634212/3
Local Museum housed in a restored Edwardian Theatre. Displays illustrate the history and artifacts of Ceredigion including archaeology, geology, agriculture, seafaring, lead mining. Fine collection of furniture and clocks. Many folk life exhibits. Temporary art and other exhibitions throughout the year.
Open: Mon-Sat 10-5 Suns in school holidays.
Admission: Free.

DRE-FACH FELINDRE

MUSEUM OF THE WELSH WOOLLEN INDUSTRY
Dre-Fach Felindre, Nr. Newcastle Emlyn SA44 5UP **Tel:** (01559) 370929
The Museum of the Welsh Woollen Industry is located at Dre-fach Felindre which was once the most important wool producing area in Wales and supplied flannel to the mining communities of the South Wales valleys. Located alongside a working woollen mill, the Museum houses working exhibitions with demonstrations tracing woollen cloth from fleece to fabric. Attention is also focused upon the contemporary products of the Welsh mills.
Open: Apr 1-Sept 30 Mon-Sat 10-5 Oct 1-Mar 31 Mon-Fri 10-5 closed Sun please ring for opening times at Christmas and New Year.
Admission: (1994) adults £1 OAPs 75p children(under 16) 50p generous discounts available for pre-booked groups of 20 or more.
Location: 4m east of Newcastle Emlyn off the A484 Carmarthen to Cardigan road.
Refreshments: Snack bar picnic area.
Bookings Contact Officer in Charge. Coaches: ample free parking. Gift/book shop. Toilets, toilets for the disabled.

HAVERFORDWEST

GRAHAM SUTHERLAND GALLERY
Rhos, Haverfordwest SA62 4AS **Tel:** (01437) 751296 **Fax:** (01437) 751322
This Gallery was specially created for the important collection of paintings, drawings and prints donated by the artist himself. The works on display are inspired largely by the lanes and estuaries of the surrounding areas. There is an excellent temporary exhibition programme throughout the season.
Open: Apr-Oct Tues-Sun 10.30-12.30 1.30-5 Nov-Mar by prior arrangement.
Admission: (1994) Adults £1 OAPs 75p children(under 16) 50p discounts for pre-booked groups.
Location: In the courtyard of Picton Castle 5 miles east of Haverfordwest.

KIDWELLY

KIDWELLY INDUSTRIAL MUSEUM
(Kidwelly Heritage Centre and Tinplate Museum Trust/Llanelli Borough Council)
Kidwelly SA17 4LW **Tel:** (01554) 891078
Open: Bank Holidays & June-August/mid Sept.
Admission: Adults £1 children/OAPs 50p family £1.50 parties special reduction.
Location: 1 mile from Kidwelly.
Refreshments: Tea & coffee.

LLANELLI

PARC HOWARD MUSEUM AND ART GALLERY
(Llanelli Borough Council)
Llanelli SA15 3AS **Tel:** (01554) 773538 **Fax:** (01554) 750125
Collection of Llanelli pottery. Exhibits of Welsh artists. Items of local interest. Travelling exhibitions.
Open: Winter 11-1 and 2-4 Summer 11-1 and 2-6.
Admission: Free.
Location: Parc Howard.
Refreshments: Yes.
Exhibitions/Events: Annual Programmme.

PUBLIC LIBRARY GALLERY
(Llanelli Borough Council)
Vaughan Street, Llanelli SA15 3AS **Tel:** (01554) 773538 **Fax:** (01554) 750125
Collection of local artists, travelling and other exhibitions.
Open: Mon-Sat 10-5.

TENBY

TENBY MUSEUM AND ART GALLERY
(Trustees of Tenby Museum)
Castle Hill, Tenby SA70 7BP **Tel:** (01834) 842809 **Fax:** (01834) 842809

An outstanding display of the geology, archaeology and natural history of Pembrokeshire. The maritime gallery commemorates Tenby's seafaring

past and its achievements as a lifeboat station; there are special exhibitions of local history. New extension to Art Gallery opening Easter 1995.
Open: Daily Easter-Oct 10-6 winter times from Nov 1 Mon-Fri 10-4.
Admission: Adults £1 reductions for children/OAPs. School parties by appointment free.

MID GLAMORGAN

BRIDGEND

SOUTH WALES POLICE MUSEUM

Cowbridge Road, Bridgend CF31 3SU **Tel:** (01656) 869315 **Fax:** (01656) 869399
Two exciting galleries chronicle the story of policing in Glamorgan from the Celts to the present day. Features include a recreated 1840s cell, an Edwardian police station and wartime tableau.
Open: Mon-Thurs 10-1 and 2-4.30 Fri 10-1 and 2-4 closed Bank Hols open by appointment only.
Admission: Free.
Refreshments: By prior arrangement.
Parties by appointment. Souvenir shop. School's service. Car parking. Not suitable for disabled persons. Research facility. Baby care facilities. Toilets.

MERTHYR TYDFIL

CYFARTHFA CASTLE MUSEUM AND ART GALLERY

(Merthyr Tydfil Borough Council)
Brecon Road, Merthyr Tydfil CF47 8RE **Tel:** (01685) 723112 **Fax:** (01685) 723112/722146
Situated in an Ironmasters gothic mansion, the collections cover paintings, ceramics, silver furniture and decorative art. There are displays on local history, industrial history, enthnography, archaeology and Egyptology. New Social History galleries now open, entitled 'Merthyr - 3000 years of History'. Programme of temporary exhibitions throughout the year. Just reopened after £280,000 refurbishment returning rooms to Regency spendour.
Open: Weekdays 10-6 Sat Sun 12-6 close one hour earlier Oct-Mar closed during Xmas week.
Admission: Adults 80p children 40p educational groups free joint Heritage tickets available for use with M.T. Heritage Trust sites.
Location: North end of Merthyr Tydfil situated in park.
Refreshments: Italian cafe.
Schoolroom available. Access for disabled.

SOUTH GLAMORGAN

CARDIFF

CARDIFF CASTLE

(Cardiff City Council)
Cardiff Castle, Cardiff CF1 2RB **Tel:** (01222) 822083 **Fax:** (01222) 231417
Castle with Roman and Norman remains. Important 19th restoration for the third Marquess of Bute. The castle is most famous for it's lavish decorated interiors by William Burges. These may be seen by guided tour.
Open: Daily throughout the year except Christmas day Boxing day and New Years day.
Admission: Adults £3.30 children/OAP £1.70.
Location: Central Cardiff.
Refreshments: Tea-rooms.
Exhibitions/Events: Please contact the castle for further information.
The castle interior is unsuitable for the disabled.

DE MORGAN FOUNDATION - CARDIFF CASTLE

(City of Cardiff)
Cardiff Castle, Cardiff CF1 2RB **Tel:** (01222) 822083 **Fax:** (01222) 231417

A dedicated room in the Castle contains an important part of the Foundation's collection of William De Morgan tiles and ceramics. These are supplemented by drawings and paintings by Evelyn De Morgan as well as by William.
Open: From Nov-Feb inc the guided tour of Castle includes a visit to the De Morgan room. At other times or for those wishing to study the exhibits and the reserve Collection for research purposes appointments to visit may be made. Please contact Matthew Williams, Keeper of Collections - Tel: (01222) 822084.
Admission: Included in Castle admission.
Location: Cardiff Castle.
Refreshments: Available.

THE NATIONAL MUSEUM OF WALES

Cathays Park, Cardiff CF1 3NP **Tel:** (01222) 397951 **Fax:** (01222) 373219
Treasurehouse of Wales, the **National Museum of Wales** in Cathays Park at the heart of Cardiff's elegant civic centre is proud of its excellent collections including paintings, silver and ceramics, coins and medals, fossils, minerals, shells, archaeological artefacts and even dinosaur skeletons. The recent refurbishment of the East Wing has provided a splendid new setting for the museum's impressive art collection showing them in their Welsh and European context. A major development opened in 1993 provides further new galleries for displaying world-renowned collections including French Impressionist paintings and an impressive new presentation on The Evolution of Wales. Special exhibitions of world-wide interest contribute to the museum's popularity as one of Wales' foremost tourist attractions. An exciting schedule of events and temporary exhibitions enhances the museum's visitor appeal.
Open: Tues-Sat 10-5 & Bank Hol Mon Sun 2.30-5 closed Mon please ring for opening times at Easter Christmas and New Year.
Admission: (1994) Adults £2.50 OAPs £1.85 children (under 16) £1.25 generous discounts available for pre-booked parties of 20 or more.
Location: Cardiff Civic Centre.
Refreshments: Restaurant.
Parties can be dropped at the main entrance to the museum. Bookings contact: Dept. of Public Services. Museum gift/book shops. Toilets for the disabled.

WELSH INDUSTRIAL AND MARITIME MUSEUM

Bute Street, Cardiff CF1 6AN **Tel:** (01222) 481919 **Fax:** (01222) 487252
These fascinating exhibits give an insight into the way industry, coal, road, rail and sea, combined to make Cardiff one of the world's premier ports and formed the basis for the rich and varied heritage it enjoys today. As well as the working machines with hands on and interactive exhibits, and a varied programme of temporary exhibitions, there are regular steam days with additional displays and demonstrations.
Open: Tues-Sat 10-5 Sun 2.30-5 closed Mon (except Bank Hols) Christmas Day New Year's Day.
Admission: (1994) Adults £1.50 OAPs £1.15 children(under 16) 75p generous discounts available for pre-booked groups of 20 or more.
Refreshments: Telephone for details.
Bookings contact: Administrative officer. Gift/book shop. Toilets for the disabled.

PENARTH

TURNER HOUSE

Plymouth Road, Penarth CF6 2TH **Tel:** (01222) 708870 or (01222) 397951

A small gallery holding temporary exhibitions of pictures and objets d'art from the National Museum of Wales and other sources.

Open: Tues-Sat 11-12.45 2-5 Sun 2-5 also Bank Holiday Mon closed phone for details.

Admission: 50p Suns free.

Location: Close to the centre of Penarth, 5 miles south of Cardiff.

For booking contact: Principal Officer. Coaches: Parking nearby. Museum Gift/book shop.

ST. FAGANS

WELSH FOLK MUSEUM

St. Fagans, Cardiff CF5 6XB **Tel:** (01222) 569441 **Fax:** (01222) 578413

One of Europe's foremost open-air museums, the **Welsh Folk Museum** features everything from a castle to the humble moorland cottage of a slate quarry worker among its unique collection of furnished re-erected buildings. Reflecting the lifestyle of the past both at home and at work, the buildings have been brought from all over Wales and re-erected within the museum's 100 acre parkland. As well as farmhouses, a terrace of six cottages and a Victorian shop complex from the industrial valleys of South Wales, there is a tollhouse, tannery, smithy, corn mill, woollen mill, bakehouse and a pottery. The museum is brought to life by the craftsmen who provide displays of traditional skills for the visitors. Galleries at the museum focus on agriculture, costume and material culture, and special events, demonstrations and temporary exhibitions are held regularly. Major annual seasonal festivals include May Fair, Mid Summer Festival, Harvest Festival and Christmas Tree.

Open: Apr 1-Oct 31 daily 10-5 Nov 1-Mar 31 Mon-Sat 10-5 closed Sun between Nov 1 and Mar 31 please ring for opening times over Easter Christmas and New Year.

Admission: (1994) Adults £4 OAPs £3 children(under 16) £2 generous discounts available for pre-booked parties of 20 or more.

Location: 4 miles west of Cardiff City Centre in the beautiful Vale of Glamorgan the Welsh Folk Museum is clearly signposted from junction 33 of the M4 Motorway direct access from the A4232 into the museum.

Refreshments: Self service restaurant picnic area and snack bar (summer).

Exhibitions/Events: Phone for details.

Bookings contact:Travel Trade Officer. Tel (01222) 397951. Guide books available. Ample free car parking. Free adm for coach driver. Gift/book shop. Toilets for disabled. Access to almost all areas for the disabled.

WEST GLAMORGAN

NEATH

CEFN COED COLLIERY MUSEUM

(West Glamorgan County Council)

Crynant, Neath SA10 8SN **Tel:** (01639) 750556

The museum vividly portrays the story of men and machines involved in the mining of coal at the former Cefn Coed Colliery.

Open: Daily Apr-Sep 10.30-6 Oct-Mar 10.30-4 closed Christmas holiday week.

GWENT

CAERLEON

ROMAN LEGIONARY MUSEUM

Caerleon NP6 1AE **Tel:** (01633) 423134

At the Roman Legionary Museum, Caerleon, the history of Roman Caerleon and the daily life of its garrison are featured in the displays of exciting finds from the area. Highlights include life-size Roman Soldiers - a centurion, standard bearer and legionary - arms, armour and equipment of the Roman Soldier, a labyrinth mosaic, a remarkable collection of engraved gemstones from the Fortress Baths and early Roman finds from the legionary base at Usk. Nearby are other impressive remains of the town's history - the amphitheatre designed to seat 5,000 spectators, the Fortress Baths which served as the main leisure and social centre for the soldiers and was one of the largest baths in the Roman province, the Roman defences and the only remains of legionary barracks on view in Europe.

Open: Mar 15-Oct 15 Mon-Sat 10-6 Sun 2-6 Oct 16-Mar 14 Mon-Sat 10-4.30 Sun 2-4.30 closed telephone for details.

Admission: Telephone for details also joint tickets available with Roman Baths administered by Cadw Welsh Historic Monuments.

Location: 2 miles north of Junction 25 of the M4 motorway.

Exhibitions/Events: Phone for details.

For bookings, contact the curator. Coaches can park at the nearby Roman Amphitheatre. Gift shop and book shop. Toilets for the disabled.

A hunter in the Severn Estuary. Circa 5,000 B.C.

1930's Room setting in John Wait Teapot display.

NEWPORT

NEWPORT MUSEUM AND ART GALLERY

(Borough of Newport)

John Frost Square, Newport NP9 1PA **Tel:** (01633) 840064

Natural science displays including geology; fine and applied art, specialising in early English watercolours, teapots and contemporary crafts; Prehistoric finds from Gwent and Romano-British remains from Caerwent; local history including the Chartist movement. Regular exhibitions and associated activities.

Open: Mon-Thurs 9.30-5 Fri 9.30-4.30 Sat 9.30-4.

Admission: Free

PONTYPOOL

THE VALLEY INHERITANCE

(Torfaen Museum Trust)

Pontypool NP4 6JH **Tel:** (01495) 752036 **Fax:** (01495) 752043

Museum telling the story of the Eastern Valley of Gwent.

Open: Feb-Dec Mon-Sat 10-5 Sun 2-5.

Admission: Adults £1.20 reduced 60p family £2.40.

Location: By Pontypool Parkgates.

Refreshments: Coffee Shop.

Car park, full disabled access, disabled toilets, reference library.

USK

GWENT RURAL LIFE MUSEUM

The Malt Barn, New Market Street, Usk NP5 1AU **Tel:** (01291) 673777

Agricultural and craft tools, wagons, vintage machinery, farmhouse, kitchen, laundry, dairy. Winner of the Prince of Wales Award.

Open: Apr 1-Oct 31 Mon-Fri 10-5 weekends 2-5 Nov-Mar please telephone museum.

Admission: Fee charged.

Parties by arrangement. An Independent Museum

GWYNEDD

BANGOR

PENRHYN CASTLE

(The National Trust)

Bangor LL57 4HN **Tel:** (01248) 353084

Penrhyn is a gigantic neo-Norman fantasy Castle by Thomas Hopper who also designed the magnificent interior decoration and much of the furniture. Built entirely by the stonemasons, joiners and carvers of North Wales, the Castle contains an important collection of old master pictures, and an industrial railway museum which houses full size and model engines.

Open: Apr-Oct daily except Tues.

Admission: Fee charged.

Refreshments: Tea-room on site.

CAERNARFON

SEGONTIUM ROMAN FORT MUSEUM

Caernarfon LL55 2LN **Tel:** (01286) 675625

The Roman Fort Museum is an archaeological branch gallery of the National Museum of Wales. Remains of the Roman Fort of Segontium and a museum of excavated relics are on display here.

Open: 9.30-5.30 Mon-Sat(Mar-Oct) 6 May-Sept 9.30-4 Nov-Feb 2-5 Sun all year closed phone to check.

Admission: Please phone to check.

Coaches: Ample parking nearby. Museum gift/book shop.

ISLE OF ANGLESEY

PLAS NEWYDD

(The National Trust)

Llanfairpwll, Isle of Angelsey LL61 6EQ **Tel:** (01248) 714795

The 16th century house was extended and redecorated in the 18th century with gothic and neo-classical interiors designed by James Wyatt. The house contains Rex Whistler's finest mural painting, and an exhibition of his work; a Military Museum with relics of the 1st Marquess of Anglesey, and the Ryan collection of uniforms and headgear. Park and gardens by Repton, in an unrivalled position beside the Menai Strait.

Open: Apr-Oct daily except Sats.

Admission: Fee charged.

Refreshments: Tea-room on site.

LLANBERIS

MUSEUM OF THE NORTH

Llanberis LL55 4UR **Tel:** (01286) 870636 **Fax:** (01286) 871331

The Museum of the North/Power of Wales is the National Museum of Wales' main centre in North Wales and is located in Llanberis, Gwynedd in an attractive setting overlooking Lake Padarn at the foot of Snowdon. The exiting 'Power of Wales' presentation gives an insight into how the natural power of water has been harnessed to produce electricity at Dinorwig Pumped Storage Power Station. There is also a continuing programme of splendid temporary exhibitions in the museum's galleries.

Open: June-Sept 9.30-6 daily Apr-May Oct 10-5 Nov-Mar groups only by appointment.

Admission: (1994) adults £5 children(under 16) £2.50 OAPs £3.75 generous discounts available for pre-booked parties of 20 or more.

Ample free parking. Museum gift/book shop. Toilets suitable for the disabled.

WELSH SLATE MUSEUM

Llanberis LL55 4TY **Tel:** (01286) 870630 **Fax:** (01286) 871906

When the extensive Dinorwig Quarry at Llanberis, Gwynedd was closed in 1969 the workshops, most of the machinery and plant were preserved and the **Welsh Slate Museum** was established. Much of the original atmosphere remains in the fitting and erecting shops, repair shops, smithy, dressing and sawing sheds, foundry office, mess room and yard. There are also demonstrations of many traditional slate crafts.

Open: 9.30-5.30 daily Easter Sat-Sept 30 Nov-Mar groups only by appointment.

Admission: (1994) Adults £1.50 children (under 16) 80p OAPs £1.20p generous discounts for pre-booked parties of 20 or more.

Location: In Padarn Country Park.

Ample coach and car parking. Museum gift/book shop. Toilets.

PORTHMADOG

FESTINIOG RAILWAY MUSEUM

(Festiniog Railway Trust)

Harbour Station, Porthmadog LL49 9NF **Tel:** (01766) 512340 **Fax:** (01766) 514576

Museum in part of former Goods Shed illustrating the Railway's history from the 1830s to the present day.

Open: Daily during train service hours.

Admission: Honesty Box.

Refreshments: Cafeteria adjoining.

Registered No. 171, 26th August 1992.

POWYS

BRECON

BRECKNOCK MUSEUM

(Powys County Council)

Captain's Walk, Brecon **Tel:** (01874) 624121

Collections illustrating the local and natural history of Brecknock. Archaeological, agriculture and domestic material, pottery, porcelain and lovespoons. Assize Court reconstruction. Library and Reference collection.

Open: Mon-Sat 10-1 and 2-5 also open Suns Apr-Sept closed Christmas Day-New Year's Day incl. and Good Friday.

Admission: Free.

LLANDRINDOD WELLS

LLANDRINDOD WELLS MUSEUM

(Powys County Council)

Temple Street, Llandrindod Wells LD1 5LD **Tel:** (01597) 824513

The social and archaeological history of the old Mid-Wales county of Radnor and the growth of Landrindod Wells as a country Spa Resort.

Open: Apr 1-Aug 31 6 days a week 10-12.30 and 2-4.30 closed Weds Sept 1-Mar 31 Mon-Fri 10-12.30 and 2-4.30 closed Weds Sat & Sun.

Admission: Free.

LLANIDLOES

LLANIDLOES MUSEUM C/O LLANDRINDOD WELLS MUSEUM

(Powys County Council)

Temple Street, Llandrindod Wells LD1 5LD **Tel:** (01597) 824513

Social and Industrial history of the town.

Open: May-Sept (under review).

Location: Llanidloes Town Centre.

NEWTOWN

W H SMITH MUSEUM

24 High Street, Newtown **Tel:** (01686) 626280

The museum is on the first floor of the Newtown branch of W H Smith. The shop has been completely restored to its 1927 appearance, when the branch first opened. It has the original oak-shop front, tiling and mirrors, plaster relief decoration and other details. Storyboards show how the history of the company, founded in 1792, is inextricably linked with the changes in social patterns, transport and printing.

Open: Mon-Sat 9-5 closed Sun and Bank Hols.

Admission: Free.

Some street parking and public car park approx 0.25 mile away. Not suitable for disabled persons.

WELSHPOOL

POWIS CASTLE

(The National Trust)

Welshpool SY21 8RF **Tel:** (01938) 554336

The castle of c. 1300 with some later reconstruction. The interior has fine plasterwork of the late 16th century; tapestries, paintings and furniture of the 17th centuries; collected by the 1st Lord Clive. Superb late 17th century terraced garden.

Open: Apr-Oct daily except Mon & Tues (open Bank Hol Mon) open Tues during July and Aug.

Admission: Fee charged.

Refreshments: Tea-room on site.

POWYSLAND MUSEUM & MONTGOMERY CANAL CENTRE

(Powys County Council)

The Canal Wharf, Welshpool SY21 7AQ **Tel:** (01938) 554656

The museum displays archaeological collections, the history of the railways and the canal, agricultural development and folk life material. The collections are housed in a converted and restored warehouse by the Montgomery Canal.

Open: From May Bank Hol-Sept 30 Mon Tues Thurs Fri 11-1 and 2-5 Sat Sun 10-1 and 2-5 closed Wed Oct-May Bank Hol Mon Tues Thurs Fri 11-1 and 2-5 Sat 2-5 closed Wed Sat morning and Sun. Also closed Dec 25-Jan 2.

Admission: Free.

IRELAND

CLONMEL

TIPPERARY (S.R.) CO. MUSEUM

(Patrick Holland M.A. Curator)

Parnell Street, Clonmel **Tel:** (052) 25399 **Fax:** (052) 24355

Tipperary (S.R.) County Museum collects, records, preserves and displays objects which show the history of South Tipperary. An extended and completely renovated display incorporating many recent acquistitions has been set up. Temporary and touring exhibitions are also hosted. In 1985 the museum received a special commendation in the Irish 'Museum of the Year' award.

Open: Tues-Sat 10-1 2-5 closed Bank Holidays etc.

Admission: Free.

Parties welcome by prior arrangement. Car park nearby. Unsuitable for disabled persons.

DUBLIN

CHESTER BEATTY LIBRARY
20 Shrewsbury Road, Dublin 4 **Tel:** 01-269 2386 **Fax:** 01-283 0983
Collections of Islamic manuscripts, Chinese, Japanese, Indian Art, Western prints & Christian manuscripts, biblical and other.
Open: Tues-Fri 10-5 and Sat 2-5 closed Sun and Mon.
Admission: Free.
Free guided tours on Wed & Sat at 2.30. Shop.

GUINNESS MUSEUM
(Guinness Ireland Ltd)
The Old Hop Store, Crane Street, Dublin 8 **Tel:** 01-536700 **Fax:** 01-546519
The Guiness Hopstore.
Open: Mon-Fri 10-4.30 last audio-visual presentation 3.30.
Admission: Adults £2 group rate (20 or more) £1.50 per person student with card £1.50 children/OAPs 50p.
Location: Crane Street, off Thomas Street, Dublin 8.
Refreshments: Sample Bar.
Temporary exhibition programme telephone for details.

THE HUGH LANE MUNICIPAL GALLERY OF MODERN ART
(Dublin Corporation)
Charlemont House, Parnell Square, Dublin **Tel:** 01-874 1903 **Fax:** 01-872 2182
Large representative collection of modern European painting and sculpture including contemporary Irish art. Artists represented include Monet, Degas, Jack B. Yeats, William Scott and Louis le Brocquy. Regular temporary exhibitions.
Open: Tues-Fri 9.30-6 Sat 9.30-5 Sun 11-5 closed Mon.
Admission: Free.
Refreshments: Restaurant open during Gallery hours.

NATIONAL GALLERY OF IRELAND
Merrion Square (West), Dublin 2 **Tel:** 01-661 5133 **Fax:** 01-661 5372

Paintings, drawings and sculptures of all European schools from 1300-1920s, also major Irish collection.
Open: Mon Tues Wed Fri and Sat 10-5.30 Thurs 10-8.30 Sun 2-5.
Refreshments: Restaurant.
Bookshop. Conducted tours of the Gallery, and lectures weekly.

NATIONAL MUSEUM OF IRELAND
(The National Museum)
Dublin **Tel:** 01-6618811 **Fax:** 01-6766116
Contains the National collections of archaeology, the decorative arts, history, folk life, zoology and geology. Outstanding exhibitions of Prehistoric gold and Early Christian metalwork. Exhibitions of silver, ceramics and textiles. Special display of Japanese decorative art. Historical exhibition focuses on Irish history 1900-1921. Archaeological, historical and decorative arts collections located at Kildare Street, Zoological collections in the Natural History Museum at Merrion street. Geological exhibitions at the Earth Science Museum 7-9 Merrion Row.
Open: Tues Thurs and Sat 10-5 Fri 10.30-5 Sun 2-5.
Admission: Free.
Refreshments: Available.

MONAGHAN

MONAGHAN COUNTY MUSEUM
(Monaghan County Council)
1-2 Hill Street, Monaghan **Tel:** (0147) 82928
Heritage and contemporary arts. Permanent exhibitions on archaeology, local history, folklife crafts and lace. Awarded 1980 Council of Europe Museum Prize and 1993 Gulberkian/Norwich Union Award.
Open: Tues-Sat 11-1 and 2-5 closed public hols.
Admission: Free.
Location: Near Town Centre.
Frequent temporary and visiting exhibitions, music and other live events.

WEXFORD

IRISH AGRICULTURAL MUSEUM
(The Irish Agricultural Museum (J.C.) Ltd)
Johnstown Castle, Wexford **Tel:** 053-42888 **Fax:** 053 42004/42213
National museum of agricultural and Irish rural life. Housed in estate farmyard set in the 50 acre gardens of Johnstown Castle. Specialist sections on rural transport, country furniture and rural crafts. New exhibitions being added annually.
Open: All year Mon-Fri 9-5 weekends (summer only) 2-5.
Admission: Adults £1.75 children/students £1.
Location: 4 miles SW of Wexford Town.
Refreshments: Café open for July/August.

NORTHERN IRELAND

ANNAGHMORE

FARMYARD DISPLAY
(The National Trust)
Ardress, Annaghmore BT62 1SQ **Tel:** (01762) 851236
Display of agricultural implements from the 19th and 20th centuries.
Open: Weekends and Bank holidays during Apr, daily except Tues May-Sept.
Admission: Fee charged.

BANGOR

NORTH DOWN HERITAGE CENTRE
(North Down Borough Council)
Town Hall, Bangor Castle, Bangor BT20 4BT **Tel:** (01247) 270371 **Fax:** (01247) 271370
Local History and works of art reflecting aspects of North Down's historical and cultural past. Audio-visual shows; varying temporary exhibitions.
Open: Tues-Sat 10.30-4.30 Sun 2-4.30 July and Aug 10.30-5.30 Sun 2-5.30.
Admission: Free.
Location: Centre of town in Castle Park.
Refreshments: Castle Garden Room Restaurant.
Parties by prior arrangement. Suitable for disabled persons. Curator I.A. Wilson B.A., Dip. Ed.

BELFAST

ULSTER MUSEUM

Botanic Gardens, Belfast BT9 5AB **Tel:** (01232) 381251 **Fax:** (01232) 665510

Irish archaeology and local history, industrial archaeology including linen textile machinery. Coins and ethnography. Geology including the Dinosaur Show, featuring a complete anatosaurus skeleton and the natural history of Ireland with the unique feature on the 'Living Sea'. Irish and European Art. Changing temporary exhibitions, lectures, films. Sunday afternoon events.
Admission: Free.
Location: Situated in Botanic Gardens just one mile from the city centre.
Refreshments: Cafe.
Shop. Disabled access: leaflet available on request.

DOWNPATRICK

DOWN COUNTY MUSEUM

(Down District Council)

The Mall, Downpatrick, Co. Down BT30 6AH **Tel:** (01396) 615218 **Fax:** (01396) 615590

The archaeology, history and natural history. Housed in 18th century county gaol.
Open: Tues-Fri 11-5 Sat 2-5 Sun afternoon and Mon opening from July-mid Sept open St. Patrick's Day Easter Mon and May Bank Holidays.
Admission: Free.
Location: The Mall Downpatrick Co. Down.
Refreshments: Tea-room.
Car Parking. Partly suitable for disabled persons.

ENNISKILLEN

ENNISKILLEN CASTLE

Enniskillen BT74 7HL **Tel:** (01365) 325000

Set within the walls of the old castle, visit the new Heritage Centre and Museum of the Inniskilling Fusiliers. Fermanagh's natural and social history are brought to life by film and award-winning displays. Special exhibitions programe.
Open: Oct-Apr Mon 2-5 Tues-Fri 10-5 May-Sept Sat 2-5 July-Aug Sun 2-5.
Admission: Adults £1 children 50p.
Disabled, partial access.

OMAGH

ULSTER-AMERICAN FOLK PARK

Castletown, Omagh, Co. Tyrone

The Ulster-American Folk Park tells of the story of migrations of Ulster people to the New World and of the contribution they made to the U.S.A. over 200 years. Restored and recreated buildings, log dwellings, Ship and Dockside Gallery linking the Old and New World exhibits, craft demonstrations, modern exhibitions.
Open: Easter-Sept Mon-Sat 11-6.30 Sun and Public Bank Hols 11.30-7 Oct-Easter Mon-Fri 10.30-5 (except Public Hols).
Admission: Adults £3 children/OAPs and disabled £1.50 reductions for parties of 20 or more.
Education service. Residential accommodation available.

SPRINGHILL

SPRINGHILL
(The National Trust)
Springhill, Moneymore, Magherafelt, Co Londonderry BT45 7NQ **Tel:** (016487) 48210
Costume museum in the grounds of a 17th century manor house.
Open: Weekends and Bank holidays, Apr, May, June and Sept. Daily (except Thursday) July and August.
Admission: Small fee charged.

SCOTLAND

COLDSTREAM

THE HIRSEL HOMESTEAD MUSEUM
(Douglas & Angus Estates)
Coldstream TD12 4LP **Tel:** (01890) 882834/882965 **Fax:** (01890) 882834
Tools from the Estate's past - archaeology, agriculture, forestry, joiners, blacksmiths, natural and family history, Craft House and Workshops.
Open: All reasonable daylight hours throughout the year.
Admission: Parking charge.
Location: Immediately W of Coldstream on A697.
Refreshments: Available in main season.
Exhibitions/Events: Spring and Autumn craft fairs.
Walks, Picnic area, Car Park, Playground. Craft Centre

HAWICK

HAWICK MUSEUM AND THE SCOTT ART GALLERY
(Roxburgh District Council)
Wilton Lodge Park, Hawick, Roxburghshire TD9 7JL **Tel:** (01450) 373457 **Fax:** (01450) 378526
Social history, local industries (particularly knitwear), natural history and fine local collections. Scottish paintings and temporary exhibitions in the Scott Gallery.
Open: Apr-Sept Mon-Sat 10-12 and 1-5 Sun 2-5 Oct-Mar Mon-Fri 1-4 Sun 2-4 closed Sat.
Admission: Adults 80p children/OAPs/students and the unemployed 40p Roxburgh District residents and Borders Regional schools free.
Location: Set in award-winning parkland.
Refreshments: Nearby.

INNERLEITHEN

NATIONAL TRUST FOR SCOTLAND
Innerleithen
Open: Please note that with this property and all other NTS properties last admissions are 45 minutes before the advertised closing times.
Admission: OAPs/students/unemployed are admitted at half the standard adult rate on production of their cards.
Only guide dogs are permitted.

ROBERT SMAIL'S PRINTING WORKS
(National Trust for Scotland)
7/9 High Street, Innerleithen EH44 6HA **Tel:** (01896) 830206
This 130-year-old printing works, a time-capsule of local history, and the printing methods of yesteryear, has a water-wheel and working machinery. All machinery has been restored to full working order and the printer may be viewed at work.
Open: Good Fri to Oct 22 Mon-Sat 10-1 and 2-5 Sun 2-5 last tour 45 minutes before closing am and pm.
Admission: Adults £1.50 children 80p adult parties £1.20 schools 60p.
Restored Printing Works and Shop.

JEDBURGH

CASTLE JAIL AND JEDBURGH MUSEUM
(Roxburgh District Council)
Castlegate, Jedburgh, Roxburghshire TD8 6QD **Tel:** (01835) 863254 **Fax:** (01450) 378526
A Howard reform jail, built in 1823, on the site of the former Jedburgh Castle and gallows. Contains articles associated with prison life and the history of the Royal Burgh.
Open: Apr-Nov Mon-Sat 10-5 Sun 1-5.
Admission: Adults £1 children/60+/students and the unemployed 50p.
Location: 200 metres from Town Centre, up steep hill.
Reductions for pre-booked parties over 20. Roxburgh District residents and Borders Regional schools free. Extensive renovations throughout 1995; please ring prior to visiting to check access.

MARY, QUEEN OF SCOTS' HOUSE
(Roxburgh District Council)
Queen Street, Jedburgh TD8 6EN **Tel:** (01835) 863331 **Fax:** (01450) 78526

Recently refurbished to an exceptional standard, the house tells the story of the life of the tragic queen, who herself visited Jedburgh in 1566.
Open: Apr-mid Nov daily 10-5.
Admission: Adults £1.20 children/OAPs/students and the unemployed 60p 5% discount for parties over 20 Roxburgh District residents and Borders Regional schools free.
Location: 200 metres from the main A68 route.
New shop for 1993 with wide range of Mary Queen of Scots material for sale.

KELSO

KELSO MUSEUM & THE TURRET GALLERY
(Roxburgh District Council)
Turret House, Abbey Court, Kelso TD5 7JA **Tel:** (01573) 225470 **Fax:** (01450) 78526
A new award winning museum in a charming 18th century building owned by the National Trust for Scotland. Once used as a skinner's workshop, the house has displays reconstructing a skinner's business as well as areas reflecting Kelso's growth as a market town and about Kelso Abbey.
Open: Apr-Oct Mon-Sat 10-12 & 1-5 Sun 2-5.
Admission: Adults 80p children/OAPs/students/unemployed 40p parties over 20 5% discount Roxburgh District residents and Borders Regional schools free.
Location: Near Kelso Abbey.
Refreshments: Good tea shop opposite.
There is also a Victorian School Room.Car park nearby (200 yds). Only ground floor display suitable for disabled.

PEEBLES

TWEEDDALE MUSEUM
(Tweeddale District Council)

Chambers Institute, High Street, Peebles EH45 3AP **Tel:** (01721) 720123
Fax: (01721) 720620

Local museum which has displays relating mainly to Tweeddale District, its history, environment and culture. Picture gallery showing monthly programme of contemporary art and craft.
Open: All year Mon-Fri 10-1 and 2-5 Apr-Oct Sat and Sun 2-5.
Admission: Free.
Location: High Street, Peebles.
Refreshments: No.
Exhibitions/Events: Programme of temporary exhibitons and workshops.

CENTRAL

ALLOA

ALLOA MUSEUM AND GALLERY
(Clackmannan District Council)

Speirs Centre, 29 Primrose Street, Alloa **Tel:** (01259) 213131

Local history and art exhibitions. Imaginative exhibitions changed monthly. Community involvement, school projects and regular lectures.
Open: Mon-Fri 10-4 Sat 10-12.30 closed Public Hols.
Admission: Free.
Refreshments: Vending machines.
Parties by prior arrangement. Car parking. Limited disabled access.

BANNOCKBURN

BANNOCKBURN HERITAGE CENTRE
(National Trust for Scotland)

Bannockburn FK7 0LJ **Tel:** (01786) 812664

Borestone site from where King Robert the Bruce commanded the battle of 1314 which gave the Scots their freedom and independence from English domination. Equestrian statue. Bannockburn is a Heritage Centre, with an exhibition 'The Kingdom of the Scots' tracing the history of Scotland by an imaginative series of displays from the Wars of Independence up to the Union of the Crowns in 1603.
Open: Site open all year. Heritage Centre & Shop 1 Feb-31Mar and 1 Nov-23 Dec daily 11-3; 1 Apr-31 Oct daily 10-5.30 (last admission half hour before closing).
Admission: Adults £2.00 children £1 adult parties £1.60 schools 80p.
Location: Off M80/M9, 2m south of Stirling.
Heritage Centre and Shop.

DOUNE

DOUNE MOTOR MUSEUM

Carse of Cambus, Doune **Tel:** (01786) 841203

A unique collection of vintage and post vintage throughbred cars. The display includes examples of Hispano Suiza, Bentley, Jaguar, Aston Martin, Lagonda and many others, including the second oldest Rolls-Royce in the world.
Open: Apr-Oct daily.
Admission: Fee charged.
Location: On the A84.
Refreshments: Cafeteria.
Gift shop. Free car parking.

DUMFRIES & GALLOWAY

DUMFRIES

ROBERT BURNS CENTRE
(Nithsdale District Council)

Mill Road, Dumfries DG2 7BE **Tel:** (01387) 264808

Exhibition on Burns and his life in Dumfries. AV theatre. Quality feature films 5 evenings a week.
Open: Apr-Sept Mon-Sat 10-8 Sun 2-5 Oct-Mar Tues-Sat 10-1 and 2-5.
Admission: Free except to AV theatre adults 80p concessions 40p. Combined ticket for Camera Obscura Burns House and Burns Centre AV theatre £1.60 only concession 80p.
Refreshments: Cafe.
Shop.

BURNS HOUSE
(Nithsdale District Council)

Burns Street, Dumfries DG1 OPS **Tel:** (01387) 255297

House in which Robert Burns lived for the three years prior to his death.
Open: Times as Dumfries Museum.
Admission: Adults 80p concessions 40p.

DUMFRIES MUSEUM
(Nithsdale District Council)
The Observatory, Dumfries DG2 7SW **Tel:** (01387) 253374 **Fax:** (01387) 265081

Natural history, archaeology and folk collections.
Open: Weekdays 10-1 and 2-5 Sun 2-5 closed Sun and Mon Oct-Mar.
Admission: Free whilst Camera obscura 80p concessions 40p obscura closed Oct-Mar.

GRACEFIELD - THE ARTS CENTRE FOR SOUTH WEST SCOTLAND
28 Edinburgh Road, Dumfries **Tel:** (01387) 62084

Situated in beautiful grounds overlooking the river Nith, the Centre has a collection of over 400 Scottish paintings. Regular exhibitions of contemporary art. Dark room. Pottery, studios.
Open: All year. Studios Tues-Fri 9-5 Galleries Tues-Fri 10-5 in summer and 12-5 in winter Galleries and Studios Sat 10-5 Sun 12-5 Galleries only.
Refreshments: Bar/Cafe.
Ample car parking.

OLD BRIDGE HOUSE MUSEUM
(Nithsdale District Council)
Mill Road, Dumfries DG2 7BE **Tel:** (01387) 256904
Seventeenth century house with six period and historical rooms.
Open: As Dumfries Museum closed Oct-Mar.
Admission: Free.

SANQUHAR MUSEUM
(Nithsdale District Council)
High Street, Sanquhar DG4 6BN
1735 Adam-designed town house; covers local history, geology knitting
Open: Apr-Sept Tues-Sat 10-1 and 2-5 Sun 2-5.
Admission: free.

ECCLEFECHAN

CARLYLE'S BIRTHPLACE
(National Trust for Scotland)
The Arched House, Ecclefechan, Lockerbie DG11 3DG **Tel:** (01576) 300666
House in which Carlyle was born in 1795 containing personal relics and manuscript letters.
Open: 28 Apr-30 Sept daily 1.30-5.30; 1-22 Oct Sat/Sun 1.30-5.30. Last admission 5.
Admission: Adults £1.50 children 80p adult parties £1.20 schools 60p.

KIRKCUDBRIGHT

BROUGHTON HOUSE
(National Trust for Scotland)
12 High Street, Kirkcudbright DG6 4JX **Tel:** (01557) 330437
17th century town house to which the artist E A Hornel of 'Glasgow Boys' renown added between 1901 and 1933 an art galley, an extensive library, a studio and a sheltered garden of Japanese design.
Open: Good Friday - 22 Oct daily 1-5.30
Admission: Adults £1.50 children 80p Adult parties £1.25 Schools 60p.

FIFE

ANSTRUTHER

THE SCOTTISH FISHERIES MUSEUM
St. Ayles, Harbourhead, Anstruther **Tel:** (01333) 310628
16th to 19th century buildings housing marine aquarium, fishing and ships' gear, model and actual fishing boats, period fisher-home interior, reference library.
Open: Apr-Oct weekdays 10-5.30 Sun 11-5 Nov-Mar weekdays 10-4.30 Sun 2-4.30.
Admission: Adults £2.20 Children/OAPs £1.20 (1994 rates) reduced rates for parties.
Refreshments: Tea-room
Shop. Wheelchair friendly.

CERES

FIFE FOLK MUSEUM
The Weigh House, High Street, Ceres, Cupar KY15 5NF **Tel:** (01334) 828250 (Messages only)
A varied local exhibition displayed in a unique setting.
Open: Easter then mid May-end Oct 2-5 (except Fri).
Admission: Adults £1.50 OAPs £1.20 children 50p.
Location: Ceres, Fife.
Exhibitions/Events: Not yet known.
Pre-booked adult parties £1 per head particularly welcome outside normal open hours.

DUNFERMLINE

DUNFERMLINE DISTRICT MUSEUM AND THE SMALL GALLERY

(Dunfermline District Council)

Viewfield Terrace, Dunfermline KY12 7HY **Tel:** (01383) 721814

Local history and natural history of the District. Small gallery: monthly art and craft exhibitions.
Open: Mon-Sat 11-5 closed Sun and public holidays.
Admission: Free.
Location: Centre of town.

PITTENCRIEFF HOUSE MUSEUM

(Dunfermline District Council)

Pittencrieff Park, Dunfermline KY12 8QH **Tel:** (01383) 722935/721814

History of the Pittencrief House and Park, costume displays; temporary paintings and photographic exhibitions.
Open: Apr 29-Oct 29 1995 daily (except Tues) 11-5.
Admission: Free.
Location: In Pittencrieff Park.
Exhibitions/Events: Audio-visual programme on the history of the house.

INVERKEITHING

INVERKEITHING MUSEUM

(Dunfermline District Council)

Queen Street, Inverkeithing KY11 1LS **Tel:** (01383) 410495/721814

Small local history museum with changing social history exhibitions.
Open: Wed-Sun 11-5 closed Mon and Tues and public holidays.
Admission: Free.
Location: Centre of town.
Car parking outside museum. Unsuitable for disabled persons.

KIRKCALDY

BURNTISLAND EDWARDIAN FAIR

(Kirkcaldy District Museums)

High Street, Burntisland, Kirkcaldy **Tel:** (01592) 260732

New displays bring back the fun, colour and noise of an Edwardian fairground. Visit the Burntisland Lion 1990 Scottish Museum of the Year Award Winner.
Open: Daily during library hours (closed 1-2).
Location: Entrance in Burntisland Library.

KIRKCALDY MUSEUM AND ART GALLERY

(Kirkcaldy District Museums)

Kirkcaldy KY1 1YG **Tel:** (01592) 260732 **Fax:** (01592) 645302

A Scottish Museum of the Year Award winner 1989. A unique collection of paintings including works by the Scottish Colourists, the Camden Town Group and contemporary artists. Fascinating historical displays and a lively changing exhibition programme.
Open: Mon-Sat 10.30-5 Sun 2-5.
Admission: Free.
Location: By Kirkcaldy Railway Station.
Refreshments: Cafe incorporating Wemyss pottery displays.
Exhibitions/Events: May - Treasures of Fife, Oct - Fotofeis, Nov - Fife Art.
Gallery shop for crafts, cards and local publications. Special enquiry and Outreach Service available.

MCDOUALL STUART MUSEUM

(Kirkcaldy District Museums)

Rectory Lane, Dysart, Kirkcaldy **Tel:** (01592) 260732

This small museum occupies one of Dysart's many National Trust for Scotland restored 'little houses' which form the 18th century burgh with its historic harbour. The house is the birthplace of John McDouall Stuart, first explorer to cross Australia 1861-2 and displays describe his harrowing journeys, the Australian wilderness and the Aborigines. Sales area and starting point for self-guided tours around this attractive burgh.
Open: June 1-Aug 31 daily incl. Sun 2-5.

ST. ANDREWS

BRITISH GOLF MUSEUM

(Royal & Ancient Golf Club of St. Andrews Trust)

Bruce Embankment, St. Andrews **Tel:** (01334) 478880 **Fax:** (01334) 473306

Everything that's best of the game's 500 year history is on display at the award winning British Golf Museum in St. Andrews; walk around the galleries and trace the development of golf. Re-live the famous golfing moments - stroke for stroke. The museum is home to the most innovative multi-media system in the UK. Thanks to Compact Disk Interactive (CDI) technology, specially designed, developed and supplied by Philips Electronics, you can listen to commentaries and see biographies of the players accompanied by video and photographs. You can even test your knowledge of the game - all at the touch of a screen.
Open: On application for 1995.
Admission: Fee charged special reductions for parties.
Location: 57 miles from Edinburgh on A91.
Car parking. Suitable for the disabled.

CRAWFORD ARTS CENTRE

93 North Street, St. Andrews KY16 9AL **Tel:** (01334) 474610

Monthly programme of temporary exhibitions including contemporary and historical Scottish and international art, photography, architecture, crafts etc. Also drama performances and workshops. Craft shop.
Open: All year Mon-Sat 10-5 Sun 2-5 closed Christmas and New Year.
Admission: Free.
Refreshments: Coffee and biscuits.
Main Gallery suitable for disabled persons.

GRAMPIAN

ABERDEEN

ABERDEEN ART GALLERY
(Aberdeen District Council)
Schoolhill, Aberdeen **Tel:** (01224) 646333
Permanent collection of 18th, 19th and 20th century art with emphasis on contemporary art - oil paintings, watercolours, prints, drawings, sculpture, decorative arts. Full programmme of special exhibitions. Music, Dance Poetry.
Open: Mon-Sat 10-5 (Thur 10-8) Sun 2-5.
Admission: Free.
Refreshments: Cafeteria.
Museum shop. Access for disabled. Parking (50m) 400 places.

ABERDEEN MARITIME MUSEUM
(Aberdeen District Council)
Provost Ross's House, Shiprow, Aberdeen **Tel:** (01224) 585788
Display themes on local shipbuilding, fishing, North Sea Oil, ship models and paintings within the restored 16th century building. Special Exhibitions.
Open: Mon-Sat 10-5.
Admission: Free.
Museum shop. Parking (50m) 400 places.

JAMES DUN'S HOUSE
61 Schoolhill, Aberdeen **Tel:** (01224) 646333
18th century town house renovated for use as a museum with temporary displays and special exhibitions.
Open: Mon-Sat 10-5.
Admission: Free.
Parking (300m) 250 places.

PROVOST ROSS'S HOUSE
(National Trust for Scotland)
The Shiprow, Aberdeen AB1 2BY **Tel:** (01224) 572215
Houses the Aberdeen Maritime Museum, operated by the City of Aberdeen District Council, in one of the oldest surviving houses in Aberdeen, built 1593.
Open: All year Mon-Sat 10-5 NTS Visitor Centre video programme and shop open May 1-Sept 30 Mon-Sat 10-4.
Admission: Free.

PROVOST SKENE'S HOUSE
(Aberdeen District Council)
Guestrow (off Broad Street), Aberdeen **Tel:** (01224) 641086
16th century furnished house with period room settings and displays of local history domestic life and archaeology
Open: Mon-Sat 10-5.
Admission: Free.
Refreshments: Provost Skene's Kitchen has been restored and serves coffee, tea and light meals.
Parking (25m) 35 places.

ALFORD

GRAMPIAN TRANSPORT MUSEUM
(Grampian Transport Museum Trust)
Alford AB33 8AD **Tel:** (019755) 62292 **Fax:** (019755) 62180

An extensive collection of road transport vehicles and items housed in purpose built exhibition hall. All types of vehicle are represented including steam and horse drawn. Most of vehicles have strong local associations. Regional road transport history is reflected by photographs and displays. Extensive summer events programme with tarmac circuit facility allowing demonstration of vehicles in a suitable road environment. A separate railway exhibition is housed in the reconstructed GNSR village station which also acts as a terminus of the Alford Valley Railway, a two foot gauge passenger carrying railway.
Open: Mar 26-Oct 29 daily 10-5.
Admission: Fee charged. Special reduction for parties.
Refreshments: 12-3.30 July and Aug Sun only in June and Sept.
Exhibitions/Events: Comprehensive summer events programme includes: Alford Cavalcade - Sun 23 July; Grampian Motorcycle Convention - Sun 10 Sept; Alford Auction and Autojumble Sun 24 Sept.
Extensive free parking. Suitable for disabled persons.

BANCHORY

BANCHORY MUSEUM
(North East of Scotland Museum Service)
Bridge Street, Banchory **Tel:** (01779) 477778
Local history and bygones featuring Victoriana and commemorative china, and new Natural History display.
Open: Easter-Oct.
Admission: Free.

BANFF

BANFF MUSEUM
(North East of Scotland Museum Service)
High Street, Banff **Tel:** (01779) 477778
Local history including silver display, award winning natural history display and geology display; James Ferguson relics.
Open: June-Sept.
Admission: Free.

BUCKIE

PETER ANSON GALLERY
(Moray District Council)
Townhouse West, Cluny Place, Buckie **Tel:** (01542) 832121
Gallery contains a selection from over 700 watercolours by marine artist, Peter Anson. It represents a unique record of fishing and the fishing communities of Scotland and elsewhere during the heyday of the British Trawler fleet.
Open: Mon-Fri 10-8 Sats 10-12 closed Christmas Day Boxing Day Jan 1 2 Good Friday and May Day holidays.
Admission: Free
Exhibitions/Events: Exhibitions throughout year.
Parties by arrangement, telephone (01309) 673701. Suitable for disabled. Parking available.

DUFFTOWN

DUFFTOWN MUSEUM
(Moray District Council)
The Tower, Dufftown **Tel:** (01309) 673701
Local history. Mortlach Kirk. Temporary exhibitions.
Open: Daily Apr-Oct telephone for details.

ELGIN

OLDMILLS WORKING MILL & VISITOR CENTRE
(Moray District Council)
Oldmills Road, Elgin **Tel:** (01309) 673701

Working watermill, visitor centre. ladeside trail.
Open: Apr-Sept Tues-Sun 10-5.

FORRES

FALCONER MUSEUM
(Moray District Council)
Tolbooth Street, Forres, Moray IV36 0PH **Tel:** (01309) 673701 **Fax:** (01309) 674166
Local history 'The Story of Forres'; Natural history; Exhibits on Hugh Falconer and other prominent local people. Temporary exhibitions.
Open: Please telephone for details.

NELSON TOWER
(Moray District Council)
Grant Park, Forres **Tel:** (01309) 673701
Historic viewpoint with temporary exhibitions.
Open: May-Sept Tues-Sun 2-4.

FYVIE

FYVIE CASTLE
(National Trust for Scotland)
Fyvie, Turiff AB53 8JS **Tel:** (01651) 891266
Probably the grandest example of Scottish baronial architecture, reflecting the opulence of the Edwardian era. Contains an exceptionally important collection of portraits including works by Batoni, Raeburn, Ramsey, Gainsborough, Opie and Hoppner. In addition there are arms and armour and 16th century tapestries. Castles of Mar exhibition.
Open: 1 Apr-June 30 and Sept 1-30 1.30-5.30 July 1-Aug 31 11-5.30 and 1-22 Oct 1.30-5.30 last admission 4.45 grounds all year daily 9.30-sunset.
Admission: Adults £3.50 children £1.80 adult parties £2.80 schools £1.40 grounds £1.
Refreshments: Tea-room.

HUNTLY

BRANDER MUSEUM
(North East of Scotland Museum Service)
Public Library Building, Huntly **Tel:** (01779) 477778
Small display of local bygones; interesting display of Scottish Communion Tokens. Special temporary exhibitions.
Open: All year.
Admission: Free.

INVERURIE

CARNEGIE MUSEUM
(North East of Scotland Museum Service)
Public Library Building, The Square, Inverurie **Tel:** (01779) 477778
Collection of Prehistoric material from locality. Photographic equipment display. Special temporary exhibitions.
Open: All year.
Admission: Free.

KENNETHMONT

LEITH HALL
(National Trust for Scotland)
Kennethmont, Huntly AB54 4NQ **Tel:** (0146 43) 216
Unusual house, built round a central courtyard. Home of the Leith family from 1650. House contains personal possessions of successive Laird's, Jacobite relics. Major exhibition - 'For Crown and Country: The Military Lairds of Leith Hall'.
Open: 14 Apr-1 Oct daily 1.30-5.30 last admission 4.45pm.
Admission: Adults £3.00 children £1.50 adult parties £2.40 schools £1.20 grounds and Gardens £1.
Refreshments: Tea-room.

PETERHEAD

ARBUTHNOT MUSEUM
(North East of Scotland Museum Service)
St. Peter Street, Peterhead AB42 6QD **Tel:** (01779) 477778
Collections illustrating local history; whaling, Arctic and fishing section; coins. Large local photograph collection; lively temporary exhibitions programme.
Open: All year.
Admission: Free.

PITMEDDEN

PITMEDDEN MUSEUM OF FARMING LIFE
(National Trust for Scotland)
Ellon, Pitmedden AB41 0PD **Tel:** (01651) 842352
Collection of agricultural and domestic artifacts.
Open: 14 Apr-1 Oct daily 10-5.30 last admission 5.
Admission: Adults £3 children £1.50 adult parties £2.40 schools £1.20.
Location: On A920, 1m W of Pitmedden village and 14m N of Aberdeen.
Refreshments: Tea-room.

SPEY BAY

TUGNET ICE HOUSE
(Moray District Council)
Spey Bay **Tel:** (01309) 673701
Exhibition of Salmon fishing and boat building on the River Spey in Scotland's largest commercial Ice House.
Open: May-Sept daily 10-4.
Public toilets - male/female/disabled available.

STONEHAVEN

TOLBOOTH MUSEUM
(North East of Scotland Museum Service)
The Harbour, Stonehaven **Tel:** (01779) 477778
Housed in one of the town's oldest buildings on the old quay, the museum has local history and fishing displays.
Open: June-Sept.
Admission: Free.

TOMINTOUL

TOMINTOUL MUSEUM
(Moray District Council)
The Square, Tomintoul **Tel:** (01309) 673701
Wildlife, landscape, geology, climate, local history, reconstructed farm kitchen and village smithy.
Open: Easter-Oct daily telephone for details.

HIGHLANDS

BETTYHILL

STRATHNAVER MUSEUM
Clachan, Bettyhill, by Thurso, Sutherland
An expansive collection of local antiquities revealing the life and times of bygone days. Special features include the Farr Stone (9th century A.D.), the Highland Clearances, the Clan Mackay Memorial Room.
Open: Easter-Oct.

CAITHNESS

LHAIDHAY CROFT MUSEUM
Dunbeath, Caithness KW6 6EH
Open: Daily Easter-end Oct 10-6.
Admission: 50p.
Location: 2 miles North of Dunbeath.

CROMARTY

HUGH MILLER'S COTTAGE
(National Trust for Scotland)
Cromarty, Inverness IV11 8XD **Tel:** (0138 17) 245
Birthplace of the renowned geologist, editor and writer, containing relics and geological specimens.
Open: 28-Apr-1 Oct Mon/Sat 10-1 and 2-5.30 Sun 2.5.30
Admission: Adults £1.50 children 80p adult parties £1.20 schools 60p.

CULLODEN

CULLODEN
(National Trust for Scotland)
Culloden Moor, Inverness IV1 2ED **Tel:** (01463) 790607
Site of defeat in 1746 of Prince Charles Edward Stuart and the end of the 1745 Jacobite Rising. Graves of the Clans, Well of the Dead, Memorial Cairn. Colourful historical display. Visitor centre including A/V and Old Leanach Cottage.
Open: Visitor Centre Feb 4-Mar 31 10-4 Apr 1-Oct 31 9-6 Nov 1-Dec 30 10-4. Shop closed Oct 31-Nov 7 for stocktaking. Audio-visual show and restaurant close 30 minutes before Visitor Centre.
Admission: Adults £2.00 children £1 adult parties £1.60 schools 80p.
Location: On B9006, 5m E of Inverness.
Refreshments: Restaurant.
Induction loop for hard-of-hearing. Raised map and audio-tape for the blind. Braille sheets. Multi-lingual a/v programme.

DINGWALL

DINGWALL MUSEUM
(Dingwall Museum Trust)
Town House, High Street, Dingwall IV15 9RY **Tel:** (01349) 865366
Collection of objects, militaria and photographs relating to the Dingwall area. Temporary exhibitions throughout the season.
Open: Mon-Sat 10-5.
Admission: Adults £1 children/OAPs 50p.

FORT WILLIAM

THE WEST HIGHLAND MUSEUM
Cameron Square, Fort William PH33 6AJ **Tel:** (01397) 702169
Historical, natural history and folk exhibits. Prince Charles Edward Stuart and the '45 Rising. Items of local interest from pre-history to modern industry. Tartans.
Open: Mon-Sat Sept-June 10-5 (please telephone for winter hours) July-Aug 9.30-5.30 Sun 2-5.
Admission: Small fee charged.

GAIRLOCH

GAIRLOCH HERITAGE MUSEUM
(Gairloch and District Heritage Society)
Gairloch IV21 2BJ **Tel:** (01445) 712287
Local history museum illustrating all aspects of past life in a West Highland Parish.
Open: Easter-end Sept daily except Sundays 10-5 Oct-Mar by prior arrangement.
Admission: Adults £1.50 children 50p OAPs £1 groups on application.
Location: Junction of A832 and B8021.
Refreshments: Licensed restaurant attached.
Children's quiz.

GLENCOE

GLENCOE AND NORTH LORN FOLK MUSEUM

Glencoe
Thatched restored 'Cruck' cottage in Glencoe village. Exhibits include domestic bygones, costume, weapons. Jacobite relics, agricultural implements and natural history.
Open: Late May-end Sept Mon-Sat 10-5.30.
Admission: Adults £1 children 50p.
Location: Glencoe village.

INVERNESS

INVERNESS MUSEUM AND ART GALLERY

(Inverness District Council)
Castle Wynd, Inverness **Tel:** (01463) 237114
Interprets the human and natural history of the highlands. Displays of highland weapons, musical instruments, costume and Jacobite memorabilia. There is a reconstruction of the highland taxidermist's workshop and a silversmith's workshop which complements the important display of local silver. There is a growing art collection and an active programme of temporary exhibitions and events.
Open: Mon-Sat 9-5 also Sun 2-5 July and Aug only.
Admission: Free.
Refreshments: Coffee shop.
Disabled access to all galleries. Museum shop stocks gifts, books and souvenirs.

ROSEMARKIE

GROAM HOUSE MUSEUM

(Groam House Museum Trust)
High Street, Rosemarkie IV10 8UF **Tel:** (01381) 620961
An award-winning Pictish Centre for Ross & Cromarty with original sculptured stones, colourful impressions and video programmes. Gift shop.
Open: May 1-Oct 1 and winter weekends daily 10-5 Sun 2.30-4.30.
Admission: Adults £2 OAPs £1 children/students/unemployed free.
Location: Ross & Cromarty.
Activities for children.

LOTHIAN

EDINBURGH

BIGGAR GASWORKS MUSEUM

(National Museums of Scotland)
Biggar, Lanarkshire, Edinburgh **Tel:** 0131-225 7534
Museum of the Gas Industry. Selection of gas lights and domestic appliances on display. Working steam engines on some Suns in mid-season.
Open: End May-end Sept daily 2-5.
Admission: Free.
Location: Biggar.

BRASS RUBBING CENTRE

(City of Edinburgh)
Trinity Apse, Chalmers Close, High Street, Edinburgh **Tel:** 0131-556 4364
Fax: 0131-558 3103
Display of replica brasses and Scottish carved stones. Facilities for making rubbings.
Open: Mon-Sat 10-5 June-Sept 10-6 and during Festival period open Sun 12-5.
Admission: Free.
Location: Opposite the Museum of Childhood.
Trinity Apse in one of Edinburgh's finest medieval buildings.

NO.7 CHARLOTTE SQUARE 'THE GEORGIAN HOUSE'

(National Trust for Scotland)
Edinburgh EH12 **Tel:** 0131-225 2160
The lower floors of this Georgian House are furnished as it might have been by its first owners, showing the domestic surroundings and reflecting the social conditions of that age.
Open: Apr 1-Oct 22 Mon-Sat 10-5, Sun 2-5 last admission 4.30.
Admission: Including audio-visual presentation adults £3.50 children £1.80 adult parties £2.80 schools £1.40.
Location: Nr west end of Princes Street.

CITY ART CENTRE

(City of Edinburgh)
2 Market Street, Edinburgh **Tel:** 0131-529 3541
Art collections of works by late 19th and 20th century artists, mostly Scottish. Frequent temporary exhibitions.
Open: Mon-Sat 10-5 June-Sept 10-6 and during Festival period open Sun 2-5.
Admission: Free.
Recently re-opened after major expansion and re-development.

GLADSTONE'S LAND
(National Trust for Scotland)
477B Lawnmarket, Edinburgh EH1 2NT **Tel:** 0131-226 5856
Built 1620. Remarkable painted wooden ceilings.
Open: Apr 1-Oct 22 Mon-Sat 10-5 Sun 1.30-5 last admission 4.30.
Admission: Adults £2.50 children £1.30 adult parties £2 schools £1.
Location: In the Royal Mile.

HUNTLY HOUSE
(City of Edinburgh)
142 Canongate, Edinburgh **Tel:** 0131-529 4143 **Fax:** 0131-557 3346
Local history and topography; important collections of Edinburgh silver, glass and Scottish pottery. Reconstruction of an old Scots kitchen. Original copy of the 'National Covenant' of 1638. Also personal collections of Field Marshal Earl Haig.
Open: Mon-Sat 10-5 or 6 June-Sept and 10-6 during Festival period Sun 2-5.
Admission: Free.

LAURISTON CASTLE
(Trust-City of Edinburgh)
Cramond Road South, Edinburgh **Tel:** 0131-336 2060
16th century with 19th century additions. Period furniture, tapestries, Blue-John, wool mosaics.
Open: Apr-Oct daily (except Fri) 11-1 and 2-5 Nov-Mar Sat and Sun only 2-4.
Admission: Adults £2 children £1.
Special events in the grounds throughout the Summer - enquire for details.

MUSEUM OF ANTIQUITIES
(National Museums of Scotland)
Queen Street, Edinburgh EH2 1JD **Tel:** 0131-255 7534
Collections cover the whole of Scotland from the Stone Age to recent times; pre-historic and Roman objects, sculptured stones, relics of the Celtic church, Scottish coins and medals, Stuart relics, Highland weapons, domestic life, costumes and textiles; also reference library. Special exhibition 'Dynasty: The Royal House of Stewart'.
Open: Mon-Sat 10-5 Sun 2-5.
Admission: Free.
Location: City Centre.
Refreshments: Tea-room.
Shop, access for disabled.

MUSEUM OF CHILDHOOD
(City of Edinburgh)
42 High Street (Royal Mile), Edinburgh **Tel:** 0131-529 4142 **Fax:** 0131-558 3103
Vast collection of toys, dolls, games, costume etc....Still the noisiest museum in the world!
Open: Mon-Sat 10-5 (Jun-Sept 10-6) during Festival period open Sun 2-5.
Admission: Free.
Exhibitions/Events: Regular temporary exhibitions throughout the year.

MUSEUM OF FIRE
(Lothian and Borders Fire Brigade, Community Education Dept.)
Lauriston Place, Edinburgh EH3 9DE **Tel:** 0131-228 2401 **Fax:** 0131-228 6662
Open: Mon-Fri 9-4.30 organised parties can book a visit during or outside these hours by writing to the Community Education Dept (address above) museum is closed the first two weeks in August for maintenance two weeks over Christmas/New Year period and public hols.
Admission: Free.
Location: 10 mins walk from West End Princes St.
Disabled facilities available. 3 local car parks 2-3 mins from museum

MUSEUM OF FLIGHT
(National Museums of Scotland)
East Fortune Airfield, nr. North Berwick, Edinburgh **Tel:** (01620) 880308 or 0131-225 7534
Over 30 aircraft and aero engines including a Comet 4C and Vulcan.
Open: Daily Apr-Sept 10.30-4.30.
Admission: Adults £2 £1 children & concessions £1 family ticket £5 free day Friday.
Location: East Lothian.
Refreshments: Tea-room.
Shop.

The National Trust for Scotland
Free brochures and helpful service
from the Marketing Department
The National Trust for Scotland Edinburgh EH24DU
Telephone 031 226 5922
FAX 031 243 9302
over 100 beautiful places for
WELCOME!
All that we do, we do for you
to visit
CASTLES
GREAT HOUSES
MUSEUMS
LITTLE HOUSES
HISTORIC PLACES
MOUNTAINS
WILD PLACES
GARDENS
PARKLANDS
EXHIBITIONS
RESTAURANTS
GIFT SHOPS
Telephone 031 226 5922
FAX 031 243 9302
Engraving of Culross from John Slezer's THEATRUM SCOTIÆ (1693)

NATIONAL GALLERY OF SCOTLAND

The Mound, Edinburgh EH2 2EL **Tel:** 0131-556 8921

An outstanding collection of paintings, drawings and prints by major artists from the Renaissance to Post Impressionism, including Velázquez, El Greco, Rembrandt, Vermeer, Gainsborough, Turner, Constable, Degas, Monet and Van Gogh. Also the national collection of Scottish art including Ramsay, Raeburn, Wilkie and McTaggart.
Open: Mon-Sat 10-5 Sun 2-5 closed Christmas, New Year and May Day.
Admission: Free except for some loan exhibitions.
Study Rooms: The Department of Prints and Drawings is open by arrangement at the front desk of the Gallery: Mon-Fri 10-12.30, 2-4.30. Further Information is available from the Information Department Tel 0131-556 8921. Facilities for disabled visitors. Gallery shop.

NEWHAVEN HERITAGE MUSEUM

(City of Edinburgh)
Fishmarket, Newhaven Harbour, Edinburgh EH6 **Tel:** 0131-557 4165
New museum telling about the fishing village of Newhaven and its People.
Open: Mon-Sun 12-5.
Admission: Free.

THE PEOPLE'S STORY

(City of Edinburgh)
Canongate Tolbooth, 163 Canongate, Edinburgh **Tel:** 0131-529 4057
Fax: 0131-557 3346
Housed in the 16th century Tolbooth, this exciting museum tells the story of the life and work of Edinburgh's people over the past 200 years.
Open: Mon-Sat 10-5 except June-Sept 10-6 and during Festival period open Sun 2-5.
Admission: Free.

QUEENSFERRY MUSEUM

(City of Edinburgh)
High Street, South Queensferry, Edinburgh **Tel:** 0131-331 5545
Fax: 0131-557 3346
Situated between the two Forth bridges in the Council Chambers of the former Royal Burgh of Queensferry. Local history collections.
Open: Thurs-Sat and Mon 10-1 & 2.15-5 Sun 2-5.
Admission: Free.

ROYAL MUSEUM OF SCOTLAND

(National Museums of Scotland)
Chambers Street, Edinburgh EH1 1JF **Tel:** 0131-225 7534 **Fax:** 0131-220 4819
Houses the national collections of decorative arts of the world, ethnography, natural history, geology, technology and science. Displays range from primitive art to space material, from ceramics to fossils, from birds to working models in the hall of power. Items of importance in all fields. Additional major displays in course of preparation. Main Hall of architectural interest. Temporary exhibitions. Lectures and films at advertised times.
Open: Mon-Sat 10-5 Sun 12noon-5.
Admission: Free.
Location: City Centre.
Refreshments: Tea-room.
Shop.

RUSSELL COLLECTION OF EARLY KEYBOARD INSTRUMENTS

(University of Edinburgh)
St. Cecilia's Hall, Niddry Street, Cowgate, Edinburgh **Tel:** 0131-650 2805
Forty-seven keyboard instruments, including harpsichords, clavichords, fortepianos, regals, spinets, virginals and chamber organs. Pictures (Pannini etc.). Tapestries and textiles.
Open: Sat and Wed 2-5 throughout the year. Daily during Edinburgh Festival (mornings)
Admission: Adults £1 concessions 50p.

SCOTCH WHISKY HERITAGE CENTRE

354 Castlehill, The Royal Mile, Edinburgh EH1 2NE **Tel:** 0131-220 0441
Fax: 0131-220 6288
The Scotch Whisky Heritage Centre provides an entertaining explanation of the making of Scotch Whisky from the barley to the bottle. Travel through 300 years of Scotch Whisky history in a Barrel Car, with commentary in English or seven other languages.
Open: Daily from 10-5 all year extended hours in summer.
Admission: Adults £3.80 students £3.20 OAPs £2.30 children 5-17 £2 family £10.60 group discounts available.
Location: Beside Edinburgh Castle.
Whisky and gift shop.

SCOTTISH AGRICULTURAL MUSEUM

(National Museums of Scotland(Outstation)
Ingliston, Newbridge, Edinburgh **Tel:** 0131-225 7534 or 0131-333 2674
Illustrates the history of agriculture in Scotland. Room settings, crafts, animal husbandry etc.
Open: May-Aug Mon-Fri 10-4.30 Sat (mid-season only) 10-4.30 closed Sun.
Admission: Free.
Location: In Royal Highland Showground.
Refreshments: Tea-room.
Shop, access for disabled.

SCOTTISH NATIONAL GALLERY OF MODERN ART

Belford Road, Edinburgh EH4 3DR **Tel:** 0131-556 8921
Scotland's finest collection of 20th-century painting, sculpture and graphic art. Includes works by established masters such as Picasso, Matisse, Ernst, Kirchner, Dix, Moore; major Scottish artists including Alan Davie, John Bellany and Stephen Conroy and the leading figures in contemporary international art.
Open: Mon-Sat 10-5 Sun 2-5 closed Christmas New Year and May Day.
Admission: Free except for some loan exhibitions.
Refreshments: Gallery Café.
Study Rooms:The Prints and Drawings Study Room is open by prior appointment only: Mon-Fri 10-12, 2.30-4.30. Further information about the National Galleries of Scotland, the collections and activities is available from the Information Department. Tel 0131-556 8921. Facilities for disabled visitors. Gallery shop.

SCOTTISH NATIONAL PORTRAIT GALLERY

1 Queen Street, Edinburgh EH2 1JD **Tel:** 0131-556 8921
Portraits in all media of people who have played a significant role in Scottish history from the 16th century to the present, recorded by the most famous artists of the day. Subjects include Mary, Queen of Scots, Robert Burns Sean Connery, The Queen Mother. Also the national collection of photography.
Open: Mon-Sat 10-5 Sun 2-5 closed Christmas New Year and May Day.
Admission: Free except for some loan exhibitions.
Refreshments: Queen Street Café.
Study Rooms: The Print Room and Reference Room is open by arrangement at the front desk of the Gallery: Mon-Fri 10-12.30, 2-4.30. Further Information is available from the Information Department Tel 0131-556 8921. Facilities for disabled visitors. Gallery Shop.

SCOTTISH UNITED SERVICES MUSEUM

(National Museums of Scotland)
Edinburgh Castle, Edinburgh **Tel:** 0131-225 7534
Illustrates by its display of uniform, head dress, arms and equipment, medals, portraits and models, the history of the armed forces of Scotland. Extensive library and comprehensive collection of prints of uniforms.
Open: Times as for Edinburgh Castle.
Admission: Free
Shop.

SHAMBELLIE HOUSE MUSEUM OF COSTUME
(National Museums of Scotland)
New Abbey, Dumfries, Edinburgh **Tel:** 0131-225 7534 (01387) 85375
Victorian Country home containing costumes from 1850s to 1920s.
Open: 1 Apr-31 Oct (end) 11-5 daily.
Admission: Adults £2 children & concessions £1.
Location: Dumfries.
Refreshments: Tea-room.
Shop.

THE WRITERS' MUSEUM
(City of Edinburgh)
Lady Stair's Close, Lawnmarket, Edinburgh **Tel:** 0131-529 4901
A reconstructed town house dating from 1622. Exhibits connected with Robert Burns, Sir Walter Scott and R.L.Stevenson.
Open: Mon-Sat 10-5 June-Sept 10-6 during Festival period open Sun 2-5.
Admission: Free.

NORTH BERWICK

NORTH BERWICK MUSEUM
(East Lothian Museum Service)
School Road, North Berwick EH39 4JU **Tel:** (01620) 895457
Local history, archaeology, wildlife and golf.
Open: Open daily Easter-end Sept.
Admission: Admission free small charge for special exhibitions.
Refreshments: No.
Special temporary exhibitions and events each summer.

PRESTONGRANGE

PRESTONGRANGE INDUSTRIAL HERITAGE MUSEUM
(East Lothian Museum Service)
Preston Road, Prestonpans, Prestongrange EH32 9RX **Tel:** 0131-653 2904
Historic site of Prestongrange Colliery and Brickworks. 1874 Cornish Beam Engine. Temporary exhibitions. Colliery locomotives steamed first Sunday of each month.
Open: Easter-Oct daily.
Refreshments: Yes.
Exhibitions/Events: Steam days first Sunday each month.
Occasional weekend craft sessions.

ORKNEY

STROMNESS

STROMNESS MUSEUM
(Orkney Natural History Society)
Stromness **Tel:** (01856) 850025
Orkney Maritime and natural history displays; Scapa Flow and the German Fleet.
Open: Oct-Apr Mon-Sat 10.30-12.30 and 1.30-5 May-Sept Sun-Sat 10.30-5.
Admission: Fee charged.

STRATHCLYDE

AYR

AYR CARNEGIE LIBRARY
(Kyle and Carrick District Council)
12 Main Street, Ayr **Tel:** (01292) 286385 **Fax:** (01292) 611593
Full exhibition programme.
Open: Mon Tues Thurs Fri 10-7.30 Wed Sat 10-5.

MACLAURIN GALLERY AND ROZELLE HOUSE
(Kyle and Carrick District Council in assoc with the Mary E. Maclaurin Trust)
Rozelle, Ayr **Tel:** (01292) 445447 **Fax:** (01292) 442065
Variety of exhibitions 3 to 5 weeks' duration. Fine art, craft, photography, contemporary art. Programme of touring exhibitions from UK & European venues.
Open: Mon-Sat 10-5 Sun 2-5 (Apr-Oct only).
Refreshments: Rozelle Pantry.

BARRHEAD

BARRHEAD COMMUNITY MUSEUM
(Renfrew District Council)
128 Main Street, Barrhead G78 1SG **Tel:** 0141-876 1994
A series of changing exhibition reflecting the historic background of Barrhead.
Open: All year Mon Wed Fri 1-5 Tue Thur 1-8 Sat 10-5 (Sun and public holidays Apr-Oct 1-5).
Admission: Free.
Limited car parking.

CLYDEBANK

CLYDEBANK DISTRICT MUSEUM

Old Town Hall, Dumbarton Road, Clydebank **Tel:** 0141-941 1331 Ext 402

A small museum situated beside the shipyard where some of the world's greatest liners were built. Displays tell the story of the shipbuilders and the town which grew up round their yards. Also on show is part of the museum's large and very fine collection of sewing machines.

Open: Mon and Wed 2-4.30 Sat 10-4.30 and other times by prior arrangement.

Admission: Free.

COATBRIDGE

SUMMERLEE HERITAGE TRUST

West Canal Street, Coatbridge ML5 1QD **Tel:** (01236) 431261 **Fax:** (01236) 440429

Winner of the award Scottish Museum of the Year 1990. Museum of social and industrial history with indoor and open air exhibits including recently extended working tramway, belt driven machinery, 19th century coal mine, miners' rows and other social history exhibitions. Ironworks gallery, regularly changing exhibitions and special events.

Open: 10-5 daily closed Dec 25 26 Jan 1 2.

Admission: Free.

Refreshments: Tea-room.

Exhibitions/Events: Special events from May until October.

Gift shop. Wheelchair accessible. Free car parking. Convenient access from BR Sunnyside and Coatbridge stations.

CULZEAN BAY

CULZEAN CASTLE

(National Trust for Scotland)

Maybole, Culzean Bay KA19 8LE **Tel:** (0165) 56269

Built 1772-1792 by Robert Adam on a spectacular cliff top site. Superb furnishings, magnificant Oval Staircase and Round Drawing Room. Eisenhower presentation explains the General's association with Culzean.

Open: Castle 1 Apr-22 Oct daily 10.30-5.30. Country Park 9.30 to sunset all year daily.

Admission: Adults £3.50 children £1.80 adult parties £4.50 schools £2.50 (last two prices include coach entry to Country Park). Please confirm admission prices by telephoning Kirkowald (016556 274). Other times by appointment.

Location: 12 miles south of Ayr.

Refreshments: Licensed restaurant.

Visitor centre and shop.

CUMNOCK

DISTRICT HISTORY CENTRE AND BAIRD INSTITUTE MUSEUM

Lugar Street, Cumnock **Tel:** (01290) 421701

A local history museum and district history centre featuring local pottery, wooden ware in conjunction with a programme of temporary exhibitions.

Open: Mon Tues Thur Fri 10-1 & 1.30-4.30 Sat 11-1.

Admission: Free.

GLASGOW

ART GALLERY AND MUSEUM

Kelvingrove, Glasgow G3 8AG **Tel:** 0141-221 9600 **Fax:** 0141-305 2639

Fine Art: Collection includes great paintings by Giorione, Botticelli, Rembrandt, Millet, Monet, Van Gogh, Derain as well as works from all major European schools, notably the Dutch 17th century and French Barbizon, Impressionist and Post-Impressionist periods. Also British painting 17th to 20th centuries with emphasis on Scottish art, especially Glasgow Boys and Scottish Colourists. Decorative Art: Collections include important specimens of Western European ceramics, glass, silver and furniture. Recently opened gallery displays Glasgow decorative arts 1880-1920. Armour: The Scott Collection of arms and armour including the Milanese Armour c.1450, the Whitelaw Collection of Scottish arms. Archaeology and History: Neolithic, Bronze and Iron Age material; items from the Egyptian, Greek and Cypriot collecctions. Ethnography: tools, clothing, weapons, religious and ceremonial objects relating to non-European societies. Natural History: Collection contains important botanical, geological and zoological material, being particularly strong in Scottish fossils, worldwide non-flowering plants (Stirton Collection), birds, fish and molluscs. Wheelchair access.

Open: Weekdays 10-5 Sun 11-5.

Refreshments: Self-service restaurant.

BURRELL COLLECTION

Pollok Country Park, Glasgow G45 1AT **Tel:** 0141-649 7151 **Fax:** 0141-636 0086

Housed in a new building opened in 1983. World famous collection of textiles, furniture, ceramics, stained glass, silver, art objects and pictures including major works by Cracach, Rembrandt, Courbet, Manet, Degas, Cezanne, gifted to Glasgow in 1944 by Sir William and Lady Burrell.

Open: Weekdays 10-5 Sun 11-5.

Admission: Free.

Refreshments: Self-service restaurant.

Wheelchair access.

FOSSIL GROVE

Victoria Park, Glasgow G14 1BN **Tel:** 0141-221 9600

In the midst of the tranquil beauty of Victoria Park, Fossil Grove provides interpretation of a 330 million year old fossilised forest of extinct scale trees.

Open: Apr-Sept 12-5.

Admission: Free.

Wheelchair access.

HAGGS CASTLE

100 St. Andrews Drive, Glasgow G41 4RB **Tel:** 0141-427 2725 **Fax:** 0141-427 7075

A museum of history for children with work space for children's activities.

Open: Weekdays 10-5 Sun 11-5.

Admission: Free.

Limited wheelchair access.

HUNTERIAN ART GALLERY

Hillhead Street, Glasgow University, Glasgow G12 8QQ **Tel:** 0141-330 5431 **Fax:** 0141-307 8017

Unrivalled collections of C.R.Mackintosh, including reconstructed interiors of the architect's house, and of J.A.M. Whistler. Works by Rembrandt, Chardin, Stubbs, Reynolds, Pissarro, Sisley, Rodin plus Scottish paintings from the 18th century to present. Large collection of Old Master and modern prints, Sculpture Courtyard. Varied programme of temporary exhibitions.

Open: Mon-Sat 9.30-5 Mackintosh House closed Mon-Sat 12.30-1.30.

Telephone enquiries to the above number.

HUNTERIAN MUSEUM

Glasgow University, Glasgow G12 8QQ **Tel:** 0141-330 4221

Scotland's oldest public museum, opened in 1807. Situated in Sir George Gilbert Scott's magnificent Victorian Gothic building. Collections include geological, archaeological, historical, ethnographic and numismatic material. Exhibitions include *Earth...Life* and *Roman Scotland: Outpost of an Empire*.

Open: Mon-Sat 9.30-5.

Refreshments: Small 18th century coffee shop.

Book shop. Enquiries: phone the above number.

MCLELLAN GALLERIES

270 Sauchiehall Street, Glasgow G2 3EH **Tel:** 0141-331 1854 **Fax:** 0141-332 9957

Reopened in January 1990 as part of Glasgow's celebrations as European City of Culture for the display of large temporary exhibitions, this handsome building originally housed Archibald McLellan's collection which became the nucleas of Glasgows Museums and Art Galleries fine art holding in 1856.

Open: Weekdays 10-5 Sun 11-5.

Admission: Varies.

For exhibition dates and admission prices see press or telephone the above number. Wheelchair access.

MUSEUM OF TRANSPORT

Kelvin Hall, 1 Bunhouse Road, Glasgow G3 8DP **Tel:** 0141-221 9600 **Fax:** 0141-305 2682

Opened Spring 1988. A new and considerably enlarged museum of the history of transport, including a reproduction of a typical 1938 Glasgow street. Other new features are a larger display of the ship models and a walk-in Motor Car Showroom with cars from the 1930s up to modern times. Other displays include Glasgow trams and buses, cycles and motorcycles, railway locomotives and a Glasgow Subway station.

Open: Weekdays 10-5 Sun 11-5.

Admission: Free.

Refreshments: Restaurant, fast food and bar facilities are shared with the adjacent indoor Sports Centre.

Wheelchair access.

PEOPLE'S PALACE

Glasgow Green, Glasgow G40 1AT **Tel:** 0141-554 0223 **Fax:** 0141-550 0892
Museum of Glasgow history from 1175 to the present day. Collections cover early Glasgow, the rise of the tabacco in the 18th century and domestic, social and political life in the 19th and 20th centuries. Wheelchair access.
Open: Weekdays 10-5 Sun 11-5.
Admission: Free.
Refreshments: Snack bar.

POLLOK HOUSE

Pollok Country Park, Glasgow G43 1AT **Tel:** 0141-632 0724 **Fax:** 0141-636 0086
House built c.1750 in Palladian style with Edwardian additions. Contains Stirling Maxwell Collection of paintings including works by El Greco, Murillo, Goya, Signorelli and William Blake, and also late 18th and early 19th century furniture and decorative arts. Set in beautiful wooded parkland.
Open: Weekdays 10-5 Sun 11-5.
Admission: Free.
Refreshments: Tea-room.
Wheelchair access on request.

PROVAND'S LORDSHIP

3 Castle Street, Glasgow G4 0RB **Tel:** 0141-552 8819
Facing the Cathedral, the only other surviving medieval building in Glasgow built 1471. Period displays ranging in date from 1500 to 1918.
Open: Weekdays 10-5 Sun 11-5.
Admission: Free.

RUTHERGLEN MUSEUM

King Street, Rutherglen, Glasgow G73 1DQ **Tel:** 0141-647 0837
A museum of the history of the former Royal Burgh of Rutherglen with regularly changing displays and temporary exhibitions. Wheelchair access.
Open: Weekdays 10-5 Sun 11-5.
Admission: Free.

SCOTLAND STREET SCHOOL MUSEUM

(Strathclyde Regional Council)
225 Scotland Street, Glasgow **Tel:** 0141-429 1202
Designed by Charles Rennie Mackintosh. The history of education in Scotland from 1872. Victorian, Second World War, 50's and 60's classrooms and Edwardian cookery room. Temporary exhibition programme includes art, education, and Mackintosh. Regular activities.
Open: Mon-Sat 10-5 Sun 2-5.
Admission: Free.
Location: Opposite Shield Road Underground Station.
Refreshments: Cafe.
Disabled access to ground floor only.

SPRINGBURN MUSEUM

(Springburn Museum Trust)
Atlas Square, Ayr Street, Glasgow G21 4BW **Tel:** 0141-557 1405
Changing exhibitions about the past and present of an area which was once the greatest centre of steam locomotive manufacture in Europe. Social and Industrial History Museum of the Year Award in 1989.
Open: Mon-Fri 10.30-5 Sat 10-4.30 Sun 2-5 enquire for public holiday opening times
Admission: Free.
Location: Adjacent to Springburn Railway Station.
Exhibitions/Events: Please phone for details
Suitable for disabled persons though no wheelchairs available.

THE ST MUNGO MUSEUM OF RELIGIOUS LIFE AND ART

2 Castle Street, Glasgow G4 0RH **Tel:** 0141-553 2557 **Fax:** 0141-552 4744
Opened in 1993, this unique museum explores the universal themes of life and death and the hereafter through beautiful and evocative art objects associated with different religious faiths. Three galleries focus on art, world religions and religion in Scottish history. Britain's only Japaneze Zen Garden contributes its own unique sense of peace.
Open: Mon-Sat 10-5 Sun 11-5.
Admission: Free.
Refreshments: Restaurant (mainly vegetarian).
Facilities for the disabled. Wheelchair access. Museum shop.

THE TENEMENT HOUSE

(National Trust for Scotland)
No. 145 Buccleuch Street, Garnethill, Glasgow G3 6QN **Tel:** 0141-333 0183
A restored first floor flat in a Victorian tenement building, built 1892, presents a picture of social significance. A second flat on the ground floor provides reception interpretative and educational facilities.
Open: 1 Mar-22 Oct daily 1.30-5 last admission 4.30 groups at other times by appointment only please. Not to exceed 15 people per tour.
Admission: Adults £2 children £1 adult parties £1.60 schools 80p.
Location: N. of Charing Cross.

HELENSBURGH

THE HILL HOUSE

(National Trust for Scotland)
Upper Colquhoun Street, Helensburgh G84 9AJ **Tel:** (01436) 73900
This is one of the finest examples of the domestic architecture of Charles Rennie Mackintosh. His original and highly idiosyncratic sense of design created this 20th century masterpiece. Exhibition.
Open: 1 Apr-23 Dec daily 1.30-5.30 last admission 5 shop closed 1-7 Nov for stocktaking.
Admission: Adults £3 children £1.50 adult parties £2.40 schools £1.20.
Refreshments: Tea-room. 1 Apr-31 Oct

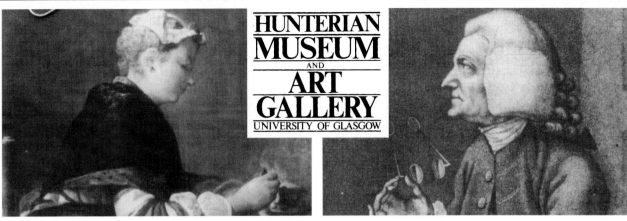

IRVINE

SCOTTISH MARITIME MUSEUM
(Scottish Maritime Museum Trust)
Laird Forge, Gottries Road, Irvine KA12 8QE **Tel:** (01294) 78283

The Scottish Maritime Museum contains, on four sites, full size ships, a Boat Shed special exhibition gallery with a new maritime theme display every year, Educational Centre and a restored Tenement Flat. There is also a Workshop and Research Unit and the site of the reconstruction of the 1872 Linthouse Engine Shop which will provide an increase in Museum Display Area over the next decade. Come and discover the world of Scotland and the sea, board the Puffer, 'Spartan', Tug and Lifeboat. Museum vessels operate in the harbour from time to time.
Open: Apr 1-Oct 31 daily 10-5 other times by appointment.
Admission: Adults £2 children and concessions £1 family £4 special rates for school and organised parties.
Refreshments: Tea-room.
Car park. Suitable for disabled (no wheelchairs available).

ISLE OF ARRAN

BRODICK CASTLE
(National Trust for Scotland)
Brodick, Isle of Arran KA27 8HY **Tel:** (01770) 302202
This ancient seat of the Dukes of Hamilton was more recently the home of the late Mary, Duchess of Montrose. The contents include superb silver, porcelain, and paintings from the collections of the Dukes of Hamilton, William Beckford and the Earls of Rochford. Sporting pictures and trophies. Castle.
Open: Castle Good Fri-Sept 30 daily 11.30-5 last entry at 4.30. 1-22 Oct Sat/Sun 11.30-5. Reception Centre restaurant and shop 10-5.
Admission: Garden adults £2 children £1 House and garden adults £4 children £2 adult parties £3.20 schools £1.60.
Refreshments: Restaurant.
Shop.

KILBARCHAN

WEAVER'S COTTAGE
(National Trust for Scotland)
The Cross, Kilbarchan PA10 2JG **Tel:** (01505) 705588
Attractive 18th century craftsman's house containing traditional weaving and domestic exhibits. Weaving demonstrations (check for times)
Open: 28 Apr-Sept 30 daily 1-5.30 1-22 Oct Sat/Sun 1.30-5.30 last admission 5pm.
Admission: Adults £1.50 children 80p adult parties £1.20 schools 60p.

KILMARNOCK

DEAN CASTLE
(Kilmarnock and Loudoun District Council)
Dean Road, off Glasgow Road, Kilmarnock **Tel:** (01563) 26401 or (01563) 22702
Medieval arms and armour, musical instruments, tapestries.
Open: Daily 12-5 closed Dec 25 26 and Jan 1 2.
Admission: £2.
Organised parties must book.

DICK INSTITUTE MUSEUM AND ART GALLERY
(Kilmarnock and Loudoun District Council)
Elmbank Avenue, Kilmarnock **Tel:** (01563) 26401
Paintings, geology, archaeology, natural history, industry. Frequent temporary exhibitions.

KIRKINTILLOCH

THE AULD KIRK MUSEUM
(Strathkelvin District Council)
Cowgate, Kirkintilloch G66 1AB **Tel:** 0141-775 1185
Permanent displays of local life and industry, plus temporary exhibitions of art, photography, local history, archaeology and social and industrial history.
Open: Tues Wed Fri 10-12 and 2-5 Thurs 10-5 Sat 10-1 and 2-5.
Admission: Free.

THE BARONY CHAMBERS MUSEUM
(Strathkelvin District Council)
The Cross, Kirkintilloch G66 1AB **Tel:** 0141-775 1185
Resource Room, temporary exhibitions only
Open: During temporary exhibitions Tues Wed Fri 10-12 and 2-5 Thurs 10-5 Sat 10-1 and 2-5.
Admission: Free.

KIRKOSWALD

SOUTER JOHNNIE'S COTTAGE
(National Trust for Scotland)
Main Road, Kirloswald KA19 8HY **Tel:** (0165 56) 603 or 274
The home of John Davidson on whom Burns modelled Souter Johnnie in his narrative poem 'Tam o' Shanter'. Life-sized sculptured figures of Souter, Tam, the innkeeper and his wife are in the restored ale house in cottage garden.
Open: 28 Apr-Sept 30 daily 1.30-5.30 1-22 Oct Sat/Sun 1.30-5.30 last admission 5.
Admission: Adults £1.50 children 80p adult parties £1.20 schools 60p.
Location: 4m south-west of Maybole.

LANARK

NEW LANARK WORLD HERITAGE VILLAGE
(New Lanark Conservation Trust)
New Lanark Mills, Lanark ML11 9DB **Tel:** (01555) 661345 **Fax:** (01555) 665738

200 year old Cotton Mill Village, site of Robert Owen's social and educational experiments, now nominated as a World Heritage site. Set in the Clyde Gorge, surrounded by beautiful woodlands and the Falls of Clyde, New Lanark is Europe's premier industrial heritage site. Award-winning Visitor Centre.
Open: Daily 11-5 closed Dec 25 26 and Jan 1 2.
Admission: Please telephone for charges. Pre-booking advisable for groups - special rates for schools.
Location: 1 mile south of Lanark.
Refreshments: Coffee Shop.
Exhibitions/Events: Various throughout the year. Speciality shopping, picnic and play areas, Millworkers' House, other attractions.
Giftshop. Edinburgh Woollen Mill shop, picnic area, children's playground, period village store, 'power trail'. Car parking in visitor car park. 'Visitor Centre' suitable for disabled persons. Two wheelchairs available. Access to village free at all times. Limited disabled parking in village square.

LOCHWINNOCH

LOCHWINNOCH COMMUNITY MUSEUM
(Renfrew District Council)
Main Street, Lochwinnoch PA12 4AG **Tel:** (01505) 842615 **Fax:** 0141-889 9240
A series of changing exhibitions reflecting the historic background of local agriculture, industry and village life.
Open: All year Mon Wed Fri 10-1 2-5 6-8 Tues Sat 10-1 and 2-5 except Bank Holidays.
Admission: Free.
Limited car parking.

MILLPORT

ROBERTSON MUSEUM AND AQUARIUM
University Marine Biological Station, Millport **Tel:** (01475) 530581/2 **Fax:** (01475) 530601
Museum and aquarium showing the natural history of the Clyde sea.
Open: All year.
Admission: Adults £1 Children 50p.

MILNGAVIE

HEATHERBANK MUSEUM OF SOCIAL WORK
163 Mugdock Road, Milngavie G62 8ND **Tel:** 0141-956 5923
A unique museum on the History of Social Work. Changing exhibitions and outreach services. A reference Library of over 2,000 books and a Picture Library.
Open: 2-5 every day except Tues Thurs Sat or by appointment for parties.
Admission: Donations only.
Location: Milngavie, Glasgow.
Refreshments: Can be served in the garden in Summertime.
Exhibitions/Events: Out of Doors, exhibition on homelessness.

LILLIE ART GALLERY
(Bearsden and Milngavie District Council)
Station Road, Milngavie G62 8BZ **Tel:** 0141-943 3247 **Fax:** 0141-943 0200
Collections of 20th century Scottish paintings; temporary and loan exhibitions of art and crafts.
Open: Mon-Fri 10-5 Sat & Sun 2-5.
Admission: Free.
Location: Close to A81 and Railway Station.

PAISLEY

COATS OBSERVATORY
(Renfrew District Council)
49 Oakshaw Street West, Paisley PA1 2DR **Tel:** 0141-889 2031 **Fax:** 0141-889 9240
Dating from 1883, the observatory plays an important role in the fields of astromomy, metereology and seismology. Displays relate to the history of the building, astronomy, metereology and space flight.
Open: All year except Bank Holidays Mon Tues Thurs 2-8 Wed Fri Sat 10-5.
Admission: Free.
Limited car parking. Unsuitable for disabled persons.

PAISLEY MUSEUM AND ART GALLERIES
(Renfrew District Council)
High Street, Paisley PA1 2BA **Tel:** 0141-889 3151 **Fax:** 0141-889 9240
A world famous collection of Paisley shawls. The collections illustrate the local, industrial and natural history of the town and district. The art collection places emphasis on 19th century artists.
Open: All year (except Bank Holidays) Mon-Sat 10-5.
Admission: Free.
Disabled access being provided under a phased programme. Please check for details.

STRATHAVEN

JOHN HASTIE MUSEUM
(East Kilbride District Council)
Threestanes Road, Strathaven ML10 6DX **Tel:** (01357) 21257
A small local history museum with displays featuring Strathaven Castle, weaving, the Covenanters, the 1820 Uprising, paintings, old photos, and the Burnbrae Collection of ceramics. A programme of temporary displays is being developed.
Open: Easter-30 Oct 1994.
Admission: Free.

TARBOLTON

BACHELORS' CLUB
(National Trust for Scotland)
Sandgate Street, Tarbolton KA5 5RB **Tel:** (01292) 541940
17th century house named after the literary society founded within by Robert Burns and his friends in 1780. Contains facsimiles of letters and poems from the poet's Lochlea days, and period furnishings.
Open: 28 Apr-30 Sep 1.30-5.30 1-22 Oct Sat/Sun 1.30-5.30 last admission 5.
Admission: Adults £1.50 children 80p adult parties £1.20 schools 60p.

TAYSIDE

ARBROATH

ARBROATH ART GALLERY
(Angus District Council)
Public Library, Hill Terrace, Arbroath **Tel:** (01241) 875598
Collection of paintings by local artists and local views, in particular the works of J.W. Herald, watercolourist. Also two oil paintings, by Peter Breughell II.
Open: Mon and Wed 9.30-8 Tues and Thurs 9.30-6 Sat 9.30-5.

ARBROATH MUSEUM
(Angus District Council)
Signal Tower, Ladyloan, Arbroath **Tel:** (01241) 875598
Local collections cover the history of Arbroath from Prehistoric Times to the Industrial Revolution. Special features include the Bellrock Lighthouse, Fishing and the Wildlife of Arbroath Cliffs.
Open: All year Mon-Sat 10-5 also July & Aug Sun 2-5.

BLAIR ATHOLL

ATHOLL COUNTRY COLLECTION
(Mr and Mrs John and Janet Cameron)
The Old School, Blair Atholl **Tel:** (01796) 481232
A unique and lively museum with interesting displays of village and glen life. Something for all ages.
Open: Easter then June-mid Oct.
Admission: Adults £1.50 children 75p.

BRECHIN

BRECHIN MUSEUM
(Angus District Council)
Public Library, St. Ninian's Square, Brechin
Local collections tell the story of the development of Brechin from the Celtic church of the 9th century to the last days of the Burgh in 1975. There is a small display of some of the works of D.Waterson, etcher and watercolourist.
Open: Mon and Wed 9.30-8 Tues and Thurs 9.30-6 Fri and Sat 9.30-5.
Enquiries: Meffan Institute.

DUNDEE

BARRACK STREET MUSEUM
(City of Dundee District Council)
Barrack Street, Dundee DD1 1PG **Tel:** (01382) 432067 **Fax:** (01382) 432052
Natural History Museum. There are currently displays on Scottish Wildlife along with the skeleton of the famous Tay Whale, a humpback whale which swam up the Tay in 1883. The Art and Nature Gallery, is devoted to temporary exhibitions exploring the influence of nature on the arts and environmental themes. New Gallery 'Head For The Hills' looks at Scottish woodland, moorland and mountain habitats.
Open: Mon 11-5 Tues-Sat 10-5 closed Sun.
Admission: Free.

BROUGHTY CASTLE MUSEUM
(City of Dundee District Council)
Broughty Ferry, Dundee DD5 2BE **Tel:** (01382) 776121 **Fax:** (01382) 432052
A 15th Century estuary fort located by the seashore in Broughty Ferry. Besieged by the English in the 16th Century and attacked by Cromwell's army under General Monk in the 17th Century, it was left as a ruin, but was restored in 1861 as part of Britain's coastal defences. It is now a museum with displays on local history, arms and armour, seashore life and Dundee's whaling story. The observation area at the top of the castle provides fine views over the Tay Estuary to N.E. Fife.
Open: Mon 11-1 and 2-5 Tues-Thurs and Sat 10-1 and 2-5 Sun July-Sept only 2-5 closed Fri.
Admission: Free.
Location: 6m East of Dundee.

MCMANUS GALLERIES
(City of Dundee District Council)
Albert Square, Dundee DD1 1DA **Tel:** (01382) 432020 **Fax:** (01382) 432052
Built in 1867 and designed by Sir George Gilbert Scott, the McManus Galleries house an art collection of national importance. It includes fine examples of 19th and 20th Century Scottish paintings, prints, drawings, sculpture, furniture, clocks, glass, ceramics and silver. The McManus Galleries also house Dundee's human history collections. Three galleries tell the story of life in Tayside from prehistoric times through to the Industrial Revolution and on into the 20th Century. The costume gallery looks at clothes and customs with thematic displays. The Archaeological Gallery also has a significant display of material from Ancient Egypt. There is a programme of changing exhibitions alongside more permanent displays using the collections.
Open: Mon 11-5 Tues-Sat 10-5 closed Sun.
Admission: Free.
Location: Dundee Centre.

MILLS OBSERVATORY
(City of Dundee District Council)

Balgay Park, Dundee DD2 2UB **Tel:** (01382) 667138

Britain's only full-time Public Observatory. It is located in Balgay Park and houses a 10-inch Cooke Refracting Telescope. During the winter months viewing of the night sky is possible under the supervision of the Resident Astronomer. It is open throughout the year and offers panoramic views across the Tay to Fife. There is a small planetarium (viewing by arrangement), an audio-visual presentation and an exhibition of telescopes and scientific instruments.

Open: Apr-Sept Mon 11-5 Tues-Fri 10-5 Sat 2-5 Oct-Mar Mon-Fri 3-10 Sat 2-5 closed Sun.

Admission: Free.

Location: 2m North West of city centre.

ST. MARY'S TOWER
(City of Dundee District Council)

Nethergate, Dundee **Tel:** (01382) 434000

Dundee's oldest building. 15th Century Steeple Tower, restored in 19th Century.

Open: Closed.

Enquiries to the McManus Galleries. For all City of Dundee Museums, enquiries should be made at the McManus Galleries, Albert Square, Dundee, DD1 1DA. Tel: As above.

FORFAR

THE ANGUS FOLK MUSEUM
(National Trust for Scotland)

Kirkwynd Cottages, Glamis, Forfar DD8 1RT **Tel:** (01307) 840288

Collection of early furnishings, clothing, domestic utensils and agricultural implements from the former County of Angus.

Open: Good Fri-2 Oct daily 11-5. 3-22 Oct Sat/Sun 11.5 last admission 4.30.

Admission: Adults £2 children £1 adult parties £1.60 schools 80p.

MUSEUM AND ART GALLERY
(Angus District Council)

Meffan Institute, 20 West High Street, Forfar DD8 1BB **Tel:** (01307) 68813

Exhibition Galleries specialising in contemporary art. **Museum**-the Forfar story to be opened in 1995.

Open: All year Mon-Sat 10-5.

All enquiries to District Curator, Museums and Art Galleries at the above address.

KIRRIEMUIR

BARRIE'S BIRTHPLACE
(National Trust for Scotland)

Kirriemuir DD8 4BX **Tel:** (01575) 72646

Contains mementoes and manuscripts of Sir James Barrie. Exhibition features 'Peter Pan' and other of Barrie's works.

Open: 11 Apr-Sept 30 Mon-Sat 11-5.30 Sun 1.30-5.30 Sat 11-5.30 and Sun 1.30-5.30 only from Oct 1-22 last admission 5.

Admission: Adults £1.50 children 80p adult parties £1.20 schools 60p.

Refreshments: Tea-room.

MONTROSE

HOUSE OF DUN
(National Trust for Scotland)

Montrose DD10 9LQ **Tel:** (01674) 810264

Palladian house overlooking the Montrose Basin. Built in 1730 for David Erskine, Lord Dun, to designs by William Adam. Exuberant plasterwork. Exhibition on the architecture of the house & garden.

Open: House Courtyard and Restaurant 14 Apr-Sept 30 daily 11-5.30 Sat and Sun only from Oct 1-22 Garden 9.30-Sunset daily all year.

Admission: Adults £3.00 children £1.50 adult parties £2.40 schools £1.20 grounds £1.

Refreshments: Restaurant.

WILLIAM LAMB MEMORIAL STUDIO
(Angus District Council)

24 Market Street, Montrose **Tel:** (01674) 673232

The working studio of the famous Montrose sculptor includes displays of his sculptures, etchings, paintings and drawings. Also featured are his workroom and tools and his living room with self-styled furniture.

Open: July and Aug Sat 2-5 or by arrangement.

MONTROSE MUSEUM
(Angus District Council)

Panmure Place, Montrose **Tel:** (01674) 673232

Extensive local collections cover the history of Montrose from prehistoric times to local government reorganisation, the maritime history of the port, the Natural History of Angus and local art. Pictish stones, Montrose silver and pottery; whaling artefacts; Napoleonic items (including a cast of his death mask). Paintings by local artists and local views, Temporary Art Exhibitions during year

Open: All year Mon-Sat 10-5.

SUNNYSIDE MUSEUM
(Angus NHS Trust)

Sunnyside Royal Hospital, Hillside, Montrose DD10 9JP **Tel:** (01674) 830361 **Fax:** (01674) 830361

This museum outlines the history of psychiatry in Scotland. Exhibits include slides, audio/visual shows.

Open: Easter-Sept every Wed 2-3.30.

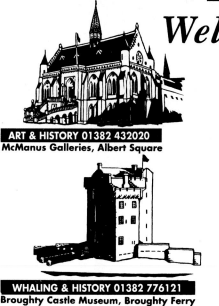

SERVICES MUSEUMS

This list of services museums gives times of opening, location and telephone numbers. Museums contain displays of uniforms, old arms, awards, campaign medals, regimental colours, pictures, trophies and souvenirs. Special items in the collection are mentioned.

THE ARGYLL & SUTHERLAND HIGHLANDERS

Stirling Castle, Stirling FK8 1EH
Tel: (01786) 475165
Display in the King's Old Building.
Open: Easter-Sept Mon-Sat 10-6 Sun 11-5 Oct-Easter Mon-Sat 10-4.30 Sun 11-4.30 closed Christmas and New Year.

ARMY PHYSICAL TRAINING CORPS MUSEUM

A.S.P.T. Queen's Avenue, Aldershot GU11 2LB
Tel: (01252) 347131
Military Museum.
Open: Mon-Fri 8.30-12.30 and 2-4.30 weekends by appointment.
Admission: Free.
Location: In Army School of Physical Training at Aldershot.

AYRSHIRE (E.C.O.) YEOMANRY MUSEUM

Rozelle House, Alloway, By Ayr **Tel:** (01292) 264091
Open: All year Mon-Sat 10-5 open also on Suns from Apr 1-Oct 30 2-5.

THE BEDFORDSHIRE & HERTFORDSHIRE REGIMENT

c/o Luton Museum Service, Wardown Park, Luton LU2 7HA **Tel:** (01582) 36941 **Fax:** (01582) 483178
Open: For times see Luton Museum & Art Gallery.
Admission: Free
Location: Luton Museum & Art Gallery, Wardown Park.
Refreshments: Refreshment area.
Shop, free car park. Facilities for people with disabilities.

THE BLACK WATCH (R.H.R.)

Balhousie Castle, Hay Street, Perth PH1 5HR
Tel: (01738) 621281 ext 8530 0131-310 8530
Fax: 0131-310 8425
Open: Mon-Fri 10-4.30 (winter 3.30) Public Hols (Easter-Sept only) 2-4.30 closed Sat Public & Military Hols for week-end opening after Easter 1995 telephone. Closed 23 Dec-4 Jan.
Location: (facing North Inch, entrance & car park by Hay Street gate).

THE BORDER REGIMENT & KING'S OWN ROYAL BORDER REGIMENT

(Curator, Mr S A Eastwood BA AMA)
Queen Mary's Tower, The Castle, Carlisle CA3 8UR
Tel: (01228) 32774 **Fax:** (01228) 21275
Two dioramas, four V.C's, treasures and battle trophies. Uniforms, records and documents from 1702.
Open: Apr 1-Oct 31 9.30-6 Sun 10-6 Nov 1-Mar 31 9.30-4 Sun 10-4.
Admission: Free after paid entry to Carlisle Castle.
Location: Queen Mary's Tower is located within the Inner Bailey of the Castle
Groups welcome. Bookings must be made through English Heritage who administer the Castle.

BUFFS REGIMENTAL MUSEUM

(Canterbury City Council and Trustees)
Royal Museum & Art Gallery, High Street, Canterbury CT1 2JE **Tel:** (01227) 452747
Fax: (01227) 455047
History and treasures of the Royal East Kent Regiment.
Open: All year Mon-Sat 10-5 closed Good Fri and Christmas week.
Admission: Free.
Location: In city centre car parks and British Rail within walking distance.

CAMBRIDGESHIRE REGIMENTAL COLLECTION/ELY MUSEUM

High Street, Ely CB7 4HL **Tel:** (01353) 666655
Unique collection of uniforms, objects and photographs illustrating the history of the Cambridgeshire Regiment. Includes the regimental drums buried at the fall of Singapore and recovered after the war.
Open: Summer Tues-Sun 10.30-1 and 2.15-5 closed Mon winter Tues-Fri 11.30-3.30 week-ends 11.30-4 closed Mon.
Admission: Fee charged.

THE CAMERONIANS (SCOTTISH RIFLES)

Mote Hill, Off Muir Street, Hamilton ML3 6BY
Tel: (01698) 428688 **Fax:** (01698) 283479
For details please telephone the above number.
Open: Mon-Sat 10-5.
Admission: Free
Location: Short walk from Hamilton Town Centre, adjacent to Hamilton District Museum.

CASTLE AND REGIMENTAL MUSEUM, MONMOUTH

The Castle, Monmouth NP5 3BS
Tel: (01600) 772175 **Fax:** (01600) 712935
Historical record of Monmouth Castle and R Mon RE(M).
Open: Daily Easter-Oct weekends only for rest of the year 2-5. Researchers may visit on weekdays by arrangement with the Administrator.
Admission: Free - Donations welcome.
Location: Castle - town centre.
Medieval style herb garden.

THE CHESHIRE MILITARY MUSEUM

The Castle, Chester CH1 2DN
5th Royal Inniskilling Dragoon Guards. 3rd Carabiniers, Cheshire Yeomanry, 22nd (Cheshire) Regiment.
Open: Daily 9-5 closed Dec 18-Jan 3.
Admission: Adults 50p children/OAPs/disabled 20p.
Enquires (01224) 327617

DERBYSHIRE YEOMANRY CAVALRY

Derby Museum & Art Gallery, The Strand, Derby DE1 1BS **Tel:** (01332) 255581
Items illustrating the history of volunteer cavalry in Derbyshire from 1794. Displays include reconstruction Scout car.
Open: For times see Derby Museum & Art Gallery.

THE DUKE OF CORNWALL'S LIGHT INFANTRY

The Keep, Bodmin **Tel:** (01208) 72810
Housed in a fine 1859 Militia Keep, this Museum covers 257 years of military history. Weapons, documents, uniforms, paintings, photographs and artefacts illustrate the wars and campaigns fought by the Duke of Cornwall's Light Infantry and its predecessors - the 32nd and 46th Foot. The Museum also contains a fine selection of medals and one of the best displays of infantry small-arms in the Country. There is a comprehensive reference library which can be used by request.
Open: Mon-Fri 8-4.45 except Public Hols.
Admission: Adults £1 children under 16 yrs 50p.

DUKE OF LANCASTER'S OWN YEOMANRY *SEE* LANCASHIRE COUNTRY AND REGIMENTAL MUSEUM

Preston

THE DUKE OF WELLINGTON'S REGIMENT MUSEUM

Calderdale Leisure Services (Museums and Arts)
Bankfield Museum, Akroyd Park, Halifax HX3 6HG
Tel: (01422) 354823 **Fax:** (01422) 349020
Recently re-displayed, the collections cover the history of the regiment from 1702 to the present day. Emphasis is on the uniforms, equipment and relics, often displayed in period settings, and some of them touchable. Along with regimental material, local volunteer and militia items are included, as is a display of relics associated with the Iron Duke himself.
Open: Tues-Sat and Bank Holidays 10-5 Sun 2-5 closed Mons Christmas Day Boxing Day and New Years Day.
Admission: Free
Location: Off the A647 Halifax-Bradford Road
The extensive reserve collection and archive can be studied by appointment.

DURHAM LIGHT INFANTRY MUSEUM

Aykley Heads, Durham City Durham DH1 5TU
Tel: 0191-384 2214 **Fax:** 0191-386 1770
The history of the D.L.I. from 1758 to 1968 (also Durham Militia and Volunteers), uniforms, medals, weapons, photographs and regimental treasures.
Open: Weekdays (except Mon but open Bank Hols) 10-5 Sun 2-5.
Admission: Adults 80p concessions 40p.
Location: 1/2m from Durham City Centre, off A691 Consett Road.
Refreshments: Cafe.
Exhibitions/Events: Art Gallery with changing programme of exhibitions.
Free car park. Suitable for the Disabled.

FLEET AIR ARM MUSEUM, ROYAL NAVAL AIR STATION
Ilchester BA22 8HT
Tel: (01935) 840565 **Fax:** (01935) 840181
Open: Daily 10-5.30 (Apr-Oct) 4.30 (Nov-Mar) closed Dec 24 25 and 26.
Admission: Charged.
Location: On the B3151 just off the A303/A37 at Ilchester
Refreshments: Licensed restaurant

THE FUSILIERS MUSEUM OF NORTHUMBERLAND
The Abbot's Tower, Alnwick Castle, Alnwick
Tel: (01665) 602152
Open: With Alnwick Castle. Easter-Oct or by appointment.
Admission: Inclusive of Alnwick Castle entrance fee.

THE GLOUCESTERSHIRE REGIMENTAL MUSEUM *SEE* REGIMENTS OF GLOUCESTERSHIRE MUSEUM
Gloucester

THE GORDON HIGHLANDERS
Viewfield Road, Aberdeen
Tel: (01224) 318174 **Fax:** (01224) 208652
Displays depicting the history of the Regiment from its raising in 1794.
Admission: Free.
Location: Off main Ring Road.
Facilities for wheelchairs available.

THE GREEN HOWARDS MUSEUM
Trinity Church Square, Richmond DL10 4QN
Tel: (01748) 822133 **Fax:** (01748) 826521
Open: Feb Mon-Fri 10-4.30 Mar & Nov Mon-Sat 10-4.30 Apr-Oct Mon-Sat 9.30-4.30 Sun 2-4.30 closed Dec & Jan.
Admission: Fee charged.

THE GUARDS MUSEUM
Wellington Barracks, Birdcage Walk SW1E 6HQ
Tel: 0171-414 3428
The story of the Foot Guards, a superb collection of uniforms, weapons and memorabilia illustrating their martial history and service to The Sovereign and The City of London for over three centuries.
Open: 10-4 inc w/ends & all Bank Hols closed Fri & Christmas.
Admission: Adults £2 children/OAPs/groups and over 25 £1 family ticket £4.
Location: Birdcage Walk, SW1
Guide available by application. Suitable for disabled. Magnificent venue for all types of functions. Details on request.

HERTFORDSHIRE YEOMANRY & ARTILLERY HISTORICAL TRUST
c/o Hitchin Museum, Paynes Park, Hitchin
Tel: (01462) 434476
Small display within Hitchin Museum.
Open: See Hitchin Museum.

HONOURABLE ARTILLERY COMPANY
Armoury House, City Road EC1Y 2BQ
Tel: 0171-606 4644
Open: By appointment 12 noon-6 on weekdays.
Admission: £2

INNS OF COURT & CITY YEOMANRY MUSEUM
10 Stone Buildings, Lincolns Inn WC2A 3TG
Tel: 0171-405 8112/831 1693
Small but interesting display of uniforms, medals and equipment of the Inns of Court Regiment and the City of London Yeomanry (the Rough Riders) which together comprise the Inns of Court and City Yeomanry covering period 1798 to date.
Open: 10-3.30 Mon-Fri (but visitors are advised to telephone beforehand).
Admission: Free but donations gratefully received.
Curator: Major R.J.B.Gentry.

THE INTELLIGENCE CORPS MUSEUM
Templer Barracks, Ashford TN23 3HH **Tel:** (01233) 657208
The only museum in Great Britain covering military intelligence in memento, document and pictorial form from Elizabethan times to present day.
Open: Tues and Thurs 9-12.30 and 2-4.30 other times by appointment only.
Admission: Free.
Prior telephone call advisable.

KENT & SHARPSHOOTERS YEOMANRY MUSEUM
Hever Castle, Edenbridge **Tel:** (01732) 865224

THE KING'S OWN ROYAL REGIMENT MUSEUM
Lancaster City Museum, Market Square, Lancaster LA1 1HT **Tel:** (01524) 64637 **Fax:** (01524) 847663
Uniforms, medals (including three VCs) campaign relics, records and documents from 1680 to 1959.
Open: See Lancaster City Museum.
Admission: Free.
Location: City Centre.
Shop.

THE KING'S OWN SCOTTISH BORDERERS
The Barracks, Berwick-upon-Tweed **Tel:** (01289) 307426 **Fax:** (01289) 331928
Open: Mon-Fri 9.15-4.30 Sat 9.15-12 Sun by appointment closed Easter and Christmas.
Admission: £2 which includes The Town Museum, English Heritage Museum and KOSB Museum.
Location: The Barracks, Berwick upon Tweed.

THE KING'S OWN YORKSHIRE LIGHT INFANTRY
Doncaster Museum and Art Gallery, Chequer Road, Doncaster DN1 2AE
Tel: (01302) 734293 **Fax:** (01302) 735409
Open: Mon-Sat 10-5 Sun 2-5.
Admission: Free.
Location: Off inner ring road/Waterdale.
Full disabled access.

THE KING'S REGIMENT COLLECTION
(Regional History Dept. Merseyside Maritime Museum)
National Museums and Galleries on Merseyside, Albert Dock, Liverpool L3 4AA **Tel:** 0151-207 0001
The King's Regiment Collection.
Open: 10-5 Mon-Sat 12-5 Sun.
Admission: Free.
Location: Liverpool Museum, William Brown Street, Liverpool.

THE 15TH/19TH THE KING'S ROYAL HUSSARS & NORTHUMBERLAND HUSSARS
c/o Newcastle Discovery, Blandford Square, Newcastle upon Tyne NE1 4JA
Tel: 0191-232 6789 **Fax:** 0191-230 2614
Open: Mon-Sat 10-5 open Bank Holiday Mons 10-5 closed Sun Good Friday Christmas Day Boxing Day New Years Day.
Admission: Free.
Refreshments: Available.
Exhibitions/Events: New Gallery opening in 1995- 'A Soldier's Life'-the story of the 15th/19th The King's Royal Hussars and Northumberland Hussars

THE 14TH/20TH KINGS HUSSARS *SEE* LANCASHIRE COUNTY & REGIMENTAL MUSEUM
Preston

LANCASHIRE COUNTY & REGIMENTAL MUSEUM
Stanley Street, Preston PR1 4YP **Tel:** (01772) 264075
This museum displays collections relating to the county of Lancashire, the Duke of Lancaster's Own Yeomanry, the 14/20th King's Hussars, Queen's Lancashire regiment and the historic Lancashire Hussars. Re-created scenes include a First World War trench, with lights, sound and smell effects.
Open: Daily except Thurs and Sun 10-5 closed Bank Hols.
Admission: Adults £1 children free.
Classroom available for schools. Car park.

THE LANCASHIRE FUSILIERS' MUSEUM
Lancashire Headquarters, The Royal Regiment of Fusiliers, Wellington Barracks, Bury BL8 2PL
Tel: 0161-764 2208 **Fax:** 0161-764 2208 (ask for Fax)
Open: Daily 9.30-4.30 (except Suns and Weds).
Admission: Adults 50p children and OAPs 25p closed Bank Hols.

LANCASHIRE HUSSARS (SEE LANCASHIRE COUNTY & REGIMENTAL MUSEUM)
Preston

LIVERPOOL SCOTTISH REGIMENTAL MUSEUM (T.A.)
Forbes House, Score Lane, Childwall, Liverpool L16 6AN **Tel:** 0151-722 7711
Open: Every Tues Evening 7.30-10 other times by appointment with D Reeves Hon Curator on 0151 647 4342 Major D S Evans TD.Hon Secretary on 0151 924 7800.

THE LOYAL REGIMENT (NL) *SEE* THE QUEEN'S LANCASHIRE REGIMENT
Preston

MILITARY VEHICLE MUSEUM
Exhibition Park Pavilion, Newcastle upon Tyne NE2 4PZ **Tel:** 0191-281 7222
Over 40 vehicles, 60 cabinets mostly from World War II including guns and artefacts relating to the war years.
Open: 10-4 (last adm) all year.
Admission: Adults £1.50 concessions 75p reductions for parties of children by arrangement.
Location: Park.
Refreshments: Cafe in Park.
Car park outside park. Exhibition park bus stop on the Great North Road or by Tyne-side Metro to Jesmond or Haymarket stations - if using public transport. Full disabled facilities (including car parking but not wheelchairs)

MUSEUM OF ARMY FLYING

Middle Wallop, Stockbridge SO20 8DY **Tel:** (01264) 384421

All aspects of Army Flying from the 19th Century to the present. Now double the size.
Open: Daily 10-4.30. Closed Christmas period.
Admission: Fee charged.
Location: A343 between Andover & Salisbury.
Shop, free cinema and coffee shop, full disabled facilities. Ample free car parking. Group visits welcome.

MUSEUM OF ARTILLERY

The Rotunda, Repository Road, Woolwich SE18
Tel: 0181-316 5402

Open: Mon-Fri 12-5 Sat and Sun 1-5 closed at 4 in winter Christmas Day Boxing Day New Years Day and Good Friday.

THE MUSEUM OF THE DUKE OF EDINBURGH'S ROYAL REGIMENT (BERKSHIRE & WILTSHIRE)

The Wardrobe, 58 The Close, Salisbury SP1 2EX
Tel: (01722) 414536

Open: Mon-Fri 10-5 (Fri 4.30) Apr-Oct open daily closed Dec & Jan.
Admission: Adults £1.80 OAPs/students £1.50 children (under 16 yrs) £1 child accompanied by an adult - free.
Location: Salisbury Cathedral Close.
Refreshments: Available.
Garden open to Museum visitors.

NORFOLK & SUFFOLK AVIATION MUSEUM LTD

Flixton, Bungay

18 historic aircraft and unique indoor exhibition of aviation items from the early days of flying to the present day.
Open: Apr-Oct Suns and Bank Holidays 10-5 Tues Weds and Thurs 10-5 school summer holiday period.
Admission: Free.
Location: Flixton Bungay.

THE NORTHAMPTONSHIRE REGIMENT

Abington Museum, Abington Park
Tel: (01604) 31454

Abington Museum will be closed for structural work until further notice.

NORTHAMPTONSHIRE YEOMANRY

Abington Museum, Abington Park
Tel: (01604) 31454

Abington Museum will be re-opening after structural work in July 1994.

THE PRINCE OF WALES'S OWN REGIMENT OF YORKSHIRE (WEST & EAST YORKSHIRE REGTS.) ROYAL DRAGOON GUARDS

Tower Street, York **Tel:** (01904) 642038

Open: Mon-Sat 9.30-4.30 closed Public Hols.
Admission: Adults 50p children/OAPs 25p.

THE PRINCESS OF WALES'S ROYAL REGIMENT AND THE QUEEN'S REGIMENT MUSEUM

Inner Bailey, Dover Castle, Dover CT16 1HU
Tel: (01304) 240121

An exhibition and exhibits from the Regiments which form todays Regiment, ie The Queen's Royal Regiment (West Surrey), The Buffs (The Royal East Kent Regiment), The East Surrey Regiment, The Royal Sussex Regiment, The Royal Hampshire Regiment, The Queen's Own Royal West Kent Regiment, The Middlesex Regiment (DCO) and The Queen's Regiment.
Open: Summer daily 10-6 winter daily 10-4.
Admission: Included in the price of admission to Castle.
Location: Inner Bailey, Dover Castle.
Permanent exhibition of the Regiment 1661-1994.

QUEEN ALEXANDRA'S ROYAL ARMY NURSING CORPS

AMS Training Centre, Keogh Barracks, Ash Vale, Aldershot **Tel:** (01252) 349301 or 349315

Open: Mon-Fri 9-12.30 afternoons by appointment no weekend opening.
Closed for relocation at above address - reopen 27 March 1995 (TBC)

1ST THE QUEEN'S DRAGOON GUARDS

Cardiff Castle, Cardiff CF1 2RB **Tel:** (01222) 227611 ext 8232 (Maindy Barracks, Cardiff) **Fax:** (01222) 227611 ext 8384

Collection includes KDG Mounted Officer tableau. Bays Drum Horse tableau. Officers Mess Dinner tableau. Hologram depicting 3 equestrian figures of different periods, VC case. Trench System, 1914-1918 war, and many other attractions.
Open: Sun Mon Tuesday 10-4.30 (Winter) Wed 10-1 (Winter) Sun Mon Tues 10-6 (Summer) Wed 10-2 (Summer).
Admission: Adults £2.20 children and OAPs £1.10.

THE QUEEN'S LANCASHIRE REGIMENT INCORPORATING THE LOYAL REGIMENT (NL)

Fulwood Barracks, Preston PR2 4AA
Tel: (01772) 260362 **Fax:** (01772) 260591

Military artefacts, medals, uniforms, library.
Open: Tues and Thurs 9-12 and 2-4 or by appointment.
Admission: Free.
Location: Preston.
Curator: Major (Retd) A.J. Maher MBE.

QUEEN'S OWN HIGHLANDERS REGIMENTAL MUSEUM

(RHQ Queen's Own Highlanders)

Cameron Barracks, Inverness IV2 3XD **Tel:** (01473) 224380

Open: April-Sept Mon-Fri 10-6 Sun 2-6 Oct-March Mon-Fri 10-4 closed Sat and Sun Dec 25 Jan 1 & 2 and Easter Spring and Summer Bank Hol week-ends and Civil Service Hols.
Admission: Free.
Location: Fort George, Ardersiet, Inverness-shire.

THE QUEEN'S OWN HUSSARS REGIMENTAL MUSEUM

Lord Leycester Hospital, High Street, Warwick CV34 4BH
Tel: (01926) 492035 **Fax:** (01926) 492035

Open: Summer Tues-Sun & Bank Holiday Mons 10.30-6 winter Tues-Sun 10.30-4.
Admission: Free to museum £2.25 to Lord Leycester Hospital. Children(under 14) £1 OAPs and students £1.50 discount for parties of 20 adults or more.
Refreshments: Summer only.

THE QUEEN'S ROYAL LANCERS REGIMENTAL MUSEUM

Belvoir Castle, Grantham NG32 1PD **Tel:** Curator (0115) 9573195/Castle Office (01476) 870262

Combined Museum of the 16th, 5th, 17th, 21st, 16th/5th Lancers and 17th/21st Lancers. Tells the story of these Regiments since their formation to the present day. Weapons, uniforms, medals, silver, pictures and personal relics. The Queen's Royal Lancers was formed on 25 July '93 by the amalgamation of 16th/5th Queen's Royal Lancers and 17th/21st Lancers.
Open: Apr-Sept inclusive daily 11-5 closed Mon & Fri (open Bank Holidays).
Admission: Castle & Museum inclusive adults £3.50 children £2.50 (subject to increase).
Location: 8m SW of Grantham.
Refreshments: Castle Cafe.

THE QUEEN'S ROYAL SURREY REGIMENT MUSEUM

(The National Trust)

Clandon Park, West Clandon, Guildford GU4 7RQ
Tel: (01483) 223419

Historical items of the former Queen's Royal Regiment, The East Surrey Regiment and The Queen's Royal Surrey Regiment.
Open: Easter-mid Oct Sat Sun Mon Tues Wed 1.30-5.30 open Bank Hol Mon.
Admission: No charges for the Museum but donations welcome.

REGIMENTS OF GLOUCESTERSHIRE MUSEUM

Custom House, Gloucester Docks GL1 2HE
Tel: (01452) 522682 **Fax:** (01452) 311116

The story of The Glosters and the Royal Gloucestershire Hussars. Life-size displays with sound effects. Fascinating photographs from the last 100 years. Archive film of the Korean War.
Open: Tues-Sun and Bank Hol Mons 10-5.
Admission: Fee charged.
Shop. Facilities for disabled visitors. Voted the Museum achieving the most with the least - National Heritage Museum of the Year Awards 1991.

ROYAL AIR FORCE MUSEUM

Grahame Park Way, Hendon NW9 5LL
Tel: 0181-205 2266 **Fax:** 0181-200 1751

Britain's national museum of aviation houses one of the world's finest collections of historic aircraft, tells the fascinating story of flight and illustrating the development of aviation from before the Wright Brothers to the present day RAF. Over 70 aircraft on display including the legendary Spitfire and Lancaster, plus German and American aircraft. Complex includes Battle of Britain Experience and Bomber Hall. Film shows, art exhibitions, flight simulator. Licensed family restaurant and Museum Shop.
Open: Daily 10-6.
Admission: Fee charged.
Location: North London.
Refreshments: Licensed restaurant.
Exhibitions/Events: Flying for Invasion and Wings over Water 17 May - 31 Oct.
Free car park.

ROYAL ARMY CHAPLAINS' DEPARTMENT

Bagshot Park GU19 5PL **Tel:** (01276) 471717 Ext 2845 **Fax:** (01276) 471717 Ext 2848

Open: Mon Tues Wed Thurs & Fri 10-4 by appointment only.
Admission: Free.

ROYAL ARMY DENTAL CORPS MUSEUM,HQ AND CENTRAL GROUP RADC

Evelyn Woods Road, Aldershot GU11 2LS
Tel: (01252) 347782 **Fax:** (01252) 347726

Instruments and items of professional interest.
Open: Mon-Fri 10-12 and 2-4.

ROYAL ARMY MEDICAL CORPS HISTORICAL MUSEUM

Keogh Barracks, Ash Vale, Aldershot GU12 5RQ
Tel: (01252) 340212 **Fax:** (01252) 340209

Open: Mon-Fri 8.30-4 evenings and weekends by appointment.
Admission: Free.
Facilities for disabled.

ROYAL ARTILLERY REGIMENTAL MUSEUM
Old Royal Military Academy, Red Lion Lane, Woolwich SE18 4DN **Tel:** 0181-781 5628
Open: Mon-Fri 12.30-4.30 closed Sat Sun and Bank Holidays.
Admission: Free.

ROYAL BERKSHIRE YEOMANRY CAVALRY
Berkshire Yeomanry Museum, TA Centre, Bolton Road, Windsor SL4 3JG **Tel:** (01753) 860600
The Berkshire Yeomanry Museum covers the history of the Regiment from 1794 to the present day. It is run by serving and ex-members of the Berkshire Yeomanry and shows items of uniform, equipment, photographs, prints, documents and ephemera associated with the Regiment over nearly 200 years.
Open: Open by appointment.

4TH/7TH ROYAL DRAGOON GUARDS
No. 3A Tower Street, York **Tel:** (01904) 642036
Open: Opening times Mon-Sat 9.30-4.30. Adults 50p children and OAPs 25p.

ROYAL ENGINEERS MUSEUM
Prince Arthur Road, Gillingham **Tel:** (01634) 406397
Large Museum tracing thelives and work of Britain's soldier engineers from 1066 to 1945. Fine medal rooms with 22 VCs. Wide survey of military and Imperial history. Rich international decorative arts collection.
Open: Open Mon-Thurs 10-5 Sat & Sun 11.30-5.
Admission: Adults £2 children/unwaged £1 service ID free.
Location: Adjacent to Brompton Barracks. Own entrance to Museum from Prince Arthur Road.
Refreshments: Vending machine.
Regular temporary exhibitions.

THE ROYAL FUSILIERS
HM Tower of London, Tower Hill EC3N 4AB
Tel: 0171-488 5611 **Fax:** 0171-481 1093
Artifacts and narrative illustrating the history of the Royal Fusiliers from formation in 1685 to present day. Ten VC's including the original prototype. Peninsular War Gold Medal etc.
Open: Weekdays summer 9.30-5 winter 9.30-4.30.
Admission: 25p.
Location: HM Tower of London.

THE ROYAL GREEN JACKETS
Peninsula Barracks, Romsey Road, Winchester
Tel: (01962) 863846
This splendid and exciting Museum tells the history of The Oxfordshire and Buckinghamshire Light Infantry, The King's Royal Rifle Corps and The Rifle Brigade and the Royal Green Jackets. With the use of graphics, models and artefacts it tells a compelling story of not only the Regiment's history but also that of the nation's, from 1741 to this present time. For schools it contains much of that history required for the national curriculum, including the Napoleonic periods, the Waterloo period and the 1st and 2nd World Wars. It also contains the largest diorama, measuring 22' x 11' in the country of the Battle of Waterloo; this diorama has some 22,000 model figures on it with sound and lighting effects.
Open: Daily throughout the year except for 14 days at Christmas Mon-Sat 10-5 Sun 12-4.
Admission: Adults £2 OAPs & children £1 groups (minimum of 10) £1.25 family Group £6.
Location: Winchester.
Schools very welcome by arrangement.

THE ROYAL HAMPSHIRE REGIMENT MUSEUM & MEMORIAL GARDEN
Serles House, Southgate Street, Winchester SO23 9EG **Tel:** (01962) 863658
Open: All year Mon-Fri 10-12.30 and 2-4 Easter-end Oct Sun and Bank Hols 12-4.
Admission: Free.

THE ROYAL HIGHLAND FUSILIERS (PRINCESS MARGARET'S OWN GLASGOW AND AYRSHIRE REGIMENT)
518 Sauchiehall Street, Glasgow G2 2LW
Tel: 0141-332 5639 **Fax:** 0141-353 1493
Regimental Museum.
Open: Mon-Thurs 8.30-4.30 Fri 8.30-4 weekends by appointment.
Admission: Free.

THE ROYAL IRISH FUSILIERS
Sovereign's House, The Mall, Armagh
Tel: (01861) 522911
Open: Mon-Fri 10-12.30 and 2-4.30.

THE 9TH/12TH ROYAL LANCERS REGIMENTAL MUSEUM
Derby Museum & Art Gallery, The Strand, Derby
Tel: (01332) 255581
Items illustrating the history of the regiment and its two predecessors from 1715 to the present day. Replica stable circa 1885 large uniform and medal displays.
Open: See Derby Museum & Art Gallery.

THE ROYAL LINCOLNSHIRE REGIMENT
Museum of Lincolnshire Life, Burton Road, Lincoln LN1 3LY **Tel:** (01522) 528448 **Fax:** (01522) 521264
Gallery devoted to over 300 Years of History of the Regiment.
Open: See under Lincoln.
Admission: Adults £1 children 50p.
Refreshments: Seasonal.

ROYAL MARINES MUSEUM
Jane Hodgkins-Marketing
Southsea PO4 9PX
Tel: (01705) 819385 **Fax:** (01705) 838420
Considered one of the finest military Museums in Britain. It is located in spacious grounds adjacent to Southsea beach and outdoor exhibits include a Whirlwind helicopter and a Falklands Landing Craft which visitors can walk into. The Museum tells the story of the Royal Marines from 1664 to the present day in a lively and fascinating way. Popular exhibitions include: the fascinating Falklands audio visual; a chilled Arctic Display. An early history gallery featuring a talking head of Hannah Snell, the first female Marine, and live maggots. Plus one of the greatest medal collections in the country. The Main Hall Exhibition Centre-including the Jungle Room. A D-Day Exhibition and new Exhibition wing.
Open: Daily 9-5 Whitsun and Aug 10-4.30 Sept-Whitsun.
Admission: Fee charged.
Location: On the Southsea seafront at the eastern end of the Esplanade.
Refreshments: Licensed Restaurant.
Exhibitions/Events: 1-4 June Camp D-Day. 3/4 Sept Daylight Tattoo.
Free parking and seafront entrance. Well stocked shop offers a wide range of quality goods for all ages. Junior Assault Course.

ROYAL MILITARY POLICE MUSEUM
The Keep, Roussillon Barracks, Broyle Road, Chichester PO19 4BN
Tel: (01243) 534225 **Fax:** (01243) 534288
Fully refurbished in 1985, tracing military police history from Tudor times to date - along with cleverly presented aspects of the RMP role in the modern professional army. Features include historic uniforms, a new medal room, nostalgic 'National Service' kit lay out and Barrack Room, North Africa diorama of desert mine field c1942 and videos.
Open: Apr-Sept Tues-Fri 10.30-12.30 and 1.30-4.30 Sat & Sun 2-5 Oct-Mar Tues-Fri 10.30-12.30 and 1.30-4.30 closed Jan.
Admission: Free.
Car parking. Suitable for disabled persons. Shop.

ROYAL MILITARY SCHOOL OF MUSIC
Kneller Hall, Twickenham TW2 7DU
Tel: 0181-898 5533/4/5
Open: By appointment only.
Curator - Major (Ret'd) R.G.Swift LRAM, ARCM, LTCL.

ROYAL NAVY SUBMARINE MUSEUM
Haslar Jetty Road, Gosport PO12 2AS
Tel: (01705) 529217 **Fax:** (01705) 511349
Underwater warfare yesterday and today.
Open: Apr-Oct 10-to last tour starting 4.30 Nov-Mar 10-to last tour starting 3.30 closed Dec 24-Jan 1.
Admission: Charged. Special rates for groups.
Location: Gosport, Hampshire
Refreshments: Coffee Shop. Picnic Area.

THE ROYAL NORFOLK REGIMENTAL MUSEUM
(Norfolk Museums Service)
Shirehall, Market Avenue, Norwich NR1 3JQ
Tel: (01603) 223649 **Fax:** (01603) 765651
The story of a County Regiment and the men who served in it from 1658 to the present day.
Open: Mon-Sat 10-5 Sun 2-5.
Admission: Adults £1.40 concessions £1.20 children 70p.
Location: Linked to Castle Museum via tunnel. Joint Norwich Museums tickets available.

THE ROYAL SCOTS REGIMENTAL MUSEUM
The Castle EH1 2YT
Tel: 0131-310 5014 **Fax:** 0131-310 5019
Open: Apr-Sept daily 9.30-4.30 Oct-Apr Mon-Fri 9.30-4 closed Sat & Sun.
Admission: No extra charge to view Regimental Museum.

ROYAL SIGNALS MUSEUM
Blandford Camp, Blandford Forum DT11 8RH
Tel: (01258) 482248
Museum shows history of army communications and the history of the Royal Signals, including Middlesex Yeomanry section.
Open: Mon-Fri 10-5 weekends June-Sept 10-4.
Admission: Free.

THE ROYAL SUSSEX REGIMENT
Redoubt Fortress, Eastbourne **Tel:** (01323) 410300
Open: Opening times see Sussex Combined Service Museum.

THE ROYAL ULSTER RIFLES
5, Waring Street, Belfast B11 2EW
Tel: (01232) 232086
Open: Mon-Fri 10-4 (prior notice may sometimes be necessary) closed Bank Hols.
Admission: Free.

THE ROYAL WELCH FUSILIERS

Queen's Tower, Caernarfon Castle
Tel: (01286) 673362
Hat ribbon worn by King William of Orange 1690. Keys of Corunna, officer's Mitre cap 1750, 10 V.C's Gold Peninsula War medals; Large collection of campaign meals, full size tableau and Royal and other portraits by Dennis Fields, Oswald Birley, Gerald Kelly.
Open: End Mar-end Oct daily 9.30-6.30 end Oct-end Mar weekdays 9.30-4 Sun 11-4.
Admission: Castle £3.50 children/OAPs £2.50 regimental Museum free.

THE SCOTTISH HORSE REGIMENTAL MUSEUM

The Cross, Dunkeld PH8 0AN
Open: Easter-end Sept daily 10-12 and 2-5.
Admission: 50p.
Location: Dunkeld, Perthshire, Scotland.

SCOTTISH UNITED SERVICES MUSEUM

The Castle, Edinburgh EH1 2NG
Tel: 0131-255 7534 **Fax:** 0131-225 3848
The Armed Forces at all periods with particular emphasis on Scottish regiments and on the Royal Navy and Royal Air Force in Scotland.
Open: Weekdays 9.30-6 (winter 9.30-5) Sun 11-5.50 (winter 12.30-4.20).
Admission: Free (charge to Castle).
Location: Museum Square & Crown Square, Edinburgh Castle.
Refreshments: Available nearby.
Museum shop, reading/research room avialable by appointment.

THE SHERWOOD FORESTERS MUSEUM (45TH/95TH FOOT)

The Castle, Nottingham NG1 6EL
Tel: (0115) 9483504
The History of the Regiment from formation of the 45th Regiment in 1741 to amalgamation with the Worcestershire Regiment in 1970. Medals, buttons, badges uniforms, weapons, pictures and Regimental trophies.
Open: See the Castle Museum.
Subsidiary displays in the Civic Museums of Derby and Newark, the latter entirely devoted to the 8th Battalion.

SHERWOOD FORESTERS (NOTTS & DERBY) REGIMENT

Derby Museum & Art Gallery, The Strand, Derby
Tel: (01332) 255581
The story of infantry in Derbyshire from 1689 through to the formation of the Sherwood Foresters in 1881 and amalgamation with the Worcestershire Regiment in 1970. Displays include items from the Militia. Volunteers, Territorials and 95th Derbyshire Regiment. Also First World War trench diorama and sentry box.
Open: See Derby Museum & Art Gallery.

THE SOMERSET MILITARY MUSEUM

Somerset County Museum, Taunton Castle, Taunton TA1 4AA **Tel:** (01823) 255504 or 333434
Open: Mon-Sat 10-5.
Admission: To the County museum £1.50 OAPs £1 children(5-18) 40p children under 5 free.
Location: County Museum, The Castle, Castle Green, Taunton. TA1 4AA.

THE SOUTH WALES BORDERERS AND MONMOUTHSHIRE REGIMENTAL MUSEUM

The Barracks, Brecon LD3 7EB
Tel: (01874) 613310 **Fax:** (01834) 613275
The museum portrays the history of the 24th Regiment (The South Wales Borderers), as well as associated Militia and Volunteer Units, from it's inception in 1689 to its amalgamation with the 41st Regiment (The Welch Regiment) in 1969. The new regiment is known as The Royal Regiment of Wales. The story of the Battle of Isandhlwana and the Defence of Rorke's Drift in the Zulu War of 1879 has a high profile. Uniforms, equipment, paintings, guns, a cinema and many trophies tell the story of over 300 years service.
Open: Apr-Sept Mon-Sat 9-1 and 2-5 Oct-Mar Mon-Fri 9-1 and 2-5.
Admission: Adults £1 children 50p.
Location: 1/4 mile east of town centre on A40.
Car parking, suitable for disabled.

ST. PETER'S BUNKER MUSEUM

St. Peter's Village, St. Peter, Jersey JE3 7AF
Tel: (01534) 481048
Museum of the German occupation of Jersey. Comprehensive collection of German Militaria of WWII including rare 'enigma' decoding machine.
Open: Mar-end of Oct 10-5 daily.
Admission: 1994 charges adults £1.80 children 90p 1995 charges not yet determined.
Refreshments: Pub and coffee lounge.
Parking in the Jersey Motor Museum car park opposite 11th century Church of St. Peter.

THE STAFFORDSHIRE REGIMENT (THE PRINCE OF WALES'S)

Whittington Barracks, Lichfield
Tel: 0121-311 3240 or 3229
Collection includes rare embroidered cap c. 1760 and medals of 8 holders of the V.C.
Open: Mon-Fri 9-4 weekends and Bank Hols by arrangement closed Christmas-New Year.
Location: Lichfield (on A51 on Lichfield side of Whittington Barracks)

THE SUFFOLK REGIMENT

Gibraltar Barracks, Out Rishygate, Bury St Edmunds
Tel: (01284) 752394
Open: Weekdays 10-12 and 2-4 closed Bank Hols.

THE SUSSEX COMBINED SERVICES MUSEUM

Redoubt Fortress, Royal Parade, Eastbourne
Tel: (01323) 410300
Includes Royal Sussex Regiment Collection and Queen's Royal Irish Hussars collections.
Open: Easter-end Oct daily 10-5.30 other times by arrangement.
Admission: Free to Fortress (including battlements and cannons). Separate charge for museum.
Refreshments: Available.

THE TANK MUSEUM (ROYAL ARMOURED CORPS AND ROYAL TANK REGIMENT MUSEUM)

Bovington BH20 6JG
Tel: (01929) 463953 **Fax:** (01929) 405360
The world's first Tank Museum, with the largest and most comprehensive collection of armoured fighting vehicles; more than 300 from over 25 countries. Also collections of medals, memorabilia, photographs including Lawrence of Arabia Exhibition and fascinating Costume Collection dedicated to the Army wife. Large reference library, national archive and research facilities.
Open: Daily 10-5 closed Dec 23-26.
Admission: Fee charged.
Refreshments: Large restaurant.
Exhibitions/Events: A number of outside events - phone for details.
Gift shop, free video theatre, picnic area, junior assault course, free car park. Easy access for disabled.

THE WARWICKSHIRE YEOMANRY MUSEUM (ENTRANCE IN CASTLE STREET)

The Court House Vaults, Jury Street, Warwick
Tel: (01926) 492212
Military museum
Open: Good Friday-end Sept Fri Sat Sun and Bank Hols 10-1 and 2-4.
Admission: Free.
Location: Centre of Warwick.

THE WELCH REGIMENT MUSEUM OF THE ROYAL REGIMENT OF WALES

The Black and Barbican Towers, Cardiff Castle CF1 2RB **Tel:** (01222) 229367
Colours, uniform and appointments of the 41st and 69th Foot, later 1st and 2nd Battalions. The Welch Regiment, as also the Militia and Volunteer Corps of South Wales, Gallantry awards and campaign medals. The national colour of the 4th American Infantry surrendered at Fort Detroit, 1812.
Open: May 1-Sept 30 Wed 1-6 Thurs Fri & Sat 10-6 other months 10-4.30 guided Tours of the Museum can be arranged on Mons and Tues in any week by appointment with the Curator. The Museum is closed on Christmas Day Boxing Day and New Year's Day.
Admission: Castle Grounds Roman Wall Norman Keep The Welch Regt and Queen's Dragoon Guards Museums £2.20 children & OAPs £1.10 special rates available for parties arranging a Guided Tour.
Location: Central.
Refreshments: Available in Castle Grounds.
Guided Tours of the Museum can be arranged on Mondays and Tuesdays in any week by appointment with the Curator. Research facility available on Mon & Tues by appointment with Curator. Regimental book shop.

THE WORCESTERSHIRE REGIMENT

City Museum & Art Gallery, Foregate Street, Worcester WR1 1DT **Tel:** (01905) 25371
Open: Mon-Fri 9.30-6 Sat 9.30-5 closed Thurs.

THE YORK & LANCASTER REGIMENTAL MUSEUM BRIAN O'MALLEY CENTRAL LIBRARY & ARTS CENTRE

Walker Place, Rotherham
Tel: (01709) 382121 ext. 3625
A history of the Regiment and its forebears the 65th and 84th foot. Displays include the Plumer Collection and nine Victoria cross Awards. The archives can be researched by appointment.
Open: Tues-Sat 10-5 closed Mons Suns & Bank Hols
Admission: Free.

SUBJECT INDEX

Enniskillen - *Northern Ireland*
Enniskillen Castle
Ewell - *Surrey*
Bourne Hall Museum
Folkestone - *Kent*
Folkestone Museum and Gallery
Forfar - *Tayside*
Museum and Art Gallery
Forres - *Grampian*
Falconer Museum
Fort William - *Highlands*
The West Highland Museum
Gairloch - *Highlands*
Gairloch Heritage Museum
Glasgow - *Strathclyde*
Art Gallery and Museum
Burrell Collection
Hunterian Museum
People's Palace
Provand's Lordship
Gloucester - *Gloucestershire*
City East Gate
City Museum and Art Gallery
Grays - *Essex*
Thurrock Museum
Great Yarmouth - *Norfolk*
The Tolhouse Museum and Brass Rubbing Centre
Guernsey - *Channel Islands*
Guernsey Museum & Art Gallery
Guildford - *Surrey*
Guildford Museum
Guisborough - *Cleveland*
Margrove South Cleveland Heritage Centre
Hastings - *East Sussex*
Museum and Art Gallery
Museum of Local History
Hatfield - *Hertfordshire*
Mill Green Museum and Mill
Hawick - *Borders*
Hawick Museum and the Scott Art Gallery
Henfield - *West Sussex*
Henfield Museum
Hereford - *Hereford & Worcester*
Hereford City Museum and Art Gallery
Hertford - *Hertfordshire*
Hertford Museum
Horsham - *West Sussex*
Horsham Museum
Huddersfield - *West Yorkshire*
Tolson Museum
Inverness - *Highlands*
Inverness Museum and Art Gallery
Inverurie - *Grampian*
Carnegie Museum
Ipswich - *Suffolk*
Ipswich Museum and High Street Exhibition Gallery
Jarrow - *Tyne & Wear*
Bedes World
Jedburgh - *Borders*
Castle Jail and Jedburgh Museum
Jersey - *Channel Islands*
La Hougue Bie Museum
Mont Orgueil Castle
Kelso - *Borders*
Kelso Museum & The Turret Gallery
Kettering - *Northamptonshire*
Manor House Museum
Kilmarnock - *Strathclyde*
Dick Institute Museum and Art Gallery
King's Lynn - *Norfolk*
The Lynn Museum
The Town House - Museum of Lynn Life
Kirkcaldy - *Fife*
Kirkcaldy Museum and Art Gallery
Kirkintilloch - *Strathclyde*
The Auld Kirk Museum
The Barony Chambers Museum
Lancaster - *Lancashire*
City Museum
Leeds - *West Yorkshire*
Kirkstall Abbey
Leeds City Museum
Museum of Leeds Waterfront Heritage Trail
Leicester - *Leicestershire*
Jewry Wall Museum
Letchworth - *Hertfordshire*
Letchworth Museum and Art Gallery
Leyland - *Lancashire*
South Ribble Museum and Exhibition Centre
Lindisfarne - *Northumberland*
Lindisfarne Priory
Littlehampton - *West Sussex*
Littlehampton Museum
Liverpool - *Merseyside*
Liverpool Museum
Llanberis - *Gwynedd*
Museum of the North
London - *London (inc Greater London)*
Bexley Museum
British Museum
Bromley Museum
Cuming Museum
Freud Museum
Greenwich Borough Museum
Gunnersbury Park Museum
Harrow Museum and Heritage Centre
Horniman Museum and Gardens
Kingston Museum
The Museum of London
Narwhal Inuit Art Gallery
National Maritime Museum
Old Speech Room Gallery, Harrow School
Sir John Soane's Museum
Wandsworth Museum
Luton - *Bedfordshire*
Luton Museum and Art Gallery
Maidstone - *Kent*
Museum and Art Gallery
Malvern - *Hereford & Worcester*
Malvern Museum
Manchester - *Greater Manchester*
Manchester Museum
Middlesbrough - *Cleveland*
Captain Cook Birthplace Museum
Dorman Museum
Monaghan - *Ireland*
Monaghan County Museum
Newcastle upon Tyne - *Tyne & Wear*
The Castle Keep Museum
Hancock Museum
Museum of Antiquities
The Shefton Museum of Greek Art and Archaeology
Newport - *Gwent*
Newport Museum and Art Gallery
Newport - *Isle of Wight*
Carisbrooke Castle Museum
North Berwick - *Lothian*
North Berwick Museum
Northampton - *Northamptonshire*
Central Museum & Art Gallery
Norwich - *Norfolk*
Norwich Castle Museum
Sainsbury Centre for Visual Arts
Nuneaton - *Warwickshire*
Nuneaton Museum and Art Gallery
Oakham - *Leicestershire*
Rutland County Museum
Okehampton - *Devon*
Museum of Dartmoor Life
Oldham - *Greater Manchester*
Saddleworth Museum & Art Gallery
Oxford - *Oxfordshire*
The Ashmolean Museum of Art and Archaeology
Museum of Oxford
Oxford University Museum
The Pitt Rivers Museum
Peebles - *Borders*
Tweeddale Museum
Penrith - *Cumbria*
Penrith Museum
Peterborough - *Cambridgeshire*
Sacrewell Farm and Country Centre
Pontefract - *West Yorkshire*
Pontefract Castle
Pontefract Museum
Poole - *Dorset*
Waterfront Museum, Poole Quay
Portsmouth - *Hampshire*
City Museum
Southsea Castle and Museum
Reading - *Berkshire*
The Museum of Reading
Redditch - *Hereford & Worcester*
Forge Mill Needle Museum and Bordesley Abbey Visitor Centre
Retford - *Nottinghamshire*
The Bassetlaw Museum
Richborough - *Kent*
Richborough Castle
Richmond - *North Yorkshire*
The Richmondshire Museum
Rochester - *Kent*
Guildhall Museum
Rosemarkie - *Highlands*
Groam House Museum
Rotherham - *South Yorkshire*
Clifton Park Museum
Royston - *Hertfordshire*
Museum
Runcorn - *Cheshire*
Norton Priory Museum
Saffron Walden - *Essex*
Saffron Walden Museum
St. Austell - *Cornwall*
Charlestown Shipwreck and Heritage Centre
St. Ives - *Cambridgeshire*
Norris Museum
Salisbury - *Wiltshire*
Salisbury and South Wiltshire Museum
Scarborough - *North Yorkshire*
Rotunda Museum
Scunthorpe - *Humberside*
Museum and Art Gallery
Selborne - *Hampshire*
The Oates Museum and Gilbert White's House
Shrewsbury - *Shropshire*
The Shrewsbury Museums
Skipton - *North Yorkshire*
Craven Museum
Southend-on-Sea - *Essex*
Central Museum: Southend Museums Service
Prittlewell Priory Museum
Southchurch Hall
Stevenage - *Hertfordshire*
Stevenage Museum
Steyning - *West Sussex*
Steyning Museum
Stockport - *Greater Manchester*
Stockport Museum
Stoke-on-Trent - *Staffordshire*
City Museum and Art Gallery
Stratford-upon-Avon - *Warwickshire*
The Shakespeare Birthplace Trust's Properties
Swindon - *Wiltshire*
Swindon Museum and Art Gallery
Taunton - *Somerset*
Somerset County Museum
Telford - *Shropshire*
Museum of Iron and Furnace Site
Tenby - *Dyfed*
Tenby Museum and Art Gallery
Thetford - *Norfolk*
The Ancient House Museum
Torquay - *Devon*
Torquay Museum
Torre Abbey Historic House and Gallery
Totnes - *Devon*
Totnes (Elizabethan) Museum
Truro - *Cornwall*
Royal Cornwall Museum
Wakefield - *West Yorkshire*
Sandal Castle
Wakefield Museum
Wall - *Staffordshire*
Wall Roman Site (Letocetum)
Wantage - *Oxfordshire*
Vale and Downland Museum Centre
Warrington - *Cheshire*
Museum and Art Gallery
Warwick - *Warwickshire*
Warwickshire Museum
Watford - *Hertfordshire*
Watford Museum
Welshpool - *Powys*
Powysland Museum & Montgomery Canal Centre
Welwyn Garden City - *Hertfordshire*
Welwyn Roman Baths
Weybridge - *Surrey*
Elmbridge Museum
Whitby - *North Yorkshire*
Whitby Museum
Wimborne Minster - *Dorset*
Priest's House Museum of East Dorset Life and Garden
Winchester - *Hampshire*
Winchester City Museum
Woodstock - *Oxfordshire*
Oxfordshire County Museum
Worcester - *Hereford & Worcester*
City Museum and Art Gallery
Worthing - *West Sussex*
Worthing Museum and Art Gallery
Wroxeter - *Shropshire*
Wroxeter Roman City
Yeovil - *Somerset*
The Museum of South Somerset
York - *North Yorkshire*
The ARC
Jorvik Viking Centre
The Yorkshire Museum

ARCHITECTURE

Bath - *Avon*
No. 1 Royal Crescent
Boston - *Lincolnshire*
Guildhall Museum
Bromsgrove - *Hereford & Worcester*
Avoncroft Museum of Historic Buildings
Budleigh Salterton - *Devon*
Otterton Mill Centre and Working Museum
Cardiff - *South Glamorgan*
Cardiff Castle
Chalfont St. Giles - *Buckinghamshire*
Chiltern Open Air Museum
Chester - *Cheshire*
Chester Heritage Centre
Chichester - *West Sussex*
Pallant House
Weald and Downland Open Air Museum
Doncaster - *South Yorkshire*
Museum of South Yorkshire Life, Cusworth Hall
Dundee - *Tayside*
St. Mary's Tower
Dunfermline - *Fife*
Pittencrieff House Museum
Faversham - *Kent*
Fleur De Lis Heritage Centre
Glasgow - *Strathclyde*
Scotland Street School Museum
Halifax - *West Yorkshire*
Shibden Hall
Hove - *East Sussex*
West Blatchington Windmill
Jarrow - *Tyne & Wear*
Bedes World
Jedburgh - *Borders*
Castle Jail and Jedburgh Museum
Mary, Queen of Scots' House
Kelso - *Borders*
Kelso Museum & The Turret Gallery
Letchworth - *Hertfordshire*
First Garden City Heritage Museum
Leyland - *Lancashire*
South Ribble Museum and Exhibition Centre
London - *London (inc Greater London)*
Carew Manor and Dovecote
Carshalton House
Church Farmhouse Museum
Dulwich Picture Gallery
Geffrye Museum
Harrow Museum and Heritage Centre
Orleans House Gallery
Queen Elizabeth's Hunting Lodge
Sir John Soane's Museum
Spencer House
Tower Bridge
Whitehall
Oakham - *Leicestershire*
Oakham Castle
Penzance - *Cornwall*
Trinity House National Lighthouse Centre
Runcorn - *Cheshire*
Norton Priory Museum
St. Andrews - *Fife*
Crawford Arts Centre
St. Asaph - *Clwyd*
Bodelwyddan Castle
St. Fagans - *South Glamorgan*
Welsh Folk Museum
Selborne - *Hampshire*
The Oates Museum and Gilbert White's House
Sheffield - *South Yorkshire*
Bishops' House
Spalding - *Lincolnshire*
Ayscoughfee Hall and Gardens
Stafford - *Staffordshire*
Ancient High House
Stafford Castle and Visitor Centre
Izaak Walton's Cottage
Stockport - *Greater Manchester*
Bramall Hall
Telford - *Shropshire*
Iron Bridge and Information Centre
Walsingham - *Norfolk*
Shirehall Museum
Weston-super-Mare - *Avon*
Weston-super-Mare Heritage Centre
Wimborne Minster - *Dorset*
Priest's House Museum of East Dorset Life and Garden
Wrexham - *Clwyd*
Wrexham Maelor Heritage Centre
York - *North Yorkshire*
Ryedale Folk Museum

ARCHIVES see HISTORICAL & LITERARY ASSOCIATIONS

ARMS & ARMOUR

Blackburn - *Lancashire*
Blackburn Museum and Art Gallery
Bridgwater - *Somerset*
Admiral Blake Museum
Canterbury - *Kent*
Buffs Regimental Museum
The West Gate Museum
Coventry - *West Midlands*
Lunt Roman Fort (Reconstruction)
Dumfries - *Dumfries & Galloway*
Dumfries Museum
Edinburgh - *Lothian*
Museum of Antiquities
Fareham - *Hampshire*
Fort Nelson
Fort William - *Highlands*
The West Highland Museum
Glasgow - *Strathclyde*
Art Gallery and Museum
Burrell Collection
Gloucester - *Gloucestershire*
Regiments of Gloucestershire Museum
Guernsey - *Channel Islands*
Castle Cornet
Harwich - *Essex*
Harwich Redoubt
Hereford - *Hereford & Worcester*
Hereford City Museum and Art Gallery
Hexham - *Northumberland*
Border History Museum
Jersey - *Channel Islands*
Elizabeth Castle
Jersey Museum
Mont Orgueil Castle
Kilmarnock - *Strathclyde*
Dean Castle
Dick Institute Museum and Art Gallery
Leicester - *Leicestershire*
Museum of the Royal Leicestershire Regiment
London - *London (inc Greater London)*
Bethnal Green Museum of Childhood
British Museum
HMS Belfast
Imperial War Museum
The Museum of London
National Army Museum
National Maritime Museum
St. John's Gate, The Museum of the Order of St. John
The Wallace Collection
Manchester - *Greater Manchester*
Manchester Museum
Market Bosworth - *Leicestershire*
Bosworth Battlefield Visitor Centre and Country Park
Middle Wallop - *Hampshire*
Museum of Army Flying
Newcastle upon Tyne - *Tyne & Wear*
The Castle Keep Museum
Museum of Antiquities
Reading - *Berkshire*
The Museum of Reading
Rochester - *Kent*
Guildhall Museum
Rossendale - *Lancashire*
Rossendale Museum
Southend-on-Sea - *Essex*
Southchurch Hall
Stafford - *Staffordshire*
Stafford Castle and Visitor Centre
Stockton-on-Tees - *Cleveland*
Preston Hall Museum
Tamworth - *Staffordshire*
Tamworth Castle and Museum Service
Tangmere - *West Sussex*
Tangmere Military Aviation Museum Trust
Weston-super-Mare - *Avon*
The International Helicopter Museum
Whitby - *North Yorkshire*
Whitby Museum
York - *North Yorkshire*
York Castle Museum

ASTRONOMICAL INSTRUMENTS see SCIENCE & INDUSTRY

AUTOGRAPHS see HISTORICAL & LITERARY ASSOCIATIONS

BELLS & BELLFOUNDING

Loughborough - *Leicestershire*
The Bell Foundry Museum

BOTANY see NATURAL HISTORY

BYGONES see FOLK COLLECTIONS

CARPETS see TAPESTRY & TEXTILES

CERAMICS & GLASS

Aberdeen - *Grampian*
Aberdeen Art Gallery
Provost Skene's House
Aberystwyth - *Dyfed*
Aberystwyth Arts Centre Exhibitions
Banchory - *Grampian*
Banchory Museum
Barnsley - *South Yorkshire*
Cannon Hall Museum
Bath - *Avon*
American Museum in Britain
Holburne Museum and Crafts Study Centre
The Museum of East Asian Art
No. 1 Royal Crescent
Batley - *West Yorkshire*
Bagshaw Museum
Bedford - *Bedfordshire*
Cecil Higgins Art Gallery and Museum
Belfast - *Northern Ireland*
Ulster Museum
Berwick-upon-Tweed - *Northumberland*
Berwick Borough Museum & Art Gallery
Birkenhead - *Merseyside*
Williamson Art Gallery & Museum
Birmingham - *West Midlands*
Birmingham Museum and Art Gallery
Blackburn - *Lancashire*
Blackburn Museum and Art Gallery
Bolton - *Greater Manchester*
Bolton Museum and Art Gallery
Bournemouth - *Dorset*
Russel-Cotes Art Gallery and Museum
Brighton - *East Sussex*
Brighton Museum and Art Gallery
Preston Manor
The Royal Pavilion
Bristol - *Avon*
Bristol City Museum and Art Gallery
Burnley - *Lancashire*
Towneley Hall Art Gallery and Museums and Museum of Local Crafts and Industries
Cambridge - *Cambridgeshire*
Kettle's Yard
Canterbury - *Kent*
The Royal Museum & Art Gallery and Buffs Regimental Museum
Cardiff - *South Glamorgan*
De Morgan Foundation - Cardiff Castle
The National Museum of Wales
Castleford - *West Yorkshire*
Castleford Museum
Ceres - *Fife*
Fife Folk Museum
Cheltenham - *Gloucestershire*
Cheltenham Art Gallery and Museum
Chertsey - *Surrey*
Chertsey Museum
Chichester - *West Sussex*
Pallant House
Cleckheaton - *West Yorkshire*
Red House
Coventry - *West Midlands*
Herbert Art Gallery and Museum
Derby - *Derbyshire*
Derby Museums & Art Gallery
Royal Crown Derby Museum
Doncaster - *South Yorkshire*
Doncaster Museum and Art Gallery
Dumfries - *Dumfries & Galloway*
Dumfries Museum
Gracefield - The Arts Centre for South West Scotland
Durham - *County Durham*
Durham University Oriental Museum
East Cowes - *Isle of Wight*
Osborne House
Edinburgh - *Lothian*
Huntly House
Lauriston Castle
Royal Museum of Scotland
Ely - *Cambridgeshire*
The Stained Glass Museum
Glasgow - *Strathclyde*
Art Gallery and Museum
Burrell Collection
People's Palace
Pollok House
Rutherglen Museum
Gloucester - *Gloucestershire*
City Museum and Art Gallery
Great Yarmouth - *Norfolk*
Elizabethan House Museum
Hartlebury - *Hereford & Worcester*
Hereford and Worcester County Museum
Hastings - *East Sussex*
Museum and Art Gallery
Hereford - *Hereford & Worcester*
Hereford City Museum and Art Gallery
Horsham - *West Sussex*
Horsham Museum
Hove - *East Sussex*
Hove Museum and Art Gallery
Huddersfield - *West Yorkshire*
Huddersfield Art Gallery
Hull - *Humberside*
University of Hull Art Collection
Wilberforce House Museum
Ilkeston - *Derbyshire*
Erewash Museum
Ipswich - *Suffolk*
Christchurch Mansion and Wolsey Art Gallery
Jersey - *Channel Islands*
Jersey Museum
Kilmarnock - *Strathclyde*
Dick Institute Museum and Art Gallery
King's Lynn - *Norfolk*
The Town House - Museum of Lynn Life
Kirkcaldy - *Fife*
Kirkcaldy Museum and Art Gallery
Lancaster - *Lancashire*
City Museum
Leamington Spa - *Warwickshire*
Leamington Spa Art Gallery and Museum
Leek - *Staffordshire*
Cheddleton Flint Mill
Leicester - *Leicestershire*
The Leicestershire Museum and Art Gallery
Letchworth - *Hertfordshire*
Letchworth Museum and Art Gallery
Lincoln - *Lincolnshire*
Usher Gallery
Liverpool - *Merseyside*
Liverpool Museum
University of Liverpool Art Gallery
London - *London (inc Greater London)*
Apsley House
Bethnal Green Museum of Childhood
Bramah Tea and Coffee Museum
British Museum
De Morgan Foundation - Old Battersea House
Fenton House
Forty Hall Museum
Harrow Museum and Heritage Centre
Kingston Museum
Leighton House Art Gallery and Museum
Medici Galleries
Museum of the Royal Pharmaceutical Society of Great Britain
National Army Museum
National Maritime Museum
Osterley Park House
Percival David Foundation of Chinese Art
Pitshanger Manor Museum
Science Museum
Victoria and Albert Museum
The Wallace Collection
Woodlands Art Gallery
Macclesfield - *Cheshire*
West Park Museum
Maidstone - *Kent*
Museum and Art Gallery
Mansfield - *Nottinghamshire*
Mansfield Museum and Art Gallery
Merthyr Tydfil - *Mid Glamorgan*
Cyfarthfa Castle Museum and Art Gallery
Middlesbrough - *Cleveland*
Cleveland Crafts Centre
Milngavie - *Strathclyde*
Lillie Art Gallery
Newcastle-under-Lyme - *Staffordshire*
Borough Museum and Art Gallery
Newcastle upon Tyne - *Tyne & Wear*
The Shefton Museum of Greek Art and Archaeology
Newport - *Gwent*
Newport Museum and Art Gallery
Newport - *Isle of Wight*
Carisbrooke Castle Museum
Norwich - *Norfolk*
Norwich Castle Museum
Sainsbury Centre for Visual Arts
Ombersley - *Hereford & Worcester*
Ombersley Gallery
Oxford - *Oxfordshire*
The Ashmolean Museum of Art and Archaeology
Christ Church Picture Gallery
Paisley - *Strathclyde*
Paisley Museum and Art Galleries
Plymouth - *Devon*
City Museum and Art Gallery
Pontefract - *West Yorkshire*
Pontefract Museum
Port Sunlight - *Merseyside*
Lady Lever Art Gallery
Portsmouth - *Hampshire*
City Museum
Preston - *Lancashire*
Harris Museum and Art Gallery
Retford - *Nottinghamshire*
The Bassetlaw Museum
Rotherham - *South Yorkshire*
Clifton Park Museum
Royston - *Hertfordshire*
Museum
Rye - *East Sussex*
Rye Museum
Saffron Walden - *Essex*
Saffron Walden Museum
St. Helens - *Merseyside*
Pilkington Glass Museum
Salford - *Greater Manchester*
Museum and Art Gallery
Salisbury - *Wiltshire*
Salisbury and South Wiltshire Museum
Sheffield - *South Yorkshire*
Graves Art Gallery
Shrewsbury - *Shropshire*
The Shrewsbury Museums
Southampton - *Hampshire*
Southampton City Art Gallery
Southend-on-Sea - *Essex*
Central Museum: Southend Museums Service
Southport - *Merseyside*
Atkinson Art Gallery
Stockport - *Greater Manchester*
Bramall Hall
Stoke-on-Trent - *Staffordshire*
City Museum and Art Gallery
The Sir Henry Doulton Gallery
Gladstone Pottery Museum
Minton Museum
Wedgwood Museum
Strathaven - *Strathclyde*
John Hastie Museum
Swindon - *Wiltshire*
Lydiard Park
Swindon Museum and Art Gallery
Taunton - *Somerset*
Somerset County Museum
Telford - *Shropshire*
Coalport China Museum
Jackfield Tile Museum
Torquay - *Devon*
Torre Abbey Historic House and Gallery
Truro - *Cornwall*
Royal Cornwall Museum
Wakefield - *West Yorkshire*
Wakefield Art Gallery
Warrington - *Cheshire*
Museum and Art Gallery
Westcott - *Surrey*
The Westcott Gallery
Whitby - *North Yorkshire*
Whitby Museum
Whitehaven - *Cumbria*
Whitehaven Museum and Art Gallery
Workington - *Cumbria*
Helena Thompson Museum
Wroxeter - *Shropshire*
Wroxeter Roman City
York - *North Yorkshire*
Fairfax House
York City Art Gallery
The Yorkshire Museum

CINEMATOGRAPHY & PHOTOGRAPHY

Aberystwyth - *Dyfed*
Aberystwyth Arts Centre Exhibitions
The Catherine Lewis Print Room
Bath - *Avon*
The Royal Photographic Society
Belfast - *Northern Ireland*
Ulster Museum
Blackburn - *Lancashire*
Blackburn Museum and Art Gallery
Bradford - *West Yorkshire*
National Museum of Photography, Film and Television
Bridgend - *Mid Glamorgan*
South Wales Police Museum
Canterbury - *Kent*
Whitstable Museum & Gallery
Chertsey - *Surrey*
Chertsey Museum
Coatbridge - *Strathclyde*
Summerlee Heritage Trust
Coventry - *West Midlands*
Herbert Art Gallery and Museum
Crich - *Derbyshire*
The National Tramway Museum
Dumfries - *Dumfries & Galloway*
Dumfries Museum
Gracefield - The Arts Centre for South West Scotland
Edinburgh - *Lothian*
Scottish National Gallery of Modern Art
Scottish National Portrait Gallery
Ewell - *Surrey*
Bourne Hall Museum
Farnham - *Surrey*
Rural Life Centre
Glasgow - *Strathclyde*
Museum of Transport
People's Palace
Glencoe - *Highlands*
Glencoe and North Lorn Folk Museum
Great Grimsby - *Humberside*
Back O' Doig's
Hitchin - *Hertfordshire*
Hitchin Museum and Art Gallery
Holmfirth - *West Yorkshire*
Holmfirth Postcard Museum
Hove - *East Sussex*
Hove Museum and Art Gallery
Huddersfield - *West Yorkshire*
Huddersfield Art Gallery
Jersey - *Channel Islands*
Jersey Museum
Kettering - *Northamptonshire*
Alfred East Gallery
Kilmarnock - *Strathclyde*
Dick Institute Museum and Art Gallery
Kingsbridge - *Devon*
Cookworthy Museum of Rural Life in South Devon
Kirkcaldy - *Fife*
Kirkcaldy Museum and Art Gallery
Lancaster - *Lancashire*
City Museum
Maritime Museum
Leicester - *Leicestershire*
Leicestershire Record Office
London - *London (inc Greater London)*
The Association Gallery
Commonwealth Institute
Kingston Museum
Linley Sambourne House
Museum of the Moving Image (MOMI)
Museum of the Royal Pharmaceutical Society of Great Britain
Science Museum
Victoria and Albert Museum
Woodlands Art Gallery
Manchester - *Greater Manchester*
The Museum of Science and Industry in Manchester
March - *Cambridgeshire*
March and District Museum
Middlesbrough - *Cleveland*
Cleveland Gallery
Middle Wallop - *Hampshire*
Museum of Army Flying
Newlyn - *Cornwall*
Newlyn Art Gallery
Oldham - *Greater Manchester*
Oldham Art Gallery
Peterhead - *Grampian*
Arbuthnot Museum
Rochdale - *Greater Manchester*
Rochdale Art Gallery
St. Andrews - *Fife*
Crawford Arts Centre
St. Asaph - *Clwyd*
Bodelwyddan Castle
Salford - *Greater Manchester*
Viewpoint Photographic Gallery
Stockport - *Greater Manchester*
Stockport Art Gallery
Stockton-on-Tees - *Cleveland*
Billingham Art Gallery
Tangmere - *West Sussex*
Tangmere Military Aviation Museum Trust
Wakefield - *West Yorkshire*
Elizabethan Exhibition Gallery
Winchcombe - *Gloucestershire*
Gloucestershire Warwickshire Railway
Winchester - *Hampshire*
Winchester City Museum
York - *North Yorkshire*
Ryedale Folk Museum

CLOCKS & WATCHES

Aberystwyth - *Dyfed*
Ceredigion Museum
Banff - *Grampian*
Banff Museum
Barnard Castle - *County Durham*
The Bowes Museum
Bath - *Avon*
Holburne Museum and Crafts Study Centre
No. 1 Royal Crescent
Victoria Art Gallery
Belfast - *Northern Ireland*
Ulster Museum
Blackburn - *Lancashire*
Blackburn Museum and Art Gallery
Brechin - *Tayside*
Brechin Museum
Brighton - *East Sussex*
Preston Manor
Chertsey - *Surrey*
Chertsey Museum
Coventry - *West Midlands*
Herbert Art Gallery and Museum
Derby - *Derbyshire*
Derby Museums & Art Gallery
Dumfries - *Dumfries & Galloway*
Dumfries Museum
Dunfermline - *Fife*
Dunfermline District Museum and the Small Gallery
Edinburgh - *Lothian*
Huntly House
Lauriston Castle
Glasgow - *Strathclyde*
Art Gallery and Museum
Burrell Collection
Gloucester - *Gloucestershire*
City Museum and Art Gallery
Ipswich - *Suffolk*
Christchurch Mansion and Wolsey Art Gallery
Jersey - *Channel Islands*
Jersey Museum
Kendal - *Cumbria*
Abbot Hall Art Gallery
Kilmarnock - *Strathclyde*
Dick Institute Museum and Art Gallery
Kirkcaldy - *Fife*
Kirkcaldy Museum and Art Gallery
Lancaster - *Lancashire*
City Museum
Leicester - *Leicestershire*
Newarke Houses Museum
Lincoln - *Lincolnshire*
Usher Gallery
London - *London (inc Greater London)*
British Museum
National Maritime Museum
Osterley Park House
Science Museum
Sir John Soane's Museum
Thomas Coram Foundation for Children
The Wallace Collection
Loughborough - *Leicestershire*
The Bell Foundry Museum
Macclesfield - *Cheshire*
West Park Museum
Newport - *Isle of Wight*
Carisbrooke Castle Museum
Northleach - *Gloucestershire*
Keith Harding's World of Mechanical Music
Norwich - *Norfolk*
Bridewell Museum of Local Industries
Oxford - *Oxfordshire*
The Ashmolean Museum of Art and Archaeology
Prescot - *Merseyside*
Prescot Museum of Clock and Watch-Making
Ramsgate - *Kent*
Maritime Museum Complex
St. Fagans - *South Glamorgan*
Welsh Folk Museum
Skipton - *North Yorkshire*
Craven Museum
Stockport - *Greater Manchester*
Lyme Hall and Park
Warrington - *Cheshire*
Museum and Art Gallery
Warwick - *Warwickshire*
St. John's House
Wrexham - *Clwyd*
Wrexham Maelor Heritage Centre
York - *North Yorkshire*
Fairfax House
York Castle Museum

COINS & MEDALS see also MILITARY

Aberdeen - *Grampian*
Aberdeen Art Gallery
Provost Skene's House
Bedford - *Bedfordshire*
Bedford Museum
Belfast - *Northern Ireland*
Ulster Museum
Birmingham - *West Midlands*
The Barber Institute of Fine Arts
Blackburn - *Lancashire*
Blackburn Museum and Art Gallery
Bolton - *Greater Manchester*
Bolton Museum and Art Gallery
Caerleon - *Gwent*
Roman Legionary Museum
Canterbury - *Kent*
Buffs Regimental Museum
The Royal Museum & Art Gallery and Buffs Regimental Museum
Cardiff - *South Glamorgan*
The National Museum of Wales
Chelmsford - *Essex*
Chelmsford and Essex Museum, Essex Regiment Museum
Clonmel - *Ireland*
Tipperary (S.R.) CO. Museum
Colne - *Lancashire*
British in India Museum
Derby - *Derbyshire*
Derby Museums & Art Gallery
Doncaster - *South Yorkshire*
The King's Own Yorkshire Light Infantry
Douglas - *Isle of Man*
Manx National Heritage
Dumfries - *Dumfries & Galloway*
Dumfries Museum
Edinburgh - *Lothian*
Huntly House
National Gallery of Scotland
Scottish National Gallery of Modern Art
Forres - *Grampian*
Falconer Museum
Glasgow - *Strathclyde*
Art Gallery and Museum
Hunterian Museum
Rutherglen Museum
Gloucester - *Gloucestershire*
City Museum and Art Gallery
Guildford - *Surrey*
British Red Cross Museum and Archives
Hawick - *Borders*
Hawick Museum and the Scott Art Gallery
Hull - *Humberside*
Wilberforce House Museum
Huntly - *Grampian*
Brander Museum
Inverness - *Highlands*
Inverness Museum and Art Gallery
Jersey - *Channel Islands*
Elizabeth Castle
Jersey Museum
King's Lynn - *Norfolk*
The Lynn Museum
Lancaster - *Lancashire*
City Museum
Leeds - *West Yorkshire*
Leeds City Museum
Leicester - *Leicestershire*
Newarke Houses Museum
Letchworth - *Hertfordshire*
Letchworth Museum and Art Gallery
London - *London (inc Greater London)*
Forty Hall Museum
Imperial War Museum
The Jewish Museum
National Army Museum
National Maritime Museum
Royal Hospital Museum
St. John's Gate, The Museum of the Order of St. John
Thomas Coram Foundation for Children
Manchester - *Greater Manchester*
Manchester Museum
Middlesbrough - *Cleveland*
Dorman Museum
Middle Wallop - *Hampshire*
Museum of Army Flying
Monaghan - *Ireland*
Monaghan County Museum
Newport - *Gwent*
Newport Museum and Art Gallery
Norwich - *Norfolk*
Norwich Castle Museum
Oxford - *Oxfordshire*
The Ashmolean Museum of Art and Archaeology
Peterhead - *Grampian*
Arbuthnot Museum
Portsmouth - *Hampshire*
Royal Marines Museum
Ramsgate - *Kent*
Maritime Museum Complex
Reading - *Berkshire*
The Museum of Reading
Rossendale - *Lancashire*
Rossendale Museum
Rotherham - *South Yorkshire*
The York and Lancaster Regiment Museum
St. Albans - *Hertfordshire*
The Verulamium Museum
Scarborough - *North Yorkshire*
Rotunda Museum
Shaftesbury - *Dorset*
Local History Museum
Southend-on-Sea - *Essex*
Central Museum: Southend Museums Service
Tamworth - *Staffordshire*
Tamworth Castle and Museum Service
Warrington - *Cheshire*
Museum and Art Gallery
Warwick - *Warwickshire*
Warwickshire Museum
Whitby - *North Yorkshire*
Whitby Museum
Winchester - *Hampshire*
Winchester City Museum

CONSERVATION

Bolventor - *Cornwall*
Potters Museum of Curiosity
Bracknell - *Berkshire*
The Look Out Countryside and Heritage Centre
Bromsgrove - *Hereford & Worcester*
Avoncroft Museum of Historic Buildings
Holmfirth - *West Yorkshire*
Holmfirth Postcard Museum
Lanark - *Strathclyde*
New Lanark World Heritage Village
Leicester - *Leicestershire*
Snibston Discovery Park
London - *London (inc Greater London)*
City & Guilds of London Art School
Spencer House
Thames Barrier Visitors' Centre
Millport - *Strathclyde*
Robertson Museum and Aquarium
Newcastle upon Tyne - *Tyne & Wear*
Hancock Museum
Northleach - *Gloucestershire*
Keith Harding's World of Mechanical Music
Portsmouth - *Hampshire*
Royal Marines Museum
Telford - *Shropshire*
Museum of the River
Weston-super-Mare - *Avon*
Weston-super-Mare Heritage Centre

CONSERVATION INDUSTRIAL HERITAGE

Bridgnorth - *Shropshire*
Daniel's Mill
Budleigh Salterton - *Devon*
Otterton Mill Centre and Working Museum
Camborne - *Cornwall*
Camborne School of Mines Geological Museum and Art Gallery
Crich - *Derbyshire*
The National Tramway Museum
Dewsbury - *West Yorkshire*
Dewsbury Museum

Epping - *Essex*
The Squadron
Glasgow - *Strathclyde*
Art Gallery and Museum
Burrell Collection
Rutherglen Museum
Hove - *East Sussex*
The British Engineerium
West Blatchington Windmill
Lanark - *Strathclyde*
New Lanark World Heritage Village
London - *London (inc Greater London)*
Museum of Garden History
The Wandle Industrial Museum
Wimbledon Windmill Museum
Lyndhurst - *Hampshire*
New Forest Museum and Visitor Centre
Manchester - *Greater Manchester*
Pump House People's History Museum
Morwellham Quay - *Devon*
Morwellham Quay Museum and 19th Century Port and Copper Mine
Pickering - *North Yorkshire*
North Yorkshire Moors Railway
Telford - *Shropshire*
Iron Bridge and Information Centre
Weybridge - *Surrey*
Brooklands Museum
Winchcombe - *Gloucestershire*
Gloucestershire Warwickshire Railway

CONTEMPORARY ART see FINE ARTS

CONTEMPORARY CRAFTS

Bedford - *Bedfordshire*
Bromham Mill
Bournemouth - *Dorset*
Russel-Cotes Art Gallery and Museum
Coldstream - *Borders*
The Hirsel Homestead Museum
Guildford - *Surrey*
Guildford House Gallery
Kettering - *Northamptonshire*
Alfred East Gallery
Leigh - *Greater Manchester*
Turnpike Gallery
London - *London (inc Greater London)*
Cabaret Mechanical Theatre
Manchester - *Greater Manchester*
The Whitworth Art Gallery
Middlesbrough - *Cleveland*
Cleveland Crafts Centre
Newlyn - *Cornwall*
Newlyn Art Gallery
Ombersley - *Hereford & Worcester*
Ombersley Gallery
Southampton - *Hampshire*
Southampton City Art Gallery
Wakefield - *West Yorkshire*
Wakefield Art Gallery
Worksop - *Nottinghamshire*
The Harley Gallery

COSTUME & ACCESSORIES see also MILITARY

Aberdeen - *Grampian*
James Dun's House
Bakewell - *Derbyshire*
The Old House Museum
Banchory - *Grampian*
Banchory Museum
Banff - *Grampian*
Banff Museum
Barnard Castle - *County Durham*
The Bowes Museum
Bath - *Avon*
Fashion Research Centre
Museum of Costume
Batley - *West Yorkshire*
Bagshaw Museum
Bedford - *Bedfordshire*
Cecil Higgins Art Gallery and Museum
Belfast - *Northern Ireland*
Ulster Museum
Blackburn - *Lancashire*
Blackburn Museum and Art Gallery
Bolton - *Greater Manchester*
Bolton Museum and Art Gallery
Bridgend - *Mid Glamorgan*
South Wales Police Museum
Brighton - *East Sussex*
Brighton Museum and Art Gallery
Bromsgrove - *Hereford & Worcester*
Bromsgrove Museum
Budleigh Salterton - *Devon*
Fairlynch Arts Centre and Museum
Canterbury - *Kent*
Buffs Regimental Museum
Ceres - *Fife*
Fife Folk Museum
Chard - *Somerset*
Chard and District Museum
Chelmsford - *Essex*
Chelmsford and Essex Museum, Essex Regiment Museum
Cheltenham - *Gloucestershire*
Pittville Pump Room Museum
Chertsey - *Surrey*
Chertsey Museum
Chester - *Cheshire*
Grosvenor Museum
Clonmel - *Ireland*
Tipperary (S.R.) CO. Museum
Colne - *Lancashire*
British in India Museum
Coventry - *West Midlands*
Herbert Art Gallery and Museum
Derby - *Derbyshire*
Pickford's House Museum
Ditchling - *West Sussex*
Ditchling Museum
Doncaster - *South Yorkshire*
The King's Own Yorkshire Light Infantry
Museum of South Yorkshire Life, Cusworth Hall
Dre-Fach Felindre - *Dyfed*
Museum of the Welsh Woollen Industry
Dumfries - *Dumfries & Galloway*
Dumfries Museum
Dunfermline - *Fife*
Pittencrieff House Museum
Durham - *County Durham*
Durham University Oriental Museum
Edinburgh - *Lothian*
Huntly House
Museum of Childhood
Museum of Fire
The People's Story
Royal Museum of Scotland
Ewell - *Surrey*
Bourne Hall Museum
Fort William - *Highlands*
The West Highland Museum
Glasgow - *Strathclyde*
Art Gallery and Museum
Glencoe - *Highlands*
Glencoe and North Lorn Folk Museum
Gloucester - *Gloucestershire*
Regiments of Gloucestershire Museum
Great Grimsby - *Humberside*
Back O' Doig's
Guildford - *Surrey*
British Red Cross Museum and Archives
Halifax - *West Yorkshire*
Bankfield Museum
Hartlebury - *Hereford & Worcester*
Hereford and Worcester County Museum
Hereford - *Hereford & Worcester*
Churchill Gardens Museum
Hitchin *Hertfordshire*
Hitchin Museum and Art Gallery
Horsham - *West Sussex*
Horsham Museum
Huddersfield - *West Yorkshire*
Tolson Museum
Hull - *Humberside*
Wilberforce House Museum
Huntly - *Grampian*
Brander Museum
Inverness - *Highlands*
Inverness Museum and Art Gallery
Ipswich - *Suffolk*
Christchurch Mansion and Wolsey Art Gallery
Jersey - *Channel Islands*
Jersey Museum
Kendal - *Cumbria*
Abbot Hall Art Gallery
Kilmarnock - *Strathclyde*
Dick Institute Museum and Art Gallery
King's Lynn - *Norfolk*
The Town House - Museum of Lynn Life
Kingsbridge - *Devon*
Cookworthy Museum of Rural Life in South Devon
Kirkcaldy - *Fife*
Kirkcaldy Museum and Art Gallery
Leicester - *Leicestershire*
Museum of Costume
Lincoln - *Lincolnshire*
Usher Gallery
Liverpool - *Merseyside*
Liverpool Museum
London - *London (inc Greater London)*
Apsley House
Bethnal Green Museum of Childhood
The Fan Museum
Forty Hall Museum
Gunnersbury Park Museum
The Museum of London
National Army Museum
St. John's Gate, The Museum of the Order of St. John
Theatre Museum
Vestry House Museum
Victoria and Albert Museum
Luton - *Bedfordshire*
Luton Museum and Art Gallery
Maidstone - *Kent*
Museum and Art Gallery
Manchester - *Greater Manchester*
Greater Manchester Police Museum
The Whitworth Art Gallery
Market Harborough - *Leicestershire*
The Harborough Museum
Middle Wallop - *Hampshire*
Museum of Army Flying
Monaghan - *Ireland*
Monaghan County Museum
Newark-on-Trent - *Nottinghamshire*
Vina Cooke Museum of Dolls & Bygone Childhood
Norwich - *Norfolk*
Strangers' Hall
Peterhead - *Grampian*
Arbuthnot Museum
Portsmouth - *Hampshire*
City Museum
Royal Marines Museum
Preston - *Lancashire*
Harris Museum and Art Gallery
Ramsey - *Isle of Man*
The Grove Museum
Reading - *Berkshire*
The Museum of Reading
Reeth - *North Yorkshire*
Swaledale Folk Museum
Rochester - *Kent*
Guildhall Museum
Ross-on-Wye - *Hereford & Worcester*
The Button Museum
Rossendale - *Lancashire*
Rossendale Museum
St. Fagans - *South Glamorgan*
Welsh Folk Museum
Salisbury - *Wiltshire*
Salisbury and South Wiltshire Museum
Shrewsbury - *Shropshire*
The Shrewsbury Museums
Shugborough - *Staffordshire*
Mansion House, Servants' Quarters, Museum of Staffordshire life and Park Farm.
Skipton - *North Yorkshire*
Craven Museum
Southend-on-Sea - *Essex*
Central Museum: Southend Museums Service
Stockport - *Greater Manchester*
Stockport Museum
Stoke-on-Trent - *Staffordshire*
City Museum and Art Gallery
Totnes - *Devon*
Totnes Costume Museum
Totnes (Elizabethan) Museum
Warwick - *Warwickshire*
St. John's House
Weybridge - *Surrey*
Elmbridge Museum
Whitby - *North Yorkshire*
Whitby Museum
Workington - *Cumbria*
Helena Thompson Museum
Worthing - *West Sussex*
Worthing Museum and Art Gallery
Yeovil - *Somerset*
The Museum of South Somerset
Yeovilton - *Somerset*
Fleet Air Arm Museum and Concorde Exhibition
York - *North Yorkshire*
York Castle Museum

CRAFTS

Aberystwyth - *Dyfed*
Aberystwyth Arts Centre Exhibitions
Acton Scott - *Shropshire*
Acton Scott Historic Working Farm
Batley - *West Yorkshire*
Batley Art Gallery
Bedford - *Bedfordshire*
Bromham Mill
Billericay - *Essex*
Barleylands Farm Museum
Birmingham - *West Midlands*
Jewellery Quarter Discovery Centre
Brecon - *Powys*
Brecknock Museum
Bristol - *Avon*
Guild Gallery
Budleigh Salterton - *Devon*
Otterton Mill Centre and Working Museum
Chichester - *West Sussex*
Weald and Downland Open Air Museum
Dre-Fach Felindre - *Dyfed*
Museum of the Welsh Woollen Industry
Ely - *Cambridgeshire*
Ely Museum
Enniskillen - *Northern Ireland*
Enniskillen Castle
Forfar - *Tayside*
Museum and Art Gallery
Gressenhall - *Norfolk*
Norfolk Rural Life Museum and Union Farm
Halifax - *West Yorkshire*
Bankfield Museum
The Piece Hall
Smith Art Gallery
Hartlebury - *Hereford & Worcester*
Hereford and Worcester County Museum
Hornsea - *Humberside*
Hornsea Museum
Hove - *East Sussex*
Hove Museum and Art Gallery
Leeds - *West Yorkshire*
Tetley's Brewery Wharf
Leigh - *Greater Manchester*
Turnpike Gallery
London - *London (inc Greater London)*
City & Guilds of London Art School
Commonwealth Institute
The Design Museum by Tower Bridge
The Fan Museum
Little Holland House
Livesey Museum
Luton - *Bedfordshire*
Stockwood Craft Museum and Gardens Home of the Mossman Collection
Maidstone - *Kent*
Museum of Kent Life
Milton Keynes - *Buckinghamshire*
Milton Keynes Exhibition Gallery
Milton Keynes Museum of Industry & Rural Life
Newport - *Gwent*
Newport Museum and Art Gallery
Nottingham - *Nottinghamshire*
Djanogly Art Gallery
Oldham - *Greater Manchester*
Oldham Art Gallery
Omagh - *Northern Ireland*
Ulster-American Folk Park
Ombersley - *Hereford & Worcester*
Ombersley Gallery
Paddock Wood - *Kent*
Whitbread Hop Farm
Reading - *Berkshire*
Museum of English Rural Life
Ross-on-Wye - *Hereford & Worcester*
The Button Museum
Runcorn - *Cheshire*
Norton Priory Museum
Ruthin - *Clwyd*
Ruthin Craft Centre
St. Andrews - *Fife*
Crawford Arts Centre
St. Fagans - *South Glamorgan*
Welsh Folk Museum
Stockport - *Greater Manchester*
Stockport Art Gallery
Stockton-on-Tees - *Cleveland*
Billingham Art Gallery
Stoke-on-Trent - *Staffordshire*
Etruria Industrial Museum
Sudbury - *Suffolk*
Gainsborough's House
Telford - *Shropshire*
Blists Hill Open Air Museum
Wakefield - *West Yorkshire*
Elizabethan Exhibition Gallery
Wexford - *Ireland*
Irish Agricultural Museum
Worksop - *Nottinghamshire*
The Harley Gallery
York - *North Yorkshire*
Ryedale Folk Museum

CUTLERY see JEWELLERY & METALWORK

DESIGN
Bradford - *West Yorkshire*
Colour Museum
Derby - *Derbyshire*
Royal Crown Derby Museum
London - *London (inc Greater London)*
Geffrye Museum
Little Holland House
Livesey Museum
William Morris Gallery
National Postal Museum
Theatre Museum
Victoria and Albert Museum
Ross-on-Wye - *Hereford & Worcester*
The Button Museum
St. Andrews - *Fife*
Crawford Arts Centre
Stoke-on-Trent - *Staffordshire*
The Sir Henry Doulton Gallery
Minton Museum

DOLLS & DOLLS HOUSES see TOYS

EFFIGIES
London - *London (inc Greater London)*
Westminster Abbey Museum
Newark-on-Trent - *Nottinghamshire*
Vina Cooke Museum of Dolls & Bygone Childhood

EGYPTOLOGY
Birmingham - *West Midlands*
Birmingham Museum and Art Gallery
Leicester - *Leicestershire*
The Leicestershire Museum and Art Gallery
London - *London (inc Greater London)*
Old Speech Room Gallery, Harrow School
Newcastle upon Tyne - *Tyne & Wear*
Hancock Museum
Oxford - *Oxfordshire*
The Ashmolean Museum of Art and Archaeology
Saffron Walden - *Essex*
Saffron Walden Museum
Warrington - *Cheshire*
Museum and Art Gallery

EMBROIDERY & NEEDLEWORK
Aberdeen - *Grampian*
Aberdeen Art Gallery
Ayr - *Strathclyde*
Maclaurin Gallery and Rozelle House
Bakewell - *Derbyshire*
The Old House Museum
Barnard Castle - *County Durham*
The Bowes Museum
Bath - *Avon*
American Museum in Britain
Batley - *West Yorkshire*
Bagshaw Museum
Berwick-upon-Tweed - *Northumberland*
Berwick Borough Museum & Art Gallery
Birstall - *West Yorkshire*
Oakwell Hall and Country Park
Brighton - *East Sussex*
Brighton Museum and Art Gallery
Budleigh Salterton - *Devon*
Fairlynch Arts Centre and Museum
Burnley - *Lancashire*
Towneley Hall Art Gallery and Museums and Museum of Local Crafts and Industries
Chertsey - *Surrey*
Chertsey Museum
Ditchling - *West Sussex*
Ditchling Museum
Dumfries - *Dumfries & Galloway*
Dumfries Museum
Edinburgh - *Lothian*
Lauriston Castle
Museum of Childhood
Glasgow - *Strathclyde*
Art Gallery and Museum
Guildford - *Surrey*
British Red Cross Museum and Archives
Guildford Museum
High Wycombe - *Buckinghamshire*
Wycombe Local History and Chair Museum
Honiton - *Devon*
Allhallows Museum
Hove - *East Sussex*
Hove Museum and Art Gallery
Ilkeston - *Derbyshire*
Erewash Museum
Ipswich - *Suffolk*
Christchurch Mansion and Wolsey Art Gallery
Jersey - *Channel Islands*
Jersey Museum
Kendal - *Cumbria*
Abbot Hall Art Gallery
Kilmarnock - *Strathclyde*
Dick Institute Museum and Art Gallery
King's Lynn - *Norfolk*
The Town House - Museum of Lynn Life
Leicester - *Leicestershire*
Museum of Costume
Lincoln - *Lincolnshire*
Usher Gallery
London - *London (inc Greater London)*
Bethnal Green Museum of Childhood
Forty Hall Museum
The Jewish Museum
William Morris Gallery
The Museum of London
National Army Museum
Osterley Park House
Macclesfield - *Cheshire*
West Park Museum
Manchester - *Greater Manchester*
The Whitworth Art Gallery
Monaghan - *Ireland*
Monaghan County Museum
Newport - *Gwent*
Newport Museum and Art Gallery
Norwich - *Norfolk*
Strangers' Hall
Nottingham - *Nottinghamshire*
The Lace Centre
Port Sunlight - *Merseyside*
Lady Lever Art Gallery
Portsmouth - *Hampshire*
City Museum
D-Day Museum and Overlord Embroidery
Ramsey - *Isle of Man*
The Grove Museum
Redditch - *Hereford & Worcester*
Forge Mill Needle Museum and Bordesley Abbey Visitor Centre
Richmond - *North Yorkshire*
The Richmondshire Museum
Royston - *Hertfordshire*
Museum
Saffron Walden - *Essex*
Saffron Walden Museum
St. Fagans - *South Glamorgan*
Welsh Folk Museum
St. Ives - *Cambridgeshire*
Norris Museum
Shaftesbury - *Dorset*
Local History Museum
Shrewsbury - *Shropshire*
The Radbrook Culinary Museum
Torquay - *Devon*
Torre Abbey Historic House and Gallery
Totnes - *Devon*
Totnes Costume Museum
Warwick - *Warwickshire*
St. John's House
Whitby - *North Yorkshire*
Whitby Museum

ENGINEERING see SCIENCE & INDUSTRY

ENTOMOLOGY see NATURAL HISTORY

ETHNOGRAPHY see ARCHAEOLOGY & PREHISTORY

FAMOUS PEOPLE
Bedford - *Bedfordshire*
The Bunyan Meeting Library and Museum
Boston - *Lincolnshire*
Guildhall Museum
Bridgwater - *Somerset*
Admiral Blake Museum
Canterbury - *Kent*
Canterbury Heritage Museum
Cheltenham - *Gloucestershire*
Holst Birthplace Museum
Derby - *Derbyshire*
Royal Crown Derby Museum
Edinburgh - *Lothian*
Scottish National Portrait Gallery
Forres - *Grampian*
Nelson Tower
Godalming - *Surrey*
Godalming Museum
Hastings - *East Sussex*
Museum of Local History
Hexham - *Northumberland*
Border History Museum
Jedburgh - *Borders*
Mary, Queen of Scots' House
Kirkcudbright - *Dumfries & Galloway*
Broughton House
London - *London (inc Greater London)*
Bromley Museum
Cuming Museum
Faraday's Laboratory and Museum
Alexander Fleming Laboratory Museum
Freud Museum
Hogarth's House
Museum of Garden History
Museum of Richmond
Museum of the Moving Image (MOMI)
Queen Elizabeth's Hunting Lodge
Theatre Museum
Macclesfield - *Cheshire*
Jodrell Bank Science Centre & Arboretum
Maryport - *Cumbria*
Maritime Museum
Merthyr Tydfil - *Mid Glamorgan*
Cyfarthfa Castle Museum and Art Gallery
Millport - *Strathclyde*
Robertson Museum and Aquarium
Milngavie - *Strathclyde*
Heatherbank Museum of Social Work
Olney - *Buckinghamshire*
Cowper and Newton Museum
Peterborough - *Cambridgeshire*
Railworld
Portsmouth - *Hampshire*
Charles Dickens' Birthplace Museum
HMS Victory
HMS Warrior 1860
Selborne - *Hampshire*
The Oates Museum and Gilbert White's House
Stafford - *Staffordshire*
Ancient High House
Izaak Walton's Cottage
Stoke-on-Trent - *Staffordshire*
The Sir Henry Doulton Gallery
Minton Museum
Wakefield - *West Yorkshire*
Wakefield Museum

FINE ARTS
Aberdeen - *Grampian*
Aberdeen Art Gallery
Aberystwyth - *Dyfed*
Aberystwyth Arts Centre Exhibitions
The Catherine Lewis Print Room
Arbroath - *Tayside*
Arbroath Art Gallery
Bangor - *Gwynedd*
Penrhyn Castle
Barnard Castle - *County Durham*
The Bowes Museum
Barnsley - *South Yorkshire*
Cooper Gallery
Bath - *Avon*
The Book Museum
Guildhall
Holburne Museum and Crafts Study Centre
The Museum of East Asian Art
No. 1 Royal Crescent
Victoria Art Gallery
Batley - *West Yorkshire*
Batley Art Gallery
Bedford - *Bedfordshire*
Bromham Mill
Cecil Higgins Art Gallery and Museum
Belfast - *Northern Ireland*
Ulster Museum
Berwick-upon-Tweed - *Northumberland*
Berwick Borough Museum & Art Gallery
Birkenhead - *Merseyside*
Williamson Art Gallery & Museum
Birmingham - *West Midlands*
The Barber Institute of Fine Arts
Birmingham Museum and Art Gallery
Birstall - *West Yorkshire*
Oakwell Hall and Country Park
Blackburn - *Lancashire*
Blackburn Museum and Art Gallery
Bolton - *Greater Manchester*
Bolton Museum and Art Gallery
Boston - *Lincolnshire*
Guildhall Museum
Bournemouth - *Dorset*
Russel-Cotes Art Gallery and Museum
Brechin - *Tayside*
Brechin Museum
Bridgwater - *Somerset*
Admiral Blake Museum
Brighton - *East Sussex*
Brighton Museum and Art Gallery
Preston Manor
The Royal Pavilion
Bristol - *Avon*
Bristol City Museum and Art Gallery
David Cross Gallery
Guild Gallery
Buckie - *Grampian*
Peter Anson Gallery
Burnley - *Lancashire*
Towneley Hall Art Gallery and Museums and Museum of Local Crafts and Industries
Cambridge - *Cambridgeshire*
Kettle's Yard
Canterbury - *Kent*
The Royal Museum & Art Gallery and Buffs Regimental Museum
Whitstable Museum & Gallery
Cardiff - *South Glamorgan*
Cardiff Castle
The National Museum of Wales
Chelmsford - *Essex*
Chelmsford and Essex Museum, Essex Regiment Museum
Cheltenham *Gloucestershire*
Cheltenham Art Gallery and Museum
Chertsey - *Surrey*
Chertsey Museum
Chester - *Cheshire*
Grosvenor Museum
Chichester - *West Sussex*
Pallant House
Chirk - *Clwyd*
Chirk Castle
Clonmel - *Ireland*
Tipperary (S.R.) CO. Museum
Cookham-on-Thames - *Berkshire*
Stanley Spencer Gallery
Coventry - *West Midlands*
Herbert Art Gallery and Museum
Cowes - *Isle of Wight*
Sir Max Aitken Museum
Darlington - *County Durham*
Darlington Art Collections
Derby - *Derbyshire*
Derby Museums & Art Gallery
Devizes - *Wiltshire*
Devizes Museum
Dewsbury - *West Yorkshire*
Dewsbury Museum
Ditchling - *West Sussex*
Ditchling Museum
Doncaster - *South Yorkshire*
Doncaster Museum and Art Gallery
Dublin - *Ireland*
The Hugh Lane Municipal Gallery of Modern Art
National Gallery of Ireland
National Museum of Ireland
Dumfries - *Dumfries & Galloway*
Dumfries Museum
Gracefield - The Arts Centre for South West Scotland
Dundee - *Tayside*
McManus Galleries
Dunfermline - *Fife*
Dunfermline District Museum and the Small Gallery
Pittencrieff House Museum
Durham - *County Durham*
Durham Light Infantry Museum and Durham Art Gallery
Eastbourne - *East Sussex*
Towner Art Gallery and Local Museum
Edinburgh - *Lothian*
City Art Centre
Huntly House
Lauriston Castle
National Gallery of Scotland
Russell Collection of Early Keyboard Instruments
Scottish National Gallery of Modern Art
Scottish National Portrait Gallery
Egham - *Surrey*
The Egham Museum
Enniskillen - *Northern Ireland*
Enniskillen Castle
Falmouth - *Cornwall*
Falmouth Art Gallery and Museum
Ford & Etal Estates - *Northumberland*
Lady Waterford Hall and Murals

Forfar - *Tayside*
Museum and Art Gallery
Glasgow - *Strathclyde*
Art Gallery and Museum
Burrell Collection
Hunterian Art Gallery
People's Palace
Pollok House
The St Mungo Museum of Religious Life and Art
Gloucester - *Gloucestershire*
City Museum and Art Gallery
Nature in Art
Goudhurst - *Kent*
Finchcocks, Living Museum of Music
Great Grimsby - *Humberside*
Back O' Doig's
Great Yarmouth - *Norfolk*
Exhibition Galleries
Guernsey - *Channel Islands*
Castle Cornet
Guernsey Museum & Art Gallery
Guildford - *Surrey*
Guildford House Gallery
Halifax - *West Yorkshire*
Bankfield Museum
The Piece Hall
Shibden Hall
Smith Art Gallery
Hastings - *East Sussex*
Museum and Art Gallery
Haverfordwest - *Dyfed*
Graham Sutherland Gallery
Hawick - *Borders*
Hawick Museum and the Scott Art Gallery
Hawkshead - *Cumbria*
Beatrix Potter Gallery
Hereford - *Hereford & Worcester*
Hereford City Museum and Art Gallery
High Wycombe - *Buckinghamshire*
Wycombe Local History and Chair Museum
Hove - *East Sussex*
Hove Museum and Art Gallery
Huddersfield - *West Yorkshire*
Huddersfield Art Gallery
Hull - *Humberside*
Ferens Art Gallery
Town Docks Museum
University of Hull Art Collection
Inverness - *Highlands*
Inverness Museum and Art Gallery
Ipswich - *Suffolk*
Christchurch Mansion and Wolsey Art Gallery
Isle of Anglesey - *Gwynedd*
Plas Newydd
Jersey - *Channel Islands*
Sir Francis Cook Gallery
Jersey Museum
Kendal - *Cumbria*
Abbot Hall Art Gallery
Kettering - *Northamptonshire*
Alfred East Gallery
Kilmarnock - *Strathclyde*
Dick Institute Museum and Art Gallery
Kirkcaldy - *Fife*
Kirkcaldy Museum and Art Gallery
Kirkcudbright - *Dumfries & Galloway*
Broughton House
Lancaster - *Lancashire*
City Museum
Leamington Spa - *Warwickshire*
Leamington Spa Art Gallery and Museum
Leicester - *Leicestershire*
The Leicestershire Museum and Art Gallery
Leigh - *Greater Manchester*
Turnpike Gallery
Letchworth - *Hertfordshire*
Letchworth Museum and Art Gallery
Lincoln - *Lincolnshire*
Usher Gallery
Littlehampton - *West Sussex*
Littlehampton Museum
Liverpool - *Merseyside*
Liverpool Museum
Sudley House
Tate Gallery Liverpool
University of Liverpool Art Gallery
Walker Art Gallery
Llanelli - *Dyfed*
Parc Howard Museum and Art Gallery
Public Library Gallery
London - *London (inc Greater London)*
Apsley House
Bankside Gallery
Barbican Art Gallery
Ben Uri Art Society and Gallery
Bethnal Green Museum of Childhood
British Dental Association Museum
Buckingham Palace, The Queen's Gallery
Cabaret Mechanical Theatre
Canadian High Commission
Carlyle's House
Chiswick House
City & Guilds of London Art School
Commonwealth Institute
Courtauld Institute Galleries
The Crafts Council
De Morgan Foundation - Old Battersea House
Dulwich Picture Gallery
The Fan Museum
Forty Hall Museum
Jill George Gallery Ltd
Goethe-Institut London
Greenwich Borough Museum
Martyn Gregory Gallery
Haringey Museum and Archives Service
Hayward Gallery, South Bank Centre
Hogarth's House
The Jewish Museum
Kenwood - The Iveagh Bequest
Kingston Museum
Leighton House Art Gallery and Museum
Linley Sambourne House
Little Holland House
Mall Galleries
Marble Hill House
Matthiesen Fine Art Ltd
Medici Galleries
William Morris Gallery
The Museum of London
Narwhal Inuit Art Gallery
National Army Museum
The National Gallery
National Maritime Museum
National Portrait Gallery
Old Speech Room Gallery, Harrow School
Orleans House Gallery
Osterley Park House
Percival David Foundation of Chinese Art
Ranger's House
Royal Academy of Arts
Royal College of Music Department of Portraits and Performance History
Royal Hospital Museum
Sir John Soane's Museum
South London Gallery
Spencer House
St. John's Gate, The Museum of the Order of St. John
Tate Gallery
Theatre Museum
Thomas Coram Foundation for Children
Victoria and Albert Museum
The Wallace Collection
Whitechapel Art Gallery
Whitehall
Woodlands Art Gallery
Zella Nine Gallery
Luton - *Bedfordshire*
Luton Museum and Art Gallery
Macclesfield - *Cheshire*
West Park Museum
Maidstone - *Kent*
Museum and Art Gallery
Manchester - *Greater Manchester*
The Whitworth Art Gallery
Mansfield - *Nottinghamshire*
Mansfield Museum and Art Gallery
Margate - *Kent*
Old Town Hall Museum
Maryport - *Cumbria*
Maritime Museum
Merthyr Tydfil - *Mid Glamorgan*
Cyfarthfa Castle Museum and Art Gallery
Middlesbrough - *Cleveland*
Cleveland Gallery
Middlesbrough Art Gallery
Milngavie - *Strathclyde*
Lillie Art Gallery
Milton Keynes - *Buckinghamshire*
Milton Keynes Exhibition Gallery
Monaghan - *Ireland*
Monaghan County Museum
Montrose - *Tayside*
William Lamb Memorial Studio
Montrose Museum
Newcastle-under-Lyme - *Staffordshire*
Borough Museum and Art Gallery
Newcastle upon Tyne - *Tyne & Wear*
Hatton Gallery
Newlyn - *Cornwall*
Newlyn Art Gallery
Newmarket - *Suffolk*
The National Horseracing Museum
Newport - *Gwent*
Newport Museum and Art Gallery
Newport - *Isle of Wight*
Carisbrooke Castle Museum
Northampton - *Northamptonshire*
Central Museum & Art Gallery
Norwich - *Norfolk*
Norwich Castle Museum
Sainsbury Centre for Visual Arts
Nottingham - *Nottinghamshire*
Djanogly Art Gallery
Nuneaton - *Warwickshire*
Nuneaton Museum and Art Gallery
Oldham - *Greater Manchester*
Oldham Art Gallery
Ombersley - *Hereford & Worcester*
Ombersley Gallery
Oxford - *Oxfordshire*
The Ashmolean Museum of Art and Archaeology
Christ Church Picture Gallery
Paisley - *Strathclyde*
Paisley Museum and Art Galleries
Peebles - *Borders*
Tweeddale Museum
Penarth - *South Glamorgan*
Turner House
Peterhead - *Grampian*
Arbuthnot Museum
Plymouth - *Devon*
City Museum and Art Gallery
Port Sunlight - *Merseyside*
Lady Lever Art Gallery
Portsmouth - *Hampshire*
City Museum
Preston - *Lancashire*
Harris Museum and Art Gallery
Ramsgate - *Kent*
Ramsgate Library Gallery
Rochdale - *Greater Manchester*
Rochdale Art Gallery
Rotherham - *South Yorkshire*
Art Gallery
Clifton Park Museum
Runcorn - *Cheshire*
Norton Priory Museum
St. Andrews - *Fife*
Crawford Arts Centre
St. Asaph - *Clwyd*
Bodelwyddan Castle
St. Ives - *Cornwall*
The Barbara Hepworth Museum
St. Ives Society of Artists
Tate Gallery St Ives
Salford - *Greater Manchester*
Lancashire Mining Museum, Salford
Museum and Art Gallery
Salisbury - *Wiltshire*
Salisbury and South Wiltshire Museum
Scarborough - *North Yorkshire*
Scarborough Art Gallery
Wood End Museum
Scunthorpe - *Humberside*
Museum and Art Gallery
Sheffield - *South Yorkshire*
City Museum and Mappin Art Gallery
Graves Art Gallery
Shrewsbury - *Shropshire*
The Shrewsbury Museums
Southampton - *Hampshire*
Southampton City Art Gallery
Southend-on-Sea - *Essex*
Beecroft Art Gallery
Southchurch Hall
Southport - *Merseyside*
Atkinson Art Gallery
Stafford - *Staffordshire*
Shire Hall Gallery and Craft Shop
Stalybridge - *Greater Manchester*
The Astley Cheetham Art Gallery
Stockport - *Greater Manchester*
Bramall Hall
Lyme Hall and Park
Stockport Art Gallery
Stockton-on-Tees - *Cleveland*
Billingham Art Gallery
Stoke-on-Trent - *Staffordshire*
Wedgwood Museum
Sudbury - *Suffolk*
Gainsborough's House
Swindon - *Wiltshire*
Lydiard Park
Swindon Museum and Art Gallery
Tenby - *Dyfed*
Tenby Museum and Art Gallery
Torquay - *Devon*
Torre Abbey Historic House and Gallery
Truro - *Cornwall*
Royal Cornwall Museum
Tunbridge Wells - *Kent*
Tunbridge Wells Museum and Art Gallery
Wakefield - *West Yorkshire*
Elizabethan Exhibition Gallery
Wakefield Art Gallery
Yorkshire Sculpture Park
Warrington - *Cheshire*
Museum and Art Gallery
Watford - *Hertfordshire*
Watford Museum
Welshpool - *Powys*
Powis Castle
Westcott - *Surrey*
The Westcott Gallery
Whitby - *North Yorkshire*
Whitby Museum
Whitehaven - *Cumbria*
Whitehaven Museum and Art Gallery
Winchester - *Hampshire*
Winchester City Museum
Worcester - *Hereford & Worcester*
City Museum and Art Gallery
Worksop - *Nottinghamshire*
The Harley Gallery
Worthing - *West Sussex*
Worthing Museum and Art Gallery
Yeovil - *Somerset*
The Museum of South Somerset
York - *North Yorkshire*
Fairfax House
York City Art Gallery

FOLK COLLECTIONS

Aberdeen - *Grampian*
James Dun's House
Provost Skene's House
Aberystwyth - *Dyfed*
Ceredigion Museum
Abingdon - *Oxfordshire*
Abingdon Museum
Aylesbury - *Buckinghamshire*
Buckinghamshire County Museum
Bakewell - *Derbyshire*
The Old House Museum
Banbury - *Oxfordshire*
Banbury Museum
Banchory - *Grampian*
Banchory Museum
Banff - *Grampian*
Banff Museum
Barton-on-Humber - *Humberside*
Baysgarth House Museum
Bath - *Avon*
American Museum in Britain
Mr Bowler's Business - Bath Industrial Heritage Centre
Batley - *West Yorkshire*
Bagshaw Museum
Bewdley - *Hereford & Worcester*
Bewdley Museum
Billericay - *Essex*
Barleylands Farm Museum
Blackburn - *Lancashire*
Blackburn Museum and Art Gallery
Lewis Textile Museum
Witton Country Park Visitor Centre
Blair Atholl - *Tayside*
Atholl Country Collection
Bolton - *Greater Manchester*
Hall i'th' Wood Museum
Bolventor - *Cornwall*
Potters Museum of Curiosity
Brecon - *Powys*
Brecknock Museum
Bridgnorth - *Shropshire*
Daniel's Mill
Brighton - *East Sussex*
Brighton Museum and Art Gallery
Cambridge - *Cambridgeshire*
Cambridge and County Folk Museum
Camelford - *Cornwall*
North Cornwall Museum and Gallery
Ceres - *Fife*
Fife Folk Museum
Chalfont St. Giles - *Buckinghamshire*
Chiltern Open Air Museum
Chelmsford - *Essex*
Chelmsford and Essex Museum, Essex Regiment Museum
Cheltenham - *Gloucestershire*
Cheltenham Art Gallery and Museum

Chertsey - *Surrey*
Chertsey Museum
Chichester - *West Sussex*
Chichester District Museum
Guildhall Museum
Coventry - *West Midlands*
Herbert Art Gallery and Museum
Darlington - *County Durham*
Darlington Museum
Dingwall - *Highlands*
Dingwall Museum
Doncaster - *South Yorkshire*
Museum of South Yorkshire Life, Cusworth Hall
Douglas - *Isle of Man*
Manx National Heritage
Dre-Fach Felindre - *Dyfed*
Museum of the Welsh Woollen Industry
Dumfries - *Dumfries & Galloway*
Dumfries Museum
Dunfermline - *Fife*
Dunfermline District Museum and the Small Gallery
Edinburgh - *Lothian*
Huntly House
Museum of Childhood
Queensferry Museum
Elgin - *Grampian*
Oldmills Working Mill & Visitor Centre
Enniskillen - *Northern Ireland*
Enniskillen Castle
Farnham - *Surrey*
Rural Life Centre
Faversham - *Kent*
Fleur De Lis Heritage Centre
Forfar - *Tayside*
The Angus Folk Museum
Fort William - *Highlands*
The West Highland Museum
Glasgow - *Strathclyde*
Art Gallery and Museum
People's Palace
Provand's Lordship
Rutherglen Museum
Glastonbury - *Somerset*
Somerset Rural Life Museum
Glencoe - *Highlands*
Glencoe and North Lorn Folk Museum
Gloucester - *Gloucestershire*
Folk Museum
Great Grimsby - *Humberside*
Back O' Doig's
Guildford - *Surrey*
Guildford Museum
Halifax - *West Yorkshire*
Shibden Hall
Harrogate - *North Yorkshire*
Nidderdale Museum
Harwich - *Essex*
Harwich Redoubt
Hastings - *East Sussex*
Museum and Art Gallery
Museum of Local History
Henfield - *West Sussex*
Henfield Museum
Heptonstall - *West Yorkshire*
Heptonstall
Hereford - *Hereford & Worcester*
Hereford City Museum and Art Gallery
Hertford - *Hertfordshire*
Hertford Museum
Hornsea - *Humberside*
Hornsea Museum
Hull - *Humberside*
Wilberforce House Museum
Huntly - *Grampian*
Brander Museum
Ilkeston - *Derbyshire*
Erewash Museum
Inverkeithing - *Fife*
Inverkeithing Museum
Inverness - *Highlands*
Inverness Museum and Art Gallery
Ipswich - *Suffolk*
Christchurch Mansion and Wolsey Art Gallery
Jedburgh - *Borders*
Castle Jail and Jedburgh Museum
Jersey - *Channel Islands*
Jersey Museum
La Hougue Bie Museum
Kelso - *Borders*
Kelso Museum & The Turret Gallery
Kilmarnock - *Strathclyde*
Dick Institute Museum and Art Gallery
Kingsbridge - *Devon*
Cookworthy Museum of Rural Life in South Devon
Lancaster - *Lancashire*
City Museum
Period Cottage
Leicester - *Leicestershire*
Newarke Houses Museum
Lincoln - *Lincolnshire*
Museum of Lincolnshire Life
Littlehampton - *West Sussex*
Littlehampton Museum
London - *London (inc Greater London)*
Church Farmhouse Museum
Church Farmhouse Museum
The Crafts Council
Cuming Museum
Horniman Museum and Gardens
The Museum of London
Vestry House Museum
Luton - *Bedfordshire*
Stockwood Craft Museum and Gardens Home of the Mossman Collection
Lyndhurst - *Hampshire*
New Forest Museum and Visitor Centre
Macclesfield - *Cheshire*
West Park Museum
March - *Cambridgeshire*
March and District Museum
Milton Keynes - *Buckinghamshire*
Milton Keynes Museum of Industry & Rural Life
Monaghan - *Ireland*
Monaghan County Museum
Morpeth - *Northumberland*
Morpeth Chantry Bagpipe Museum
Newark-on-Trent - *Nottinghamshire*
Vina Cooke Museum of Dolls & Bygone Childhood
Newent - *Gloucestershire*
The Shambles Museum
Newport - *Gwent*
Newport Museum and Art Gallery
Newport - *Isle of Wight*
Carisbrooke Castle Museum
National Wireless Museum
Northleach - *Gloucestershire*
Keith Harding's World of Mechanical Music
Oakham - *Leicestershire*
Rutland County Museum
Okehampton - *Devon*
Museum of Dartmoor Life
Omagh - *Northern Ireland*
Ulster-American Folk Park
Oxford - *Oxfordshire*
Museum of Oxford
The Pitt Rivers Museum
Paddock Wood - *Kent*
Whitbread Hop Farm
Penrith - *Cumbria*
Penrith Museum
Peterborough - *Cambridgeshire*
Sacrewell Farm and Country Centre
Peterhead - *Grampian*
Arbuthnot Museum
Pickering - *North Yorkshire*
Beck Isle Museum of Rural Life
Plymouth - *Devon*
City Museum and Art Gallery
Pocklington - *Humberside*
Penny Arcadia
Port St. Mary - *Isle of Man*
The Cregneash Village Folk Museum
Portsmouth - *Hampshire*
City Museum
Ramsey - *Isle of Man*
The Grove Museum
Reading - *Berkshire*
Museum of English Rural Life
Reeth - *North Yorkshire*
Swaledale Folk Museum
Rossendale - *Lancashire*
Rossendale Museum
St. Albans - *Hertfordshire*
The Museum of St. Albans
St. Fagans - *South Glamorgan*
Welsh Folk Museum
St. Ives - *Cambridgeshire*
Norris Museum
Salford - *Greater Manchester*
Museum and Art Gallery
Ordsall Hall Museum
Scarborough - *North Yorkshire*
Rotunda Museum
Scunthorpe - *Humberside*
Museum and Art Gallery
Shaftesbury - *Dorset*
Local History Museum
Sheffield - *South Yorkshire*
Abbeydale Industrial Hamlet
Kelham Island Museum
Shrewsbury - *Shropshire*
The Radbrook Culinary Museum
Shugborough - *Staffordshire*
Mansion House, Servants' Quarters, Museum of Staffordshire life and Park Farm.
Southend-on-Sea - *Essex*
Prittlewell Priory Museum
Spalding - *Lincolnshire*
Ayscoughfee Hall and Gardens
Stevenage - *Hertfordshire*
Stevenage Museum
Stoke-on-Trent - *Staffordshire*
Ford Green Hall
Stonehaven - *Grampian*
Tolbooth Museum
Stowmarket - *Suffolk*
Museum of East Anglian Life
Stratford-upon-Avon - *Warwickshire*
The Shakespeare Birthplace Trust's Properties
Swindon - *Wiltshire*
Swindon Museum and Art Gallery
Tewkesbury - *Gloucestershire*
The John Moore Countryside Museum
Thirsk - *North Yorkshire*
Thirsk Museum
Tomintoul - *Grampian*
Tomintoul Museum
Torquay - *Devon*
Torquay Museum
Tunbridge Wells - *Kent*
Tunbridge Wells Museum and Art Gallery
Usk - *Gwent*
Gwent Rural Life Museum
Warwick - *Warwickshire*
St. John's House
Welshpool - *Powys*
Powysland Museum & Montgomery Canal Centre
Wexford - *Ireland*
Irish Agricultural Museum
Whitby - *North Yorkshire*
Whitby Museum
Wimborne Minster - *Dorset*
Priest's House Museum of East Dorset Life and Garden
Woodstock - *Oxfordshire*
Oxfordshire County Museum
Worthing - *West Sussex*
Worthing Museum and Art Gallery
York - *North Yorkshire*
Ryedale Folk Museum
York Castle Museum

FOOD & DRINK PREPARATION

Aberdeen - *Grampian*
Provost Skene's House
Beetham - *Cumbria*
Heron Corn Mill and Museum of Papermaking
Birstall - *West Yorkshire*
Oakwell Hall and Country Park
Cheltenham - *Gloucestershire*
Holst Birthplace Museum
Cleckheaton - *West Yorkshire*
Red House
Donington-le-Heath - *Leicestershire*
The Manor House
Douglas - *Isle of Man*
Manx National Heritage
Dublin - *Ireland*
Guinness Museum
East Cowes - *Isle of Wight*
Osborne House
Edinburgh - *Lothian*
Lauriston Castle
Royal Museum of Scotland
Glasgow - *Strathclyde*
Burrell Collection
People's Palace
Provand's Lordship
Great Yarmouth - *Norfolk*
Elizabethan House Museum
Old Merchant's House, Row 111 Houses and Greyfriars' Cloisters
Hereford - *Hereford & Worcester*
Churchill Gardens Museum
The Old House
Hull - *Humberside*
Wilberforce House Museum
Ipswich - *Suffolk*
Christchurch Mansion and Wolsey Art Gallery
Kilmarnock - *Strathclyde*
Dick Institute Museum and Art Gallery
Lancaster - *Lancashire*
City Museum
Leeds - *West Yorkshire*
Tetley's Brewery Wharf
Leicester - *Leicestershire*
Newarke Houses Museum
London - *London (inc Greater London)*
Bethnal Green Museum of Childhood
Bramah Tea and Coffee Museum
Carlyle's House
Chiswick House
Church Farmhouse Museum
Courtauld Institute Galleries
Fenton House
Forty Hall Museum
Gunnersbury Park Museum
Harrow Museum and Heritage Centre
Kenwood - The Iveagh Bequest
Leighton House Art Gallery and Museum
Marble Hill House
Osterley Park House
Valence House Museum and Art Gallery
Wimbledon Windmill Museum
Matlock - *Derbyshire*
Caudwell's Mill
Ombersley - *Hereford & Worcester*
Ombersley Gallery
Peterborough - *Cambridgeshire*
Sacrewell Farm and Country Centre
St. Albans - *Hertfordshire*
The Verulamium Museum
Salford - *Greater Manchester*
Ordsall Hall Museum
Shrewsbury - *Shropshire*
The Radbrook Culinary Museum
Southend-on-Sea - *Essex*
Southchurch Hall
Stoke-on-Trent - *Staffordshire*
Ford Green Hall

FURNITURE & WOODWORK

Aberystwyth - *Dyfed*
Ceredigion Museum
Bangor - *Gwynedd*
Penrhyn Castle
Barnard Castle - *County Durham*
The Bowes Museum
Barnsley - *South Yorkshire*
Cannon Hall Museum
Bath - *Avon*
American Museum in Britain
Mr Bowler's Business - Bath Industrial Heritage Centre
The Museum of East Asian Art
No. 1 Royal Crescent
Bedford - *Bedfordshire*
Cecil Higgins Art Gallery and Museum
Belfast - *Northern Ireland*
Ulster Museum
Birstall - *West Yorkshire*
Oakwell Hall and Country Park
Blackburn - *Lancashire*
Blackburn Museum and Art Gallery
Lewis Textile Museum
Bolton - *Greater Manchester*
Bolton Museum and Art Gallery
Hall i'th' Wood Museum
Smithills Hall Museum
Brecon - *Powys*
Brecknock Museum
Bridgend - *Mid Glamorgan*
South Wales Police Museum
Brighton - *East Sussex*
Brighton Museum and Art Gallery
Preston Manor
The Royal Pavilion
Budleigh Salterton - *Devon*
Otterton Mill Centre and Working Museum
Cambridge - *Cambridgeshire*
Kettle's Yard
Cheltenham - *Gloucestershire*
Cheltenham Art Gallery and Museum
Holst Birthplace Museum
Chertsey - *Surrey*
Chertsey Museum
Chichester - *West Sussex*
Pallant House
Chirk - *Clwyd*
Chirk Castle
Derby - *Derbyshire*
Pickford's House Museum
Dumfries - *Dumfries & Galloway*
Dumfries Museum
Edinburgh - *Lothian*
Russell Collection of Early Keyboard Instruments
Glasgow - *Strathclyde*
Art Gallery and Museum
Guildford - *Surrey*
Guildford House Gallery

Halifax - *West Yorkshire*
Shibden Hall
Hereford - *Hereford & Worcester*
The Old House
High Wycombe - *Buckinghamshire*
Wycombe Local History and Chair Museum
Isle of Anglesey - *Gwynedd*
Plas Newydd
King's Lynn - *Norfolk*
The Town House - Museum of Lynn Life
Kirkcudbright - *Dumfries & Galloway*
Broughton House
Leicester - *Leicestershire*
Belgrave Hall and Gardens
Lincoln - *Lincolnshire*
Usher Gallery
Liverpool - *Merseyside*
Sudley House
London - *London (inc Greater London)*
British Dental Association Museum
Cabaret Mechanical Theatre
Geffrye Museum
Linley Sambourne House
Little Holland House
William Morris Gallery
Sir John Soane's Museum
Spencer House
The Wallace Collection
Norwich - *Norfolk*
Strangers' Hall
Port Sunlight - *Merseyside*
Lady Lever Art Gallery
Portsmouth - *Hampshire*
Charles Dickens' Birthplace Museum
St. Asaph - *Clwyd*
Bodelwyddan Castle
St. Fagans - *South Glamorgan*
Welsh Folk Museum
Salford - *Greater Manchester*
Ordsall Hall Museum
Sheffield - *South Yorkshire*
Bishops' House
Stockport - *Greater Manchester*
Bramall Hall
Lyme Hall and Park
Stoke-on-Trent - *Staffordshire*
Ford Green Hall
Stratford-upon-Avon - *Warwickshire*
The Shakespeare Birthplace Trust's Properties
Swindon - *Wiltshire*
Great Western Railway Museum
Tamworth - *Staffordshire*
Tamworth Castle and Museum Service
Torquay - *Devon*
Torre Abbey Historic House and Gallery
Tunbridge Wells - *Kent*
Tunbridge Wells Museum and Art Gallery
Warwick - *Warwickshire*
Warwickshire Museum
Welshpool - *Powys*
Powis Castle
Wexford - *Ireland*
Irish Agricultural Museum
Wrexham - *Clwyd*
Erddig

GARDEN CITIES

Letchworth - *Hertfordshire*
First Garden City Heritage Museum
London - *London (inc Greater London)*
Museum of Garden History

GARDENING

Bath - *Avon*
Georgian Garden
Bridlington - *Humberside*
Bridlington Art Gallery and Museum
Chichester - *West Sussex*
Pallant House
Coldstream - *Borders*
The Hirsel Homestead Museum
Farnham - *Surrey*
Rural Life Centre
Goudhurst - *Kent*
Finchcocks, Living Museum of Music
Gressenhall - *Norfolk*
Norfolk Rural Life Museum and Union Farm
Guernsey - *Channel Islands*
Castle Cornet
Harrogate - *North Yorkshire*
Harlow Carr Museum of Gardening
Kirkcudbright - *Dumfries & Galloway*
Broughton House
Lacock - *Wiltshire*
Lackham Country Attractions - Gardens, Museum and Rare Animal Breeds
Leicester - *Leicestershire*
Belgrave Hall and Gardens
London - *London (inc Greater London)*
Carshalton House
Geffrye Museum
Museum of Garden History
Luton - *Bedfordshire*
Stockwood Craft Museum and Gardens Home of the Mossman Collection
Macclesfield - *Cheshire*
Jodrell Bank Science Centre & Arboretum
Olney - *Buckinghamshire*
Cowper and Newton Museum
Runcorn - *Cheshire*
Norton Priory Museum
Selborne - *Hampshire*
The Oates Museum and Gilbert White's House
Wimborne Minster - *Dorset*
Priest's House Museum of East Dorset Life and Garden

GEOLOGY

Ashburton - *Devon*
Ashburton Museum
Axbridge - *Somerset*
Axbridge Museum: King John's Hunting Lodge
Ayr - *Strathclyde*
Maclaurin Gallery and Rozelle House
Banff - *Grampian*
Banff Museum
Barton-on-Humber - *Humberside*
Baysgarth House Museum
Bath - *Avon*
The Museum of East Asian Art
Bedford - *Bedfordshire*
Bedford Museum
Belfast - *Northern Ireland*
Ulster Museum
Blackburn - *Lancashire*
Blackburn Museum and Art Gallery
Bolton - *Greater Manchester*
Bolton Museum and Art Gallery
Brecon - *Powys*
Brecknock Museum
Brighton - *East Sussex*
The Booth Museum of Natural History
Bristol - *Avon*
Bristol City Museum and Art Gallery
Budleigh Salterton - *Devon*
Fairlynch Arts Centre and Museum
Camborne - *Cornwall*
Camborne School of Mines Geological Museum and Art Gallery
Cardiff - *South Glamorgan*
The National Museum of Wales
Chelmsford - *Essex*
Chelmsford and Essex Museum, Essex Regiment Museum
Chichester - *West Sussex*
Chichester District Museum
Guildhall Museum
Coventry - *West Midlands*
Herbert Art Gallery and Museum
Cromer - *Norfolk*
The Cromer Museum
Darlington - *County Durham*
Darlington Museum
Derby - *Derbyshire*
Derby Industrial Museum
Derby Museums & Art Gallery
Devizes - *Wiltshire*
Devizes Museum
Douglas - *Isle of Man*
Manx National Heritage
Dublin - *Ireland*
National Museum of Ireland
Folkestone - *Kent*
Folkestone Museum and Gallery
Forres - *Grampian*
Falconer Museum
Fort William - *Highlands*
The West Highland Museum
Gairloch - *Highlands*
Gairloch Heritage Museum
Glasgow - *Strathclyde*
Art Gallery and Museum
Hunterian Museum
Gloucester - *Gloucestershire*
City Museum and Art Gallery
Guernsey - *Channel Islands*
Guernsey Museum & Art Gallery
Guisborough - *Cleveland*
Margrove South Cleveland Heritage Centre
Hartland - *Devon*
Hartland Quay Museum
Hastings - *East Sussex*
Museum and Art Gallery
Hereford - *Hereford & Worcester*
Hereford City Museum and Art Gallery
Hertford - *Hertfordshire*
Hertford Museum
Horsham - *West Sussex*
Horsham Museum
Inverness - *Highlands*
Inverness Museum and Art Gallery
Ipswich - *Suffolk*
Ipswich Museum and High Street Exhibition Gallery
Jersey - *Channel Islands*
La Hougue Bie Museum
Kettering - *Northamptonshire*
Manor House Museum
King's Lynn - *Norfolk*
The Lynn Museum
Kirkcaldy - *Fife*
Kirkcaldy Museum and Art Gallery
Leeds - *West Yorkshire*
Leeds City Museum
Museum of Leeds Waterfront Heritage Trail
Leicester - *Leicestershire*
The Leicestershire Museum and Art Gallery
Letchworth - *Hertfordshire*
Letchworth Museum and Art Gallery
Llanberis - *Gwynedd*
Museum of the North
Welsh Slate Museum
London - *London (inc Greater London)*
Bexley Museum
British Museum
Erith Museum
Greenwich Borough Museum
Lyme Regis - *Dorset*
Dinosaurland
Malvern - *Hereford & Worcester*
Malvern Museum
Manchester - *Greater Manchester*
Manchester Museum
Millport - *Strathclyde*
Robertson Museum and Aquarium
Montrose - *Tayside*
Montrose Museum
Much Wenlock - *Shropshire*
Much Wenlock Museum
Newcastle upon Tyne - *Tyne & Wear*
Hancock Museum
Newport - *Gwent*
Newport Museum and Art Gallery
Norwich - *Norfolk*
Norwich Castle Museum
Oxford - *Oxfordshire*
Oxford University Museum
Peebles - *Borders*
Tweeddale Museum
Penrith - *Cumbria*
Penrith Museum
Peterhead - *Grampian*
Arbuthnot Museum
Portsmouth - *Hampshire*
City Museum
Reeth - *North Yorkshire*
Swaledale Folk Museum
Richmond - *North Yorkshire*
The Richmondshire Museum
Rossendale - *Lancashire*
Rossendale Museum
Rotherham - *South Yorkshire*
Clifton Park Museum
Saffron Walden - *Essex*
Saffron Walden Museum
Salford - *Greater Manchester*
Lancashire Mining Museum, Salford
Scarborough - *North Yorkshire*
Wood End Museum
Scunthorpe - *Humberside*
Museum and Art Gallery
Shrewsbury - *Shropshire*
The Shrewsbury Museums
Skipton - *North Yorkshire*
Craven Museum
Southend-on-Sea - *Essex*
Central Museum: Southend Museums Service
Stevenage - *Hertfordshire*
Stevenage Museum
Stockport - *Greater Manchester*
Stockport Museum
Swindon - *Wiltshire*
Swindon Museum and Art Gallery
Telford - *Shropshire*
Jackfield Tile Museum
Tar Tunnel
Tenby - *Dyfed*
Tenby Museum and Art Gallery
Tomintoul - *Grampian*
Tomintoul Museum
Torquay - *Devon*
Torquay Museum
Truro - *Cornwall*
Royal Cornwall Museum
Warrington - *Cheshire*
Museum and Art Gallery
Warwick - *Warwickshire*
Warwickshire Museum
Weybridge - *Surrey*
Elmbridge Museum
Whitby - *North Yorkshire*
Whitby Museum
Winchester - *Hampshire*
Winchester City Museum
Worcester - *Hereford & Worcester*
City Museum and Art Gallery
Worthing - *West Sussex*
Worthing Museum and Art Gallery
York - *North Yorkshire*
The Yorkshire Museum

GLASS see CERAMICS & GLASS

HISTORICAL & LITERARY ASSOCIATIONS

Aberdeen - *Grampian*
James Dun's House
Provost Skene's House
Anstruther - *Fife*
The Scottish Fisheries Museum
Banchory - *Grampian*
Banchory Museum
Banff - *Grampian*
Banff Museum
Bath - *Avon*
Mr Bowler's Business - Bath Industrial Heritage Centre
The Royal Photographic Society
Bedford - *Bedfordshire*
The Bunyan Meeting Library and Museum
Belfast - *Northern Ireland*
Ulster Museum
Berwick-upon-Tweed - *Northumberland*
Berwick Borough Museum & Art Gallery
Birstall - *West Yorkshire*
Oakwell Hall and Country Park
Bolton - *Greater Manchester*
Hall i'th' Wood Museum
Brighton - *East Sussex*
Preston Manor
Broadstairs - *Kent*
Dickens' House Museum
Budleigh Salterton - *Devon*
Fairlynch Arts Centre and Museum
Cambridge - *Cambridgeshire*
Kettle's Yard
Canterbury - *Kent*
Buffs Regimental Museum
Canterbury Heritage Museum
Chawton - *Hampshire*
Jane Austen's House
Chelmsford - *Essex*
Chelmsford and Essex Museum, Essex Regiment Museum
Chertsey - *Surrey*
Chertsey Museum
Cleckheaton - *West Yorkshire*
Red House
Clonmel - *Ireland*
Tipperary (S.R.) CO. Museum
Clydebank - *Strathclyde*
Clydebank District Museum
Colne - *Lancashire*
British in India Museum
Crich - *Derbyshire*
The National Tramway Museum
Dewsbury - *West Yorkshire*
Dewsbury Museum
Douglas - *Isle of Man*
Manx National Heritage
Dunwich - *Suffolk*
Dunwich Museum
Durham - *County Durham*
Durham Light Infantry Museum and Durham Art Gallery
East Cowes - *Isle of Wight*
Osborne House
Edinburgh - *Lothian*
Museum of Fire
The Writers' Museum

Gairloch - *Highlands*
Gairloch Heritage Museum
Glasgow - *Strathclyde*
People's Palace
Gloucester - *Gloucestershire*
Regiments of Gloucestershire Museum
Grasmere - *Cumbria*
Dove Cottage and Wordsworth Museum
Great Yarmouth - *Norfolk*
Old Merchant's House, Row 111 Houses and Greyfriars' Cloisters
The Tolhouse Museum and Brass Rubbing Centre
Guildford - *Surrey*
British Red Cross Museum and Archives
Harwich - *Essex*
Harwich Redoubt
Port of Harwich Maritime Museum
Hastings - *East Sussex*
Museum and Art Gallery
Horsham - *West Sussex*
Horsham Museum
Hull - *Humberside*
Wilberforce House Museum
Huntingdon - *Cambridgeshire*
The Cromwell Museum
Jedburgh - *Borders*
Castle Jail and Jedburgh Museum
Mary, Queen of Scots' House
Kirkcudbright - *Dumfries & Galloway*
Broughton House
Leicester - *Leicestershire*
Leicestershire Record Office
Lincoln - *Lincolnshire*
Lincoln Cathedral Library
Liverpool - *Merseyside*
The King's Regiment Collection
Llandrindod Wells - *Powys*
Llandrindod Wells Museum
London - *London (inc Greater London)*
Age Exchange Reminiscence Centre
Apsley House
Bankside Gallery
Bramah Tea and Coffee Museum
The British Library
British Museum
BT Museum - The Story of Telecommunications
Cabinet War Rooms
Carlyle's House
The Dickens House Museum
Freud Museum
Haringey Museum and Archives Service
HMS Belfast
Hogarth's House
Imperial War Museum
The Jewish Museum
Kingston Museum
The London Museum of Jewish Life
William Morris Gallery
Museum of the Royal Pharmaceutical Society of Great Britain
National Army Museum
National Maritime Museum
Pitshanger Manor Museum
Royal Academy of Arts
Royal College of Music Department of Portraits and Performance History
Royal Hospital Museum
Sherlock Holmes Museum
Theatre Museum
Thomas Coram Foundation for Children
Vestry House Museum
Loughborough - *Leicestershire*
The Bell Foundry Museum
Lyndhurst - *Hampshire*
New Forest Museum and Visitor Centre
Manchester - *Greater Manchester*
Greater Manchester Police Museum
March - *Cambridgeshire*
March and District Museum
Margate - *Kent*
Old Town Hall Museum
Middle Wallop - *Hampshire*
Museum of Army Flying
Newport - *Isle of Wight*
Carisbrooke Castle Museum
Newtown - *Powys*
W H Smith Museum
Norwich - *Norfolk*
St. Peter Hungate Church Museum
Nuneaton - *Warwickshire*
Nuneaton Museum and Art Gallery
Olney - *Buckinghamshire*
Cowper and Newton Museum
Oxford - *Oxfordshire*
Christ Church Library
Plymouth - *Devon*
City Museum and Art Gallery
Portsmouth - *Hampshire*
Charles Dickens' Birthplace Museum
Royal Marines Museum
The Royal Naval Museum, Portsmouth
Ramsgate - *Kent*
Ramsgate Museum
Ripon - *North Yorkshire*
Ripon Prison and Police Museum
Rossendale - *Lancashire*
Rossendale Museum
Rye - *East Sussex*
Rye Museum
St. Asaph - *Clwyd*
Bodelwyddan Castle
Stafford - *Staffordshire*
Ancient High House
Izaak Walton's Cottage
Stoke-on-Trent - *Staffordshire*
City Museum and Art Gallery
Ford Green Hall
Stratford-upon-Avon - *Warwickshire*
The Shakespeare Birthplace Trust's Properties
Sudbury - *Suffolk*
Gainsborough's House
Swindon - *Wiltshire*
Richard Jefferies Museum
Lydiard Park
Tenby - *Dyfed*
Tenby Museum and Art Gallery
Tewkesbury - *Gloucestershire*
The John Moore Countryside Museum
Torquay - *Devon*
Torquay Museum
Welshpool - *Powys*
Powysland Museum & Montgomery Canal Centre
Weybridge - *Surrey*
Brooklands Museum
Winchester - *Hampshire*
Winchester City Museum
Wrexham - *Clwyd*
Erddig
York - *North Yorkshire*
York Story
Yorkshire Air Museum

INDUSTRIAL HERITAGE

Alford - *Grampian*
Grampian Transport Museum
Barton-on-Humber - *Humberside*
Baysgarth House Museum
Bath - *Avon*
Mr Bowler's Business - Bath Industrial Heritage Centre
Beaulieu - *Hampshire*
Maritime Museum
National Motor Museum
Bedford - *Bedfordshire*
Bromham Mill
Beetham - *Cumbria*
Heron Corn Mill and Museum of Papermaking
Bickenhill - *West Midlands*
National Motorcycle Museum
Birmingham - *West Midlands*
Birmingham Museum and Art Gallery
Jewellery Quarter Discovery Centre
Bracknell - *Berkshire*
The Look Out Countryside and Heritage Centre
Bradford - *West Yorkshire*
Colour Museum
Bressingham - *Norfolk*
Bressingham Steam Museum and Gardens
Bridgnorth - *Shropshire*
Daniel's Mill
Bridgwater - *Somerset*
Westonzoyland Pumping Station
Bromsgrove - *Hereford & Worcester*
Avoncroft Museum of Historic Buildings
Camborne - *Cornwall*
Camborne School of Mines Geological Museum and Art Gallery
Chard - *Somerset*
Chard and District Museum
Coatbridge - *Strathclyde*
Summerlee Heritage Trust
Cromford - *Derbyshire*
Arkwright's Mill
Derby - *Derbyshire*
Royal Crown Derby Museum
Didcot - *Oxfordshire*
Didcot Railway Centre
Droitwich Spa - *Hereford & Worcester*
Droitwich Heritage Centre
Dudley - *West Midlands*
Black Country Museum
Edinburgh - *Lothian*
Scotch Whisky Heritage Centre
Egham - *Surrey*
The Egham Museum
Gillingham - *Kent*
Small Exhibits and Locos
Gloucester - *Gloucestershire*
National Waterways Museum
Grays - *Essex*
Thurrock Museum
Gressenhall - *Norfolk*
Norfolk Rural Life Museum and Union Farm
Halifax - *West Yorkshire*
Shibden Hall
Hatfield - *Hertfordshire*
Mill Green Museum and Mill
Hove - *East Sussex*
The British Engineerium
West Blatchington Windmill
Keighley - *West Yorkshire*
Vintage Railway Carriage Museum
Kidwelly - *Dyfed*
Kidwelly Industrial Museum
Lanark - *Strathclyde*
New Lanark World Heritage Village
Leeds - *West Yorkshire*
Tetley's Brewery Wharf
Leek - *Staffordshire*
Cheddleton Flint Mill
Leicester - *Leicestershire*
John Doran Gas Museum
Snibston Discovery Park
Leyland - *Lancashire*
The British Commercial Vehicle Museum
Lincoln - *Lincolnshire*
Museum of Lincolnshire Life
Llanidloes - *Powys*
Llanidloes Museum c/o Llandrindod Wells Museum
London - *London (inc Greater London)*
Bramah Tea and Coffee Museum
Markfield Beam Engine and Museum
North Woolwich Old Station Museum
Tower Bridge
The Wandle Industrial Museum
Wimbledon Windmill Museum
Manchester - *Greater Manchester*
The Museum of Science and Industry in Manchester
Market Harborough - *Leicestershire*
The Harborough Museum
Maryport - *Cumbria*
Maritime Museum
Merthyr Tydfil - *Mid Glamorgan*
Cyfarthfa Castle Museum and Art Gallery
Milton Keynes - *Buckinghamshire*
Milton Keynes Museum of Industry & Rural Life
Neath - *West Glamorgan*
Cefn Coed Colliery Museum
Okehampton - *Devon*
Museum of Dartmoor Life
Oldham - *Greater Manchester*
Saddleworth Museum & Art Gallery
Penzance - *Cornwall*
Trinity House National Lighthouse Centre
Pickering - *North Yorkshire*
North Yorkshire Moors Railway
Pocklington - *Humberside*
Penny Arcadia
Pontypool - *Gwent*
The Valley Inheritance
Porthmadog - *Gwynedd*
Festiniog Railway Museum
Portsmouth - *Hampshire*
HMS Victory
HMS Warrior 1860
Prestongrange - *Lothian*
Prestongrange Industrial Heritage Museum
Reading - *Berkshire*
National Dairy Museum
Redcar - *Cleveland*
Kirkleatham Old Hall Museum
Redditch - *Hereford & Worcester*
Forge Mill Needle Museum and Bordesley Abbey Visitor Centre
Rochdale - *Greater Manchester*
Rochdale Pioneers Co-operative Museum
St. Austell - *Cornwall*
Charlestown Shipwreck and Heritage Centre
Salford - *Greater Manchester*
Lancashire Mining Museum, Salford
Sheffield - *South Yorkshire*
Kelham Island Museum
Spalding - *Lincolnshire*
Ayscoughfee Hall and Gardens
Stockport - *Greater Manchester*
Stockport Museum
Stockton-on-Tees - *Cleveland*
Green Dragon Museum and Tourist Information Centre
Stoke-on-Trent - *Staffordshire*
The Sir Henry Doulton Gallery
Etruria Industrial Museum
Minton Museum
Wedgwood Museum
Telford - *Shropshire*
Blists Hill Open Air Museum
Museum of Iron and Furnace Site
Tar Tunnel
Truro - *Cornwall*
Royal Cornwall Museum
Wakefield - *West Yorkshire*
Yorkshire Mining Museum
Weston-super-Mare - *Avon*
The International Helicopter Museum
Wigan - *Greater Manchester*
Wigan Pier
Winchcombe - *Gloucestershire*
Gloucestershire Warwickshire Railway
Windermere - *Cumbria*
Windermere Steamboat Museum
Workington - *Cumbria*
Helena Thompson Museum
Wrexham - *Clwyd*
King's Mill Visitor Centre
Wrexham Maelor Heritage Centre
York - *North Yorkshire*
National Railway Museum

INTERIOR DECORATION

Barnard Castle - *County Durham*
The Bowes Museum
Barnsley - *South Yorkshire*
Cannon Hall Museum
Batley - *West Yorkshire*
Batley Art Gallery
Berwick-upon-Tweed - *Northumberland*
The Cell Block Museum
Boston - *Lincolnshire*
Guildhall Museum
Bournemouth - *Dorset*
Russel-Cotes Art Gallery and Museum
Bradford - *West Yorkshire*
Colour Museum
Brighton - *East Sussex*
Brighton Museum and Art Gallery
Preston Manor
The Royal Pavilion
Budleigh Salterton - *Devon*
Otterton Mill Centre and Working Museum
Cardiff - *South Glamorgan*
Cardiff Castle
Cheltenham - *Gloucestershire*
Pittville Pump Room Museum
Chichester - *West Sussex*
Pallant House
Douglas - *Isle of Man*
Manx National Heritage
East Cowes - *Isle of Wight*
Osborne House
Glasgow - *Strathclyde*
Burrell Collection
Great Yarmouth - *Norfolk*
Old Merchant's House, Row 111 Houses and Greyfriars' Cloisters
Guildford - *Surrey*
Guildford Museum
Hastings - *East Sussex*
Museum and Art Gallery
Hull - *Humberside*
Wilberforce House Museum
Inverness - *Highlands*
Inverness Museum and Art Gallery
London - *London (inc Greater London)*
Carshalton House
Linley Sambourne House
Little Holland House
Sir John Soane's Museum
Spencer House
Victoria and Albert Museum
Portsmouth - *Hampshire*
Charles Dickens' Birthplace Museum
St. Albans - *Hertfordshire*
The Verulamium Museum
Sheffield - *South Yorkshire*
Bishops' House
Wakefield - *West Yorkshire*
Wakefield Museum
York - *North Yorkshire*
Fairfax House

JEWELLERY & METALWORK

Aberdeen - *Grampian*
Aberdeen Art Gallery
Banff - *Grampian*
Banff Museum
Bath - *Avon*
American Museum in Britain
The Museum of East Asian Art
Bedford - *Bedfordshire*
Cecil Higgins Art Gallery and Museum
Birmingham - *West Midlands*
Jewellery Quarter Discovery Centre
Canterbury - *Kent*
The Roman Museum
Cheltenham - *Gloucestershire*
Cheltenham Art Gallery and Museum
Pittville Pump Room Museum
Chertsey - *Surrey*
Chertsey Museum
Chester - *Cheshire*
Grosvenor Museum
Edinburgh - *Lothian*
Huntly House
Lauriston Castle
Inverness - *Highlands*
Inverness Museum and Art Gallery
Ipswich - *Suffolk*
Christchurch Mansion and Wolsey Art Gallery
Lancaster - *Lancashire*
City Museum
Liverpool - *Merseyside*
University of Liverpool Art Gallery
London - *London (inc Greater London)*
Apsley House
British Museum
The Jewish Museum
Kenwood - The Iveagh Bequest
Osterley Park House
St. John's Gate, The Museum of the Order of St. John
Victoria and Albert Museum
The Wallace Collection
Woodlands Art Gallery
Middlesbrough - *Cleveland*
Cleveland Crafts Centre
Montrose - *Tayside*
Montrose Museum
Norwich - *Norfolk*
Sainsbury Centre for Visual Arts
Strangers' Hall
Oxford - *Oxfordshire*
The Ashmolean Museum of Art and Archaeology
The Pitt Rivers Museum
Plymouth - *Devon*
City Museum and Art Gallery
Portsmouth - *Hampshire*
City Museum
Reading - *Berkshire*
The Museum of Reading
Salisbury - *Wiltshire*
Salisbury and South Wiltshire Museum
Sheffield - *South Yorkshire*
Kelham Island Museum
Southend-on-Sea - *Essex*
Southchurch Hall
Stockport - *Greater Manchester*
Stockport Art Gallery
Telford - *Shropshire*
Museum of Iron and Furnace Site
Torquay - *Devon*
Torre Abbey Historic House and Gallery
Warwick - *Warwickshire*
Warwickshire Museum
York - *North Yorkshire*
Fairfax House

LEATHER

Bakewell - *Derbyshire*
The Old House Museum
Brighton - *East Sussex*
Preston Manor
Market Harborough - *Leicestershire*
The Harborough Museum
Northampton - *Northamptonshire*
Central Museum & Art Gallery
Norwich - *Norfolk*
Bridewell Museum of Local Industries

LOCAL HISTORY

Aberdeen - *Grampian*
James Dun's House
Provost Skene's House
Aberystwyth - *Dyfed*
Ceredigion Museum
Abingdon - *Oxfordshire*
Abingdon Museum
Acton Scott - *Shropshire*
Acton Scott Historic Working Farm
Alford - *Grampian*
Grampian Transport Museum
Alloa - *Central*
Alloa Museum and Gallery
Arbroath - *Tayside*
Arbroath Museum
Arundel - *West Sussex*
Museum and Heritage Centre
Ashburton - *Devon*
Ashburton Museum
Ashby-de-la-Zouch - *Leicestershire*
Ashby-De-La-Zouch Museum
Ashton-under-Lyne - *Greater Manchester*
Portland Basin Industrial Heritage Centre
Axbridge - *Somerset*
Axbridge Museum: King John's Hunting Lodge
Bakewell - *Derbyshire*
The Old House Museum
Banbury - *Oxfordshire*
Banbury Museum
Banchory - *Grampian*
Banchory Museum
Bangor - *Northern Ireland*
North Down Heritage Centre
Barnard Castle - *County Durham*
The Bowes Museum
Barrhead - *Strathclyde*
Barrhead Community Museum
Barton-on-Humber - *Humberside*
Baysgarth House Museum
Batley - *West Yorkshire*
Batley Art Gallery
Belfast - *Northern Ireland*
Ulster Museum
Berwick-upon-Tweed - *Northumberland*
Berwick Borough Museum & Art Gallery
The Cell Block Museum
Bettyhill - *Highlands*
Strathnaver Museum
Bewdley - *Hereford & Worcester*
Bewdley Museum
Billericay - *Essex*
Barleylands Farm Museum
Birkenhead - *Merseyside*
Birkenhead Priory
Shore Road Pumping Station
Williamson Art Gallery & Museum
Woodside Visitor Centre
Birmingham - *West Midlands*
Jewellery Quarter Discovery Centre
Birstall - *West Yorkshire*
Oakwell Hall and Country Park
Blackburn - *Lancashire*
Sunnyhurst Wood Visitor Centre
Witton Country Park Visitor Centre
Blair Atholl - *Tayside*
Atholl Country Collection
Bolton - *Greater Manchester*
Bolton Museum and Art Gallery
Boston - *Lincolnshire*
Guildhall Museum
Bracknell - *Berkshire*
The Look Out Countryside and Heritage Centre
Brechin - *Tayside*
Brechin Museum
Brecon - *Powys*
Brecknock Museum
Bridgend - *Mid Glamorgan*
South Wales Police Museum
Bridgwater - *Somerset*
Admiral Blake Museum
Westonzoyland Pumping Station
Bridlington - *Humberside*
Bridlington Art Gallery and Museum
Brighton - *East Sussex*
Brighton Museum and Art Gallery
Preston Manor
Brixham - *Devon*
Brixham Museum
Bromsgrove - *Hereford & Worcester*
Bromsgrove Museum
Budleigh Salterton - *Devon*
Fairlynch Arts Centre and Museum
Otterton Mill Centre and Working Museum
Caerleon - *Gwent*
Roman Legionary Museum
Caernarfon - *Gwynedd*
Segontium Roman Fort Museum
Camberley - *Surrey*
Surrey Heath Museum
Cambridge - *Cambridgeshire*
Cambridge and County Folk Museum
Canterbury - *Kent*
Canterbury Heritage Museum
The Roman Museum
The West Gate Museum
Whitstable Museum & Gallery
Cardiff - *South Glamorgan*
Cardiff Castle
Welsh Industrial and Maritime Museum
Castleford - *West Yorkshire*
Castleford Museum
Castletown - *Isle of Man*
The Nautical Museum
Caterham - *Surrey*
East Surrey Museum
Ceres - *Fife*
Fife Folk Museum
Chalfont St. Giles - *Buckinghamshire*
Chiltern Open Air Museum
Chard - *Somerset*
Chard and District Museum
Chelmsford - *Essex*
Chelmsford and Essex Museum, Essex Regiment Museum
Cheltenham - *Gloucestershire*
Cheltenham Art Gallery and Museum
Pittville Pump Room Museum
Chertsey - *Surrey*
Chertsey Museum
Chester - *Cheshire*
Chester Heritage Centre
King Charles Tower
Water Tower
Chesterfield - *Derbyshire*
Chesterfield Museum and Art Gallery
Revolution House
Chichester - *West Sussex*
Chichester District Museum
Guildhall Museum
Clonmel - *Ireland*
Tipperary (S.R.) CO. Museum
Clydebank - *Strathclyde*
Clydebank District Museum
Coatbridge - *Strathclyde*
Summerlee Heritage Trust
Coldstream - *Borders*
The Hirsel Homestead Museum
Coventry - *West Midlands*
Herbert Art Gallery and Museum
Lunt Roman Fort (Reconstruction)
Cowes - *Isle of Wight*
Sir Max Aitken Museum
Cromer - *Norfolk*
The Cromer Museum
Cromford - *Derbyshire*
Arkwright's Mill
Cumnock - *Strathclyde*
District History Centre and Baird Institute Museum
Darlington - *County Durham*
Darlington Art Collections
Darlington Museum
Derby - *Derbyshire*
Derby Industrial Museum
Derby Museums & Art Gallery
Dewsbury - *West Yorkshire*
Dewsbury Museum
Dingwall - *Highlands*
Dingwall Museum
Ditchling - *West Sussex*
Ditchling Museum
Doncaster - *South Yorkshire*
Doncaster Museum and Art Gallery
Museum of South Yorkshire Life, Cusworth Hall
Douglas - *Isle of Man*
Manx National Heritage
Downpatrick - *Northern Ireland*
Down County Museum
Droitwich Spa - *Hereford & Worcester*
Droitwich Heritage Centre
Dudley - *West Midlands*
Black Country Museum
Dufftown - *Grampian*
Dufftown Museum
Dunfermline - *Fife*
Dunfermline District Museum and the Small Gallery
Pittencrieff House Museum
Dunwich - *Suffolk*
Dunwich Museum
Durham - *County Durham*
Durham Light Infantry Museum and Durham Art Gallery
East Cowes - *Isle of Wight*
Osborne House
Eastbourne - *East Sussex*
Towner Art Gallery and Local Museum
Edinburgh - *Lothian*
Museum of Fire
Queensferry Museum
Egham - *Surrey*
The Egham Museum
Ely - *Cambridgeshire*
Ely Museum
Ewell - *Surrey*
Bourne Hall Museum
Fareham - *Hampshire*
Fort Nelson
Farnham - *Surrey*
Museum of Farnham
Faversham - *Kent*
Fleur De Lis Heritage Centre
Folkestone - *Kent*
Folkestone Museum and Gallery
Forfar - *Tayside*
Museum and Art Gallery
Forres - *Grampian*
Falconer Museum
Gairloch - *Highlands*
Gairloch Heritage Museum
Gillingham - *Kent*
Small Exhibits and Locos
Glasgow - *Strathclyde*
Haggs Castle
People's Palace
Provand's Lordship
Rutherglen Museum
Springburn Museum
The St Mungo Museum of Religious Life and Art
Glencoe - *Highlands*
Glencoe and North Lorn Folk Museum
Gloucester - *Gloucestershire*
Folk Museum
National Waterways Museum
Regiments of Gloucestershire Museum
Godalming - *Surrey*
Godalming Museum
Grasmere - *Cumbria*
Dove Cottage and Wordsworth Museum
Grays - *Essex*
Thurrock Museum
Great Grimsby - *Humberside*
Back O' Doig's
Great Yarmouth - *Norfolk*
Maritime Museum for East Anglia
Old Merchant's House, Row 111 Houses and Greyfriars' Cloisters
The Tolhouse Museum and Brass Rubbing Centre
Gressenhall - *Norfolk*
Norfolk Rural Life Museum and Union Farm
Guernsey - *Channel Islands*
Castle Cornet
German Occupation Museum
Guernsey Museum & Art Gallery
Guildford - *Surrey*
Guildford Museum
Guisborough - *Cleveland*
Margrove South Cleveland Heritage Centre
Halifax - *West Yorkshire*
Bankfield Museum
Hartland - *Devon*
Hartland Quay Museum
Harwich - *Essex*
Harwich Redoubt
Port of Harwich Maritime Museum
Hastings - *East Sussex*
Museum and Art Gallery
Museum of Local History
Hatfield - *Hertfordshire*
Mill Green Museum and Mill
Hawick - *Borders*
Hawick Museum and the Scott Art Gallery
Henfield - *West Sussex*
Henfield Museum
Hertford - *Hertfordshire*
Hertford Museum
Hexham - *Northumberland*
Border History Museum
High Wycombe - *Buckinghamshire*
Wycombe Local History and Chair Museum
Hitchin - *Hertfordshire*
Hitchin Museum and Art Gallery
Holmfirth - *West Yorkshire*
Holmfirth Postcard Museum
Honiton - *Devon*
Allhallows Museum
Hornsea - *Humberside*
Hornsea Museum
Hove - *East Sussex*
West Blatchington Windmill
Hull - *Humberside*
Ferens Art Gallery
Old Grammar School

Streetlife - Hull Museum of Transport
Town Docks Museum
Wilberforce House Museum
Huntly - *Grampian*
Brander Museum
Ilkeston - *Derbyshire*
Erewash Museum
Inverkeithing - *Fife*
Inverkeithing Museum
Inverness - *Highlands*
Inverness Museum and Art Gallery
Inverurie - *Grampian*
Carnegie Museum
Ipswich - *Suffolk*
Ipswich Museum and High Street Exhibition Gallery
Irvine - *Strathclyde*
Scottish Maritime Museum
Jarrow - *Tyne & Wear*
Bedes World
Jedburgh - *Borders*
Castle Jail and Jedburgh Museum
Mary, Queen of Scots' House
Kelso - *Borders*
Kelso Museum & The Turret Gallery
Kendal - *Cumbria*
Abbot Hall Art Gallery
Kettering - *Northamptonshire*
Manor House Museum
Kidwelly - *Dyfed*
Kidwelly Industrial Museum
Kingsbridge - *Devon*
Cookworthy Museum of Rural Life in South Devon
Kirkcaldy - *Fife*
Kirkcaldy Museum and Art Gallery
McDouall Stuart Museum
Kirkintilloch - *Strathclyde*
The Auld Kirk Museum
The Barony Chambers Museum
Lancaster - *Lancashire*
City Museum
Leamington Spa - *Warwickshire*
Leamington Spa Art Gallery and Museum
Leeds - *West Yorkshire*
Museum of Leeds Waterfront Heritage Trail
Leek - *Staffordshire*
Brindley Water Mill and Museum
Cheddleton Flint Mill
Leicester - *Leicestershire*
John Doran Gas Museum
Leicestershire Record Office
Newarke Houses Museum
Snibston Discovery Park
Letchworth - *Hertfordshire*
First Garden City Heritage Museum
Leyland - *Lancashire*
South Ribble Museum and Exhibition Centre
Lincoln - *Lincolnshire*
Museum of Lincolnshire Life
Littlehampton - *West Sussex*
Littlehampton Museum
Llanberis - *Gwynedd*
Museum of the North
Welsh Slate Museum
Llanelli - *Dyfed*
Parc Howard Museum and Art Gallery
Lochwinnoch - *Strathclyde*
Lochwinnoch Community Museum
London - *London (inc Greater London)*
Age Exchange Reminiscence Centre
Bethnal Green Museum of Childhood
Bromley Museum
Carew Manor and Dovecote
Carshalton House
Church Farmhouse Museum
Cuming Museum
Erith Museum
Forty Hall Museum
Geffrye Museum
Greenwich Borough Museum
Gunnersbury Park Museum
Hampstead Museum
Haringey Museum and Archives Service
Harrow Museum and Heritage Centre
The Jewish Museum
Kingston Museum
Linley Sambourne House
Livesey Museum
The London Museum of Jewish Life
Markfield Beam Engine and Museum
Museum of Garden History
Museum of Richmond
Orleans House Gallery
Queen Elizabeth's Hunting Lodge
South London Gallery
Thames Barrier Visitors' Centre
Valence House Museum and Art Gallery
Vestry House Museum
The Wandle Industrial Museum
Wandsworth Museum
Whitehall
The Wimbledon Lawn Tennis Museum
Wimbledon Society's Museum
Loughborough - *Leicestershire*
The Bell Foundry Museum
Luton - *Bedfordshire*
Luton Museum and Art Gallery
Lyndhurst - *Hampshire*
New Forest Museum and Visitor Centre
Macclesfield - *Cheshire*
Paradise Mill
West Park Museum
Maidstone - *Kent*
Museum and Art Gallery
Malvern - *Hereford & Worcester*
Malvern Museum
Manchester - *Greater Manchester*
Greater Manchester Police Museum
Manchester Jewish Museum
Museum of Transport
Pump House People's History Museum
Mansfield - *Nottinghamshire*
Mansfield Museum and Art Gallery
March - *Cambridgeshire*
March and District Museum
Margate - *Kent*
Old Town Hall Museum
Market Harborough - *Leicestershire*
The Harborough Museum
Maryport - *Cumbria*
Maritime Museum
Melton Mowbray - *Leicestershire*
Melton Carnegie Museum
Merthyr Tydfil - *Mid Glamorgan*
Cyfarthfa Castle Museum and Art Gallery
Middlesbrough - *Cleveland*
Dorman Museum
Middle Wallop - *Hampshire*
Museum of Army Flying
Monaghan - *Ireland*
Monaghan County Museum
Montrose - *Tayside*
Montrose Museum
Morpeth - *Northumberland*
Morpeth Chantry Bagpipe Museum
Morwellham Quay - *Devon*
Morwellham Quay Museum and 19th Century Port and Copper Mine
Neath - *West Glamorgan*
Cefn Coed Colliery Museum
Newcastle-under-Lyme - *Staffordshire*
Borough Museum and Art Gallery
Newport - *Gwent*
Newport Museum and Art Gallery
Newport - *Isle of Wight*
Carisbrooke Castle Museum
North Berwick - *Lothian*
North Berwick Museum
Northampton - *Northamptonshire*
Central Museum & Art Gallery
Norwich - *Norfolk*
Bridewell Museum of Local Industries
St. Peter Hungate Church Museum
Nuneaton - *Warwickshire*
Nuneaton Museum and Art Gallery
Oakham - *Leicestershire*
Rutland County Museum
Okehampton - *Devon*
Museum of Dartmoor Life
Oldham - *Greater Manchester*
Saddleworth Museum & Art Gallery
Olney - *Buckinghamshire*
Cowper and Newton Museum
Omagh - *Northern Ireland*
Ulster-American Folk Park
Oxford - *Oxfordshire*
Museum of Oxford
The Oxford Story
Paddock Wood - *Kent*
Whitbread Hop Farm
Paisley - *Strathclyde*
Paisley Museum and Art Galleries
Peebles - *Borders*
Tweeddale Museum
Penrith - *Cumbria*
Penrith Museum
Peterborough - *Cambridgeshire*
Railworld
Sacrewell Farm and Country Centre
Peterhead - *Grampian*
Arbuthnot Museum
Pickering - *North Yorkshire*
Beck Isle Museum of Rural Life
Plymouth - *Devon*
City Museum and Art Gallery
Merchant's House
Pontefract - *West Yorkshire*
Pontefract Castle
Pontefract Museum
Pontypool - *Gwent*
The Valley Inheritance
Poole - *Dorset*
Scaplen's Court
Waterfront Museum, Poole Quay
Port St. Mary - *Isle of Man*
The Cregneash Village Folk Museum
Porthmadog - *Gwynedd*
Festiniog Railway Museum
Portsmouth - *Hampshire*
City Museum
Prescot - *Merseyside*
Prescot Museum of Clock and Watch-Making
Prestongrange - *Lothian*
Prestongrange Industrial Heritage Museum
Ramsgate - *Kent*
Maritime Museum Complex
Ramsgate Museum
Reading - *Berkshire*
Blake's Lock Museum
The Museum of Reading
Redcar - *Cleveland*
Kirkleatham Old Hall Museum
Redditch - *Hereford & Worcester*
Forge Mill Needle Museum and Bordesley Abbey Visitor Centre
Reeth - *North Yorkshire*
Swaledale Folk Museum
Retford - *Nottinghamshire*
The Bassetlaw Museum
Richmond - *North Yorkshire*
The Richmondshire Museum
Ripon - *North Yorkshire*
Ripon Prison and Police Museum
Rochdale - *Greater Manchester*
Rochdale Pioneers Co-operative Museum
Rochester - *Kent*
Guildhall Museum
Rosemarkie - *Highlands*
Groam House Museum
Rossendale - *Lancashire*
Rossendale Museum
Rotherham - *South Yorkshire*
Clifton Park Museum
Royston - *Hertfordshire*
Museum
Rye - *East Sussex*
Rye Museum
St. Albans - *Hertfordshire*
Clocktower
The Museum of St. Albans
St. Austell - *Cornwall*
Charlestown Shipwreck and Heritage Centre
St. Ives - *Cambridgeshire*
Norris Museum
Salford - *Greater Manchester*
Lancashire Mining Museum, Salford
Museum and Art Gallery
Ordsall Hall Museum
Viewpoint Photographic Gallery
Salisbury - *Wiltshire*
Salisbury and South Wiltshire Museum
Scarborough - *North Yorkshire*
Rotunda Museum
Scunthorpe - *Humberside*
Museum and Art Gallery
Shaftesbury - *Dorset*
Local History Museum
Sheffield - *South Yorkshire*
Abbeydale Industrial Hamlet
Bishops' House
Kelham Island Museum
Shipley - *West Yorkshire*
Furever Feline
Shrewsbury - *Shropshire*
The Radbrook Culinary Museum
Shugborough - *Staffordshire*
Mansion House, Servants' Quarters, Museum of Staffordshire life and Park Farm.
Slough - *Berkshire*
Slough Museum
Southend-on-Sea - *Essex*
Beecroft Art Gallery
Prittlewell Priory Museum
Southchurch Hall
Southport - *Merseyside*
Botanic Gardens Museum
Spalding - *Lincolnshire*
Ayscoughfee Hall and Gardens
Spey Bay - *Grampian*
Tugnet Ice House
Stafford - *Staffordshire*
Ancient High House
Shire Hall Gallery and Craft Shop
Stafford Castle and Visitor Centre
Izaak Walton's Cottage
Stevenage - *Hertfordshire*
Stevenage Museum
Steyning - *West Sussex*
Steyning Museum
Stockport - *Greater Manchester*
Stockport Museum
Stockton-on-Tees - *Cleveland*
Billingham Art Gallery
Green Dragon Museum and Tourist Information Centre
Stoke-on-Trent - *Staffordshire*
City Museum and Art Gallery
The Sir Henry Doulton Gallery
Etruria Industrial Museum
Ford Green Hall
Minton Museum
Stonehaven - *Grampian*
Tolbooth Museum
Stowmarket - *Suffolk*
Museum of East Anglian Life
Strathaven - *Strathclyde*
John Hastie Museum
Stromness - *Orkney*
Stromness Museum
Swindon - *Wiltshire*
Great Western Railway Museum
Richard Jefferies Museum
Lydiard Park
Railway Village Museum
Swindon Museum and Art Gallery
Tamworth - *Staffordshire*
Tamworth Castle and Museum Service
Taunton - *Somerset*
Somerset County Museum
Tenby - *Dyfed*
Tenby Museum and Art Gallery
Tenterden - *Kent*
Tenterden and District Museum
Tewkesbury - *Gloucestershire*
The Museum
Thetford - *Norfolk*
The Ancient House Museum
Thirsk - *North Yorkshire*
Thirsk Museum
Tomintoul - *Grampian*
Tomintoul Museum
Torquay - *Devon*
Torre Abbey Historic House and Gallery
Totnes - *Devon*
Totnes (Elizabethan) Museum
Tunbridge Wells - *Kent*
Tunbridge Wells Museum and Art Gallery
Usk - *Gwent*
Gwent Rural Life Museum
Wakefield - *West Yorkshire*
Elizabethan Exhibition Gallery
Wakefield Museum
Walsingham - *Norfolk*
Shirehall Museum
Waltham Abbey - *Essex*
Epping Forest District Museum
Wantage - *Oxfordshire*
Vale and Downland Museum Centre
Warrington - *Cheshire*
Museum and Art Gallery
Warwick - *Warwickshire*
Warwickshire Museum
Watford - *Hertfordshire*
Watford Museum
Welshpool - *Powys*
Powysland Museum & Montgomery Canal Centre
Weston-super-Mare - *Avon*
Weston-super-Mare Heritage Centre
Weybridge - *Surrey*
Brooklands Museum
Elmbridge Museum
Whitehaven - *Cumbria*
Whitehaven Museum and Art Gallery
Wigan - *Greater Manchester*
Wigan Pier
Wimborne Minster - *Dorset*
Priest's House Museum of East Dorset Life and Garden
Winchcombe - *Gloucestershire*
Gloucestershire Warwickshire Railway
Winchester - *Hampshire*
Winchester City Museum

Windermere - *Cumbria*
Windermere Steamboat Museum
Witney - *Oxfordshire*
Combe Mill Beam Engine and Working Museum
Woodbridge - *Suffolk*
Suffolk Horse Museum
Woodstock - *Oxfordshire*
Oxfordshire County Museum
Workington - *Cumbria*
Helena Thompson Museum
Worksop - *Nottinghamshire*
Worksop Museum
Wrexham - *Clwyd*
Wrexham Maelor Heritage Centre
Yeovil - *Somerset*
The Museum of South Somerset
York - *North Yorkshire*
The ARC
Jorvik Viking Centre

MEDICAL

Edinburgh - *Lothian*
Museum of Childhood
Royal Museum of Scotland
Guildford - *Surrey*
British Red Cross Museum and Archives
Hitchin - *Hertfordshire*
Hitchin Museum and Art Gallery
Kingsbridge - *Devon*
Cookworthy Museum of Rural Life in South Devon
London - *London (inc Greater London)*
British Dental Association Museum
Alexander Fleming Laboratory Museum
Freud Museum
Museum of the Royal Pharmaceutical Society of Great Britain
Royal Hospital Museum
Science Museum
St. John's Gate, The Museum of the Order of St. John
Middlesbrough - *Cleveland*
Dorman Museum
Montrose - *Tayside*
Sunnyside Museum
Shugborough - *Staffordshire*
Mansion House, Servants' Quarters, Museum of Staffordshire life and Park Farm.
Stratford-upon-Avon - *Warwickshire*
The Shakespeare Birthplace Trust's Properties
Thirsk - *North Yorkshire*
Thirsk Museum
Winchester - *Hampshire*
Winchester City Museum

METALWORK see JEWELLERY & METALWORK

MILITARY

Aberdeen - *Grampian*
James Dun's House
Aldershot - *Hampshire*
Army Physical Training Corps Museum
Ashton-under-Lyne - *Greater Manchester*
The Museum of the Manchesters: A Social and Regimental History
Barnsley - *South Yorkshire*
Cannon Hall Museum
Barton-on-Humber - *Humberside*
Baysgarth House Museum
Berwick-upon-Tweed - *Northumberland*
Berwick Borough Museum & Art Gallery
The Cell Block Museum
Birkenhead - *Merseyside*
Historic Warships
Bolton - *Greater Manchester*
Bolton Museum and Art Gallery
Bovington - *Dorset*
The Tank Museum
Brechin - *Tayside*
Brechin Museum
Bury St. Edmunds - *Suffolk*
The Suffolk Regiment
Caernarfon - *Gwynedd*
Segontium Roman Fort Museum
Canterbury - *Kent*
Buffs Regimental Museum
The Roman Museum
The Royal Museum & Art Gallery and Buffs Regimental Museum
The West Gate Museum
Cardiff - *South Glamorgan*
The National Museum of Wales
Carlisle - *Cumbria*
The Border Regiment & King's Own Royal Border Regiment
Chatham - *Kent*
Fort Amherst
Chelmsford - *Essex*
Chelmsford and Essex Museum, Essex Regiment Museum
Chichester - *West Sussex*
Royal Military Police Museum
Colne - *Lancashire*
British in India Museum
Coventry - *West Midlands*
Lunt Roman Fort (Reconstruction)
Derby - *Derbyshire*
Derby Industrial Museum
Dingwall - *Highlands*
Dingwall Museum
Doncaster - *South Yorkshire*
Doncaster Museum and Art Gallery
The King's Own Yorkshire Light Infantry
Douglas - *Isle of Man*
Manx National Heritage
Durham - *County Durham*
Durham Light Infantry Museum and Durham Art Gallery
Edinburgh - *Lothian*
Huntly House
Scottish United Services Museum
Enniskillen - *Northern Ireland*
Enniskillen Castle
Epping - *Essex*
The Squadron
Fareham - *Hampshire*
Fort Nelson
Gloucester - *Gloucestershire*
Regiments of Gloucestershire Museum
Guernsey - *Channel Islands*
Castle Cornet
German Occupation Museum
Guildford - *Surrey*
British Red Cross Museum and Archives
Guildford Museum
Halifax - *West Yorkshire*
Bankfield Museum
Harwich - *Essex*
Harwich Redoubt
Port of Harwich Maritime Museum
Hitchin - *Hertfordshire*
Hitchin Museum and Art Gallery
Hull - *Humberside*
Wilberforce House Museum
Inverkeithing - *Fife*
Inverkeithing Museum
Isle of Anglesey - *Gwynedd*
Plas Newydd
Jersey - *Channel Islands*
Elizabeth Castle
La Hougue Bie Museum
Mont Orgueil Castle
Lancaster - *Lancashire*
The King's Own Royal Regiment Museum
Leicester - *Leicestershire*
Leicestershire Record Office
Museum of the Royal Leicestershire Regiment
Liverpool - *Merseyside*
The King's Regiment Collection
London - *London (inc Greater London)*
Apsley House
British Museum
Cabinet War Rooms
HMS Belfast
HMS Belfast
Imperial War Museum
National Army Museum
National Maritime Museum
Royal Air Force Museum
Luton - *Bedfordshire*
Luton Museum and Art Gallery
Macclesfield - *Cheshire*
West Park Museum
Maidstone - *Kent*
Museum and Art Gallery
March - *Cambridgeshire*
March and District Museum
Margate - *Kent*
Old Town Hall Museum
Middle Wallop - *Hampshire*
Museum of Army Flying
Newcastle-under-Lyme - *Staffordshire*
Borough Museum and Art Gallery
Newport - *Gwent*
Newport Museum and Art Gallery
Newport - *Isle of Wight*
National Wireless Museum
Norwich - *Norfolk*
Royal Norfolk Regimental Museum
Oakham - *Leicestershire*
Rutland County Museum
Portsmouth - *Hampshire*
City Museum
D-Day Museum and Overlord Embroidery
Mary Rose Ship Hall and Exhibition
The Royal Naval Museum, Portsmouth
Southsea Castle and Museum
Richmond - *North Yorkshire*
The Green Howards Museum
Ross-on-Wye - *Hereford & Worcester*
The Button Museum
Rossendale - *Lancashire*
Rossendale Museum
Rotherham - *South Yorkshire*
The York and Lancaster Regiment Museum
Rye - *East Sussex*
Rye Museum
St. Austell - *Cornwall*
Charlestown Shipwreck and Heritage Centre
St. Ives - *Cambridgeshire*
Norris Museum
Shifnal - *Shropshire*
The Aerospace Museum
Stromness - *Orkney*
Stromness Museum
Tangmere - *West Sussex*
Tangmere Military Aviation Museum Trust
Taunton - *Somerset*
Somerset County Museum
Warwick - *Warwickshire*
St. John's House
Watford - *Hertfordshire*
Watford Museum
Weston-super-Mare - *Avon*
The International Helicopter Museum
Whitby - *North Yorkshire*
Whitby Museum
Worcester - *Hereford & Worcester*
City Museum and Art Gallery
Yeovilton - *Somerset*
Fleet Air Arm Museum and Concorde Exhibition
York - *North Yorkshire*
Yorkshire Air Museum

MINERALS see GEOLOGY

MINING see SCIENCE & INDUSTRY

MUSIC & MUSICAL INSTRUMENTS

Banchory - *Grampian*
Banchory Museum
Barnard Castle - *County Durham*
The Bowes Museum
Brighton - *East Sussex*
Brighton Museum and Art Gallery
Cheltenham - *Gloucestershire*
Cheltenham Art Gallery and Museum
Holst Birthplace Museum
East Cowes - *Isle of Wight*
Osborne House
Edinburgh - *Lothian*
Russell Collection of Early Keyboard Instruments
Glasgow - *Strathclyde*
Art Gallery and Museum
Goudhurst - *Kent*
Finchcocks, Living Museum of Music
Guildford - *Surrey*
Guildford Museum
Hereford - *Hereford & Worcester*
Hereford City Museum and Art Gallery
Inverness - *Highlands*
Inverness Museum and Art Gallery
Ipswich - *Suffolk*
Christchurch Mansion and Wolsey Art Gallery
Jersey - *Channel Islands*
Jersey Museum
Kilmarnock - *Strathclyde*
Dean Castle
Leicester - *Leicestershire*
Newarke Houses Museum
London - *London (inc Greater London)*
British Museum
Commonwealth Institute
Fenton House
Horniman Museum and Gardens
The Jewish Museum
The Musical Museum
Ranger's House
Royal College of Music Department of Portraits and Performance History
Royal College of Music Museum of Instruments
Thomas Coram Foundation for Children
Victoria and Albert Museum
Loughborough - *Leicestershire*
The Bell Foundry Museum
Manchester - *Greater Manchester*
Pump House People's History Museum
Merthyr Tydfil - *Mid Glamorgan*
Cyfarthfa Castle Museum and Art Gallery
Morpeth - *Northumberland*
Morpeth Chantry Bagpipe Museum
Newport - *Isle of Wight*
Carisbrooke Castle Museum
Northleach - *Gloucestershire*
Keith Harding's World of Mechanical Music
Norwich - *Norfolk*
St. Peter Hungate Church Museum
Strangers' Hall
Oxford - *Oxfordshire*
The Ashmolean Museum of Art and Archaeology
The Pitt Rivers Museum
Rossendale - *Lancashire*
Rossendale Museum
St. Albans - *Hertfordshire*
St. Albans Organ Museum
Wareham - *Dorset*
A World of Toys
Warwick - *Warwickshire*
St. John's House

NATURAL HISTORY

Arbroath - *Tayside*
Arbroath Museum
Banchory - *Grampian*
Banchory Museum
Banff - *Grampian*
Banff Museum
Batley - *West Yorkshire*
Bagshaw Museum
Bedford - *Bedfordshire*
Bedford Museum
Bromham Mill
Belfast - *Northern Ireland*
Ulster Museum
Birmingham - *West Midlands*
Birmingham Museum and Art Gallery
Blackburn - *Lancashire*
Blackburn Museum and Art Gallery
Sunnyhurst Wood Visitor Centre
Witton Country Park Visitor Centre
Bolton - *Greater Manchester*
Bolton Museum and Art Gallery
Bolventor - *Cornwall*
Potters Museum of Curiosity
Bracknell - *Berkshire*
The Look Out Countryside and Heritage Centre
Brecon - *Powys*
Brecknock Museum
Brighton - *East Sussex*
The Booth Museum of Natural History
Bristol - *Avon*
Bristol City Museum and Art Gallery
Burnley - *Lancashire*
Towneley Hall Art Gallery and Museums and Museum of Local Crafts and Industries
Canterbury - *Kent*
Whitstable Museum & Gallery
Cardiff - *South Glamorgan*
The National Museum of Wales
Chelmsford - *Essex*
Chelmsford and Essex Museum, Essex Regiment Museum
Chester - *Cheshire*
Grosvenor Museum
Coldstream - *Borders*
The Hirsel Homestead Museum
Coventry - *West Midlands*
Herbert Art Gallery and Museum
Lunt Roman Fort (Reconstruction)
Darlington - *County Durham*
Darlington Museum
Derby - *Derbyshire*
Derby Museums & Art Gallery
Devizes - *Wiltshire*
Devizes Museum
Doncaster - *South Yorkshire*
Doncaster Museum and Art Gallery
Douglas - *Isle of Man*
Manx National Heritage
Downpatrick - *Northern Ireland*
Down County Museum
Dublin - *Ireland*
National Museum of Ireland
Dumfries - *Dumfries & Galloway*
Dumfries Museum
Dundee - *Tayside*
Barrack Street Museum

Dunfermline - *Fife*
Dunfermline District Museum and the Small Gallery
Edinburgh - *Lothian*
Royal Museum of Scotland
Elgin - *Grampian*
Oldmills Working Mill & Visitor Centre
Enniskillen - *Northern Ireland*
Enniskillen Castle
Folkestone - *Kent*
Folkestone Museum and Gallery
Forres - *Grampian*
Falconer Museum
Fort William - *Highlands*
The West Highland Museum
Glasgow - *Strathclyde*
Art Gallery and Museum
Gloucester - *Gloucestershire*
City Museum and Art Gallery
Nature in Art
Guernsey - *Channel Islands*
Guernsey Museum & Art Gallery
Guisborough - *Cleveland*
Margrove South Cleveland Heritage Centre
Hartland - *Devon*
Hartland Quay Museum
Hastings - *East Sussex*
Museum and Art Gallery
Hawick - *Borders*
Hawick Museum and the Scott Art Gallery
Hereford - *Hereford & Worcester*
Hereford City Museum and Art Gallery
Hertford - *Hertfordshire*
Hertford Museum
Honiton - *Devon*
Allhallows Museum
Huddersfield - *West Yorkshire*
Tolson Museum
Inverness - *Highlands*
Inverness Museum and Art Gallery
Ipswich - *Suffolk*
Ipswich Museum and High Street Exhibition Gallery
Jersey - *Channel Islands*
Jersey Museum
Kilmarnock - *Strathclyde*
Dick Institute Museum and Art Gallery
King's Lynn - *Norfolk*
The Lynn Museum
Leeds - *West Yorkshire*
Leeds City Museum
Museum of Leeds Waterfront Heritage Trail
Leicester - *Leicestershire*
The Leicestershire Museum and Art Gallery
Letchworth - *Hertfordshire*
Letchworth Museum and Art Gallery
Liverpool - *Merseyside*
Liverpool Museum
Llanberis - *Gwynedd*
Museum of the North
London - *London (inc Greater London)*
Bexley Museum
British Museum
East Ham Nature Reserve
Greenwich Borough Museum
Horniman Museum and Gardens
Museum of Garden History
Narwhal Inuit Art Gallery
Old Speech Room Gallery, Harrow School
Thames Barrier Visitors' Centre
University College Museum of Zoology and Comparative Anatomy
Luton - *Bedfordshire*
John Dony Field Centre
Luton Museum and Art Gallery
Lyndhurst - *Hampshire*
New Forest Museum and Visitor Centre
Maidstone - *Kent*
Museum and Art Gallery
Museum of Kent Life
Manchester - *Greater Manchester*
Manchester Museum
Mansfield - *Nottinghamshire*
Mansfield Museum and Art Gallery
Merthyr Tydfil - *Mid Glamorgan*
Cyfarthfa Castle Museum and Art Gallery
Middlesbrough - *Cleveland*
Captain Cook Birthplace Museum
Dorman Museum
Millport - *Strathclyde*
Robertson Museum and Aquarium
Monaghan - *Ireland*
Monaghan County Museum
Montrose - *Tayside*
Montrose Museum
Morwellham Quay - *Devon*
Morwellham Quay Museum and 19th Century Port and Copper Mine
Much Wenlock - *Shropshire*
Much Wenlock Museum
Newcastle upon Tyne - *Tyne & Wear*
Hancock Museum
Newport - *Gwent*
Newport Museum and Art Gallery
North Berwick - *Lothian*
North Berwick Museum
Norwich - *Norfolk*
Norwich Castle Museum
Oakham - *Leicestershire*
Rutland County Museum
Oldham - *Greater Manchester*
Oldham Museum
Oxford - *Oxfordshire*
Oxford University Museum
Paisley - *Strathclyde*
Paisley Museum and Art Galleries
Peebles - *Borders*
Tweeddale Museum
Peterborough - *Cambridgeshire*
Sacrewell Farm and Country Centre
Peterhead - *Grampian*
Arbuthnot Museum
Plymouth - *Devon*
City Museum and Art Gallery
Portsmouth - *Hampshire*
City Museum
Natural Science Museum and Butterfly House
Redcar - *Cleveland*
Kirkleatham Old Hall Museum
Rossendale - *Lancashire*
Rossendale Museum
Rotherham - *South Yorkshire*
Clifton Park Museum
St. Albans - *Hertfordshire*
The Museum of St. Albans
Scarborough - *North Yorkshire*
Wood End Museum
Scunthorpe - *Humberside*
Museum and Art Gallery
Selborne - *Hampshire*
The Oates Museum and Gilbert White's House
Shrewsbury - *Shropshire*
The Shrewsbury Museums
Skipton - *North Yorkshire*
Craven Museum
Southend-on-Sea - *Essex*
Central Museum: Southend Museums Service
Prittlewell Priory Museum
Southport - *Merseyside*
Botanic Gardens Museum
Spey Bay - *Grampian*
Tugnet Ice House
Stevenage - *Hertfordshire*
Stevenage Museum
Stockport - *Greater Manchester*
Stockport Museum
Stoke-on-Trent - *Staffordshire*
City Museum and Art Gallery
Stromness - *Orkney*
Stromness Museum
Swindon - *Wiltshire*
Richard Jefferies Museum
Taunton - *Somerset*
Somerset County Museum
Tenby - *Dyfed*
Tenby Museum and Art Gallery
Tewkesbury - *Gloucestershire*
The John Moore Countryside Museum
Thetford - *Norfolk*
The Ancient House Museum
Tomintoul - *Grampian*
Tomintoul Museum
Torquay - *Devon*
Torquay Museum
Tunbridge Wells - *Kent*
Tunbridge Wells Museum and Art Gallery
Wakefield - *West Yorkshire*
Wakefield Museum
Warrington - *Cheshire*
Museum and Art Gallery
Warwick - *Warwickshire*
Warwickshire Museum
Weybridge - *Surrey*
Elmbridge Museum
Whitby - *North Yorkshire*
Whitby Museum
Worcester - *Hereford & Worcester*
City Museum and Art Gallery
York - *North Yorkshire*
The Yorkshire Museum

PANELLING

Glasgow - *Strathclyde*
Burrell Collection
Great Yarmouth - *Norfolk*
Old Merchant's House, Row 111 Houses and Greyfriars' Cloisters
Guildford - *Surrey*
Guildford House Gallery
St. Fagans - *South Glamorgan*
Welsh Folk Museum
Sheffield - *South Yorkshire*
Bishops' House
Stockport - *Greater Manchester*
Bramall Hall

PHILATELY

Blackburn - *Lancashire*
Blackburn Museum and Art Gallery
Jersey - *Channel Islands*
Jersey Museum
Kilmarnock - *Strathclyde*
Dick Institute Museum and Art Gallery
London - *London (inc Greater London)*
Haringey Museum and Archives Service
National Postal Museum

PRIMITIVE ART

Bath - *Avon*
The British Folk Art Collection
Batley - *West Yorkshire*
Bagshaw Museum
Blackburn - *Lancashire*
Blackburn Museum and Art Gallery
Glasgow - *Strathclyde*
Art Gallery and Museum
Hunterian Museum
Guisborough - *Cleveland*
Margrove South Cleveland Heritage Centre
Hastings - *East Sussex*
Museum and Art Gallery
Kilmarnock - *Strathclyde*
Dick Institute Museum and Art Gallery
London - *London (inc Greater London)*
British Museum
Bromley Museum
Narwhal Inuit Art Gallery
Middlesbrough - *Cleveland*
Captain Cook Birthplace Museum
Norwich - *Norfolk*
Sainsbury Centre for Visual Arts
Oxford - *Oxfordshire*
The Pitt Rivers Museum
Saffron Walden - *Essex*
Saffron Walden Museum
Sheffield - *South Yorkshire*
Graves Art Gallery
Thetford - *Norfolk*
The Ancient House Museum

PREHISTORY see ARCHAEOLOGY& PREHISTORY

PHOTOGRAPHY see CINEMATOGRAPHY & PHOTOGRAPHY

REGIMENTAL see SERVICES MUSEUMS SECTION

RELIGION

Beaulieu - *Hampshire*
Beaulieu Abbey & Exhibition of Monastic Life
Bedford - *Bedfordshire*
The Bunyan Meeting Library and Museum
Dublin - *Ireland*
National Gallery of Ireland
Durham - *County Durham*
Durham University Oriental Museum
Glasgow - *Strathclyde*
Art Gallery and Museum
The St Mungo Museum of Religious Life and Art
Hull - *Humberside*
Old Grammar School
London - *London (inc Greater London)*
Ben Uri Art Society and Gallery
The London Museum of Jewish Life
Wesley's Chapel
Manchester - *Greater Manchester*
Manchester Jewish Museum
Milngavie - *Strathclyde*
Heatherbank Museum of Social Work
Norwich - *Norfolk*
St. Peter Hungate Church Museum
Olney - *Buckinghamshire*
Cowper and Newton Museum
Oxford - *Oxfordshire*
The Oxford Story
Reeth - *North Yorkshire*
Swaledale Folk Museum
Southend-on-Sea - *Essex*
Prittlewell Priory Museum
Telford - *Shropshire*
Rosehill House
Walsingham - *Norfolk*
Shirehall Museum

SCIENCE & INDUSTRY

Alford - *Grampian*
Grampian Transport Museum
Anstruther - *Fife*
The Scottish Fisheries Museum
Ashton-under-Lyne - *Greater Manchester*
Portland Basin Industrial Heritage Centre
Banff - *Grampian*
Banff Museum
Bath - *Avon*
Mr Bowler's Business - Bath Industrial Heritage Centre
Beetham - *Cumbria*
Heron Corn Mill and Museum of Papermaking
Belfast - *Northern Ireland*
Ulster Museum
Birmingham - *West Midlands*
Birmingham Museum and Art Gallery
Blackburn - *Lancashire*
Lewis Textile Museum
Witton Country Park Visitor Centre
Bolton - *Greater Manchester*
Bolton Museum and Art Gallery
Bracknell - *Berkshire*
The Look Out Countryside and Heritage Centre
Bradford - *West Yorkshire*
Colour Museum
Bridgwater - *Somerset*
Westonzoyland Pumping Station
Bristol - *Avon*
The Exploratory Hands-On Science Centre
Burnley - *Lancashire*
Towneley Hall Art Gallery and Museums and Museum of Local Crafts and Industries
Burton-upon-Trent - *Staffordshire*
Bass Museum, Visitor Centre and Shire Horse Stables
Camborne - *Cornwall*
Camborne School of Mines Geological Museum and Art Gallery
Cardiff - *South Glamorgan*
Welsh Industrial and Maritime Museum
Chelmsford - *Essex*
Chelmsford and Essex Museum, Essex Regiment Museum
Clydebank - *Strathclyde*
Clydebank District Museum
Coatbridge - *Strathclyde*
Summerlee Heritage Trust
Crich - *Derbyshire*
The National Tramway Museum
Darlington - *County Durham*
Darlington Museum
Derby - *Derbyshire*
Derby Industrial Museum
Dre-Fach Felindre - *Dyfed*
Museum of the Welsh Woollen Industry
Dublin - *Ireland*
Guinness Museum
Dumfries - *Dumfries & Galloway*
Dumfries Museum
Dundee - *Tayside*
Mills Observatory
Dunfermline - *Fife*
Dunfermline District Museum and the Small Gallery
Edinburgh - *Lothian*
Royal Museum of Scotland
Faversham - *Kent*
Fleur De Lis Heritage Centre
Glasgow - *Strathclyde*
Hunterian Museum
Museum of Transport
People's Palace
Springburn Museum
Gloucester - *Gloucestershire*
National Waterways Museum
Halifax - *West Yorkshire*
Calderdale Industrial Museum
The Piece Hall
Hatfield - *Hertfordshire*
Mill Green Museum and Mill

Holmfirth - *West Yorkshire*
Holmfirth Postcard Museum
Hove - *East Sussex*
The British Engineerium
Huddersfield - *West Yorkshire*
Tolson Museum
Huntly - *Grampian*
Brander Museum
Inverkeithing - *Fife*
Inverkeithing Museum
Kidwelly - *Dyfed*
Kidwelly Industrial Museum
Kilmarnock - *Strathclyde*
Dick Institute Museum and Art Gallery
Leeds - *West Yorkshire*
Armley Mills
Leek - *Staffordshire*
Brindley Water Mill and Museum
Leicester - *Leicestershire*
John Doran Gas Museum
Museum of Technology
Snibston Discovery Park
Llanberis - *Gwynedd*
Museum of the North
Welsh Slate Museum
London - *London (inc Greater London)*
BT Museum - The Story of Telecommunications
Chartered Insurance Institute Museum
Faraday's Laboratory and Museum
HMS Belfast
Kew Bridge Steam Museum
Markfield Beam Engine and Museum
Museum of Richmond
National Maritime Museum
Science Museum
Thames Barrier Visitors' Centre
Tower Bridge
The Wandle Industrial Museum
Wimbledon Windmill Museum
Loughborough - *Leicestershire*
The Bell Foundry Museum
Macclesfield - *Cheshire*
Jodrell Bank Science Centre & Arboretum
Manchester - *Greater Manchester*
The Museum of Science and Industry in Manchester
Museum of Transport
Matlock - *Derbyshire*
Caudwell's Mill
Merthyr Tydfil - *Mid Glamorgan*
Cyfarthfa Castle Museum and Art Gallery
Middlesbrough - *Cleveland*
Dorman Museum
Middle Wallop - *Hampshire*
Museum of Army Flying
Morwellham Quay - *Devon*
Morwellham Quay Museum and 19th Century Port and Copper Mine
Neath - *West Glamorgan*
Cefn Coed Colliery Museum
Newport - *Gwent*
Newport Museum and Art Gallery
Newport - *Isle of Wight*
National Wireless Museum
Oxford - *Oxfordshire*
The Oxford Story
Paisley - *Strathclyde*
Coats Observatory
Penzance - *Cornwall*
Trinity House National Lighthouse Centre
Peterborough - *Cambridgeshire*
Railworld
Peterhead - *Grampian*
Arbuthnot Museum
Pickering - *North Yorkshire*
North Yorkshire Moors Railway
Porthmadog - *Gwynedd*
Festiniog Railway Museum
Portsmouth - *Hampshire*
City Museum
Prescot - *Merseyside*
Prescot Museum of Clock and Watch-Making
Prestongrange - *Lothian*
Prestongrange Industrial Heritage Museum
Reading - *Berkshire*
Blake's Lock Museum
Redcar - *Cleveland*
Kirkleatham Old Hall Museum
Redditch - *Hereford & Worcester*
Forge Mill Needle Museum and Bordesley Abbey Visitor Centre
Rotherham - *South Yorkshire*
Clifton Park Museum
St. Austell - *Cornwall*
Charlestown Shipwreck and Heritage Centre
St. Helens - *Merseyside*
Pilkington Glass Museum
Salford - *Greater Manchester*
Lancashire Mining Museum, Salford
Shaftesbury - *Dorset*
Local History Museum
Sheffield - *South Yorkshire*
Abbeydale Industrial Hamlet
Kelham Island Museum
Southend-on-Sea - *Essex*
Central Museum: Southend Museums Service
Prittlewell Priory Museum
Stowmarket - *Suffolk*
Museum of East Anglian Life
Telford - *Shropshire*
Blists Hill Open Air Museum
Museum of Iron and Furnace Site
Totnes - *Devon*
Totnes (Elizabethan) Museum
Wakefield - *West Yorkshire*
Yorkshire Mining Museum
Weston-super-Mare - *Avon*
The International Helicopter Museum
Whitby - *North Yorkshire*
Whitby Museum
Wigan - *Greater Manchester*
Wigan Pier
Witney - *Oxfordshire*
Combe Mill Beam Engine and Working Museum
Wrexham - *Clwyd*
King's Mill Visitor Centre
Wroughton - *Wiltshire*
Science Museum
York - *North Yorkshire*
National Railway Museum

SCULPTURE see FINE ARTS

SERVICES MUSEUMS see separate section

SHIPPING, SHIPBUILDING & MARINE MODELS

Aberdeen - *Grampian*
Aberdeen Art Gallery
Aberdeen Maritime Museum
Aberystwyth - *Dyfed*
Ceredigion Museum
Anstruther - *Fife*
The Scottish Fisheries Museum
Beaulieu - *Hampshire*
Maritime Museum
Birkenhead - *Merseyside*
Historic Warships
Boston - *Lincolnshire*
Guildhall Museum
Bridgwater - *Somerset*
Admiral Blake Museum
Brighton - *East Sussex*
Brighton Museum and Art Gallery
Canterbury - *Kent*
Whitstable Museum & Gallery
Cardiff - *South Glamorgan*
Welsh Industrial and Maritime Museum
Chatham - *Kent*
The Historic Dockyard, Chatham
Clydebank - *Strathclyde*
Clydebank District Museum
Cowes - *Isle of Wight*
Sir Max Aitken Museum
Cromer - *Norfolk*
The Cromer Museum
Glasgow - *Strathclyde*
Museum of Transport
Gloucester - *Gloucestershire*
National Waterways Museum
Grays - *Essex*
Thurrock Museum
Great Grimsby - *Humberside*
Back O' Doig's
Great Yarmouth - *Norfolk*
Maritime Museum for East Anglia
Guernsey - *Channel Islands*
Castle Cornet
Fort Grey Shipwreck Museum
Hartland - *Devon*
Hartland Quay Museum
Harwich - *Essex*
Harwich Redoubt
Port of Harwich Maritime Museum
Hastings - *East Sussex*
Museum of Local History
Hull - *Humberside*
Town Docks Museum
Irvine - *Strathclyde*
Scottish Maritime Museum
Jersey - *Channel Islands*
Jersey Museum
Kilmarnock - *Strathclyde*
Dick Institute Museum and Art Gallery
Lancaster - *Lancashire*
Maritime Museum
Littlehampton - *West Sussex*
Littlehampton Museum
London - *London (inc Greater London)*
Cutty Sark Clipper Ship
Erith Museum
HMS Belfast
National Maritime Museum
Science Museum
Margate - *Kent*
Old Town Hall Museum
Maryport - *Cumbria*
Maritime Museum
Middlesbrough - *Cleveland*
Captain Cook Birthplace Museum
Montrose - *Tayside*
Montrose Museum
Newport - *Gwent*
Newport Museum and Art Gallery
North Berwick - *Lothian*
North Berwick Museum
Omagh - *Northern Ireland*
Ulster-American Folk Park
Penzance - *Cornwall*
Trinity House National Lighthouse Centre
Peterhead - *Grampian*
Arbuthnot Museum
Portsmouth - *Hampshire*
City Museum
HMS Victory
HMS Warrior 1860
Mary Rose Ship Hall and Exhibition
The Royal Naval Museum, Portsmouth
Ramsgate - *Kent*
Maritime Museum Complex
Redcar - *Cleveland*
Kirkleatham Old Hall Museum
Rochester - *Kent*
Guildhall Museum
Rye - *East Sussex*
Rye Museum
St. Austell - *Cornwall*
Charlestown Shipwreck and Heritage Centre
Scarborough - *North Yorkshire*
Rotunda Museum
Stonehaven - *Grampian*
Tolbooth Museum
Stromness - *Orkney*
Stromness Museum
Tenterden - *Kent*
Tenterden and District Museum
Whitby - *North Yorkshire*
Whitby Museum
Whitehaven - *Cumbria*
Whitehaven Museum and Art Gallery
Windermere - *Cumbria*
Windermere Steamboat Museum
Workington - *Cumbria*
Helena Thompson Museum

SILVERSMITHS see JEWELLERY & METALWORK

SOCIAL HISTORY

Alford - *Grampian*
Grampian Transport Museum
Ashton-under-Lyne - *Greater Manchester*
The Museum of the Manchesters: A Social and Regimental History
Portland Basin Industrial Heritage Centre
Bath - *Avon*
Mr Bowler's Business - Bath Industrial Heritage Centre
Bedford - *Bedfordshire*
Bedford Museum
Birmingham - *West Midlands*
Birmingham Museum and Art Gallery
Bolventor - *Cornwall*
Potters Museum of Curiosity
Bracknell - *Berkshire*
The Look Out Countryside and Heritage Centre
Brechin - *Tayside*
Brechin Museum
Bressingham - *Norfolk*
Bressingham Steam Museum and Gardens
Bridgend - *Mid Glamorgan*
South Wales Police Museum
Bridgwater - *Somerset*
Westonzoyland Pumping Station
Bromsgrove - *Hereford & Worcester*
Avoncroft Museum of Historic Buildings
Bromsgrove Museum
Cambridge - *Cambridgeshire*
Cambridge and County Folk Museum
Cardiff - *South Glamorgan*
Cardiff Castle
Castleford - *West Yorkshire*
Castleford Museum
Chalfont St. Giles - *Buckinghamshire*
Chiltern Open Air Museum
Chard - *Somerset*
Chard and District Museum
Cheltenham - *Gloucestershire*
Holst Birthplace Museum
Chester - *Cheshire*
Grosvenor Museum
Chichester - *West Sussex*
Weald and Downland Open Air Museum
Coatbridge - *Strathclyde*
Summerlee Heritage Trust
Crich - *Derbyshire*
The National Tramway Museum
Devizes - *Wiltshire*
Devizes Museum
Dingwall - *Highlands*
Dingwall Museum
Dre-Fach Felindre - *Dyfed*
Museum of the Welsh Woollen Industry
Dudley - *West Midlands*
Black Country Museum
Dundee - *Tayside*
McManus Galleries
Edinburgh - *Lothian*
Museum of Fire
Faversham - *Kent*
Fleur De Lis Heritage Centre
Folkestone - *Kent*
Folkestone Museum and Gallery
Forfar - *Tayside*
Museum and Art Gallery
Forres - *Grampian*
Nelson Tower
Glencoe - *Highlands*
Glencoe and North Lorn Folk Museum
Gloucester - *Gloucestershire*
National Waterways Museum
Regiments of Gloucestershire Museum
Goudhurst - *Kent*
Finchcocks, Living Museum of Music
Grays - *Essex*
Thurrock Museum
Gressenhall - *Norfolk*
Norfolk Rural Life Museum and Union Farm
Guernsey - *Channel Islands*
Guernsey Museum & Art Gallery
Guisborough - *Cleveland*
Margrove South Cleveland Heritage Centre
Halifax - *West Yorkshire*
Calderdale Industrial Museum
Hastings - *East Sussex*
Museum of Local History
Hatfield - *Hertfordshire*
Mill Green Museum and Mill
Henfield - *West Sussex*
Henfield Museum
Hitchin - *Hertfordshire*
Hitchin Museum and Art Gallery
Horsham - *West Sussex*
Horsham Museum
Hove - *East Sussex*
West Blatchington Windmill
Hull - *Humberside*
Old Grammar School
Ilkeston - *Derbyshire*
Erewash Museum
Jedburgh - *Borders*
Castle Jail and Jedburgh Museum
Keighley - *West Yorkshire*
Vintage Railway Carriage Museum
Kelso - *Borders*
Kelso Museum & The Turret Gallery
King's Lynn - *Norfolk*
The Lynn Museum
Kirkintilloch - *Strathclyde*
The Auld Kirk Museum
The Barony Chambers Museum
Lanark - *Strathclyde*
New Lanark World Heritage Village
Lancaster - *Lancashire*
Period Cottage
Leamington Spa - *Warwickshire*
Leamington Spa Art Gallery and Museum

Leeds - *West Yorkshire*
Tetley's Brewery Wharf
Leicester - *Leicestershire*
Belgrave Hall and Gardens
John Doran Gas Museum
Leicestershire Record Office
Lincoln - *Lincolnshire*
Museum of Lincolnshire Life
Littlehampton - *West Sussex*
Littlehampton Museum
Llandrindod Wells - *Powys*
Llandrindod Wells Museum
Llanidloes - *Powys*
Llanidloes Museum c/o Llandrindod Wells Museum
London - *London (inc Greater London)*
Age Exchange Reminiscence Centre
Bexley Museum
British Dental Association Museum
Bromley Museum
BT Museum - The Story of Telecommunications
Cuming Museum
East Ham Nature Reserve
Erith Museum
The Fan Museum
Alexander Fleming Laboratory Museum
Forty Hall Museum
Geffrye Museum
Greenwich Borough Museum
Gunnersbury Park Museum
Harrow Museum and Heritage Centre
Hogarth's House
The Jewish Museum
Linley Sambourne House
The London Museum of Jewish Life
Markfield Beam Engine and Museum
Museum of Richmond
Museum of the Royal Pharmaceutical Society of Great Britain
North Woolwich Old Station Museum
Queen Elizabeth's Hunting Lodge
Thames Barrier Visitors' Centre
Thomas Coram Foundation for Children
Vestry House Museum
Wandsworth Museum
Luton - *Bedfordshire*
Stockwood Craft Museum and Gardens Home of the Mossman Collection
Maidstone - *Kent*
Museum of Kent Life
Malvern - *Hereford & Worcester*
Malvern Museum
Manchester - *Greater Manchester*
Greater Manchester Police Museum
Manchester Jewish Museum
The Museum of Science and Industry in Manchester
Pump House People's History Museum
Margate - *Kent*
Old Town Hall Museum
Market Harborough - *Leicestershire*
The Harborough Museum
Maryport - *Cumbria*
Maritime Museum
Merthyr Tydfil - *Mid Glamorgan*
Cyfarthfa Castle Museum and Art Gallery
Milngavie - *Strathclyde*
Heatherbank Museum of Social Work
Milton Keynes - *Buckinghamshire*
Milton Keynes Museum of Industry & Rural Life
Morpeth - *Northumberland*
Morpeth Chantry Bagpipe Museum
Morwellham Quay - *Devon*
Morwellham Quay Museum and 19th Century Port and Copper Mine
Neath - *West Glamorgan*
Cefn Coed Colliery Museum
Newcastle-under-Lyme - *Staffordshire*
Borough Museum and Art Gallery
Newent - *Gloucestershire*
The Shambles Museum
Newmarket - *Suffolk*
The National Horseracing Museum
Northleach - *Gloucestershire*
Keith Harding's World of Mechanical Music
Norwich - *Norfolk*
Royal Norfolk Regimental Museum
Oakham - *Leicestershire*
Rutland County Museum
Okehampton - *Devon*
Museum of Dartmoor Life
Oldham - *Greater Manchester*
Oldham Museum
Saddleworth Museum & Art Gallery
Oxford - *Oxfordshire*
The Oxford Story
Peebles - *Borders*
Tweeddale Museum
Pocklington - *Humberside*
Penny Arcadia
Pontefract - *West Yorkshire*
Pontefract Museum
Pontypool - *Gwent*
The Valley Inheritance
Portsmouth - *Hampshire*
D-Day Museum and Overlord Embroidery
Charles Dickens' Birthplace Museum
HMS Victory
HMS Warrior 1860
Royal Marines Museum
Preston - *Lancashire*
Harris Museum and Art Gallery
Prestongrange - *Lothian*
Prestongrange Industrial Heritage Museum
Ramsgate - *Kent*
Maritime Museum Complex
Reading - *Berkshire*
Museum of English Rural Life
National Dairy Museum
Redcar - *Cleveland*
Kirkleatham Old Hall Museum
Redditch - *Hereford & Worcester*
Forge Mill Needle Museum and Bordesley Abbey Visitor Centre
Rochdale - *Greater Manchester*
Rochdale Pioneers Co-operative Museum
Rotherham - *South Yorkshire*
Clifton Park Museum
St. Albans - *Hertfordshire*
The Museum of St. Albans
Salford - *Greater Manchester*
Lancashire Mining Museum, Salford
Shaftesbury - *Dorset*
Local History Museum
Sheffield - *South Yorkshire*
Bishops' House
Shrewsbury - *Shropshire*
The Radbrook Culinary Museum
Skipton - *North Yorkshire*
Craven Museum
Spalding - *Lincolnshire*
Ayscoughfee Hall and Gardens
Stafford - *Staffordshire*
Ancient High House
Izaak Walton's Cottage
Steyning - *West Sussex*
Steyning Museum
Stockton-on-Tees - *Cleveland*
Preston Hall Museum
Stowmarket - *Suffolk*
Museum of East Anglian Life
Strathaven - *Strathclyde*
John Hastie Museum
Tamworth - *Staffordshire*
Tamworth Castle and Museum Service
Telford - *Shropshire*
Blists Hill Open Air Museum
Coalport China Museum
Rosehill House
Tewkesbury - *Gloucestershire*
The Museum
Torquay - *Devon*
Torquay Museum
Totnes - *Devon*
Totnes Costume Museum
Wakefield - *West Yorkshire*
Elizabethan Exhibition Gallery
Wakefield Museum
Yorkshire Mining Museum
Wantage - *Oxfordshire*
Vale and Downland Museum Centre
Weston-super-Mare - *Avon*
Weston-super-Mare Heritage Centre
Weybridge - *Surrey*
Brooklands Museum
Elmbridge Museum
Wigan - *Greater Manchester*
Wigan Pier
Wimborne Minster - *Dorset*
Priest's House Museum of East Dorset Life and Garden
Winchcombe - *Gloucestershire*
Gloucestershire Warwickshire Railway
Windermere - *Cumbria*
Windermere Steamboat Museum
Witney - *Oxfordshire*
Combe Mill Beam Engine and Working Museum
Woodbridge - *Suffolk*
Suffolk Horse Museum
Workington - *Cumbria*
Helena Thompson Museum
Wrexham - *Clwyd*
Wrexham Maelor Heritage Centre
York - *North Yorkshire*
Ryedale Folk Museum

SPORT

Dumfries - *Dumfries & Galloway*
Dumfries Museum
Edinburgh - *Lothian*
Museum of Childhood
Glasgow - *Strathclyde*
People's Palace
London - *London (inc Greater London)*
MCC Museum
The Wimbledon Lawn Tennis Museum
Much Wenlock - *Shropshire*
Much Wenlock Museum
Newmarket - *Suffolk*
The National Horseracing Museum
St. Andrews - *Fife*
British Golf Museum
Thirsk - *North Yorkshire*
Thirsk Museum
Watford - *Hertfordshire*
Watford Museum

TAPESTRY & TEXTILES

Barnard Castle - *County Durham*
The Bowes Museum
Bath - *Avon*
American Museum in Britain
No. 1 Royal Crescent
Batley - *West Yorkshire*
Batley Art Gallery
Bedford - *Bedfordshire*
Cecil Higgins Art Gallery and Museum
Belfast - *Northern Ireland*
Ulster Museum
Berwick-upon-Tweed - *Northumberland*
Berwick Borough Museum & Art Gallery
Blackburn - *Lancashire*
Blackburn Museum and Art Gallery
Bolton - *Greater Manchester*
Bolton Museum and Art Gallery
Hall i'th' Wood Museum
Bradford - *West Yorkshire*
Colour Museum
Cardiff - *South Glamorgan*
The National Museum of Wales
Cheltenham - *Gloucestershire*
Cheltenham Art Gallery and Museum
Chertsey - *Surrey*
Chertsey Museum
Cleckheaton - *West Yorkshire*
Red House
Coventry - *West Midlands*
Herbert Art Gallery and Museum
Dre-Fach Felindre - *Dyfed*
Museum of the Welsh Woollen Industry
Dumfries - *Dumfries & Galloway*
Dumfries Museum
Dunfermline - *Fife*
Dunfermline District Museum and the Small Gallery
Durham - *County Durham*
Durham University Oriental Museum
Edinburgh - *Lothian*
Lauriston Castle
Glasgow - *Strathclyde*
Burrell Collection
People's Palace
Halifax - *West Yorkshire*
Bankfield Museum
Hawick - *Borders*
Hawick Museum and the Scott Art Gallery
Hereford - *Hereford & Worcester*
Hereford City Museum and Art Gallery
Huddersfield - *West Yorkshire*
Tolson Museum
Ipswich - *Suffolk*
Christchurch Mansion and Wolsey Art Gallery
Jedburgh - *Borders*
Mary, Queen of Scots' House
Kettering - *Northamptonshire*
Alfred East Gallery
Kilmarnock - *Strathclyde*
Dean Castle
Dick Institute Museum and Art Gallery
Leeds - *West Yorkshire*
Leeds City Museum
Leigh - *Greater Manchester*
Turnpike Gallery
London - *London (inc Greater London)*
Freud Museum
William Morris Gallery
Osterley Park House
Victoria and Albert Museum
The Wandle Industrial Museum
Lyndhurst - *Hampshire*
New Forest Museum and Visitor Centre
Macclesfield - *Cheshire*
Paradise Mill
West Park Museum
Manchester - *Greater Manchester*
The Museum of Science and Industry in Manchester
The Whitworth Art Gallery
Newport - *Gwent*
Newport Museum and Art Gallery
Norwich - *Norfolk*
Bridewell Museum of Local Industries
Oldham - *Greater Manchester*
Saddleworth Museum & Art Gallery
Omagh - *Northern Ireland*
Ulster-American Folk Park
Paisley - *Strathclyde*
Paisley Museum and Art Galleries
Port Sunlight - *Merseyside*
Lady Lever Art Gallery
Reading - *Berkshire*
The Museum of Reading
Rossendale - *Lancashire*
Rossendale Museum
St. Fagans - *South Glamorgan*
Welsh Folk Museum
Stockport - *Greater Manchester*
Bramall Hall
Lyme Hall and Park
Stoke-on-Trent - *Staffordshire*
Ford Green Hall
Strathaven - *Strathclyde*
John Hastie Museum
Truro - *Cornwall*
Royal Cornwall Museum
Warwick - *Warwickshire*
St. John's House
Welshpool - *Powys*
Powis Castle
Whitby - *North Yorkshire*
Whitby Museum
Wigan - *Greater Manchester*
Wigan Pier
York - *North Yorkshire*
Fairfax House

THEATRE

Glasgow - *Strathclyde*
People's Palace
Leeds - *West Yorkshire*
Tetley's Brewery Wharf
London - *London (inc Greater London)*
Bethnal Green Museum of Childhood
Theatre Museum
Malvern - *Hereford & Worcester*
Malvern Museum
Manchester - *Greater Manchester*
Pump House People's History Museum
St. Albans - *Hertfordshire*
St. Albans Organ Museum
Shipley - *West Yorkshire*
Furever Feline
Wigan - *Greater Manchester*
Wigan Pier

TOWN PLANNING

Letchworth - *Hertfordshire*
First Garden City Heritage Museum
London - *London (inc Greater London)*
Thames Barrier Visitors' Centre
Stevenage - *Hertfordshire*
Stevenage Museum
Weston-super-Mare - *Avon*
Weston-super-Mare Heritage Centre

TOYS

Abingdon - *Oxfordshire*
Abingdon Museum
Barnard Castle - *County Durham*
The Bowes Museum
Bath - *Avon*
Museum of Costume
Bedford - *Bedfordshire*
Bedford Museum
Bolton - *Greater Manchester*
Bolton Museum and Art Gallery
Bolventor - *Cornwall*
Potters Museum of Curiosity
Brading - *Isle of Wight*
Lilliput Museum of Antique Dolls and Toys
Brighton - *East Sussex*
Preston Manor

Bromsgrove - *Hereford & Worcester*
Bromsgrove Museum
Cambridge - *Cambridgeshire*
Cambridge and County Folk Museum
Cardiff - *South Glamorgan*
Cardiff Castle
Chelmsford - *Essex*
Chelmsford and Essex Museum, Essex Regiment Museum
Cheltenham - *Gloucestershire*
Cheltenham Art Gallery and Museum
Chertsey - *Surrey*
Chertsey Museum
Derby - *Derbyshire*
Derby Industrial Museum
Dewsbury - *West Yorkshire*
Dewsbury Museum
Dumfries - *Dumfries & Galloway*
Dumfries Museum
East Cowes - *Isle of Wight*
Osborne House
Edinburgh - *Lothian*
Museum of Childhood
Ewell - *Surrey*
Bourne Hall Museum
Glasgow - *Strathclyde*
Haggs Castle
People's Palace
Gloucester - *Gloucestershire*
Folk Museum
Great Yarmouth - *Norfolk*
Elizabethan House Museum
Guildford - *Surrey*
Guildford Museum
Halifax - *West Yorkshire*
Eureka! The Museum for Children
Hereford - *Hereford & Worcester*
Hereford City Museum and Art Gallery
Hove - *East Sussex*
Hove Museum and Art Gallery
Ipswich - *Suffolk*
Christchurch Mansion and Wolsey Art Gallery
Kirkcaldy - *Fife*
Kirkcaldy Museum and Art Gallery
Leicester - *Leicestershire*
Belgrave Hall and Gardens
Newarke Houses Museum
London - *London (inc Greater London)*
Bethnal Green Museum of Childhood
Cabaret Mechanical Theatre
Lytham St. Annes - *Lancashire*
Toy and Teddy Bear Museum
Macclesfield - *Cheshire*
West Park Museum
Maidstone - *Kent*
Museum and Art Gallery
New Romney - *Kent*
Romney Toy and Model Museum
Newark-on-Trent - *Nottinghamshire*
Vina Cooke Museum of Dolls & Bygone Childhood
Newcastle-under-Lyme - *Staffordshire*
Borough Museum and Art Gallery
Newent - *Gloucestershire*
The Shambles Museum
Newport - *Isle of Wight*
Carisbrooke Castle Museum
Northleach - *Gloucestershire*
Keith Harding's World of Mechanical Music
Norwich - *Norfolk*
Strangers' Hall
Ribchester - *Lancashire*
Museum of Childhood
Rochester - *Kent*
Guildhall Museum
Rotherham - *South Yorkshire*
Clifton Park Museum
Salford - *Greater Manchester*
Ordsall Hall Museum
Sandwich - *Kent*
The Precinct Toy Collection
Shipley - *West Yorkshire*
Furever Feline
Shugborough - *Staffordshire*
Mansion House, Servants' Quarters, Museum of Staffordshire life and Park Farm.
Southend-on-Sea - *Essex*
Central Museum: Southend Museums Service
Stockton-on-Tees - *Cleveland*
Preston Hall Museum
Tunbridge Wells - *Kent*
Tunbridge Wells Museum and Art Gallery
Wantage - *Oxfordshire*
Vale and Downland Museum Centre
Wareham - *Dorset*
A World of Toys
Warwick - *Warwickshire*
Doll Museum
Worthing - *West Sussex*
Worthing Museum and Art Gallery
York - *North Yorkshire*
York Castle Museum

TRANSPORT

Alford - *Grampian*
Grampian Transport Museum
Bangor - *Gwynedd*
Penrhyn Castle
Batley - *West Yorkshire*
Batley Art Gallery
Beaulieu - *Hampshire*
National Motor Museum
Bickenhill - *West Midlands*
National Motorcycle Museum
Birkenhead - *Merseyside*
Historic Warships
Blackburn - *Lancashire*
Witton Country Park Visitor Centre
Bolton - *Greater Manchester*
Bolton Museum and Art Gallery
Bressingham - *Norfolk*
Bressingham Steam Museum and Gardens
Bridgend - *Mid Glamorgan*
South Wales Police Museum
Brighton - *East Sussex*
Brighton Museum and Art Gallery
Bromsgrove - *Hereford & Worcester*
Bromsgrove Museum
Burton-upon-Trent - *Staffordshire*
Bass Museum, Visitor Centre and Shire Horse Stables
Canterbury - *Kent*
Canterbury Heritage Museum
Cardiff - *South Glamorgan*
Welsh Industrial and Maritime Museum
Ceres - *Fife*
Fife Folk Museum
Chard - *Somerset*
Chard and District Museum
Cheltenham - *Gloucestershire*
Cheltenham Art Gallery and Museum
Coventry - *West Midlands*
Midland Air Museum
Museum of British Road Transport
Crich - *Derbyshire*
The National Tramway Museum
Derby - *Derbyshire*
Derby Industrial Museum
Didcot - *Oxfordshire*
Didcot Railway Centre
Doncaster - *South Yorkshire*
Museum of South Yorkshire Life, Cusworth Hall
Dublin - *Ireland*
Guinness Museum
Dudley - *West Midlands*
Black Country Museum
Dumfries - *Dumfries & Galloway*
Dumfries Museum
Edinburgh - *Lothian*
Museum of Fire
Egham - *Surrey*
The Egham Museum
Ellesmere Port - *Cheshire*
The Boat Museum
Epping - *Essex*
The Squadron
Gillingham - *Kent*
Small Exhibits and Locos
Glasgow - *Strathclyde*
Museum of Transport
Springburn Museum
Gloucester - *Gloucestershire*
National Waterways Museum
Transport Museum
Halifax - *West Yorkshire*
Shibden Hall
Hartlebury - *Hereford & Worcester*
Hereford and Worcester County Museum
Hereford - *Hereford & Worcester*
Hereford City Museum and Art Gallery
Hull - *Humberside*
Streetlife - Hull Museum of Transport
Jersey - *Channel Islands*
La Hougue Bie Museum
Keighley - *West Yorkshire*
Vintage Railway Carriage Museum
Kilmarnock - *Strathclyde*
Dick Institute Museum and Art Gallery
Lancaster - *Lancashire*
City Museum
Maritime Museum
Leeds - *West Yorkshire*
Museum of Leeds Waterfront Heritage Trail
Leek - *Staffordshire*
Brindley Water Mill and Museum
Cheddleton Flint Mill
Leicester - *Leicestershire*
Snibston Discovery Park
Leyland - *Lancashire*
The British Commercial Vehicle Museum
London - *London (inc Greater London)*
BT Museum - The Story of Telecommunications
Buckingham Palace, The Royal Mews
Gunnersbury Park Museum
HMS Belfast
Museum of Richmond
National Postal Museum
Royal Air Force Museum
Science Museum
Luton - *Bedfordshire*
Stockwood Craft Museum and Gardens Home of the Mossman Collection
Lutterworth - *Leicestershire*
Stanford Hall Motorcycle Museum
Manchester - *Greater Manchester*
The Museum of Science and Industry in Manchester
Museum of Transport
Middle Wallop - *Hampshire*
Museum of Army Flying
Milton Keynes - *Buckinghamshire*
Milton Keynes Museum of Industry & Rural Life
Morwellham Quay - *Devon*
Morwellham Quay Museum and 19th Century Port and Copper Mine
New Romney - *Kent*
Romney Toy and Model Museum
Norwich - *Norfolk*
Bridewell Museum of Local Industries
Oldham - *Greater Manchester*
Saddleworth Museum & Art Gallery
Peterborough - *Cambridgeshire*
Railworld
Pickering - *North Yorkshire*
North Yorkshire Moors Railway
Plymouth - *Devon*
City Museum and Art Gallery
Porthmadog - *Gwynedd*
Festiniog Railway Museum
Portsmouth - *Hampshire*
City Museum
Prestongrange - *Lothian*
Prestongrange Industrial Heritage Museum
Ramsgate - *Kent*
Maritime Museum Complex
Reading - *Berkshire*
Blake's Lock Museum
National Dairy Museum
Richmond - *North Yorkshire*
The Richmondshire Museum
Ross-on-Wye - *Hereford & Worcester*
The Button Museum
Shackerstone - *Leicestershire*
Shackerstone Railway Museum
Sheffield - *South Yorkshire*
Kelham Island Museum
Sheffield Park - *East Sussex*
Bluebell Railway
Shifnal - *Shropshire*
The Aerospace Museum
Shugborough - *Staffordshire*
Mansion House, Servants' Quarters, Museum of Staffordshire life and Park Farm.
Steyning - *West Sussex*
Steyning Museum
Stowmarket - *Suffolk*
Museum of East Anglian Life
Swindon - *Wiltshire*
Great Western Railway Museum
Tangmere - *West Sussex*
Tangmere Military Aviation Museum Trust
Telford - *Shropshire*
Blists Hill Open Air Museum
Museum of Iron and Furnace Site
Museum of the River
Tenterden - *Kent*
Tenterden and District Museum
Wells-next-the-Sea - *Norfolk*
Wells and Walsingham Light Railway
Weston-super-Mare - *Avon*
The International Helicopter Museum
Weston-super-Mare Heritage Centre
Wexford - *Ireland*
Irish Agricultural Museum
Weybridge - *Surrey*
Brooklands Museum
Whitby - *North Yorkshire*
Whitby Museum
Winchcombe - *Gloucestershire*
Gloucestershire Warwickshire Railway
Wroughton - *Wiltshire*
Science Museum
York - *North Yorkshire*
National Railway Museum
Yorkshire Air Museum

TRAVEL

Penzance - *Cornwall*
Trinity House National Lighthouse Centre
Peterborough - *Cambridgeshire*
Railworld
Shifnal - *Shropshire*
The Aerospace Museum

WITCHCRAFT

Dumfries - *Dumfries & Galloway*
Dumfries Museum
Forfar - *Tayside*
Museum and Art Gallery
Huddersfield - *West Yorkshire*
Tolson Museum
Lancaster - *Lancashire*
City Museum

ZOOLOGY see NATURAL HISTORY

LOCATION INDEX

ALPHABETICAL LIST OF MUSEUMS AND ART GALLERIES

NOTES

NOTES